PUBLIC RADIO
——— A N D ———
TELEVISION
— I N —
AMERICA

*For Ed and Irene,
Synnöve, Jan, and Alina*

PUBLIC RADIO
—— A N D ——
TELEVISION
—— I N ——
AMERICA

A Political History

Ralph Engelman

SAGE Publications
International Educational and Professional Publisher
Thousand Oaks   London   New Delhi

For information address:

SAGE Publications, Inc.
2455 Teller Road
Thousand Oaks, California 91320
E-mail: order@sagepub.com

SAGE Publications Ltd.
6 Bonhill Street
London EC2A 4PU
United Kingdom

SAGE Publications India Pvt. Ltd.
M-32 Market
Greater Kailash I
New Delhi 110 048 India

Printed in the United States of America

Library of Congress Cataloging-in-Publication Data

Engelman, Ralph.
    Public radio and television in America : a political history /
Ralph Engelman
      p.—cm.
    Includes bibliographical references (p.) and index.
    ISBN 0-8039-5406-9 (cloth : acid-free paper).—ISBN
0-8039-5407-7 (pbk. : acid-free paper)
    1. Public broadcasting—Political aspects—United States—History.
    2. Radio broadcasting—Political aspects—United States—History
    3. Television broadcasting—Political aspects—United States—
History.   I. Title.
HE8689.8.E53   1996   95-50232

This book is printed on acid-free paper.

97 98 99 10 9 8 7 6 5 4 3 2

Production Editor: Astrid Virding
Typesetter: Marion Warren
Copy Editor: Joyce Kuhn

Contents

Acknowledgments

This study, a work of synthesis and analysis, owes a great deal to the community of media scholars and activists committed to expanding public participation and control in American telecommunications. The manuscript profited from critical readings by Patricia Aufderheide and Robert McChesney, who of course bear no responsibility for its shortcomings. I was fortunate to have the opportunity to interview a number of pioneers in public radio and television, among them William Siemering, George Stoney and DeeDee Halleck. Operating in the shadow of the communication industry, these innovators and their associates made a significant contribution to American radio and television no less than their more celebrated counterparts in commercial broadcasting.

Others who shared their experiences and perspectives in interviews included Jo Ann Allen, Carol Anshien, Ira Flatow, Robert Krulwich, Samori Marksman, Paul Ryan, Theodora Sklover, Daniel del Solar, Martha Wallner and John F. White. I am indebted to David Shulman for sharing with me material on the history of public access cable television he assembled for his 1990 documentary *Everyone's Channel.* The Union for Democratic Communications has provided a forum for both academics and practitioners to discuss many of the issues addressed in this volume. I wish to thank Professor Nick Jankowski of the University of Nijmegen, the Netherlands, for inviting me to participate in the colloquium of the European Institute of Communication and Culture on "Rethinking Access," held in September 1994 in Piran, Slovenia, where I was exposed to the work of European as well as American colleagues on the problem of the public sphere and contemporary communications. The Winter 1995 issue of the journal *Javnost—The Public, 2*(4), contains papers presented at the colloquium, including my own, "Public Access versus Public Control in the American Media Reform Movement," a distillation of some of the themes developed in this book.

My experience as a member of the national board of the Pacifica Foundation from 1973 to 1979 and of the local advisory board of WBAI-FM in New York whetted my interest in the history and politics of noncommercial radio and television. Hence, I write as a participant observer as well as a historian and critic of public radio and television.

I am grateful for the support received from Long Island University, where I have taught in the Journalism Department for the past decade. The Board of Trustees and Research Awards Committee generously awarded released time for work on this study. Robert Spector, division director of Communications, Fine and Performing Arts, and Donald Allport Bird, my colleague and predecessor as chair in the Journalism Department, created a supportive environment for both teaching and scholarship. Joan Nusbaum Schaller, Journalism Department secretary, and student aides under her supervision, assisted this undertaking in innumerable ways.

I would also like to thank Sophy Craze, my editor at Sage, for her encouragement and patience.

A section of Chapter 8 originally appeared as "From Ford to Carnegie: The Private Foundation and the Rise of Public Television" in Sari Thomas (Ed.), *Culture and Communication* (Ablex, 1987, pp. 233-243), and is reprinted with permission from the Ablex Publishing Corporation. An earlier version of Chapter 11 was published as "The Origins of Public Access Cable Television, 1966-1972" in *Journalism Monographs,* No. 123 (October 1990), by the Association for Education in Journalism and Mass Communication.

Key to Abbreviated Terms

FAE	Fund for Adult Education
FAIR	Fairness and Accuracy in Reporting
FCC	Federal Communications Commission
FRC	Federal Radio Commission
FSM	Free Speech Movement
ITVS	Independent Television Service
JCET	Joint Committee on Educational Television
NAB	National Association of Broadcasters
NACRE	National Advisory Council on Radio in Education
NAEB	National Association of Educational Broadcasters
NBC	National Broadcasting Company
NCCET	National Citizens' Committee for Educational Television
NCER	National Committee on Education by Radio
NCTA	National Cable Television Association
NEA	National Educational Association
NER	National Educational Radio
NET	National Educational Television
NFCB	National Federation of Community Broadcasters
NFLCP	National Federation of Local Cable Programmers
NPACT	National Public Affairs Center for Television
NPR	National Public Radio
NTIA	National Telecommunications and Information Administration
PBL	*Public Broadcasting Laboratory*
PBS	Public Broadcasting System
PISA	Public Interest Satellite Association
RCA	Radio Corporation of America
SLA	Symbionese Liberation Army
USIA	United States Information Agency

CHAPTER

Introduction
The Politics of Public Radio and Television

The Public Broadcasting Act of 1967 represented the apparent triumph of the movement to establish a noncommercial broadcasting system in the United States dating back to the earliest days of radio. The legislative victory followed nearly a half-century of promising initiatives dashed by political defeats. Commercial forces crushed the movement to reserve noncommercial channels on the AM band during the 1920s and 1930s. Following World War II, noncommercial broadcasters appeared doomed to an obscure existence on the FM dial, and risked being excluded from the newly developing medium of television. The landmark report of the Carnegie Commission on Educational Television (1967), which set the stage for the Public Broadcasting Act, sought to reverse the fortunes of noncommercial broadcasting in the United States. It advanced a notion of public—as opposed to mere educational—broadcasting that promised to transform broadcasting into a great national resource. The report stressed the potential of public television as a democratic instrument capable of affirming American diversity and reviving civic life:

> Public television programming can deepen a sense of community in local life. It should show us our community as it really is. It should be a forum for debate and controversy. It should bring into the home meetings, now generally untelevised, where major public decisions are hammered out, and occasions where people of the community express their hopes, their protests, their enthusiasms, and their will. It should provide a voice for groups in the community that may otherwise be unheard. (p. 92)

The report of the Carnegie Commission provided a theoretical rationale and a practical blueprint for the Public Broadcasting Act, which established the Corporation for Public Broadcasting (CPB). The legislation gave the CPB responsibility to provide federal funds and political insulation for public broadcasting and its two networking arms, National Public Radio (NPR) and the Public Broadcasting System (PBS), which were established shortly thereafter. Roughly a quarter-century later, an impressive public broadcasting infrastructure was in place. NPR boasted a nationwide system of over 500 affiliate, associate, and auxiliary stations (NPR, 1995). PBS's network embraced nearly 350 stations in every state, Puerto Rico, the Virgin Islands, Guam, and American Samoa. By the mid-1990s, over 100 million people representing more than 60% of American television households watched public television each week (PBS, 1994, p. 13). Public broadcasting made significant strides in news and public affairs programming, as recommended by the Carnegie Commission. Seven million people listen to NPR's news magazines *All Things Considered* and *Morning Edition,* which many consider the best news programs in all of broadcasting. PBS's flagship news report *The MacNeil/Lehrer NewsHour,* the first hour-long network news program in television history and winner of countless citations for excellence, has a growing audience now a third as large as that of nightly newscasts on CBS and NBC. In public affairs programming, series like *Soundprint* on public radio and *Frontline* on public TV have virtually cornered the market on major documentary journalism awards.

    Ervin S. Duggan (1995), president of PBS, recently characterized public broadcasting as a great national asset, "a treasure not unlike our national parks, or the Smithsonian Institution" (p. 24). However, Duggan said this not to affirm the coming of age of public broadcasting but in defense of its continued existence. Following the Republican sweep of the 1994 mid-term elections, the new leaders of Congress called for the elimination of federal funding for public broadcasting. House Speaker Newt Gingrich endorsed the crusade of the radical right to question the legitimacy of public broadcasting as an American institution and to liquidate the CPB. In January 1995, Gingrich's colleagues in the House of Representatives introduced a bill to repeal CPB's statutory authority. At the same time, Senator Larry Pressler advocated a fundamental reorientation of public broadcasting—namely, its privatization. Pressler chaired the Senate Commerce, Science, and Transportation Committee, which considers reauthorization of CPB funding. CPB Chairman Henry Cauthen declared in January 1995, "There has never been a day more threatening to the existence of public broadcasting than the one we face now" (cited in Behrens, 1995, p. 1).

How are we to explain public television's current plight, and, more generally, its historic difficulty in gaining a significant and secure place on the American communications landscape? We need to place the most recent crisis in the framework of the troubled history of noncommercial radio and TV in the United States as a whole. This means going below the surface of American electoral politics as represented, for example, by the congressional elections of 1994 and examining the full range of forces—ideological and social— that have impinged on the development of public broadcasting. A reconsideration of problematic aspects of the Carnegie Commission on Educational Television and the Public Broadcasting Act of 1967 may provide insights into public broadcasting's current predicament. So may a scrutiny of the development of educational broadcasting from the end of World War II up to 1967. Moreover, the early battles for noncommercial broadcasting in the 1920s and 1930s could be instructive for contemporary media activists seeking to defend and extend the practice of public radio and television.

Public Radio and Television in America: A Political History provides an interpretive overview of the development of noncommercial radio and television in the United States since World War II. It is a political history in a number of respects. Its approach is rooted in the critical school of communication studies that seeks to examine mass media in a broad social (i.e., political, economic, and ideological) context. The underlying tenet of the critical approach is that "social relations of communication are inseparable from social relations of power" (Good, 1989, p. 53). It is the task of communication scholars to demystify and analyze these relationships. Radio and television can be agents of social change or social control in their noncommercial form no less than in their commercial form. The orientation is also critical in the sense that it considers the unrealized potential as well as the achievements of noncommercial broadcasting. The history of public radio and television reflects what Czitrom (1982) termed the recurring "tension between the progressive or utopian possibilities offered by new communications technologies and their disposition as instruments of domination and exploitation" (p. 184).

The book's point of departure, its prologue, is an account of the defeat of noncommercial broadcasters by commercial broadcasters in the period between the two world wars. It draws upon revisionist scholarship on radio history by Susan Douglas, Eugene E. Leach, Robert W. McChesney, David Paul Nord, and Werner J. Severin, among others. This body of work challenged the legend of a commercial system of advertiser-supported network broadcasting emerging inevitably and without major opposition in the interwar period. The outcome of the bitter political conflict between commercial and noncommercial forces in broadcasting's early history provided the framework for the development of public radio and television as secondary or supplemental systems after World War II. This study also examines the revival of noncommercial broadcasting after 1945 in relation to commercial broadcasting and commercial culture. For public radio and television have, at turns, both challenged and helped legitimate the dominant commercial system. Special attention is given to the central role of private foundations such as the Carnegie Corporation and the Ford Foundation as a "third force" mediating between the private and public sectors in the development of public radio and TV.

Public Radio and Television in America: A Political History does not aspire to provide a definitive institutional history of noncommercial radio and TV. It is an interpretive narrative seeking to pose a series of questions and to illuminate certain patterns in regard to the trajectory of public broadcasting in American history. Educational broadcasting in the limited sense of using the airwaves to teach courses lies outside the book's purview: noncommercial radio and television systems that aspire to extend the possibilities for the exchange of information and for action by the public. Treatment of programming is similarly selective, emphasizing attempts to provide alternatives to the news and public affairs programming of the commercial system. The book explores the origins of the major institutions of noncommercial radio and television in the United States after World War II: the founding of Pacifica Radio in 1949, the creation of NPR and PBS after 1967, and Federal Communication Commission (FCC) recognition of public access channels as a requirement for cable television franchises in 1972. Due to the scope of the study and its emphasis on public radio and TV models, systems, and networks, no attempt is made to document in a systematic fashion the achievements of individual local programmers and stations. It is my hope that the present volume will encourage further study of all facets of the history of public radio and TV. Deirdre Boyle's (in press) book, *Subject to Change: Guerrilla Television Revisited,* is an example of the type of monograph that examines in depth the legacies of specific experiments and episodes of importance in the development of public broadcasting.

Public Radio and Television in America: A Political History focuses broadly on the social forces that converged to launch and to shape the major institutions of public radio and television. For example, the political climate in the immediate post-World War II period and the ideological objectives of its founder, Lewis Hill, provide the backdrop for the emergence of Pacifica Radio. Scrutiny of the very different political forces at play that led to passage of the Public Broadcasting Act of 1967 provides insight into the character of the legislation's offspring, the CPB, NPR, and PBS. The convergence of a complex set of technological, political, and economic factors led to the emergence of public access as a new form of noncommercial television in the early 1970s. The evolution as well as the origins of these institutions is examined in relation to changing social conditions in the United States.

To what extent have the aspirations of the founders of public radio and television been fulfilled? How can we weigh the achievements and failures of the institutions they created in relation to the considerable constraints upon their development? A political history that poses such questions must dispense with the rarefied image of cultural uplift and apolitical highmindedness associated by many with public broadcasting. A critical approach renders public broadcasting less pure but immeasurably richer and dynamic. This study reveals the political wars, often fought behind the scenes, that shaped noncommercial radio and TV. Here is contested terrain, with a variety of incompatible visions of what public telecommunications should be. It is a story of strange bedfellows and shifting alliances. Participants in the struggle over noncommercial radio and TV run the social and political gamut, ranging from educators to corporate executives, from prophets of a counterculture to foundation technocrats, from leftists in the streets to conservatives in the White House. All these players, their different agendas notwithstanding, understood the potential of public radio and TV as a social instrument.

A note about terminology is in order. This study examines a variety of forms of noncommercial radio and TV whose public policy goals transcend instructional programming. Yet the appellation "noncommercial" is descriptively and conceptually inadequate, a negative definition inadvertently confirming the primacy of commercial broadcasting. The term "public" in the book's title refers to *all* forms of noncommercial radio and TV. The term "public broadcasting" is not ceded here exclusively to its mainstream expression, NPR and PBS. Instead, a fundamental distinction emerges between *federal* and *community* forms of public radio and television, with the former rooted in the Public Broadcasting Act of 1967, the latter in more decentralized and participatory practices.

"Public" is retained in the book's title as a general category because it signifies the relationship of noncommercial radio and television to the larger problem of the public sphere. A vast literature written by American social scientists and social critics exists on the subject of the public, dating back to John Dewey and Walter Lippmann. Jürgen Habermas's (1989) *The Structural Transformation of the Public Sphere,* which was first published in Germany in 1962, prompted renewed interest in the subject. Habermas described the cultural and social apparatus that developed out of the Enlightenment to enable citizens to engage in rational and critical discourse about public issues of the day. According to Habermas, this public sphere, in which reasoned debate transcended narrow class interests and promoted democratic participation, had largely evaporated in the 20th century. Rooted in the tradition of the Frankfurt School and Theodor Adorno's critique of the culture industry, Habermas lamented the decline of public opinion from the expression of a rationally and critically participatory populace into its opposite, a realm in which an alienated mass audience was manipulated for political and especially commercial purposes. Hardt (1994) emphasized how Habermas's book inspired American media scholars and activists critical of the commercial system of public communication to explore possibilities of a refashioned contemporary public sphere:

> In fact, the idea of the public sphere became the cornerstone of reformist writings on social relations in society and on the need for addressing the relationship between media and society. They contained a new urgency—since the old ones of the 1920s had been abandoned—which was based on

the realization that political impotence, social marginalization, and increasing alienation, with their roots in a loss of access to power and participation in public affairs, were somehow related to the functioning of communication and the role of the media in American society. (p. 1)

Sholle (1994) suggested that renewed interest in the problem of the public sphere could provide the basis for greater dialogue—which this book seeks to promote—between media scholars and activists seeking to democratize American mass communication.

Habermas's (1989) seminal book on the public sphere together with the critique and reconceptualization of his analysis undertaken by a group of scholar-activists provide a valuable theoretical framework for a study of public radio and television in America. Negt and Kluge (1972/1993) elaborated that critique in *Öffentlichkeit und Erfahrung*; a collection of American commentary is contained in Calhoun's (1992) *Habermas and the Public Sphere*. Miriam Hansen, in her foreword to Negt and Kluge (1993 English edition), noted why media critics and activists took issue with Habermas's emphasis on the disintegration of the public sphere and criticism of electronic mass media: "Taken literally, that vision preempted the very idea of an alternative media practice on both aesthetic and sociological grounds, because of the media's technological basis and because of their imbrication with mass consumption" (p. xx).

McLaughlin (1994) made a suggestive synthesis of the critiques of Habermas's view of the public sphere and analysis of their implications. She noted that Habermas's book presented an idealized portrait of a bourgeois public sphere of propertied, educated males that excluded popular, radical democratic movements. She drew upon the Gramscian notion of "hegemony" to suggest that Habermas in fact portrayed an official or pseudopublic sphere in which a dominant group controlled public life. McLaughlin posited instead the historic existence of multiple publics or counterpublics made up of workers, women, and ethnic minorities, among others. She argued that "a post-liberal conception of the public sphere will enable a critique of the limits of existing democracy and the attainment of a radical democracy based on the notion of a heterogeneous public" (p. 8). Counterpublics, therefore, need to form coalitions to gain access to mass media; the public sphere should be reconceptualized and reconstituted. Sholle (1994) characterized the role of the alternative media in this process as "the production of a counter-public sphere whose discourse is primarily oppositional to what is conceived as the public sphere proper" (p. 5). Hansen has noted that inherent in the concept of the public sphere is a critical and utopian dimension:

> The utopia of such a self-determined public sphere, which is ultimately a radical form of democracy, involves not just the empowerment of constituencies hitherto exluded from the space of public opinion, but also a different principle of organization, a different concept of public life. (Negt & Kluge, 1972/1993, p. xxxi)

The categories that emerged out of the debate on the public sphere are relevant for our purposes. For example, one needs to ask to what extent have public radio and television reproduced the claim to unity and the exclusionary aspects of the liberal bourgeois public sphere, and, conversely, to what extent have they provided access to oppositional counterpublics absent from mainstream commercial broadcasting? This study seeks to address this question by examining the different forms of public radio and television as a whole, including public access on cable television. I have taken to heart the work of Mander (1978) and other American media critics who, like the Frankfurt School, have questioned the capacity of the mass media, especially radio and television, to extend the public sphere and to serve as a progressive social instrument. Yet Hoynes (1994) notes how Stuart Hall and other media theorists have made an effective case for the two-sided nature of mass media, especially television. Hierarchical and isolating effects coexist with tendencies toward a democratization of communication and diverse social uses and readings of programs. Hoynes stressed that, given these contradictory qualities, media reformers need to navigate between the Scylla and Charybdis of technological revulsion and romanticism. What Hoynes recommends instead is especially applicable to public radio and television: "We need to do the hard work of identifying the principles of a democratic communications system, locating those existing structures that are most likely to contribute to it and clarifying the obstacles to the realization of such a system" (p. 165).

The premise underlying this volume—written at a moment when the legitimacy of public broadcasting, indeed the very notion of a public sphere, is under attack—is the enduring emancipatory potential of mass media. Enzensberger (1974), in opposing the reduction of the study of mass media to the concept of manipulation, wrote, "The open secret of the electronic media, the decisive political factor, which has been waiting, suppressed or crippled, for its moment to come, is their mobilizing power" (p. 96).

PART I

Prologue, 1914–1945

CHAPTER  2

The Public Origins of American Broadcasting

Public radio and television as we know it today in the United States developed after World War II. However, any study of the evolution of noncommercial broadcasting must reckon with the period between the two world wars that ended with the ascendancy of a commercial system of advertiser-supported network broadcasting. As a result, noncommercial radio and television, irrespective of the forms they might assume after 1945, were fated to serve a secondary or supplemental function.

An examination of the interwar period dispels the myth that a consensus existed from the outset about the desirability of a predominantly commercial system of broadcasting. Indeed, it has been said that "the early history of public radio is, in fact, the early history of radio itself" (Carnegie Commission, 1979, p. 186). As with other new communication technologies, amateurs and educators played a leading role in the development of radio before the medium's commercial potential was fully understood. Moreover, a broad-based coalition launched a major ideological and political attack on commercial broadcasters during the Depression. Because history is usually written by the victors, the memory of this coalition's near success in limiting the dominance of commercial broadcasters was repressed. Yet this defeat is a critical factor in understanding the subsequent development of public radio and television.

The history of the telegraph was a harbinger of the conflict between public and private control of broadcasting, between public aspirations and corporate control. Czitrom (1982) noted the great popular hopes linked to the invention in 1844 of the telegraph, which had been subsidized by the U.S. Congress. Samuel Morse's invention, inaugurating the modern era of communication, had important social implications. Proponents viewed the telegraph as a means to foster a new level of national communion or participation through instantaneous electronic communication. Here was a tool that could be used to realize a Whitmanesque democratic vision, uniting a young and expanding American republic. "I see the electric telegraphs of the earth/I see the filaments of the news of the wars, deaths, losses, gains, passions of my race," Whitman wrote in 1856 (cited in Czitrom, 1982, pp. 188-189). Successful completion of the Atlantic cable two years later led to street demonstrations and celebrations throughout the United States.

Samuel Morse had hoped to sell his invention to the federal government to take its fate out of the hands of speculators and to ensure its development as a public means of communication. His fears proved to be prophetic. During the 1850s, the telegraph industry—with 50 competing companies, duplicate lines, unequal rates, and poor quality—was in a state of chaos. These conditions permitted Western Union to consolidate its control of the industry, becoming America's largest company and its first industrial monopoly. In 1909, Western Union came under the control of AT&T, a corporate giant that would play a critical role in the development of broadcasting. Czitrom (1982) stressed the disenchantment of those who had opposed the privatization of the telegraph system and had feared its development as a private monopoly rather than as a public resource: "Behind the various political proposals for telegraph reform lay a sense of betrayal of the telegraph's original promise to be the common carrier of intelligence" (p. 21).

In its early history, radio, like the telegraph, caught the popular imagination. Wireless telegraphy based on electromagnetic waves traveling through space revived the dream of "universal communication" originally inspired by Samuel Morse's wire telegraphy. Amateur "ham" operators embodied that dream. The discovery that cheap crystals could serve as detectors of radio waves launched the amateur boom around 1907, democratizing the wireless. Many of the hobbyists were young and operated their receivers and transmitters from attics and garages. Besides monitoring naval stations, they communicated with fellow amateurs, usually in Morse code. Sometimes, a speech or a song could be heard. They were not "broadcasters" offering regularly scheduled transmissions to a general public, but they did play a critical role in the transition from wireless telegraphy to radio broadcasting by experimenting with voice and music transmissions. As Barnouw (1966) emphasized, these tinkerers advanced radio technology and provided the foundation for the first generation of radio listeners and professionals: "Almost everything that became 'broadcasting' was being done or had been done" (p. 37). Barnouw added that the importance of the ham movement prior to World War I was not only technical: "Equally important was the bond it provided for a growing brotherhood, scattered far and wide, that already numbered thousands; a host of experimenters, of every age and status" (p. 27).

Douglas (1987) stressed the significance of the ham movement as a form of rebellion against the pressures of increased centralization and bureaucratization of American society. Marconi's corporate application of his invention posed a potential threat to the use the wireless in the spirit of the country's democratic and participatory principles. Amateurs seemed to dominate the airwaves in the years prior to World War I, by which time over 1,000 ham transmitters were in operation. A growing number of wireless clubs met on the air on a prearranged wavelength. Ham operators were unlike traditionally passive audiences. By 1910 they had established what Douglas characterized as a grassroots radio network:

> To the amateurs, the ether was neither the rightful province of the military nor a resource a private firm could appropriate or monopolize. . . . Social order and social control were defied. In this realm the individual voice did not have to defer to the authority of business or the state. This realm, argued the amateurs, did not belong to hierarchical bureaucracies: it belonged to "the people." (p. 214)

The dramatic growth of the ham movement led to conflict with the U.S. Navy over control of the airwaves. The wireless emerged as a vital means of communication from ship to ship or ship to shore at a time of fierce naval competition during the era of the new imperialism of the 1890s. The British

Marconi Company supplied the navy of the British empire with the wireless. In the United States, the importance of naval expansion had been popularized by the writings of Alfred Thayer Mahan prior to the annexation of Hawaii and the Spanish-American War. The U.S. Navy protested that interference from the growing number of amateurs on the air hampered naval communications and could threaten national security in time of war. Often, stronger and better equipped amateur stations drowned out their naval counterparts. Hams would monitor naval communications and, on occasion, send obscene messages or deliberately false information to ships at sea. Naval officials began lobbying for restrictions on amateur operations. The hams opposed giving the Navy priority on the airwaves, arguing that naval interests could be preserved without encroaching upon their domain.

The Navy instigated passage of the Radio Act of 1912 primarily to address the problem of interference from hams. The legislation required a license for radio transmission. Interstate stations could only operate on channels not assigned to government stations. The Secretary of Commerce could not deny a license but could assign wavelengths and time limits. Preferred portions of the spectrum were awarded to the military and to the commercial wireless companies, with the least desirable wavelengths assigned to citizens not affiliated with the government or corporations.

The new restrictions contained in the Radio Act of 1912 were opposed by most hams, who banded together in 1915 to form their own national organization, Hiram Percy Maxim's American Radio Relay League, which sought to create a national system of amateur radio. Douglas (1987) noted that on Washington's birthday in 1916 Maxim demonstrated that amateurs could constitute a national communication network through a countrywide relay of the following message: "A democracy requires that a people who govern and educate themselves should be so armed and disciplined that they can protect themselves" (p. 296). The relay received considerable publicity and increased the prestige of amateurs. Despite the constraints of the Radio Act of 1912, by 1920 about a quarter-million hams monitored 15,000 amateur stations. The hams represented a key factor, as radio pioneers who asserted the prerogatives of the public over the airwaves, in the early history of broadcasting.

Along with amateur radio enthusiasts, educators played an indispensable role in the origins of broadcasting in the United States. The earliest experiments in wireless transmission in the United States dating back to the 1890s took place in college physics and electricity laboratories. Probably the first person to broadcast intentionally to a general audience was Charles D. "Doc" Herrold of the College of Engineering and Wireless in San Jose, California. The term "broadcast" designates the use of the airwaves to transmit on a regular basis speech or music intended for the general public. Herrold engaged in a series of sound experiments, assisted by wireless students. Beginning in 1909, Herrold began transmitting from a bank building in San Jose and installed receivers for the public in local hotel lobbies. The experiment expanded into weekly broadcasts—with news bulletins, phonograph records, and an occasional live singer—monitored by amateurs as far away as San Francisco. Radio pioneer Lee De Forest said that Herrold's station "can rightfully claim to be the oldest broadcasting station of the whole world" (cited in Sterling & Kittross, 1978, p. 40).

Prior to World War I, besides the experiment operated by Herrold's technical college, four universities (Wisconsin, Nebraska, North Dakota, and Nebraska Wesleyan) operated radio stations to broadcast weather forecasts, market reports, and news bulletins. The land-grant colleges pioneered in the use of radio for the general public as a result of their mission to make higher education more of a community resource through the practical arts and sciences. As a result, Justin Morrill, who led the movement for land-grant colleges in the 1860s, has been called the spiritual father of educational and public broadcasting (Witherspoon & Kovitz, 1987). The University of Wisconsin, under the influence of the Progressive movement, played a leadership role in the educational broadcasting movement. Robert M. La Follette, Wisconsin governor from 1901 to 1906 and subsequently a U.S. senator, fostered the "Wisconsin idea" of public service by the university to all people of the state and the application of that principle to broadcasting. Given the role of the land-grant colleges of the Midwest, it is noteworthy that the etymological root of the word "broadcasting" was agrarian, signifying a method of sowing seeds in all directions.

Severin (1978) emphasized that by transmitting regularly scheduled messages intended for scattered audiences the pioneering educational stations demonstrated the potential of radio for broadcasting at a time when commercial radio companies only used radio as a means of point-to-point communication. By 1916 the Department of Commerce had issued licenses for wireless transmission to 15 educational institutions. The number of high school and college radio clubs engaged in regular broadcasts continued to grow. Up until the First World War, much of the early activity and experiments in radio took place in the homes of ordinary citizens and on the campuses of public universities. When the United States entered the war in 1917, all amateur radio transmitters as well as those owned by commercial interests were closed down as the Navy assumed operational control of all stations. Local police seized and dismantled independent stations that refused to cooperate. During the war, the Navy drew on the expertise of amateurs to expand and operate its communication facilities.

According to Sterling and Kittross (1978), at the end of World War I "the belief recurred that Congress had made a wrong turn in the late 1840s when, after providing capital for Morse, it allowed the telegraph to revert to private hands" (p. 51). Some members of Congress did not want the same mistake to be repeated in regard to radio. An attempt was made to revive the Alexander Bill of 1916, which would have enabled the government to compete with commercial interests in acquiring radio stations and potentially in establishing a government network. The bill, named after the congressman who introduced the legislation, was supported by the Secretary of the Navy and by Hiram Percy Maxim, the inventor who headed the American Radio Relay League. However, the call for the return of government-operated stations to private hands led by the Marconi interests and AT&T, followed by the Republican congressional sweep of 1918, killed the Alexander Bill. President Wilson ordered all stations returned to their owners as of March 1, 1920.

Instead of a direct governmental stake in radio, a governmentally sanctioned private enterprise would play a key role in the development of radio. Fear that a foreign company, the Marconi interests, would gain a monopoly in overseas radio communication after the war led to the creation in 1919 of the Radio Corporation of America (RCA) as a private "chosen instrument" of American policy in international communications (Sterling & Kittross, 1978, p. 53). RCA was a joint venture of General Electric, Westinghouse, and AT&T. General Electric and Westinghouse would manufacture, and RCA sell, radio receiving sets; AT&T would manufacture transmitters and use radio telephony for its domestic business. The partners also agreed to share patents. Initially, the founders of RCA did not intend to engage in broadcasting itself because they assumed that profits would derive from the sale of radios, not from programming. At the time the leaders of the radio industry did not grasp the potential of the medium for *broadcasting* on a regular basis to a mass audience but envisaged it as a means of transmitting messages between private parties.

In the immediate aftermath of the war, as the popular radio boom gathered momentum, hobbyists and educational broadcasters resumed and expanded their prewar activities. The American Radio Relay League distributed its publication *QST* within the ham community and helped lay the groundwork for the establishment of an International Amateur Radio Union. The number of ham stations continued to grow: By 1920 there were 15 times more amateur stations than all other types combined. By 1923 radio licenses had been issued to over 70 educational institutions. "To bring their dreams to fruition," Gibson (1977) noted, "colleges broadcast from stadiums, auditoriums, and lecture halls. They offered sporting events for public relations and publicity, dramas and concerts for adult entertainment and education, and complete courses for college credit" (p. 3). Witherspoon and Kovitz (1987) underscored how the early educational stations viewed their mandate broadly, carrying public affairs programming and consciously providing a broadcasting service distinct from commercial radio:

> While many of the early stations were at educational institutions, their programming mission was never seen as heavily instructional. Formal education was seen as a valuable facet of the service . . . but public programming has always ranged from stock market reports to drama and self-improvement for adults at home. (p. 61)

Noncommercial organizations such as churches and municipalities also acquired radio stations. Even the department stores, newspapers, theaters, banks, and other commercial enterprises that operated radio stations in the early 1920s did so as a sideline for publicity purposes rather than as a profit-making enterprise.

Douglas (1987) documented the revival during the radio boom of the early 1920s of the utopian aspirations originally inspired by the telegraph. Articles in magazines of the period hailed radio as a tool for making the concept of nationhood a reality. At the same time, stations rooted in diverse regions could affirm the nation's cultural diversity. The medium's potential as a resource for education and political discourse was discussed. Magazine articles portrayed radio as a democratizing agent that would "tend strongly to level the class distinctions, which depend so largely on the difference in opportunity for information and culture" (p. 309). Douglas also noted the hope that radio would promote mutual understanding and a stronger social fabric: "Those isolated from the mainstream of American culture would now be brought into the fold. Farmers, the poor, the housebound, and the uneducated were repeatedly mentioned as the main beneficiaries" (p. 306).

During the same period, commercial interests expanded their radio activities. In 1920, Westinghouse, part of the RCA consortium, launched radio station KDKA in Pittsburgh with its broadcast of the Harding-Cox election returns. Many broadcast historians define this event as the official beginning of American broadcasting in its commercial form. KDKA contributed to the radio boom, which resulted in the licensing of 400 stations by 1922. Westinghouse, General Electric, and RCA established stations throughout the country to create a nationwide audience. However, radio manufacturers initially established stations solely to encourage the sale of radios, which was seen as the basis of their profits; there was no conception yet of advertising revenue from broadcasts. Barnouw (1978) observed that "although the broadcasting era had been launched, the time-buying 'sponsor' was not yet a part of it. None of the first four hundred stations had sold time—for advertising or for any other purpose" (pp. 9-10).

As Barnouw (1966) indicated, the question of how to pay for programming was unresolved in the early 1920s. The maiden issue of *Radio Broadcast* magazine in 1922 suggested various systems of public financing. One proposal involved funding from state tax revenues; the states had already established a record of supporting radio stations at state universities. Municipal financing was presented as an alternative: In 1922, money for WNYC, a municipal radio station in New York City, was appropriated. Another plan called for a national system based on a common fund administered by elected officials. Advertising was not even contemplated as an option. Legislative attempts were made to address the problem of financing. Twenty laws related to broadcasting were placed before the 67th Congress in the period from 1921 to 1923, including proposals for nationalization and a government network. However, the impulse for public financing of broadcasting would be eclipsed by the emergence of commercial broadcasting.

In 1922, AT&T established WEAF in New York City, a new kind of station based on "toll broadcasting." It represented the first plan for selling airtime. AT&T viewed the station—and a planned national network of 38 stations linked by its telephone lines—as a common carrier for reaching the public via radio. It was conceived as a kind of radio telephone for which anyone who wished to talk to the public could pay a toll for the time. According to the original plan, AT&T would not provide programming but channels for use by paying customers. The paucity of individual users led WEAF to improvise and to expand its approach.

> Through WEAF . . . broadcasting had discovered its own saleable commodity: time. WEAF . . . sold both time and "talent"—bands, singers and speakers—to business firms who quickly found that "sponsoring," which meant attaching brand names to a programme, was more profitable than using time for direct advertising. When WEAF developed the strategy of signing contracts with advertising agencies rather than with "sponsors," and then paying the agencies 15 per cent commission . . . the pattern of public broadcasting in America was set. (Burns, 1979, pp. 5-6)

WEAF's system of sponsorship was sharply criticized in 1922 at the first of a series of Washington Radio Conferences organized by Secretary of Commerce Hoover to address the future of American broadcasting. Publicly, Hoover bowed to widespread criticism of radio advertising, declaring it "inconceivable that we should allow such so great a possibility for service and for news and for entertainment and education, for vital commercial purposes to be drowned in advertising chatter" (cited in Czitrom, 1982, p. 6). Both radio and general-interest publications condemned the plan as a mercenary attempt to exploit a public resource for private gain. Barnouw (1978) indicated that AT&T responded cautiously to such criticisms. Advertising on WEAF consisted of indirect, trade-name sponsorship. Company names were attached to programs such as the Goodrich Silvertown Orchestra and the Kodak Chorus, but the mention of prices and store locations became taboo. During the early and mid-1920s, commercial broadcasting remained a controversial experiment during a period in which over 200 noncommercial stations were on the air.

Despite Hoover's public statements, his policies as Secretary of Commerce favored commercial broadcasters or at least private stewardship of a public trust. Besides relying on the advice of the large radio companies, he permitted the sale of stations and their assigned wavelengths. This weakened the original notion of the government granting temporary licenses, and "in effect made a radio channel private property" (Czitrom, 1982, p. 76). At the second Washington Radio Conference in 1923, WEAF received a major boost from Hoover, who sought to address the growing chaos on the airwaves caused by the unchecked proliferation of stations. He responded by establishing a three-tiered hierarchy of stations: clear-channel stations with maximum power and reach, mid-size regional stations, and local stations serving small areas and often restricted to daytime hours. WEAF successfully argued that its toll station served the general public and deserved a clear channel, whereas educational stations represented special-interest programming and deserved only secondary status. Hoover awarded WEAF a clear channel, and most educational and other nonprofit stations received local status, which severely restricted the power of their transmitters and hours of broadcast. This would become a far-reaching precedent in the conflict between commercial and noncommercial broadcasters.

In 1923, AT&T established its second station, WCAP, in Washington, D.C. and developed a special cable for linking stations for "chain" broadcasts. The Bell system's telephone lines permitted the earliest network broadcasts such as *The Everready Hour* and remote broadcasts of political and sports events. AT&T, which refused to provide telephone lines to nonaffiliated commercial stations, seemed positioned for great profits and domination of national network broadcasting. RCA, General Electric, and Westinghouse, alarmed at AT&T's supremacy in programming and monopoly on networking technology, also began to sell time. Their sponsorship system, like AT&T's, would be indirect, somewhat akin to what later would be called "underwriting." For example, *Harper's Bazaar* presented a fashion show, *Field and Stream* a sports show, but neither paid for airtime, which was provided at no cost. However, AT&T contested the right of its RCA partners to engage in any form of sponsored toll broadcasting, which it considered an extension of the telephone business.

The bitter dispute between the so-called telephone and radio groups in the mid-1920s was resolved in large measure under the threat of antitrust hearings by the Federal Trade Commission. The resulting compromise, formalized in 1926, was of critical importance in establishing the structure of commercial broadcasting in the United States. AT&T agreed to divest itself of WEAF and WCAP, and indeed to quit the broadcast field entirely, for a lucrative quid pro quo. As part of the agreement, a new broadcasting network was established, the National Broadcasting Company (NBC), linking the stations of RCA, GE, and Westinghouse. The NBC stations and future affiliates would be linked by AT&T lines for terms guaranteeing the telephone company substantial fees. On November 15, 1926, the NBC network was launched with great fanfare. CBS came into existence a year later. Sponsored programming entered, in the words of Barnouw (1978), "its nationwide network phase" (p. 21).

The position of the networks would be strengthened by the Radio Act of 1927. The four national radio conferences convened by Secretary of Commerce Hoover in the period 1922-1925 laid the foundation for the Radio Act of 1927, a piece of emergency legislation with long-term consequences for noncommercial broadcasters. Hoover had convened the first conference in 1922 because of his concern that he lacked authority under the Radio Act of 1912 to deal with the regulatory problems posed by the explosive growth of radio, a fear that subsequent litigation proved well founded. Hoover asked educators, hams, and other interested parties to join representatives of the radio industry in developing proposals to help Congress enact appropriate legislation. Gibson (1977) noted that at the very first radio conference of 1922 the three fundamental tenets of American broadcasting were enunciated: The airwaves belonged to the public, the federal government should regulate broadcasting to establish order on the broadcast spectrum, and privately owned stations could broadcast in the public interest. Here was the notion of a "trusteeship model" that became the basis of the Radio Act of 1927 and all subsequent broadcast legislation. The concept of the private interests serving the public good in broadcasting with minimal government supervision was in accord with Hoover's belief in the leadership of a socially responsible business elite in American society.

The failure of Congress to enact legislation led Hoover to call subsequent radio conferences, out of which developed the three-tiered hierarchy of stations mentioned above. However, Zenith mounted a successful court challenge in 1926 to the Secretary of Commerce's authority to regulate the broadcast spectrum. The specter of a return to the uncontrolled growth of stations, resulting in interference on the airwaves and a chaotic broadcast environment, threatened the orderly expansion of the new networks. NBC and other commercial broadcasters together with Hoover intensified their campaign for congressional action. The Radio Act of 1927, passed originally as emergency legislation establishing the Federal Radio Commission (FRC) on a one-year basis, created the regulatory foundation for American broadcasting. Congress renewed the FRC in 1928 for one year and in 1929 indefinitely. The FRC allocated licenses and reduced the number of stations. Commercial broadcasters had successfully lobbied for the principle that licensing criteria be determined by a federal administrative agency rather than Congress, which was more responsive to the general public. For McChesney (1990), enactment of the Radio Act of 1927 and subsequent legislation suggested that "the modern system emerged not through consensus but through broadcasters' concerted efforts to limit public and congressional impact on policy" (p. 29).

As Congress enacted the Radio Act, educational broadcasters sought protection against the inroads of commercialism. The Association of College and University Broadcasting Stations (ACUBS), founded in 1925 during the fourth national radio conference, lobbied unsuccessfully for Congress to assign a block of channels to the states for use by land-grant state universities. House and Senate conferees declined to adopt the proposal for fear of establishing a precedent for other "special interest groups." The Act simply instructed the FRC to regulate broadcasting "in the public interest, convenience, and necessity." The amorphous phrase, borrowed from 19th-century public utility legislation, established little guidance for the balancing of public and private interests by the FRC and little comfort for increasingly hard-pressed educational broadcasters (Gibson, 1977). This formulation was perpetuated in subsequent legislation and remains the basis of contemporary broadcasting law.

In 1928, the FRC instituted its comprehensive allocation of wavelengths known as General Order No. 40. The FRC devised the allocation plan together with the networks and the National Association of Broadcasters without soliciting input from the ACUBS or other noncommercial broadcasters. Forty of the 90 available channels were assigned to 50,000-watt stations, which had exclusive national use of clear channels. The other 50 channels served the remaining 600 stations that broadcast with low power in different regions on the same frequency or shared airtime on individual stations in the same locale. The FRC also instituted a process by which the frequency assignments of existing broadcasters could be challenged, initiating a period of cutthroat competition.

In effect, the FRC extended the approach initiated by Hoover to deal with interference on the airwaves and competing license applications by creating a hierarchy of stations favoring commercial broadcasters. In its annual report for 1929 the FRC reiterated the rationale originally accepted by Hoover in 1923 in connection with WEAF. The underlying assumption was that in seeking to maximize their profits, commercial stations would inevitably engage in programming of interest to the broadest general public. Such general public service broadcasters would be favored in license allocations over so-called special interests, which ranged from educational outsets to what the FRC termed propaganda stations. The FRC placed in this category stations like WLWL, the progressive Catholic station in New York

City, and WCFL, the labor movement's outlet in Chicago. "There is no room in the broadcast band," the FRC declared in 1929, "for every school of thought, religious, political, social, and economic, each to have its separate broadcasting station, its mouthpiece in the ether" (cited in McChesney, 1987a, p. 120). Advertising was not considered a private or selfish interest by the FRC because it provided the financial basis for programming, especially entertainment, for a mass audience. McChesney (1987a) aptly characterized the FRC's logic in endorsing private, commercial control of the airwaves:

> Consequently, since every group could not have its own "mouthpiece," then, according to the FRC, no such group should be entitled to have the privilege of a broadcast license. If a group's message was desired by the public, the reasoning went, the listeners would make this known through the marketplace and "general public service" [commercial] broadcasters would provide this type of material as part of their "well-rounded" programming. (p. 120)

Commercialization and centralization would go hand in hand: "The need to maximize audiences and to achieve economies of scale drives commercial operators towards syndication of programme material and the formation of networks" (Lewis & Booth, 1990, p. 5). The FRC's spectrum reallocation plan dramatically strengthened the position of the commercial networks. All but three of the 40 clear-channel stations were owned by or affiliated with NBC or CBS. In the four years following the Radio Act of 1927, the percentage of radio stations affiliated with the two networks jumped from 6% to 30%. It has been estimated that NBC and CBS accounted for nearly 70% of American broadcasting by 1931, when number of hours broadcast and level of power are taken into consideration.

Advertising on radio, which hitherto had assumed a largely experimental and unsystematic form, became the very foundation of American broadcasting. Major corporations recognized the advertising potential of the networks that dominated the nation's airwaves after 1928. Advertising on radio changed qualitatively as well as quantitatively. At first, NBC continued the practice established by AT&T of eschewing direct advertising in favor of trade-name publicity.

The first code of the National Association of Broadcasters, issued in 1928, limited commercial messages to daytime hours under the assumption that the period from 7 p.m. to 11 p.m. were inviolate family hours (Barnouw,

1978). However, indirect advertising became obsolete following the stock market crash and the aggressive advertising policies of NBC's less-established rival, CBS. For example, CBS President William Paley proudly took credit for initiating the regular mention of prices in radio advertising in selling tobacco. In transcending such traditional constraints on commercials and establishing the modern affiliate system, Paley helped transform commercial broadcasting into a powerful national advertising medium. In the words of Halberstam (1979), "He made the American home the focal point of the American marketplace" (p. 38). In 1933, NBC reversed its policy barring direct advertising. A year later, revenues from direct advertising approached $75 million. Radio was moving out of the hands of the amateur hams and into the clutches of commercial broadcasters, out of the garage and into the living room:

> Installed in a modishly designed cabinet, it was transformed from a laboratory apparatus into a piece of furniture. It began to be thought of as a family pastime, not a lone flight of the imagination. It meant listening, not transmitting; consuming, not creating. A once venturesome pursuit appeared to have become domesticated and passive. (Covert, 1992, p. 304)

Whereas the Radio Act of 1927 and General Order No. 40 permitted the commercial networks to expand dramatically, educational broadcasting went into a tailspin. In 1927, 94 educational institutions had broadcast licenses; by 1931, only 49 were left. The process by which the FRC pressured an educational or otherwise nonprofit station off the air often worked as follows. First, the educational station would be reassigned a less desirable frequency so that a commercial station could have a more powerful signal. Second, the educational station would have to share its time on the new limited frequency with a local commercial station, which received the evening hours critical for adult education. Third, there would be a sudden requirement for expensive new equipment. Fourth, the expense of trips to Washington and litigation to preserve a license finally led many educational broadcasters to throw in the towel (Severin, 1978, p. 497).

Originally, the RCA consortium's interest in radio was limited to the sale of hardware until the experimentation of amateurs and educational broadcasters revealed radio's potential. As Douglas (1987) emphasized, commercial interests repositioned themselves with the aid of the state:

The radio trust was thus able to co-opt the amateur vision of how radio should be used, and to use the airwaves for commercial ends, to try to promote cultural homogeneity, to mute or screen out diversity and idiosyncrasy, and to advance values consonant with consumer capitalism. (p. 320)

CHAPTER

The Defeat of the
Broadcast Reform
Movement of the 1930s

The ACUBS, representing the Midwest's land-grant college stations, sought to counter the threat to the future of educational broadcasting posed by the expansion of the commercial networks during the late 1920s. The FRC, established by the Radio Act of 1927, ignored the appeals of ACUBS President Charles A. Culver to aid college stations. The ACUBS was also unsuccessful in rallying support for the Davis Amendment of 1928 to the bill prolonging the existence of the FRC. The Amendment, supported by educational broadcasters, sought to end discrimination against local and nonprofit radio stations. At the ACUBS's first national convention in 1930, a resolution was passed endorsing the reservation of radio channels for educational stations by the FRC—the first formal call for special noncommercial channel allocations on the broadcast spectrum (Nord, 1978). The FRC responded that it did not have the authority to do so and recommended that educational broadcasters seek congressional action.

McChesney (1990) noted how after 1928 "a coherent and unrepentant opposition to the emerging capitalist domination of the airwaves developed for the first time" (p. 34). The standard-bearer of that opposition during the 1930s was the National Committee on Education by Radio (NCER), which became the leading advocate of educational channel reservations after its establishment in 1930. The NCER represented nine leading educational organizations, including the National Educational Association (NEA), the National Catholic Educational Association, and the Association of Land Grant Colleges and Universities. The NCER received a five-year $200,000 grant from the Payne Fund to conduct research, aid the survival of existing educational stations, publish a bulletin, and engage in lobbying activities (Gibson, 1977). The Payne Fund had been founded by a wealthy Cleveland family to explore the impact of new mass media on youths and education and was best known for sponsoring a series of studies on the impact of movies on audiences. Its serious interest in radio dated from a visit by its president, H. M. Clymer, to observe the educational program of the British Broadcasting Corporation (BBC) in 1926.

Leach (1983) stressed the NCER's ties to midwestern populism in its antitrust perspective and criticism of electric utility monopolies such as General Electric and Westinghouse, parent companies of RCA and NBC. He wrote that through the NEA, the Payne Fund and the militant advocates of educational radio the NCER "could trace its blood lines back to the public school crusades of the 19th century" and "claim as ancestors the agrarian protestors and the progressives of the pre-World War I years." The NCER's leadership "envisioned educational broadcasting as the redemption of Jeffersonian democracy, restoring the means of informed citizenship and self improvement to everyone with a radio set" (p. 8). States with strong populist traditions, like Wisconsin, had the most vigorous educational radio stations. The rhetoric of crusading populism was applied to the "radio power trust" and to the critique of commercial broadcasting.

The driving force behind the NCER was Joy Elmer Morgan of the NEA. Morgan believed that a great public resource—the airwaves—was being plundered by private interests as a result of federal policy. Morgan's advocacy of a separate noncommercial system involved not only his belief in radio's educational potential but a critique of the commercial system as a whole. Morgan was a veteran of the public utilities movement of the progressive era. According to Nord (1978), Morgan "believed that it was monopoly business interests which had brought on the Great Depression and which were now undermining the high purpose of radio" (pp. 329-330). In 1931, he predicted that out of the Depression would develop either a century of chaos or a new world order:

> Whether it will be one or the other will depend largely upon whether broadcasting will be used as a tool of education or as an instrument of selfish greed. So far, our American radio interests have thrown their major influence on the side of greed. . . . There has never been in the entire history of the United States an example of mismanagement and lack of vision so colossal and far-reaching in its consequences as our turning of the radio channels almost exclusively into commercial hands. (cited in McChesney, 1990, p. 35)

A wide spectrum of broadcast reformers representing various sectors of American society echoed the NCER's call to convince Congress to reserve noncommercial channels. Agrarian interests in the Midwest were represented by the ACUBS, whose stations engaged in broadcasting farm extension and general educational programming. Church leaders and religious broadcasters were an important factor in the broadcasting reform movement. They included Gross W. Alexander of the Federal Council of Churches of Christ and Rev. John B. Harney of the Paulist Fathers, who operated WLWL in New York. The Paulist Fathers, a progressive order founded in the 19th century to spread the social gospel, established WLWL, the first Catholic radio station in the United States, in 1925. One of the nation's most powerful stations, its programming was nondenominational and directed especially toward the working class and the disadvantaged. Within two years of its founding, WLWL's existence was threatened by federal regulatory policies favoring commercial broadcasters and by commercial station WMCA in particular, with which it was forced to share its frequency.

Harney became a sharp critic of the power wielded by NBC and CBS, which he characterized as monopolistic networks in increasing control of the educational, social, and political content of the airwaves. Harney argued—on the air, in his writings, and before government bodies—that the programming of a centralized broadcasting system based on advertising would favor the existing social order and marginalize dissident perspectives.

Another casualty of the FRC's reallocation policies was Chicago's pioneering labor radio station WCFL, founded in 1926 by Edward N. Nockels, secretary of the Chicago Federation of Labor. Nockels envisaged WCFL as a key vehicle of the labor movement and progressive politics in the United States. He conceived it as a nonprofit station to be funded by listener donations and by income from the quarterly *WCFL Radio Magazine,* which had a circulation approaching 100,000. However, WCFL had to resort to commercial advertising to survive. Its programming mixed entertainment and public affairs so as to attract a wide audience. WCFL sponsored development of an inexpensive radio set that working-class households could afford. Nockels wanted WCFL, which became a powerful community force in Chicago, to be a national clear-channel station, the cornerstone of a progressive broadcasting system providing an alternative to the commercial networks. He thought that, after the right to organize, the most important task facing the American labor movement was to establish its own national broadcasting network (McChesney, 1994).

General Order No. 40 led to the reduction of broadcast power and airtime hours for WCFL and to the requirement that it share its new frequency with an NBC affiliate. The elimination of evening broadcast time undercut the size of WCFL's listenership. Questioning the FRC's allocation criteria, Nockels asked, "Was it in the public interest, convenience and necessity that all of the 90 channels for radio broadcasting be given to capital . . . and not even one channel to the millions that toil?" (cited in McChesney, 1992, p. 16). Nockels would be frustrated in his campaign to get a clear-channel independent labor station. After 1929, Nockels despaired of gaining a sympathetic hearing before the FRC and called for congressional action and government control of broadcasting. Nockels believed that access to the airwaves represented "the modern phase of the right of free speech," and that "whoever controls radio broadcasting in the future will eventually control the nation" (cited in McChesney, 1992, p. 16).

As Edward Nockels, Joy Elmer Morgan, and other broadcast reformers emphasized, freedom of speech was at stake in the struggle over the airwaves. These critics questioned the willingness of commercial broadcasters to air controversial issues and critiques of the existing economic and social order. The American Civil Liberties Union (ACLU) joined the broadcast reform movement because of the danger of censorship posed by growing network control of radio. As early as 1926, Morris Ernst of the ACLU complained in *The Nation* magazine about the failure to consider the First Amendment implications of radio policy (McChesney, 1987b). In the mid-1930s, as the result of a stream of complaints of censorship, the ACLU created a radio committee, chaired by Bethuel M. Webster, Jr., former general counsel of the FRC, to deal with what Roger Baldwin considered the constraints on free speech inherent in the commercial broadcasting system. The ACLU's radio committee advanced a comprehensive critique of the radio industry and joined the NCER in calling for an independent government study to rethink the structure of the broadcast industry.

The broadcast reform movement embraced broad constituencies in American society: educators, agricultural interests, the labor movement, the church, and civil libertarians as well as intellectuals such as John Dewey and Bruce Bliven, editor of *The New Republic*. This movement—generally situated under the rubric of "educational" radio—was not exclusively academic or pedagogical but included various groups of citizens whose needs were not being met by commercial broadcasters. During the first half of the 1930s, broadcast reformers, led by the NCER, advocated a variety of plans to restructure American broadcasting. One leading plan involved the establishment of a network of noncommercial government stations on a regional and national basis. A second approach called for the government to set aside a percentage of broadcast channels for the exclusive use of noncommercial broadcasters without addressing the question of how such stations would be funded. The broadcast reform movement of the 1930s underscored the oligopolistic character of the commercial network system. Its leaders argued that a private, network-dominated, advertising-supported broadcast system could never satisfy the communication requirements of a democratic society. The different elements of the broadcast reform movement did not sufficiently coordinate their efforts to limit the power of the commercial networks and to develop an alternative structure for American broadcasting. Nonetheless, they advanced a searching critique of the broadcasting status quo and proposed alternative structures that gained considerable support during the 1930s.

Another organization, also founded in 1930, took an approach diametrically opposed to that of the NCER. The National Advisory Council on Radio in Education (NACRE) advocated offering educational programming on commercial stations rather than through a separate noncommercial system. Its director, Levering Tyson, believed that educators should collaborate with commercial broadcasters and function within the framework of the free enterprise system. He held that educational broadcasters needed to base their programming on business and market principles and viewed the dull programs and miniscule audiences of noncommercial stations with contempt. Tyson, an administrator of extension education at Columbia University and a pioneer in educational radio, was well positioned to foster cooperation between the academy and the industry. He had been approached in 1924 by WEAF to produce a series of educational broadcasts. Columbia University had rebuffed some of Tyson's proposals for educational radio, after which he gravitated to the commercial networks to realize his plans. In 1930, a bitter conflict developed between Morgan's NCER and Tyson's NACRE. The former supported independent noncommercial stations and systems, the latter, conversely, the educational use of airtime provided by commercial broadcasters:

> At best, broadcast reformers regarded NACRE members as the "unwitting patsies" of the commercial broadcasters; at worst, the NACRE was regarded as a conscious effort by the commercial broadcasters and their corporate allies to drive a wedge in the resolve of the educational community for broadcast reform. (McChesney, 1992, pp. 20-21)

The NCER/NACRE split signaled a conflict within the ranks of public broadcasters between "separatists" and "collaborationists" vis-à-vis commercial forces that persists to the present.

The NCER and the NACRE reflected the different approaches of their principal foundation supporters, the Payne Fund and the Carnegie Corporation of New York. Leach (1983) wrote that "in contrast to the Payne Fund, with its roots in Ohio and its commitment to public education, the Carnegie Corp. was fully at home on Wall Street and comfortable with private initiatives in education" (p. 4). He suggested that the NACRE could be understood as an expression of corporate liberalism: "It might be argued, in fact, that the NACRE belonged to one wing of the progressive movement—the Eastern wing, long at odds with Midwestern protest, that proposed the efficiency and generosity of big business as the answer to the nation's problems" (p. 10). The Carnegie Corporation became involved in educational broadcasting in 1926 through its subsidiary, the American Association for Adult Education (AAAE). Beginning in the late 1920s, the major eastern private foundations played a pivotal role in the history of educational and noncommercial broadcasting that has continued to the present. Indeed, nearly a half-century after the Carnegie Commission's initial involvement in educational broadcasting, the report of the Carnegie Commission on Educational Television in 1967 provided the blueprint for legislation creating the contemporary public radio and television system.

The AAAE together with NBC took the lead in establishing the NACRE with major grants from the Carnegie Corporation and John D. Rockefeller, Jr.

Tyson had already worked as an investigator for the AAAE. Carnegie Corporation President Frederick Keppel exercised final control over the activities of the NACRE, which was the outgrowth of collaboration between the Carnegie Foundation's AAAE and NBC at the end of the 1920s, when the network feared that critics of broadcast commercialism and monopoly would rally to the example of the newly established BBC in Britain. The AAAE had virtually no ties to educational organizations: "Plainly, the Carnegie-AAAE-NBC entente was designed to sidestep the Independents and establish educational radio on a new Cooperative footing" (Leach, 1983, p. 5).

Funding by the Carnegie Corporation and the Rockefeller Foundation enabled the NACRE to establish an advisory and informational service at its New York headquarters and to mount a national program to promote educational programming on commercial stations. The NACRE appointed committees in all academic disciplines to develop programs and fostered collaboration among colleges, networks, government agencies, and civic organizations. Each state was assigned a NACRE representative. The capstone of the NACRE's activities was its annual assembly. The fact that the President of the United States and the Secretary of the Interior addressed the 500 participants of the first assembly in 1931 in New York City suggested that the federal government looked favorably upon the NACRE's approach (Gibson, 1977). The 1931-1932 period represented a high point in cooperative programming by educators and commercial broadcasters sponsored by the NACRE. For example, Aspects of the Depression, produced in association with the Brookings Institution, featured 32 weekly talks over 50 NBC stations by prominent economists such as Rexford Tugwell and Frances Perkins. In fall 1931, NBC committed itself to a weekly half-hour for civic education for a four-year period. This resulted in *You and Your Government,* heard on 45 NBC stations in 1932, with the participation of distinguished academics such as Charles Beard and Charles Merriam. The most noteworthy show based on the cooperative principle was *The University of Chicago Roundtable.* The university's president, Robert Hutchins, was a member of the NACRE board. The show, featuring the faculty of the University of Chicago in a lively format, drew praise from across the country. Programming under NACRE auspices in this period represented one of the most successful experiments in educational broadcasting in the United States to date.

The FRC and commercial broadcasters favored the NACRE's doctrine of Cooperation over NCER's insistence on an independent noncommercial system. In 1931, a bill conceived by the NCER reserving a minimum of 15% of all radio channels for noncommercial educational use was introduced by Senator Simeon Fess. The FRC reiterated its position that educational programmers should rely on studio time offered by commercial stations. In the debate over the bill, Senator Clarence C. Dill of Washington complained that "the greatest weakness of radio in this country today is the lack of educational and informational broadcasting" and that the FRC was equating the public interest with the interests of commercial broadcasting (cited in Severin, 1978, pp. 496-497). Despite considerable popular and congressional support, the Fess Bill failed to get out of committee due to the lobbying efforts of the commercial broadcasting industry.

The New Deal seemed to offer broadcast reformers a second chance to reverse the precipitous decline of noncommercial radio stations. The Roosevelt administration proposed legislation to replace the Radio Act of 1927 by creating a central agency to regulate telephone, telegraph, cable, and radio. Roosevelt decided to support a bill that would consolidate federal regulatory authority in the new Federal Communications Commission (FCC) but not address the question of reforming the structure of broadcasting or the other communications industries. However, educational broadcasters recognized an opportunity in the proposed legislation to launch a counterattack before Congress and the American public. Here was a rallying point for educators and other critics of commercial broadcasting in the early years of the New Deal. The NCER held a conference in Washington, D.C. on the "Use of Radio as a Cultural Agency in a Democracy" to coincide with debate on the bill. Noncommercial broadcasters from across the land converged on the nation's capital to testify at congressional hearings.

As part of the reform campaign, Father Harney of WLWL in New York published *Education and Religion vs. Commercial Radio,* a polemic against control of broadcasting by the networks and commercial interests. In congressional testimony he proposed an amendment to the communications bill requiring the new regulatory commission, after 90 days, to allocate 25% of the channels to noncommercial broadcasters. Harney argued that these nonprofit broadcasters should be permitted to support their operations through advertising, a position officially opposed by the NCER, which advocated a radical reconstruction of American broadcasting with a direct system of funding for nonprofit stations. Harney's proposal, which threatened the preeminence of commercial broadcasters, was introduced by Senators Robert F. Wagner of New York and Henry D. Hatfield of West Virginia in

1934. Harney and Nockels worked on the language of the amendment to the administration's communications legislation together with its congressional sponsors. The Wagner-Hatfield Bill would have made all existing licenses null and void, and established a system by which one fourth of the most desirable frequencies would be allotted to educational, religious, cooperative and other nonprofit institutions. Wagner said, "Let's not be too solicitous over the large stations who through the favor of government have secured a practical monopoly" (cited in Gibson, 1977, p. 26). Harney generated over 60,000 signatures in support for the Wagner-Hatfield Bill, and Nockels also rallied support for the measure. The trade publication *Variety* reported that the bill was likely to be adopted. Many NCER associates favored the bill, although the NCER did not officially support the legislation because a substantial number of its members preferred the establishment of a BBC-like government network to complement the commercial networks.

The broadcasting industry struck back. By this time the National Association of Broadcasters (NAB) had become one of the most powerful and effective lobbying forces in Washington. A member of the House of Representatives sympathetic to the reformers, under attack from broadcasters in his district, wrote a confidential letter to the NCER in 1932 explaining that he was backing down from supporting a broadcasting reform bill in order to preserve his political career: "I am mentioning these facts because you may not fully understand the complete control that the broadcasting stations have over the Members of Congress" (cited in McChesney, 1992, p. 24). The NAB ridiculed a provision of the Wagner-Hatfield Bill that allowed the nonprofit groups to sell part of their allotted time to help finance the stations. The networks stepped up the offer of their unsold time for educational projects such as NBC's *University of Chicago Roundtable* and CBS's *American School of the Air* and promised a new era of cooperative broadcasting. The NAB devised a stratagem to defuse momentum toward passage of the bill by having a clause inserted in the Communications Act of 1934 requiring the new FCC to hold hearings on the plan to reserve 25% of channels for noncommercial broadcasters and to report back to Congress in 1935. The Wagner-Hatfield Bill, whose passage had earlier seemed likely, went down to defeat in the Senate. The bill, McChesney (1987a) noted, represented "the most serious challenge ever to the private, oligopolistic and commercially subsidized nature of American broadcasting." With its defeat, "the era of legitimately challenging the private, commercial basis of American broadcasting had passed" (p. 128).

The Communications Act of 1934, passed after the defeat of the Wagner-Hatfield Bill, was limited to combining jurisdiction for the regulation of broadcasting and the telephone industry in the new FCC. The legal structure for broadcasting contained in the Radio Act of 1927 was incorporated into the Communications Act of 1934, which remains the fundamental law of American telecommunications. The FCC was given the old FRC's authority to license radio in the public interest, convenience, and necessity. The Communications Act of 1934 merely required the FCC to study the proposal that Congress allocate fixed percentages of channels to nonprofit institutions and report its findings a year later.

The 1934 FCC hearings, in which 135 witnesses were heard and 14,000 pages of testimony recorded, resulted in another defeat for noncommercial broadcasting. When President Roosevelt appointed the seven members to the new FCC, the pro-industry chair and vice chair were holdovers from the FRC, whereas its sole reformist, James Hanley, was not reappointed. In testimony before the FCC, the nonprofit organizations lacked unity and offered a plethora of different approaches to the question of educational broadcasting, ranging from government ownership of a national system of radio stations and the creation of state and local systems to setting aside airtime on commercial stations. The lack of a coordinated plan played into the hands of the networks, who staged a highly polished performance to make the case for their ability to meet all the broadcasting needs of the American public. The FCC recommended against fixed channel allocations for noncommercial broadcasting and indicated its intention to promote Cooperation between commercial and noncommercial broadcasters. Never again would a fundamental restructuring of American broadcasting be seriously considered by a government body.

The NACRE model for Cooperation between educational and commercial broadcasters was an important factor in the defeat of the Wagner-Hatfield Bill in 1934 and in the FCC hearings on channels reservations in 1935. However, the cause of Cooperation, which reached its high-water mark in 1931-1932, was in retreat by mid-decade. By 1934, Tyson concluded that the NACRE would not attain the mass audience he aspired to reach. There was growing disenchantment among proponents of Cooperation as the networks cut back on the hours and funds allocated to educational broadcasting after 1934. Major defections took place at a NACRE conference in Washington coinciding with the FCC hearings in 1935, as Robert M. Hutchins of the University of Chicago and other educational leaders questioned the viability of the Cooperative approach and called for legislative action. Arthur G. Crane, president of the University of Wyoming, angrily declared that

> the present American system of broadcasting is an almost incredible absurdity for a country that stakes its existence upon universal suffrage, upon the general intelligence of its citizens, upon the spread of reliable information . . . , and then consigns a means of general communication exclusively to private interests, making public use for general welfare subordinate and incidental.
> . . . The absurdity passes comprehension when we not only give up our public birthright but tax ourselves to support commissions, to protect private monopoly in the use and control of what belongs to the nation. The absurdity becomes tragic when the total values of radio communication to a democracy are considered. (cited in McChesney, 1987b, note 68)

The "sustaining" programming of the networks during the latter part of the 1930s—with such highlights as Archibald MacLeish's drama *The Fall of the City* and *Ballad for Americans* with Paul Robeson—consisted of in-house productions rather than collaborative efforts with educators. Leach (1983) concluded that ultimately "Cooperation proved a hollow principle" (p. 2). He noted the irony that the myth of Cooperation triumphed in 1934-1935 at the same time it was failing in practice: "NACRE wasn't able to make Cooperation work, but the rhetoric of Cooperation survived. Ironically, NACRE played its biggest advocacy role precisely when NACRE leaders were starting to admit the inadequacies of their broadcasting experiments" (p. 14).

In 1937, a disillusioned Tyson resigned as head of the NACRE, which went out of existence a year later. 1937 was a time of transition for other broadcast reformers. Edward Nockels died that year, after which WCFL lost its focus as a labor movement station, and Father Harney's WLWL, bereft of sufficient airtime and funds, was sold. The components of the media reform movement, reeling from the defeat of 1934, broke apart and reoriented themselves in relation to the status quo (McChesney, 1994). The ACLU, for example, abandoned its critique of the broadcast industry and accepted the view defining free speech in terms of the rights of commercial broadcasters. Within the NCER, moderate leadership deposed the militants and reversed the organization's advocacy of structural reform and opposition to collaboration with the commercial networks. The NCER's official history, compiled after 1935, virtually purged from the record its critique of the broadcasting industry, the call for a noncommercial system, and the role of Joy Elmer Morgan. The NCER ceased operations in 1941. The ACUBS, with its heritage in the land-grant schools of the Midwest and the distinction of initiating the call for the reservation of noncommercial channels, was reconstituted as the National Association of Educational Broadcasters (NAEB). However, the NAEB, which became the standard-bearer for noncommercial broadcasting, conceived its mission more narrowly as representing the professional interests of educational broadcasters rather than spearheading a movement to reform the structure of American broadcasting. The process by which the militant—and nearly successful—effort to reform American broadcasting in the 1930s was airbrushed away made it more difficult for future generations of media reformers to resume the struggle for public control of the airwaves.

In 1938, the FCC, in a gesture to the marginalized educational broadcasting movement, reserved several channels in a new experimental high frequency band for noncommercial stations. The channels, in the band that would later be used by FM, were not of interest to commercial broadcasters at the time. An NCER official predicted that federal regulators would once again "let the educational stations do the experimental work," as college stations had done on the AM band in the 1920s, "and then perhaps would take away the channels and allocate them for commercial use" (cited in McChesney, 1994, p. 233).

* * *

The stages of development of radio in the period between the two world wars broadly paralleled that of the telegraph in the 19th century: first, popular enthusiasm, later a chaotic marketplace, and finally, government-fostered corporate monopoly. By the end of the interwar period, educational radio had been virtually eliminated from the American airwaves. The majority of the more than 200 educational licenses issued by the 1920s ceased to exist by the 1930s. Of the four university stations that had engaged in broadcasting prior to World War I, only one—that of the University of Wisconsin—succeeded in remaining on the air without interruption. By 1945, a mere 29 educational stations remained on the AM band, and of those only 13 had 5,000 watts or more power, and just 2 were permitted to broadcast during nighttime hours (Severin, 1978).

The Radio Act of 1927 provided the foundation for the institutionaliza-
tion of commercial broadcasting in the United States in the same year in
which the BBC was launched on a noncommercial basis in Great Britain.
Historical and ideological factors help explain the differences between the
dominant forms of broadcasting in the United States and Britain. A parlia-
mentary commission recommended the creation of the BBC as a public
corporation with a monopoly over broadcasting, financed by license fees
from owners of radio sets. Although ultimately answerable to Parliament, the
BBC was controlled by a board of governors and enjoyed broad independence from state control in the conduct of its affairs. Williams (1974)
attributed the character of the BBC to the English elite's "effective paternalist
definition of both service and responsibility" (p. 33). This tradition was
epitomized by John Reith, later Lord Reith, general director of the BBC from
1927 to 1938, who approached the task of bringing culture and information
into the homes of the British people with a missionary spirit. To be sure, the
public service principle behind the BBC was highly paternalistic and helped
legitimate and perpetuate the old elite, but it nonetheless provided a social
rationale for broadcasting that transcended the commercial marketplace.

Potter (1954) posited that the absence of a medieval civilization in the
United States meant that American capitalism would assume a purer form
and be less tempered by an aristocratic culture than in Europe. Furthermore,
the 1920s, the critical decade for broadcasting, was a period of economic
boom and political conservatism in America. The United States emerged
from World War I as the world's leading economic power. The Ford Motor
Company introduced its Model A and mass production techniques. A consumer revolution embracing products such as ready-made clothes, canned
foods, and electric ice-boxes and washing machines, transformed the home
and the workplace. As Allen (1964) noted in his classic study of the 1920s,
it was a period in which business was venerated as a higher calling and often
associated with religion; thus, in Bruce Barton's best-seller, *The Man Nobody
Knows,* Jesus is presented as "the founder of modern business," whose
parables were "the best advertisements of all time" and who "picked up
twelve men from the bottom ranks of business and forged them into an
organization that conquered the world" (cited in Allen, 1964, p. 149). It was
in this climate that the de facto privatization of the airwaves occurred and
that the commercial networks crushed educational broadcasting by the end
of the decade.

Herbert Hoover is the representational figure in the early history of American broadcasting as Lord Reith is for British broadcasting. The belief in the leadership of an enlightened business elite provides a continuum linking Hoover's radio conferences, the policies of the FRC, and the Cooperation program of the Carnegie Commission of New York. Unlike the public service principle in Britain, the state's role in the American broadcasting system was to engage in regulation limited to ensuring an orderly marketplace. It represented what Williams (1974) called "a classic kind of market-regulatory control, into which were asserted, always with difficulty and controversy, notions of a non-market public interest" (p. 35).

As part of the consumer revolution of the 1920s, a national advertising industry came into being. A necessity for driving the consumer revolution, advertising was hailed as integrating heterogeneous groups into a national market and way of life. Ewen (1989) cited an evangelical champion of consumerism in the late 1920s who said that the greatest doctrine America can offer the world is "the idea that workmen and the masses be looked upon not simply as workers and producers but as consumers" (p. 90). With the advent of modern advertising, based in part on the psychological insights gained from wartime propaganda and on the development of the science of market research, radio was an ideal means for the consumer culture to penetrate the home. Advertising would play a central role in a new economic order. In this historical context, Herbert Hoover, and subsequently the FRC, made the paradoxical ruling that commercial radio served the general public whereas noncommercial broadcasters represented special interests.

The research unit of the BBC reiterated in 1985 the fundamental difference between public service and commercial broadcasting: "Public service broadcasting is an attempt to embody, in the age of electronic communication, the notion of a public sphere as central to the democratic polity." A broadcasting system rooted in the public sphere, that arena of social interaction in which public opinion is formed and mobilized, is juxtaposed to a market-based system of broadcasting: "The two systems mobilize fundamentally different concepts of their audience and of the set of social relations which bind them to their audience and each member of that audience to other members" (cited in Schiller, 1989, pp. 322-323). The marketplace model approached its audience as individual consumers motivated by self-interest; the public service model defined its audience as citizens who require information to participate fully in the nation's political and cultural life.

If commercial broadcasters in the United States made great strides during the consumer and advertising revolution of the 1920s, the crisis of the Great Depression enabled noncommercial broadcasters to mount a significant counteroffensive in the period 1930-1935 led by the NCER. The NCER's program for an independent noncommercial system of broadcasting was countered by the principle of Cooperation between educators and commercial broadcasters advanced by the NACRE. The triumph of the advocates of Cooperation was ideological as well as political:

> In the second half of the [1930s], as the industry became economically and politically consolidated, the commercial broadcasters strove for ideological closure. In this campaign they triumphantly located commercial broadcasting . . . as an icon of American freedom and culture and, with considerable historical revisionism if not outright fabrication, removed it from critical contemplation. The opposition movement was correspondingly written out of the dominant perspective on the development of U.S. broadcasting, and the conflict of the early 1930s was erased from historical memory. (McChesney, 1990, p. 47)

David Sarnoff told a nationwide audience over NBC in the late 1930s that commercial broadcasting was a natural outgrowth of private enterprise, the basis of American freedom. By the 1940s, challenges to the network and advertising-dominated broadcasting system were outside the pale of legitimate discourse.

PART II

Public Radio

CHAPTER 4

Pacifica Radio

The Vision of Lewis K. Hill

Commercial broadcasters crushed the media reform movement of the 1930s politically and ideologically. Hence, in 1937 CBS President William S. Paley could assert that whoever attacks the structure of the "American system" of advertising-supported network broadcasting "attacks democracy itself" (cited in McChesney, 1994, p. 251). By World War II, noncommercial broadcasting had all but disappeared from the AM band. Participation in the war effort helped the broadcast industry fortify its position, which seemed impregnable in the cold war climate of the 1950s. Yet at precisely this moment, starting virtually from scratch, a small-scale experiment provided an alternative model for radio and inaugurated the modern movement for public broadcasting. This venture consciously sought to counter the constraints on public discourse in a period of political and cultural repression.

In 1946, Lewis K. Hill and a group of associates incorporated the Pacifica Foundation for the purpose of establishing a new kind of radio station. Poet Kenneth Rexroth recalled his first encounter with Hill in

California shortly after World War II, when Pacifica's founder appeared unannounced at a large meeting:

> Lew himself was astonishing . . . a tall thin man with a long, dead white face and a soft, propulsive manner of speaking. . . . He presented what was really a very simple thesis. There had been a great structural change in society, and the days of street meetings and little pamphlets were over. New, far more effective means of communication were available. It was comparatively easy and inexpensive to set up a listener supported FM radio station whose signal would cover at least the entire Bay Area, and which could be supported by the subscriptions without any commercials. (cited in Land, 1994, p. 163)

Following World War II, Pacifica received "the first noncommercial license that did not go to an educational or religious institution and was consequently important as a precedent" (Lewis & Booth, 1990, p. 116). Hill was critical of the direction most educational radio stations had taken:

> We must face the fact that the main use of university radio stations has not been to form a cultural bridge between centers of learning and occupational classes. . . . Moreover, the people in charge of educational stations are tied either to state legislatures or to boards of trustees which inevitably represent tendencies close to the commercial and conservative part of the community. (cited in Land, 1994, pp. 222-223)

In 1949, Pacifica's KPFA-FM went on the air in Berkeley, California. The history of public and community broadcasting after World War II, conceived as a social instrument transcending the traditional conceptual framework of educational radio, begins with KPFA.

There is no evidence that Hill was familiar with the history of the heterogeneous broadcast reform movement of the Depression years. Yet he resurrected and synthesized many of the principles voiced by broadcast reformers like Joy Elmer Morgan, Father John B. Harney, Edward Nockels, and Roger Baldwin during the 1930s. Unlike his spiritual ancestors of the 1930s, Hill was forced to recognize the domination of mainstream broadcasting by the commercial networks as a given. The attempt to establish a noncommercial broadcasting system on AM radio parallel with the commercial networks had ended with the defeat of the Wagner-Hatfield Bill. This is not to say that KPFA represented an accommodation with the status quo. The opposite was the case: KPFA represented a radical model for a nonprofit, community-based radio station operating outside the parameters of mainstream broadcasting. Lewis Hill based KPFA on principles that defied the social and political conventions of his day. On the eve of the postwar economic boom, Hill concluded that only a noncommercial broadcasting system financed by listener sponsorship could be free. On the eve of the McCarthy era, he envisaged KPFA as an electronic gadfly, providing access to groups and perspectives otherwise absent from the airwaves. In light of the hegemony of the networks, KPFA was fashioned as an *alternative* radio station. Hill (1966) described his venture as a "supplemental form of radio," a pilot project he hoped would be duplicated across the nation (p. 25). KPFA's historic significance has been characterized as providing "a conceptual and operational prototype" of an independent form of radio (Lumpp, 1979, p. 4). Pacifica Radio—comprising KPFA and a national system of four other stations by the 1980s—became a comprehensive alternative model to commercial broadcasting in terms of its internal structure, funding, programming, and relationship to the audience.

Lewis Hill was the prime mover among the five founders of the Pacifica Foundation. Born in 1919 in Kansas City into a wealthy family, Hill built at the age of 6 a working crystal radio in a shoe box during the radio craze of the mid-1920s. Here was a thread linking the ham movement and the origins of Pacifica, where nonprofessional volunteers would play a central role in all aspects of station operations. Hill drew on his experience as a peace activist, civil libertarian, and broadcaster in launching KPFA. A conscientious objector, Hill refused to serve in the military during World War II, working instead on a reclamation project run by the Civilian Public Service (CPS) before being discharged for poor health caused by arthritis of the spine. Hill moved to Washington, D.C., where he worked at the office of the ACLU counseling draft resisters as head of the National Committee of Conscientious Objectors. He also worked as an announcer at a commercial radio station, WINX-AM, and was promoted to night news editor when the station was bought by the *Washington Post.* Hill left the station in protest over the rip-and-read news format of the commercial station and its one-sided coverage of domestic and international affairs (Raimi, 1979).

Land (1994) documents how Hill's vision for Pacifica was rooted in the pacifist movement of the 1930s and 1940s. Hill began to discuss and to develop the concept of alternative radio at the CPS camp in Coleville, California. The string of 151 CPS camps nationwide, modeled on Work Progress Administration projects, were made up exclusively of conscientious objectors to war, mostly pacifists and anarchists. The camp experience, permitting like-minded resisters to engage in intense political discussion and to establish a heightened sense of solidarity, radicalized the pacificism of the participants. Important leaders of the antiwar movement of the 1950s and 1960s came from the ranks of the CPS camps. Hill, who, like many of his co-religionists, knew about the repression of dissent during and after World War I, linked the peace movement and civil liberties. The more radical elements of the CPS population feared that American society would take a totalitarian turn at the end of World War II inhospitable to a broad exercise of freedom of expression, especially by dissenters. Land emphasized that the radicalism emerging from the CPS camps—tempered by individualism, by the pacifist's commitment to personal witness—had its roots in the American experience.

Hill selected the San Francisco Bay Area for his experiment because it was a haven for pacifists, anarchists, and other nonconformists. The name "Pacifica" suggested both the organization's philosophical roots in the peace movement and geographical roots on the West Coast. In that milieu, Hill developed his conception of a radio station that would be controlled by programmers and responsible to listeners rather than to advertisers. The "Radio Prospectus," written when Pacifica incorporated in 1946, bemoaned the isolation of pacifist organizations and suggested that broadcasting could be instrumental in promoting the cause of peace, echoing Joy Elmer Morgan's position during the Depression that radio had the potential to become a powerful agent of progress in a period of world crisis. The "Radio Prospectus" indicated that Pacifica was dedicated to promoting broad human understanding rather than serving the cause of peace and social justice in a sectarian spirit. KPFA would have three objectives: cultural, journalistic, and social. The first was to provide an outlet for the musical, literary, and theatrical talent of the local community. The second goal was to engage in comprehensive news coverage using a wider variety of sources than commercial broadcasters. Finally, the founders indicated their intention to examine the causes of social conflict and "to engage in any activity that shall contribute to a lasting understanding between nations and between the individuals of all nations, races, creeds and colors" (cited in Lumpp, 1979, p. 90).

The "Radio Prospectus" implicitly constituted a critique of commercial broadcasting. For example, it proposed an experimental theater workshop as an alternative to the mediocre quality of commercial radio drama. Pacifica would feature folk music for the workers from the Midwest and South, who had migrated to California during the war. Pacifica planned regular coverage of the labor movement in light of the failure of the major wire services and broadcast outlets to treat the affairs of workers with any sympathy or depth. Standard news sources were also criticized for their treatment of African Americans and other minorities: "They commonly ignore the struggle of all minority groups everywhere in the world. Their treatment of national and international events is superficial and often unintelligibly confused. Their copy is loaded with inflammatory prejudices and platitudes" (cited in Lumpp, 1979, p. 98).

In its application to the FCC for a radio station, Pacifica anticipated the FCC's concern that KPFA would be a "propaganda" station with a particular point of view by framing its objectives in terms of extending the marketplace of ideas by offering a wide range of programs and perspectives absent from the networks. Hill, whose work at the ACLU strengthened his commitment to the First Amendment, emphasized the importance of creating a public affairs forum that "provides an opportunity for ideas to gain currency in the presence of their opposing ideas" (cited in Stebbins, 1978, p. 59). Smith (1988), a member of KPFA's local board in the late 1980s who researched Pacifica's history, detected tension between principles of civil libertarianism and political engagement in Hill's plan. Although Hill repeatedly character-ized Pacifica's mission as providing an arena for an open marketplace of ideas in which no attempt would be made to form public opinion in a preconceived way, Smith also attributed to Hill an unsigned memorandum from 1952 that stated, "This project was begun in an attempt to carry radical war resistance program into a mass medium." The memorandum indicated that

> the formula conceived at the outset was that mass education for war resistance would take place in direct proportion to the radio station's growth in stature as a source of non-ideological entertainment and artistic activity. We were willing to take the "long view." . . . Our whole project was a war-resistance weapon. (pp. 24-25)

Whatever the provenience of this memorandum, contradictions implicit in Hill's vision would alternately energize and haunt Pacifica throughout its history—conflicts between open-ended and partisan approaches to program-ming, between conflicting appeals to elite and mass audiences, and between hierarchical and egalitarian forms of station management. Hill's vision of Pacifica radio had both liberal and radical elements, defined in turn as providing a neutral marketplace of ideas and a vehicle for social action. The liberal component was reflected in Hill's view of the intelligentsia as Pacifica's primary constituency and his individualistic conception of broadcaster and audience. He endorsed the authenticity of the personal perspective of each programmer, who was encouraged to envisage his audience as another individual, "not an aggregate of any description" (cited in Raimi, 1979, p. 50). The radical factor was Hill's rejection of the undemocratic media structures and overriding commitment to use the medium of radio to promote the peace movement and social change.

Hill was compelled to modify two operational aspects of his original plan for a radio station: location on the AM band and limited use of advertising to help finance operations. Pacifica's first application was for a 1,000-watt AM station in Richmond, California, which had no AM station. The application was turned down in 1947 because the proposed frequency overlapped with the signals of powerful NBC and CBS stations in the area, a ruling that Hill bitterly claimed reflected the FCC's bias in favor of network broadcasting. The lack of another available AM frequency led Pacifica to apply for an FM station in Berkeley, for which it received a construction permit from the FCC in 1948. If FM radio had not been in its infancy, it is unlikely that Hill's experiment would have taken root. Recall that in 1938, in the aftermath of the purge of educational broadcasters from the AM dial, the FCC reserved channels for noncommercial stations in frequencies above the then standard broadcast band. A few years earlier, engineer Edwin Armstrong had demonstrated the new system of "frequency modulation," or FM, and petitioned the FCC for spectrum allocations. David Sarnoff of RCA had not supported Armstrong's petition, fearing it would make existing AM radios obsolete and interfere with the development of television, which shared the upper frequencies with FM. Armstrong committed suicide after protracted litigation against RCA. Because FM broadcasts could not be received by standard AM radios, and RCA's power as a radio manufacturer and owner of NBC was initially arrayed against FM's development, the new radio system was of little interest to commercial broadcasters.

After World War II, the FCC revised allocations in the higher frequency bands, which included television as well as FM radio. Twenty percent of the FM radio channels were reserved for noncommercial use. Pacifica Radio was launched at a time when FM was a new frontier on the broadcasting spectrum with few radios to receive its signals and when the attention of the commercial networks was riveted on the new medium of television. Berkeley was selected by Pacifica's founders as the site for KPFA in part because of the presumption that an academic community centered around a campus of the University of California would be more likely to support an experimental FM station.

Besides abandoning his plan for an AM station, Hill reassessed Pacifica's proposal for a commercially supported nonprofit station. As initially conceived, income from limited advertising would finance the station, but no stock would be issued that could return profit. Hill hoped that commercial sponsorship might provide seed money for additional Pacifica projects, but he envisaged listener sponsorship as ultimately the sole means of supporting KPFA once the station was securely established. The FCC and the Internal Revenue Service indicated that even limited commercial support could jeopardize Pacifica Radio's noncommercial and tax-exempt status, and Hill decided that advertising support was neither feasible nor desirable. Instead, KPFA's application was resubmitted based exclusively on a listener subscription plan: The station would be funded by individual subscriptions of $10 a year and become self-supporting in two years. The FCC ruling was a blessing in disguise. The split over commercial sponsorship of noncommercial radio had weakened the broadcast reform movement of the 1930s and confused the public about the distinct mission of what was then called educational broadcasting. As Land (1994) emphasized, listener sponsorship was the linchpin that freed Pacifica "from the tether of corporate or state control, differentiating its programming from that of every other media outlet in the United States" (p. 13).

In 1949, KPFA-FM began broadcasting on an interim basis in the hope of generating sufficient listener support to put the station on a permanent footing. Hill wrote that interim status would permit Pacifica "to work out an infinitude of operational matters for which commercial radio provides no precedent" (cited in Lumpp, 1979, p. 105). During the first five months, 600 people participated in live programs, which constituted nearly half of KPFA's broadcasts. Offerings ranged from live musical performances from KPFA's studios and children's programs to discussions of great books and recorded plays from the BBC. The station placed a strong emphasis on news and public affairs programming. Individual commentaries and panel discussions contained many perspectives seldom if ever heard on the American airwaves.

The format and content of KPFA's programs differed from commercial and noncommercial broadcasts. McKinney (1966), one of the five founders of Pacifica Radio and a KPFA programmer, recalled how KPFA dispensed with the conventions and clichés of traditional broadcasts: "There were no fanfares, no themes, no organ strings. Duration of programs was designed to fulfill natural content—not to be chopped off in regular segments by the stop watch" (p. 12). Gaps in programming were filled by prose, poetry or musical interludes. KPFA communicated a spirit of spontaneity and informality at odds with the conventions of commercial broadcasting. In a move to demystify radio operations for the audience and to permit listener interaction, the station broadcast Hill's *Report to Listeners* and *Inside KPFA*. The latter permitted listeners to comment on programming and staff members to explain their policies and the internal operation of the station. During the interim period, many listeners visited the offices of KPFA, resulting in the creation of a large volunteer staff, an enduring feature of Pacifica stations. The interactive character of KPFA was emphasized in a KPFA program guide that suggested that radio should serve as "the modern equivalent of the old town meeting," if the medium "is to make its contribution to the democratic process" (cited in Lumpp, 1979, p. 110). During the early years of KPFA, Hill wrote to his father,

> In the admissibility of heresies and the absence of philosophical censorship there has been nothing like it in American radio, and we have found that the public hunger for a frank speaking out, a radical ethical confrontation of major issues, greatly exceeds the public dispepsia [sic]. A more general fact about the project, its complete independence, shores up the confidence and respect this kind of activity requires. (cited in Stebbins, 1978, p. 102)

Interim KPFA generated widespread local interest and national press attention. Yet by summer 1950, KPFA had fewer than 300 subscribers and considerable debt, including over $10,000 in back pay owed to its staff. KPFA went off the air temporarily as the Pacifica Foundation sought to put its station on a sounder financial footing. The viability of listener sponsorship remained unproved. After a nine-month campaign mounted by the Pacifica Foundation and KPFA's subscribers, the station returned to the air in 1951.

Pacifica tried to mobilize manufacturers and stores to make inexpensive FM units available in its listening area. Pacifica even considered distributing an FM model made to its own specifications directly to the listeners of KPFA,

Berkeley's only FM outlet. Hill revived his plan to acquire an AM station. Meanwhile, KPFA again fell seriously into debt, and only a grant from the Fund for Adult Education (FAE) of the Ford Foundation, established in 1951 to support educational radio and television, saved the Pacifica experiment from extinction. Robert Hutchins, former president of the University of Chicago and a veteran of the conflicts over educational radio during the 1930s, was now an associate director of the Ford Foundation. In the application process Hill dealt with Robert Hudson and Scott Fletcher, Ford Foundation officials who wielded considerable influence in the development of noncommercial radio and television in the years to come. It has been said that "the FAE grant [to Pacifica] was of great significance in U.S. radio and television history—it was the first of hundreds of millions of dollars the Ford Foundation (and others) were to donate to 'public' broadcasters" (Lumpp, 1979, p. 128).

The Ford Foundation awarded Pacifica an immediate grant of $7,800 and a three-year development grant of $150,000. The funds permitted KPFA to subsidize its operational expenses and purchase new equipment, acquire greater studio and office space, and engage in promotional activity. KPFA was able to establish a professional radio facility so that it could apply to the FCC for a permanent broadcast license. By virtue of the Ford Foundation grant, Hill bought time to test his experiment as Pacifica Radio entered into a three-year period of relative financial stability. The grant would also mean greater national visibility for Pacifica because Hill committed KPFA to supplying programs for the tape network of the NAEB, which the FAE also sought to strengthen. Although the grant saved the Pacifica experiment from oblivion and inaugurated a new era in the history of public broadcasting, it was fraught with danger for KPFA. The money from the Ford Foundation was intended to facilitate the plan for listener sponsorship but threatened to create a dependency on large infusions of funds, which Hill considered anathema to his experiment in independent, community-based radio. The FAE grant entailed contractual obligations on the part of Pacifica, and the FAE held a 50% lien on Pacifica's property against KPFA's failure to fulfill its obligations. The FAE also reserved the right to review the grant in the event of significant changes in KPFA's structure or operations. In general, private philanthropies linked to the business world like the Ford Foundation would be in the position to exert considerable leverage over the development of noncommercial broadcasting comparable to that wielded by the Carnegie Corporation of New York prior to World War II.

As a result of the FAE grant, KPFA gained a new office and transmitter and a respite from financial pressure, and the focus shifted to organizational issues. Hill conceived KPFA as an alternative radio station by virtue of its internal organization and its programming. According to his design, the KPFA staff was responsible for what would normally be the authority of management at a commercial station or of a college administration at an educational station. All staff members were paid equally, and the station was operated on a collective basis. An executive membership of approximately 12 KPFA staff members and volunteers originally functioned as the licensee or legal authority for KPFA. All employees were eligible regardless of function. The executive membership elected a smaller committee of directors that appointed Pacifica's officers and conducted the day-to-day affairs of the station. Alongside these, an advisory committee of civic leaders and representatives of the local community provided outreach and accountability. Downing (1984) suggested that the internal structure of KPFA was the most innovative feature of Hill's project:

> The experimental policy of paying all members equally and of having majority votes on programming policy after open discussion, was the most nearly revolutionary feature of the early KPFA. It was a policy framed in the conscious rejection of the undemocratic structures of national media in the U.S. (p. 80)

For Downing, KPFA represented an example of "prefigurative politics" in which the practice of alternative institutions anticipate a more equitable society of the future. Downing stressed the importance of emancipatory communication systems like Hill's that engage in "movement-building with self-managed media" by remaining open to popular social currents (pp. 22-23).

The democratic structure devised by Hill worked relatively well in the early period when KPFA was founded and broadcast on an interim basis. Decisions were arrived at by consensus shaped largely by Hill. But as the KPFA staff expanded beyond a tight-knit group of founders to a larger and more disparate staff, the difficulties of self-management took a serious toll on KPFA's affairs and on Hill himself. In 1952, a group of staff members revolted against a perceived overcentralizaton of power in the hands of Hill and two other Pacifica founders. This was the first of a succession of palace revolutions in Pacifica history that entailed debilitating emergency meetings, bitter personal and ideological conflict, firings and resignations, reinstatements, and reorganization plans. One of the consequences of the turmoil was that it threatened Pacifica's relationship with the FAE, which held a lien on Pacifica's property and considered Hill personally responsible for fulfilling the obligations of the $150,000 grant. In fact, the FAE did withhold its third-year grant funds pending what it considered the successful resolution of Pacifica's organizational problems. Also put at risk was a $30,000 award by the Educational Television and Radio Center to provide programs to the tape network of the NAEB.

Hill offered a plan to restructure Pacifica that included a reduced role for himself and a reconsideration of the practicality of self-management. The reorganization approved in 1954 resulted in Hill assuming a new and more circumscribed position as president of Pacifica; at the same time, egalitarianism was tempered along lines recommended by Hill as staff membership on the executive committee was limited to a third. In the months that followed the reorganization, subscriptions to KPFA grew, reaching 5,000 in 1956. The NAEB tape exchange program had increased the number of KPFA programs distributed nationally. Yet the station was not self-sustaining. Hill unsuccessfully applied to the FAE for new grants to fund KPFA and to acquire an AM station at a time when the Ford Foundation was shifting its interest to noncommercial television. He also initiated a project to acquire an FM station in Los Angeles to carry KPFA's offerings and engage in local programming. Serious health problems forced Hill to take a leave of absence. When he returned to KPFA in 1957, he became embroiled in a bitter personnel dispute. What one staff member called "the contradiction of leadership in the midst of organizational 'equality'" had not been resolved (cited in Stebbins, 1978, p. 172). Firings ordered by Hill were reversed by the Pacifica board in the course of the dispute. The next day after the firings, 38-year-old Lewis Hill, his rheumatoid arthritis and general ill health exacerbated by the organizational problems at KPFA, committed suicide.

Despite Hill's death in 1957, Pacifica survived and expanded. In 1958, KPFA became the first FM radio station to receive the George Foster Peabody Award for Public Service. As a result of its offerings of classical and folk music, live drama, in-depth documentaries, and news reports, KPFA had established a permanent niche for itself in the San Francisco Bay Area. Lawrence Ferlinghetti, West Coast poet, bookstore owner, and publisher, recalled how

> KPFA had a large influence in the fifties. This was before everyone had a
> TV. KPFA was really a focal point for a lot of the underground. . . . When
> I arrived [in San Francisco] in 1951, it was in full force. It was the center of
> the intellectual community right up on through the early sixties. (cited in
> Armstrong, 1981, p. 75)

KPFA, which broadcast the music of Paul Robeson and Pete Seeger, Alan
Watts' discussions of Eastern philosophy, the literary and film criticism of
Kenneth Rexroth and Pauline Kael, and a wide range of minority perspectives during an epoch of conservatism and conformity, helped nourish an
emerging counterculture.

KPFA remained the nation's sole listener-sponsored station until 1959,
when its sister station, KPFK-FM in Los Angeles, went on the air. In 1960,
WBAI-FM in New York City became Pacifica's third station, a gift from
philanthropist Louis Schweitzer, who had originally bought the station for
his own amusement and become familiar with Pacifica through KPFA tapes
broadcast on WBAI. Within a two-year period Pacifica had entered two new
and highly visible communication markets. In the same period, Pacifica also
applied for a station in Washington, D.C. The FCC sought to discourage the
application by requesting voluminous supporting documentation. The FCC
challenged the nonprofit status of Pacifica radio, asking why the "sale" of
listener subscriptions for program guides should not render its stations
ineligible for a noncommercial license. The communication from the FCC
also made reference to accusations of obscenity and attacks against religion
and government.

Besides pressure from the FCC, Pacifica was attacked by the political
right because of its new level of visibility in the major communication
centers on the east and west coasts. Thus, a time of expansion, when threats
to Pacifica's existence came from external forces, followed the period of
internal strife that ended with the suicide of Pacifica's founder. Pacifica was
the target of the February 5, 1960 issue of *Counterattack,* the red-baiting
publication that had spearheaded the broadcasting blacklist and issued *Red
Channels: The Report of Communist Influence in Radio and Television.* The
issue on Pacifica was headed "Radio Station Promotes Communism." In fact,
Hill and the other libertarian pacifists who founded Pacifica were anticom-
munist but had opened KPFA's airwaves to all groups on the left and to
representatives of the center and the right, for that matter. *Counterattack*
criticized the appearance over the air of American Marxist Herbert Aptheker,

Soviet specialist William Mandel, black leader W. E. B. DuBois, socialist Norman Thomas, and *Nation* editor Carey McWilliams, among others. This issue of *Counterattack* was brought to the attention of the FCC, which continued to raise questions about the legitimacy of Pacifica Radio. In the early 1960s, the FCC also received complaints about obscene programming as it considered the status of Pacifica's broadcast licenses. Such complaints were made, for example, about KPFK's broadcast of Edward Albee's play, *A Zoo Story,* and of *Live and Let Live,* an unprecedented discussion of homosexuality by a panel of gays on KPFK in 1963 that the *New York Times* television critic called the most open and extensive consideration of the subject in the history of American broadcasting (Lumpp, 1979).

The FCC had initially declined to grant WBAI a permanent license and permission to install a new transmitter when it became a Pacifica station. KPFK had also not yet received a permanent license. Furthermore, the FCC balked at a speedy renewal of KPFA's license. Hence, all three Pacifica stations were operating under "interim authorization" when Pacifica experienced a new challenge in the form of congressional scrutiny. In 1963, Pacifica became a target of the Senate Judiciary Subcommittee on Internal Security's investigation of communist infiltration of the mass media. Six Pacifica officials and programmers and one subscriber were subpoenaed to testify. The inquisition into communist infiltration of Pacifica focused on the political affiliations of its officers and staff and the content of specific programs. It singled out such broadcasts as the examination of U.S.-Cuban relations and a lengthy interview with an ex-FBI agent, which revealed the Bureau's infiltration of organizations like the ACLU and the NAACP, its use of phone taps, mail interception, and other violations of the rights of citizens. The interview with the agent, who had unsuccessfully approached *The New York Times* and other mainstream news organizations, represented the first substantial public critique of the agency and its director, J. Edgar Hoover. The program generated considerable attention and most likely precipitated the Senate investigation into Pacifica's affairs at the behest of Hoover. The broadcasting industry did not come forward to defend Pacifica's First Amendment's right to engage in controversial programming and to be free of government inquisition. Indeed, the Senate investigation into Pacifica's programming and funding gave currency to the threat made by William Paley in the late 1930s that those who challenged the practices of mainstream broadcasting brought their loyalty as Americans into question.

The Senate subcommittee hearings posed a threat to Pacifica's applications for permanent licenses for its three stations. Following the hearings, the FCC requested that Pacifica officers and managers complete a questionnaire about membership in the Communist Party or other organizations advocating the violent overthrow of the government. The *San Francisco Examiner* predicted that the FCC would shut down Pacifica's stations. A delegation from the Pacifica board met with the chairman of the FCC, which continued to press for a loyalty oath. The meeting resulted in a compromise statement in which Pacifica affirmed its adherence to the U.S. Constitution but also upheld the right of individuals to refuse to answer government inquiries into their beliefs. The FCC chairman agreed to accept the Pacifica statement provided the Commission could submit several members of Pacifica to further questions. One of the persons the FCC wished to question was Jerome Shore, executive vice president of Pacifica, who was slated to become its next president. Shore had testified before the subcommittee that he was not presently a member of the Communist Party but had refused to answer questions about alleged membership prior to 1954.

The Pacifica board sought to square a circle, condoning compliance with the FCC's request while objecting in principle, reaffirming the right of individuals to refuse to cooperate on First Amendment grounds. Feeling isolated and without the full support of the board, Shore removed himself as a factor in the FCC proceedings by resigning from Pacifica. Some saw Shore as a sacrificial lamb to the FCC: One month after his resignation, the FCC awarded Pacifica stations permanent licenses. The Senate and FCC witch-hunts took a toll on Pacifica's internal resources and morale. The ordeal contributed to a strike and a call for reduced board and managerial authority at KPFA, where there was widespread feeling among the staff that Pacifica's leadership had compromised on important matters of principle. Nonetheless, the acquisition in 1964 of permanent licenses for the Berkeley, Los Angeles, and New York stations set the stage for Pacifica's radicalization during the second half of the 1960s, when Pacifica would more readily accept confrontation with governmental authority.

Free-form radio represented a manifestation of Pacifica's transformation of programming in form as well as content. The new format drew upon the sensibility of the Beat Generation, the cultural revolt of a new generation of youth, and the example of the disk jockeys of African American radio, who provided a "'grapevine' for the flow of information in their respective communities" (Barlow, 1988, p. 84). Bob Fass's late-night program, *Radio*

Unnameable, pioneered free-form radio at Pacifica beginning in 1963. John Leonard had originated *Nightsounds* at KPFA. KPFK began its own free-form experiment, *Radio Free Oz,* in Los Angeles with Paul Robbins and Peter Bergman, who had ties to the Southern California counterculture. Two other popular free-form shows originated at WBAI in the mid-1960s: Steve Post's Saturday night show *The Outside* and Larry Josephson's weekday morning program *In the Beginning.* Each practitioner of free-form radio created a personal montage of talk, music, and call-ins that shattered traditional programming structures.

Fass was the first to develop the full potential of free-form radio and make it a major vehicle of the counterculture. Fass's program, based on a wide range of live and recorded material, became a community switchboard for a generation of cultural and political dissidents. Often, folk and rock musicians such as Bob Dylan, Richie Havens, José Feliciano, and Arlo Guthrie—long before they became well known—would appear and perform on Fass's show. As Land (1994) noted,

> With his instinctive psychological acumen, his avuncular demeanor, and extraordinary dexterity on the soundboard, Fass was a master radio artisan. More important than his effortless skill using [W]BAI's archaic equipment was the ineffable immediacy to the tone of his show. There has perhaps never been such an authentic human *presence* on radio as Fass. (p. 344)

Events organized by Fass through *Radio Unnameable* such as the 1967 "fly in" at the International Arrivals Building at Kennedy Airport, an apolitical "happening," nonetheless suggested the power of radio to mobilize people for action. Indeed, a year later, Fass's program would serve as a communication center for the student occupation at Columbia University, broadcasting telephone calls from within and outside the occupied buildings.

Radio Unnameable represented a radical departure not only from mainstream commercial broadcasting but from Pacifica practices as well. Although the content of Pacifica programming constituted an alternative to mainstream broadcasting from the outset, the programming style and relationship with the audience remained rather formal. Some Pacifica veterans considered *Radio Unnameable* anarchistic, excessively subjective, and even frivolous but tolerated the show because it was broadcast during off-hours after midnight. The programming format perfected by Fass began to forge a new relationship between programmers and listeners at Pacifica, reaching beyond the intelligentsia to new constituencies. Free-form radio struck a responsive chord for a generation of disaffected youths that would play a central role in the protest movements of the 1960s. For Land (1994), free-form radio, based on an individual human voice and the element of the unexpected, evoked the magic for the wireless's earliest listeners. Moreover, "with the broadcast day dominated by Post, Josephson, Fass, [Julius] Lester, and others [W]BAI demonstrated that radio could stimulate an immense, ceaseless conversation about the possibilities of the new age" (p. 349).

Pacifica's radicalization was also overtly political. It involved going beyond Lewis Hill's gentle pacifism, the emphasis on intellectual discourse, and his intention to engage individual listeners in the consideration of social issues. As the protest movements of the 1960s took shape, Pacifica approached its audience more as collective entities—minorities, women, and the antiwar movement, for example. Pacifica programmers, in a changed political context, extended Hill's original vision of alternative radio as an agent of human understanding and social justice. A key figure bridging the two eras of Pacifica's history was Elsa Knight Thompson, KPFA's public affairs director from 1957 to 1971. Thompson was responsible for molding Pacifica's innovative public affairs and news programming and served as a mentor to members of a new generation of Pacifica programmers like Chris Koch and Dale Minor. During the 1960s, Pacifica became the broadcasting counterpart to the new activism as the result of its comprehensive coverage of political protest. Seminal events took place in the San Francisco Bay Area, Pacifica's birthplace. KPFA offered extensive coverage of demonstrations against the hearings of the House Un-American Activities Committee in San Francisco in 1960 and produced a remarkable documentary that captured the tumultuous proceedings both inside and outside the hearing room. Here and elsewhere, Pacifica Radio transported listeners to sites of political conflict and captured the sounds of protest.

The Free Speech Movement (FSM) at the Berkeley campus of the University of California in 1964, a critical event in the crystallization of the new left, also had important repercussions for Pacifica. There was an affinity—indeed, a synergy—between the FSM and KPFA, whose offices were a block away from the campus. KPFA preempted regular programming to offer continuous coverage, which became a model for subsequent Pacifica-wide coverage of political protest. The university's ban on distribution of material by civil rights and antiwar groups made the issue of free expression the organizing principle around which a host of political and cultural taboos were challenged. A new generation of Pacifica staff members perceived a link between First Amendment rights and collective acts of civil disobedience in addition to individual acts of conscience. Years later, Thompson, KPFA's former director of public affairs, would suggest that the station's presence in the Bay Area since the 1950s helped sow the seeds for Berkeley's role as a center of protest in the 1960s. Berkeley shaped KPFA, but KPFA also shaped Berkeley.

Pacifica provided special coverage of national and international developments as well as of more proximate events like the Berkeley revolt. Dale Minor of WBAI initiated Pacifica's early and continuous coverage of the civil rights movement of the 1960s. Instead of the spot coverage given by other newscasters, Minor's graphic and sustained reporting was the result of extended periods spent in the Deep South accompanying civil rights activists with whom he had developed a close working relationship. As a result, the cumulative effect of Minor's news reports and documentaries illuminated not only specific demonstrations and crises but the growth of a movement. Some argued that such journalism was more partisan than objective. Minor's sympathy with the objectives of the civil rights movement was a given; indeed, the vividness, intimacy, and depth of his coverage could be attributed to the fact that in effect he became a part of that movement. Yet this did not diminish Minor's professional standards and critical capacity as a journalist.

Minor's reporting was rooted in Pacifica's historic mission—stated in its articles of incorporation two decades earlier—to foster the examination of social conflict and to promote understanding among all peoples. Seeking to further that mission by straddling the line between participant and reporter, Minor anticipated the direction that Pacifica programming would take in the years to follow (see Minor, 1970). A 1972 article in WBAI's *Folio* on "Phonecasts" illustrated how Dale Minor's style of committed journalism would be grafted onto the use of the telephone introduced by free-form radio:

> We are . . . not just an institution supported by the community, but the community itself—the people in microcosm. By combining the economic model of listener-support with the electronic mode of the "Phonecast," our community has created for itself an entirely new forum for public dialogue, an electronic Town Hall. . . . So when women are discussing women's issues on the air, we are not reporting an event, we are an event—another meeting of the community through a "Phonecast." . . . When war resisters discuss war resistance; when junkies discuss junk; when homosexuals discuss homosexuality; and when prisoners and jailors discuss jail—we are not a news organi-

> zation; there is no mediation, no outtakes. We are a publicly financed public instrument for public discourse. We are, in effect, the streets. (cited in Post, 1974, p. 161)

Pacifica, whose founders were pacifists, gave extensive coverage to the war in Vietnam and to the antiwar movement as well as to the civil rights struggle. Here, too, Pacifica broke out of the traditional confines of news and public affairs reporting. In 1965, KPFA, KPFK, and WBAI collaborated to produce Vietnam Day, a day-long national broadcast on the war and the issues it raised. Soon thereafter, Pacifica's stations carried live a national "teach-in" on the war from Washington, D.C. and another from Berkeley. Besides examining the ramifications of the Vietnam war by broadcasting teach-ins, a member of the WBAI staff sought to add a new dimension to coverage of the war itself. In 1965, Chris Koch, program director of WBAI, without the prior knowledge of his Pacifica colleagues traveled to North Vietnam from France with several other journalists. On the basis of this visit, Koch prepared several hour-long programs based on his observations and taped interviews.

Supporters of the American war effort attacked Koch's visit and sympathetic treatment of the "enemy" as treasonous. The Pacifica board was divided over Koch's undertaking: Some among the old guard were uncomfortable with Pacifica's radicalization and concerned about issues of advocacy and balance. The board was noncommittal in response to Koch's request for support if the government prosecuted him for the trip. Attempts were made to force Koch to delete and revise portions of his programs. Finally, Koch and five other staff members resigned in protest. Post (1974) referred to the incident as a tragic violation of the principles of Pacifica, "a case of self censorship within an institution whose unbending dedication was to the First Amendment." In the aftermath, thousands canceled their subscriptions to WBAI—nearly a third of its membership. "It was an astonishing display of the power of our subscribers," Post observes, "and, in its tragic way, a reaffirmation of the validity of a communications medium supported, and therefore controlled, by broad-based community participation" (pp. 75-76).

Pacifica once again recovered from a failure of nerve, as it had after the Jerome Shore affair, and went on to provide ground-breaking coverage of the war in Vietnam and the antiwar movement in the latter part of the 1960s and early 1970s. Pacifica stations drew on their own Washington news bureau established in 1968, independent sources such as the old Indochina hands of Agence France-Presse, and a broad spectrum of scholars and activists. The fact that Pacifica news broadcasts did not have a set length but contracted and expanded depending on the day's events gave Pacifica's news departments flexibility in covering major developments in depth. An article entitled "News on a Shoestring" in the May 26, 1973 issue of *The New Yorker* magazine, appearing during the Vietnam war era, suggested that WBAI provided the best broadcast news program on radio or television in New York City. The article noted that the meager salary of WBAI's news director, Paul Fischer, was six weeks in arrears due to cash flow problems and that the $50,000 budget of WBAI's news department would pay half the salary of a network TV weatherman.

Pacifica gave extensive coverage not only to the war itself but to the antiwar movement as well. Regular programming was preempted for full live coverage of major demonstrations. Often, Pacifica airtime would be used to announce and help organize these and other antiwar activities. Pacifica became the radio equivalent of the underground press of the 1960s. Nonetheless, it did not treat the antiwar movement in a monolithic fashion. Pacifica became a vehicle through which the disparate elements of the antiwar movement—embracing liberals, anarchists, and Maoists, among others—could discuss differences in ideology, strategy, and tactics. Pacifica also served as a resource for the women's, environmental, and gay movements. Gitlin (1980) exposed the mechanisms by which the mainstream press distorted, and even helped contain, the radical currents of the 1960s. Conversely, Pacifica served as a genuine resource for the heterogeneous forces of the new left. Spark (1987), a volunteer at KPFK since 1969 who later became its program director, made the case for Pacifica as a platform for the left comparable to journals of opinion:

> Our conception of Pacifica in this light was not as a monolithic organ of leftist propaganda but as a center that would permit the formulation of a cogent ideological perspective on political and cultural issues—a perspective allowing full room for debate from both within and outside the left. (p. 578)

Pacifica's role in the movement against the war in Vietnam and as a vehicle for dissent and social change in general was in keeping with the objectives of its founder. The new left transformed but did not did not betray the vision of Lewis Hill. A radical interpretation of the First Amendment served as the foundation of Pacifica Radio—of its programming and of its defense of that programming before the FCC, the Senate Internal Securities Subcommittee, and other government bodies. The civil libertarian emphasis posited that a people armed with the right of free expression rather than the state constituted the basis of democratic government. Supreme Court Justice Hugo Black and legal scholar Alexander Meiklejohn, among others, articulated this expansive view of the First Amendment over KPFA's airwaves during the 1950s. After World War II, when the cold war threatened democratic institutions and practices, Lewis Hill initiated his project to create a free and critical sphere on the broadcast spectrum. Hill did not conceive free expression as a symbolic exercise or safety valve for discontent but, in the spirit articulated by Wini Breines,

> "free" in the sense of liberated, unrestricted communication that may foster political forms that transcend the existing framework, enabling utopian ideas to inspire individuals toward becoming political actors on the basis of their unmet collective and individual needs. (cited in Land, 1994, p. 316)

CHAPTER 5

The Spread of Community Radio and Pacifica's Institutional Crisis

In the years following its transformation by the new left, Pacifica became a locus of social conflict, helped inspire a community radio movement, and experienced a wrenching institutional crisis. At first, attacks came from elements of the public offended by Pacifica's programming, especially its coverage of the affairs of African Americans. In 1968, for example, the reading of an anti-Semitic poem on WBAI became a cause célèbre in New York City. During a teachers' strike fraught with conflict over community control of public schools and with racial tension in the Oceanhill-Brownsville section of Brooklyn, one teacher read a vitriolic anti-Semitic poem written by one of his students on the program of African American writer Julius Lester. The controversy provoked a storm of criticism and a complaint to the FCC calling for the revocation of WBAI's license. Pacifica responded to its critics that although it deplored anti-Semitism it would not censor a program that documented growing tensions between the African American and Jewish communities of New York. In its response to an FCC inquiry, Pacifica noted that in a two-year period WBAI had aired over 250 programs on African Americans and race relations and 90 separate programs devoted to Jewish affairs. Pacifica also stressed that the First Amendment protected the expression of controversial and even repugnant ideas.

The FCC upheld Pacifica's position. A concurring statement by Nicholas Johnson—the young, maverick commissioner appointed to the FCC by President Johnson—constituted a passionate defense of listener-sponsored radio and indictment of commercial broadcasters. Johnson (1969) noted the emergence of a new school of First Amendment law led by Professor Jerome Barron that stressed the public's need for access to electronic media to make freedom of speech a reality in contemporary society. Noting the civil disorders in black ghettos and the Kerner Commission's indictment of press coverage of minorities, Johnson praised WBAI for offering an uncensored forum for African Americans. He added that the FCC "should be particularly reluctant to impose restraints upon the programming of a station so actively sponsored by its listener community" (p. 5).

Johnson contrasted Pacifica's willingness to risk airing controversial material with the pervasive self-censorship practiced by the networks for fear of disrupting the advertising marketplace. He criticized the industry magazine *Broadcasting* for editorializing against WBAI while on the same page decrying the FCC's proposal to ban cigarette commercials from the air as a violation of the First Amendment. According to Johnson, the broadcasting industry invoked free speech only when its monetary interests were at stake—for example, when the FCC sought to limit the number of commercials per hour on television. Yet when Pacifica was the target of Senate inquisitors or when its permanent licenses were deferred for three years by the FCC because of complaints about programming the industry remained silent. Johnson (1969) concluded that

> if truly free speech is to flourish in broadcasting, and if individual citizens are to be given rights of access to the media to exercise their First Amendment freedoms to any meaningful extent, then it is apparent to all that the public must seek its First Amendment champions among other than industry spokesmen. (p. 11)

WBAI was not the only Pacifica station to become a center of controversy and conflict. The Ku Klux Klan campaigned against the establishment of a new Pacifica station, KPFT-FM, in Houston, Texas. Soon after it went on the air in 1970, 15 sticks of dynamite shattered the station's transmitter and narrowly missed killing its engineer. A second bombing occurred later that year. Pacifica stations also became involved in a series of controversial cases involving protection of news sources in the period 1970-1975 as a result of its special relationship with dissident groups. Pacifica did not necessarily agree with the views of the sources it protected, but, as its national board declared, "our adherence to the letter and the spirit of the first amendment and applicable state statutes leads the Pacifica Foundation to reassert its determination to protect the identity and confidentiality of our news sources when necessary to preserve the free flow of information" (cited in Lumpp, 1979, p. 285). In 1972, for example, the station manager of WBAI was imprisoned for contempt of court while Pacifica appealed a subpoena for 30 hours of telephone interviews with inmates of the Men's House of Detention broadcast during a prison insurrection in 1970. WBAI's manager was released from jail after three days, and the subpoena was subsequently quashed. WBAI also fought in the courts—ultimately unsuccessfully—a subpoena for a Weather Underground letter announcing a bombing of the New York Corrections Commission's office.

On the West Coast, KPFA and KPFK became engaged in conflicts over the protection of news sources in 1973 and 1974. These cases resulted from communiqués from a number of radical groups that undertook bombings: the Weather Underground, the New World Liberation Front, and the Symbionese Liberation Army (SLA). For example, the latter had taken responsibility for the killing of an educator in Oakland, and later it kidnapped newspaper heiress Patricia Hearst. KPFK in Los Angeles received a subpoena for a taped message with the voices of Patricia Hearst and SLA members. The station manager gave copies of a tape to the FBI and local police but refused to answer questions about the station's news operations and the source of the documents. He was imprisoned for contempt of court for 16 days until ordered released by Supreme Court Justice William O. Douglas pending the outcome of Pacifica's appeal. In 1975, the Supreme Court allowed the contempt citation to stand, and KPFK's manager complied with an order to hand over the original documents. Shortly after the Supreme Court decision in the SLA case, KPFA in Berkeley received a communiqué from the New World Liberation Front announcing a bombing at the Sheraton Airport Hotel. Here, Pacifica's refusal to hand over the original tape led to a police search of KPFK in which the police ransacked files, confiscated material, and copied phone numbers. The station broadcast live an account of the search. The mainstream press disassociated itself from Pacifica's resistance to government efforts to turn the news media as a whole into an arm of law enforcement. Larry Bensky, manager of KPFA, who was subpoenaed before a federal grand jury because of another New World Liberation Front communiqué, testified that such proceedings took a heavy toll on Pacifica's meager material resources: "Nevertheless, we intend to continue to broadcast controversial material, as we have done for the past twenty-five years" (cited in Lumpp, 1979, p. 295).

Pacifica, after two decades of broadcasting, helped inspire a broad community radio movement in the United States. Lewis Hill originally envisioned a Pacifica radio network of at least a dozen strategically located stations across the country with a combined listening audience of 50 million people. At Pacifica, as late as 1968, Stuart Cooney dreamed of expanding Pacifica to a 30-station network. Cooney assembled a team of lawyers and technical experts who, together with media activists scattered throughout the country, filed a flurry of applications for noncommercial FM licenses. Barlow (1992) notes that although these applications did not result in additional Pacifica stations they provided the groundwork for the emergence of a community radio movement in the 1970s.

One proponent of this movement was Lorenzo Milam, a former KPFA volunteer who used his inheritance in 1962 to acquire a license for KRAB-FM in Seattle. The sale of a second station, KDNA-FM in St. Louis, for $1.1 million enabled Milam to set up "KRAB Nebula," 14 community radio stations across the nation, among them KBOO in Portland, Oregon; KTAO in Los Gatos, California; KCHU in Dallas, Texas; WORT in Madison, Wisconsin; and KPOO in San Francisco. No wonder Milam has been called "the Johnny Appleseed of community radio" (Armstrong, 1981, p. 78). In 1974, he expressed his philosophy of broadcasting in a community radio manifesto, *Sex and Broadcasting: A Handbook on Starting a Radio Station for the Community.* American radio, once wild and free, had been ruined by the "toads" (commercial broadcasters) and the "bores" (educational broadcasters). Milam sought to recapture the anarchic excitement and the spirit of equality of the earliest days of radio. Like Lewis Hill, Milam wished to invigorate radio by establishing listener-supported stations in which volunteers would play a leading role. Nonetheless, there were differences in emphasis between Pacifica stations and the new community radio movement.

Land (1994) wrote of Lewis Hill's article on "The Theory of Listener-Sponsored Radio" that

> unbeknownst to Hill in 1951, over time his listeners' engagement would lead them to do more than simply sponsor programs or volunteer to answer phones; they would come to feel they had the right to participate in all aspects of station activity, from broadcasting to management policy. (p. 22)

In his overview of community radio in the United States, Barlow (1988) noted that "Lew Hill believed in community service, support and involvement through volunteer association, but not community control—which he felt was unworkable because there would be too many factions in competition with each other" (pp. 85-86). Pacifica stations were ultimately responsible to a central entity, a self-perpetuating board that held the stations' licenses. Barlow states that Milam represented "a decentralized, anarchist wing of the growing community radio movement" (p. 93). His stations were more freewheeling operations in which the local community had greater degree of direct influence. The KRAB Nebula owed much to the antiauthoritarian counterculture, and some of the stations were torn by racial conflict between white staff members and minority community activists. Such conflict led to the sale of KDNA in St. Louis and the demise of KCHU in Dallas but was more productive at KPOO, "Poor People's Radio," founded in San Francisco. Criticism of station policies led Milam and the station's board to turn the station over to a coalition of Hispanics, Asians, Filipinos, and Native Americans, making it, according to Barlow (1988), "the country's first multi-ethnic community oriented radio station" (p. 95).

By the mid-1970s, the model provided by Pacifica and by Lorenzo Milam's stations—their differences notwithstanding—helped inspire a broader community radio movement. Ethnic-oriented foreign-language broadcasters and African American stations constituted another model for community radio. All Pacifica stations were located in major metropolitan areas, whereas the new generation of alternative noncommercial stations were more diverse in character, often serving smaller and more sharply defined communities across the nation. These ranged from bilingual stations in Hispanic and Native American communities to progressive stations located in college and university towns. As Hochheimer (1993) noted, the community radio movement raised difficult issues of praxis that were largely unaddressed in the Pacifica experience:

Who speaks for which community interest? Who decides what are legitimate voices to be heard? . . . What happens when ideas and technical skills are at odds? How are community views solicited, encouraged? In other words, to what degree does/can the station bring its audiences into the process of programme production for themselves? (p. 476)

The community radio movement received its institutional expression in the National Federation of Community Broadcasters (NFCB), which was established in 1975 in Washington, D.C. by 25 stations. Under its bylaws, the NFCB was open to noncommercial stations governed by the community they served and committed to local access, especially for women, Third World people, and other groups ordinarily excluded from the airwaves. NFCB policy encouraged training volunteers from the local community and giving staff members a say in station policy. The NFCB provided an important impetus to the establishment of new community radio stations as well as support to existing stations through its newsletter, training conferences, tape exchange program, and advocacy before the FCC and other governmental bodies. Within a decade, the NFCB had 70 members and 120 associates.

The community radio movement reached a plateau and faced mounting obstacles during the 1980s. The expansion of the NPR network—accomplished through grants from the CPB for established stations with sufficient levels of power, broadcast hours, paid staff and budgets—marginalized smaller operations. Most larger community stations, with the exception of Pacifica's outlets, were affiliated with NPR. The elimination of CETA (Civilian Employment Training Assistance) grants hit minority community radio stations especially hard, and some were forced to fold. During this period, leadership of the NFCB passed from Tom Thomas, a veteran of the community radio movement in St. Louis, to Carol Schatz from Alaska, where the state government actively supported a group of community-oriented stations. Barlow (1988) suggests that the NFCB became absorbed into the world of more mainstream, government-supported public radio during the difficult years of the Reagan administration. Under Schatz, the NFCB and NPR "came to something of a 'gentlemen's agreement' with respect to the demarcations in the public radio domain": NPR would represent the larger, CPB-qualified stations, including community stations, and the NFCB would represent the smaller 100-3,000-watt operations (Barlow, 1988, pp. 97-99).

In a conservative political climate characterized by a decline in community activism and reduced government support for the public sector, the

NFCB, like NPR, reached out for private support. NFCB literature promised potential underwriters that community radio was a cost-effective way to "enhance your image," to "reach your market," and to "influence the buying decisions of your listeners" (National Federation of Community Broadcasters, n.d., pp. 65-67). Community stations issued rate cards and demographic breakdowns of their audiences. The evolution of WORT-FM, serving Madison, Wisconsin, was characteristic of many NFCB stations. WORT, a charter member of the NFCB, was forced to adjust to new conditions by modifying its noncommercial character. During the mid-1980s the station introduced "noncommercial advertising." At the end of the process WORT had adopted a tighter format and strategies for "audience development." A piece of WORT's promotional literature stated, "For underwriting purposes, we have divided WORT's schedule into several rotations, designed to provide underwriters with an opportunity to match their station support with their target market" (WORT, 1989, p. 73). Originally one of Lorenzo Milam's anarchistic experiments in militantly alternative radio, WORT gained the reputation for being "at the commercial end of community radio" (Lewis & Booth, 1990, p. 122).

The more conservative political climate of the 1970s affected Pacifica stations along with other member stations of the NFCB. Whereas most community radio stations moved to the center, accepting business underwriting and entering the public radio mainstream, Pacifica maintained its radical posture under increasingly difficult circumstances. Pacifica experienced a far-reaching crisis—organizational, political, and fiscal—as the new left became fragmented and went into eclipse in the mid-1970s. The crisis came to a head in bitter strikes at KPFA in Berkeley in 1974 and at WBAI in New York in 1977. Women, blacks, Latinos, Asian Americans, homosexuals, and organizations of the poor, among others, began to demand greater authority within Pacifica stations. Many viewed the call for empowerment by minority groups and control of segments of airtime as consistent with Pacifica's principles. Others within Pacifica opposed what they considered the loss of a common vision and the unleashing of centrifugal forces that could threaten the continued viability of the Pacifica project. The resulting conflicts threatened to tear Pacifica apart. Pacifica was shouldering an impossible burden not wholly of its own making as it remained virtually the only national broadcasting organization to which insurgent groups could have direct access.

The women's movement had an important impact on Pacifica's internal affairs. As early as 1972, Liza Cowen, a WBAI staff member, charged that despite progressive rhetoric a male power clique ran the station, unconscious of the exclusion of women from positions of authority. Cowen's protest took the form of an open letter to the WBAI staff and was reprinted in a manifesto put out by a group of feminist media activists. KPFT staff member Pat Dowell said that women faced the same problem in Pacifica's Houston station and that this was part of a larger problem: that too often Pacifica programs were produced for minorities rather than by them (Lumpp, 1979). As KPFK's Spark (1987) put it, "If we want to build a larger, more robust and expressive liberated community, we should be looking at all the ways we, as 'alternative' media people, have been trapped in social relations and institutional practices of the dominant culture" (p. 588). In 1977, after a nine-year legal battle, WPFW went on the air in Washington, D.C. as the first Pacifica station to be managed by African American media activists.

At KPFA, a Third World project within the station together with a local media reform organization sought changes at Pacifica's original station. The coalition demanded the creation of a Third World department at KPFA with a full-time paid coordinator, control of minority hiring and programming, and a guarantee of 10 hours of airtime per week. The station manager conceded that the KPFA local advisory board had no African American members and only 2 half-time African American employees on a staff of 16, but he argued that KPFA's limited resources and its commitment to programming that cut across demographic boundaries made the demands unacceptable. The resulting bitterness was such that in 1973 the KPFA Third World project and its allies petitioned the FCC to deny Pacifica's application for a fifth station in Washington, D.C. Tension at KPFA led to a bitter strike in 1974 in which the station was off the air for a month. The issue of minority representation became linked, at a time of fiscal crisis, with conflict over layoffs, unionization of the staff, full staff rights for volunteers, and demands that the station manager be fired. The KPFA staff was deeply divided, and a local board member noted that behind the strike were contradictory agendas for Pacifica:

> Some want a station with a national affairs emphasis; some want a community access station; . . . some believe a collective structure can work while others seek a hierarchy; some want volunteers, others a staff run station; some want equal pay, others do not. (cited in Lumpp, 1979, p. 280)

A negotiated settlement a month after the station went off the air met strikers' demands for the resignation of the station manager and recognition of volunteers as unpaid staff members and full participants in the decision-making process. The agreement represented a victory for organized local constituencies seeking more airtime and input at KPFA. In the aftermath of the strike, the Pacifica National Board revised its by-laws to require the concurrence of local boards and staffs in the hiring and firing of managers, a victory for local over central authority. The outcome of the KPFA strike reinforced the trend toward Balkanization within Pacifica. Pacifica stations had coalesced and flourished in response to great national controversies such as the civil rights struggle, the war in Vietnam, and Watergate. Now programming increasingly reflected identity politics, with producers targeting their own groups primarily, if not exclusively. Edwin Goodman, Pacifica president and former WBAI manager, noted in his report to the national board in 1973 that a Pacifica brochure claimed "Sacred cows find no sanctuary in our studios." He then went on to suggest that the statement "is less true than it once was, that too often we allow our political inclinations to skew, if not corrupt, our intellectual honesty," threatening to make Pacifica stations "more political, more predictable and less interesting and less worthy of support" (cited in Lumpp, 1979, p. 303).

WBAI's strike in 1977, like KPFA's three years earlier, revolved around related issues of finance, race, and power. The crisis at WBAI was precipitated by financial problems resulting from a decline in listener subscriptions, once numbering 30,000 in 1972, to 17,000. Two station managers who sought to address the problem had resigned under pressure from the staff. A third station manager and a new program director, Pablo Guzman, sought to reverse the decline by introducing a new programming format with the support of the local WBAI board. Guzman was one of the founders in 1968 of the militant Puerto Rican party, the Young Lords, serving as its Minister of Information until 1972. Guzman believed WBAI had failed to broaden its audience by ignoring the interests of Latinos and African Americans. He wished to rectify this through what he called "inner-city programming" in which the schedule would be built around more structured programming clusters.

The reorganization of the staff into production teams supervised by the program director represented a sharp departure from the practice of independent producers having complete control over their time slots. Guzman envisaged the programming clusters as tightly produced blocks of time featuring a mix of pretaped reportage, brisk conversation, and popular music aimed at broadening the station's appeal to minorities while maintaining its progressive orientation. To carry out the new format, Guzman planned to add new black and Latin programmers to WBAI's existing staff.

The WBAI staff revolted against the station's management and the new format, indicating over the air its refusal to accept layoffs and implement programming changes. The local advisory board voted to take the station off the air because Pacifica could not guarantee control of transmissions as required of licensees by the FCC. Rebel staff members seized the station's transmitter in the Empire State Building and continued broadcasting via a telephone patch for five hours before WBAI went off the air. Staff members declared a strike and their intention to unionize and proceeded to occupy the broadcast studios of the station, which would remain silent for 48 days. Many staff members viewed Guzman's proposed format as slick and authoritarian, a betrayal of Pacifica's most sacred traditions of noncommercialism and individualism. The approach to programming was at odds with what Land (1994) termed the "idiosyncratic, personality-centered programming which the station had cultivated since the mid-sixties" (p. 367). A structured format seemed the very antithesis of free-form radio, and Bob Fass emerged as one of the leaders of the staff revolt.

Supporters of change at WBAI countered that the strikers were defending a status quo in which the station's programmers and listeners consisted primarily of middle-class whites. The rhetoric of antiauthoritarianism was being used to resist change and a more inclusionary approach. The KPFA staff and local board issued a statement expressing alarm at the "pervasively unrepresentative nature of WBAI's staff and programming" and at illegal broadcasts of one-sided information that "risked all Pacifica licenses in a society where the survival of radio stations like ours has proved extremely difficult in the past." A statement signed by management and staff of Pacifica's newest station, WPFW-FM in Washington, D.C., which had just begun broadcasting, also criticized the strikers:

> No matter what those opposing change at WBAI may perceive themselves as protecting—their jobs, their own access to the airwaves, their own idea of whom the First Amendment is meant to serve—the effect of their actions and demands is the antithesis of public radio: a closed shop, where certain points of view are entrenched at the expense of a broader forum in which other disenfranchised voices might also be heard. (WPFW, 1977, p. 2)

During the conflict, WBAI lost a long-fought battle for New York City tax exemption, adding $250,000 to its debt. After a 7-week period of being off the air, a 45-day interim agreement led to the resumption of broadcasting, albeit without the concessions to decentralization following the strike at KPFA. Former adversaries among the local board, management, and staff mounted a successful effort to save WBAI from financial extinction. However, as an editorial in *The New York Times* on February 28, 1977, suggested, the larger issue of WBAI's identity and future as a Pacifica station had not been resolved:

> Behind the static of charges and countercharges, including the inevitable cries of "racism" on both sides, the reality is that WBAI's combination of adversary politics and relatively highbrow culture has never appealed to many New Yorkers outside of a young, white, middle-class, fairly well-educated group. Now, the excitement of the 1960s gone, its once loyal cadre grown older, the station has not succeeded either in restocking its audience or in reaching beyond it. Whether a very different kind of audience can be attracted without damaging the inimitable quality of WBAI . . . is the question. ("A Station in Search," 1977, p. 26. Copyright © 1977 by the New York Times Company. Reprinted by permission.)

The problems faced by Pacifica in the 1970s, which culminated in the strikes at KPFA and WBAI, were compounded by the conservative political ascendency in the 1980s beginning with the election of Ronald Reagan as president. In 1981, the program directors of Pacifica's five stations met to address the problem of ideological and organizational crisis. One of the participants was Clare Spark, program director of KPFK in Los Angeles, who wrote about the meeting in an essay entitled "Pacifica Radio and the Politics of Culture." The assembled program directors raised fundamental questions about the dilemmas they faced and the relevance of Lewis Hill's founding principles in addressing them. "Was Pacifica to be a community-access open forum, an instrument for social change, or both?" (Spark, 1987, p. 577). How could the concept of Pacifica as a vanguard medium be squared with its role as an open platform for diverse perspectives and interests? Might competition for control of that platform lead to its destruction?

The program directors sought to address Pacifica's institutional crisis by integrating the lessons of the 1960s and 1970s with the original vision of Lewis Hill, who, after all, had launched Pacifica during the 1940s and 1950s, an earlier period of conservative ascendency. Now the task was to overcome sexism, racism, and authoritarianism through a collaborative process in which both the staff and listeners from the community sought to transform themselves and Pacifica's stations. Otherwise sectarian fights over airtime would continue to pit groups against each and perpetuate their isolation and powerlessness. Spark (1987) emphasized that centrifugal forces within Pacifica had to be overcome if its stations were to flourish:

> The Pacifica agenda—our legal mandate— . . . is unambiguous in its language and intent: the study of the causes of conflict, with the goal of a lasting understanding among all peoples. Pacifica programs and programmers, therefore, are mandated to create programs and social processes that show what people must do to *heal* conflicts. People whose agenda it is to *exacerbate* conflict in order to perpetuate structures of domination are, it seems to us, not to be in control of our air (i.e., present themselves as representing Pacifica or as exempt from critical dialogue). (p. 580)

Future programming would emphasize how issues of class, gender, and race intersect. The five program directors committed themselves to exploring the full spectrum of established and oppositional culture and to fostering critical, independent thinking. Central to the task of reinvigorating Pacifica would be activating listeners to participate more fully in Pacifica's affairs so as to nurture an alternative, progressive culture: "Developing open and reciprocal relations with our 'audience' is necessary if we are to uproot, expose, and eventually destroy the illegitimate control that pervades everyday life" (p. 589). The approach of the program directors stressed greater communication and collaboration on all levels—among programmers within Pacifica and the five stations and their combined listeners. Their hope was that this approach would help Pacifica realize its potential as the most influential alternative radio network in the United States.

During the 1970s and 1980s, as Pacifica sought to resolve its internal conflicts, it experienced an external challenge with the growth of NPR, the subject of Chapter 6. NPR, a federally funded public radio production and distribution system, was created as a result of the Public Broadcasting Act of 1967. NPR eventually acquired over 200 affiliates and became the dominant force in noncommercial radio. The station manager of KPFK had represented Pacifica on the original NPR board established in 1970. However, the Pacifica national board concluded that a federal public radio system, funded largely by government appropriations and centralized along network lines, was at odds with Pacifica's mission. Indicating that Pacifica stations would not join NPR and continue to serve on its board, Pacifica's president wrote,

> We are sympathetic with, and wish to encourage, NPR's efforts to create a viable national coalition of public radio broadcasters, but feel that Pacifica's most appropriate and effective role, under present circumstances, is as an independent source of good programs and effective programming in non-commercial broadcasting. (cited in Haney, 1981, p. 70)

To be sure, indirect cross-fertilization between Pacifica and NPR has taken place over the years. NPR continued intermittently to court Pacifica, and for a period a divided Pacifica national board reluctantly permitted KPFT in Houston, which had marginal financial and programming resources, to enter into a limited partnership with NPR. NPR has repeatedly hired away Pacifica staff members, especially for *All Things Considered,* its flagship news program. Nonetheless, Pacifica declined to blur its distinct identity and mission by affiliating with NPR.

NPR aside, another challenge to Pacifica tradition emerged in the 1970s and 1980s: consideration of corporate underwriting or other forms of limited advertising by Pacifica stations. Underwriting, a euphemism for a discrete form of advertising, involves financial support for a specific program or series, for which the sponsor received an on-air credit or "tag." Government guidelines placed limits on direct advertising of products or services and the mention of prices for underwriting credits given on noncommercial stations. Such underwriting, akin to the earliest form of indirect commercial advertising on WEAF in the early 1920s, aimed to promote goodwill and an enhanced image for corporate sponsors. Pacifica made a distinction between public and private funding. As a result of the Public Broadcasting Act of 1967, government funds became available to Pacifica for the first time. Following debate about the dependency such funding might create, Pacifica began accepting nonspecific community service grants from the CPB, which were available to all noncommercial radio stations meeting basic requirements for station operations. Pacifica also started to receive program underwriting grants from governmental entities disbursing public funds, such as the National Endowment for the Humanities. However, in 1977 the Pacifica national board passed a resolution calling for a halt to expansion of program underwriting, ruling out sponsorship of programs by private enterprises. In 1982, Pacifica's two youngest and neediest stations—KPFT in Houston and

WPFW in Washington, D.C.—petitioned the national board to reconsider Pacifica's policy of accepting private capital for equipment and general operating expenses but not for programming. Advocates of program underwriting at WPFW in Washington, D.C. noted the difficulty of raising sufficient funds from a predominantly low-income, inner-city, minority audience. In addition to putting constraints on raising private funds for specific programs, Pacifica's policy prevented its stations from broadcasting programs with underwriting credits produced by independent producers or noncommercial production centers and distributed by tape or satellite. The conflict over underwriting, which pitted Pacifica's president and executive director against each other, came to a head in 1983, and was widely reported in the press.

According to Peter Franck, Pacifica president at the time, the controversy over underwriting, like the question of affiliation with NPR, involved the organization's very identity: Is Pacifica to be part of mainstream public broadcasting or the media voice of the progressive movement? The Pacifica Radio News bureau prepared a position paper for the 1983 board meeting arguing that Pacifica should maintain its distinct tradition, which entailed an adversarial relationship with corporate interests. Acceptance of corporate funds would signal a significant defeat, an inability to produce programming to maintain a progressive listenership, "in short a failure to use our medium as a political challenge and as an organizing tool." The statement concluded, "A failure of this magnitude should not be compounded with a gross violation of principle such as corporate backing" (Pacifica Radio News, 1983, pp. 101-102). The Pacifica national board voted in 1983 to continue Pacifica's ban on business sponsorship of programming. The board reaffirmed that "listener-sponsorship is the core of [Pacifica's] support," and called for increased reliance on subscribers in order to reduce and eventually eliminate all government and nonlistener support (Smith, 1988, p. 28).

Pacifica policy was bucking an accelerating trend within public radio and television of decreased public and increased corporate support. In 1984, the FCC approved "enhanced underwriting," which expanded the permissible scope of corporate tags to include detailing brand names and the donors' products and services. At the end of the 1980s, the issue of underwriting again came to a head within Pacifica and was the focal point of its national board meeting in Los Angeles in January 1989, Pacifica's 40th anniversary. To inform those deliberations, a packet containing historical accounts of Pacifica policies, position papers, and supporting materials was assembled and titled *Underwriting: An Evaluation of Pacifica Policy.* Advocates of a relaxation of underwriting restraints estimated that as of 1988 only 60% of Pacifica's revenue could be considered listener support and that the goal of 100% listener funding stated by the national board in 1983 was unattainable. It was recalled that Lewis Hill's experiment probably would have collapsed in the 1950s without the support of the Ford Foundation. Noncommercial radio stations belonging to the NFCB were said to have established adequate standards and safeguards in their underwriting guidelines. Also, Pacifica's ban on underwriting credits meant, for example, that its stations could not carry the BBC news broadcast distributed by American Public Radio (APR) or reports from National Native News/Alaska Public Radio Network, which both received corporate underwriting. More generally, some viewed Pacifica's policy on corporate underwriting as self-righteous posturing that perpetuated the organization's poverty, limited its political impact, and resulted in the turnover of many of its most talented staff members.

Corless Smith, who prepared a report for the KPFA local board, emphasized the impact of mounting corporate underwriting on public television. She suggested that public broadcasting had become a strategic if indirect and supplemental vehicle for corporations to promote their products, general goodwill, and positions on public policy. Smith (1988) cited Les Brown's contention that "there is a studious avoidance of controversy in PBS programs with corporate underwriting" (p. 33). Underwriters preferred to support benign programs of high culture over hard-hitting public affairs programming and documentaries. Smith noted examples of censorship on public television attributable to corporate influence. However, the self-censorship involved in pitching programs to suit corporate sponsors was more insidious and far-reaching in its impact on public television, especially on the increasing scarcity of minority and dissident perspectives. In general, corporate underwriting had rendered less clear public television's mission as an alternative to commercial TV. In effect, Smith argued that the impact of corporate underwriting on Pacifica would be anathema to the principles of Lewis Hill.

At its 1989 meeting, the Pacifica national board unanimously reaffirmed listeners' sponsorship as the core of its financial support and "the prohibition of soliciting and or acceptance of business underwriting for programming" (Pacifica Foundation, 1989, p. 11). A second resolution authorized Pacifica's two hard-strapped stations, WPFW in Washington, D.C., and KPFT in Houston, to solicit "business memberships" for general support on an experimental basis for a two-year period. Guidelines were to be established for the solicitation and acknowledgment of such business support so as not to compromise Pacifica's listener-sponsored, noncommercial character.

Larry Bensky, veteran Pacifica programmer and station manager, had demonstrated how the Pacifica tradition of innovative public affairs programming could be maintained despite—also, in part, thanks to—limited material resources. For three months during summer 1987, Bensky integrated the investigative reporting legacy of Elsa Knight Thompson with the techniques of free-form radio of Bob Fass when he anchored Pacifica's gavel-to-gavel coverage of the Iran-Contra hearings. Bensky supplemented live testimony with informed commentary and interviews with both a wide range of figures in the United States and abroad involved in the controversy and a host of experts and reporters. He also conducted nationwide phone-ins several times a week during breaks in the hearings in which listeners called Bensky in the hearing room and were put on the air. His coverage was carried by Pacifica's 5 stations and by more than 20 community radio stations across the nation. Bensky received a George Polk Award for providing the most comprehensive coverage of the hearings in American broadcasting. In its awards citation, the Polk Committee noted that Bensky received a paltry salary, shared a rented room in Washington, D.C., and biked to the hearings every day. The entire cost of Bensky's coverage did not equal the weekly salary of a network news anchor. As a result of Pacifica's coverage of the hearings, listenership jumped throughout the system. "The question that haunts Pacifica now," Fisher (1989) wrote in *Mother Jones* magazine in that period, "is how to keep those unexpected recruits" (p. 51), a reference to Pacifica's dependency on the cycles of political crisis off which it has fed since the 1960s.

Despite periodic programming triumphs during the 1980s and 1990s that coalesced forces within Pacifica and gave it national visibility, Pacifica continued to be plagued by internal conflict. In the early 1980s, as a result of a major ideological split over issues of race and class within KPFK in Los Angeles, Program Director Claire Spark and News Director Marc Cooper were fired. Spark and Cooper went public with their grievances, and a local committee agitated for their reinstatement. During the same period Peter Franck, president of Pacifica's board from 1980 to 1984, and Executive Director Sharon Maeda became embroiled in a bitter personal and political fight whose reverberations continued well into the 1990s. Franck, whose ties to KPFA reached back to his days as a student activist on the Berkeley campus during the 1950s, accused Maeda of aspiring to move Pacifica away from its radical roots and reposition it as the liberal wing of mainstream public radio. Franck, accused by Maeda of abusing his authority, was forced to resign (Barlow, 1992). In 1994, the former Pacifica president, reflecting in retrospect on his three-decade involvement with Pacifica, concluded that "Pacifica has to be redesigned from top to bottom—no small task." Franck, arguing that Pacifica suffered from a loss of vision, blandness in news and public affairs, and a general lack of internal review and accountability, added: "Without a well-articulated vision of what progressive media could do for the country it's hard to focus on how badly the Pacifica mission is fading" (cited in Noton, 1994, pp. 56-57).

Similar sentiments were echoed by Andrew Phillips (1993) at the end of his four-year tenure as program director of WBAI in New York. Bemoaning the trend toward centralization in programming, the impossibility of meeting the needs of myriad constituencies, and the low level of subscribers' support, Phillips asserted that "Pacifica has a crisis of identity. There is no leadership; no vision" (p. 4). An article by Rauber (1993) in Berkeley's *East Bay Express* described KPFA, conceived at the outset of the cold war, in a state of "near-total stasis" (p. 13) in the post-cold-war era, riddled by factionalism and under attack by alienated listener groups. Pacifica's unresolved institutional crisis and trying working conditions caused the defection of many of its most talented programmers, who quit Pacifica for the more stable if less iconoclastic world of mainstream public radio. Larry Josephson, one of Pacifica's most gifted practitioners of free-form radio and the art of radio documentary and a former manager of WBAI, expressed the bittersweet feelings shared by many Pacifica alumni upon his departure:

> I am tired. Tired of the anarchy, the penury, the physical disorder, and the collective insanity that romantics among us insist are the necessary preconditions to the chemistry of WBAI, and more important, to the perception of an extended WBAI family that we all love/hate. (cited in Lumpp, 1979, p. 326)

* * *

Pacifica approaches the half-century mark—it was incorporated in 1946 and went on the air in 1949—in a mixed state of health. Lewis Hill's quest for a viable democratic model for the internal operation of Pacifica and its stations remains elusive. Pacifica and the community broadcasting movement as a whole have only begun to address the issues of democratic praxis posed by Hochheimer (1993). The institutional crisis continues. Yet if many Pacifica workers experience burnout, the institution itself displays a remarkable resiliency. Perhaps there is something to be said for an organization that resists being captured by any single group or orientation that could impose political and structural discipline. As noted by Barlow (1992), Pacifica absorbed three distinct generations of media activists— rooted in the old left, the new left, and the multicultural left—making it "one of a very select number of progressive and democratic media organizations in the U.S. which has managed to survive, grow and even prosper, relatively speaking, during the political and cultural upheavals and dislocations of the last four decades" (p. 2).

If fundamental organizational and programmatic questions remain unresolved, Pacifica has not lost its way. Listener subscriptions continue to be the cornerstone of Pacifica's funding, constituting roughly 66% of its income. CPB grants amount to only 15% of station budgets and have not cowed Pacifica into dependency. For example, Pacifica was the only CPB-funded organization to publicly oppose legislation in 1992 requiring CPB monitoring of "objectivity and balance" of programming. During the 15-year period beginning in 1980, listener donations more than tripled, and total revenues grew from $2.3 million to nearly $8 million (Salniker, 1994). Pat Scott (1994), national affairs director, wrote in response to Peter Franck's critique,

> Proposing ultra-left, "horse and buggy" solutions to Pacifica's problems and future doesn't cut it in the 1990s. Pacifica's plans are to remain a major force for multi-racial and multi-cultural expression in its broadcasts and policies and to harness the new technologies to this end. (p. 4)

Despite the years of turmoil caused by Pacifica's post-1960s institutional crisis, the challenge posed by National Public Radio, and the lure of corporate underwriting, Pacifica opted to maintain its institutional integrity as an alternative radio system based primarily on direct listener sponsorship. Pacifica's triumphs and failures would continue to take place within the framework established by Lewis Hill. That framework permitted a degree of freedom unparalleled in American broadcasting but entailed a continuous struggle—internal and external—for survival. Hill's historic contribution was to forge a third model of broadcasting in addition to the two dominant models that emerged in the 1920s. The first was the commercial model of advertiser-supported network broadcasting in the United States; the second was public service broadcasting in Britain. The third, listener-sponsored community radio, launched after World War II, represented a synthesis and extension of the noncommercial experiments and broadcast reform movement of the prewar period. This approach differed from the two established systems in a fundamental respect: "While the commercial and public service models both treat listeners as objects, to be captured for advertisers or improved and informed, community radio aspires to treat its listeners as subjects and participants" (Lewis & Booth, 1990, p. 8).

Pacifica represented the first, and the most radical, model for public broadcasting after World War II. Lewis Hill initiated the practice of basing station funding on listener sponsorship, modeled on subscriptions for periodicals, a plan that Edward Nockels was unable to realize for labor station WCFL in the 1920s and 1930s. Subscriptions now support over 100 community radio stations and provide an increasing percentage of the income of public radio stations. Pacifica prepared the groundwork for the emergence of NPR in the 1960s, the NFCB in the 1970s, and the World Association of Community Radio Broadcasters (AMARC) in the 1980s. Hill also influenced the development of public television. He played a leading role in the formation in 1951 of the Bay Area Educational Television Association, which developed the pioneering noncommercial television station KQED in San Francisco on the basis of subscription funding. Membership contributions remain a major source of money for PBS stations and will assume increased importance as a result of reductions in federal aid. Hill provided the spark that ignited the public broadcasting movement after 1945, which grew to include NPR, PBS, the NFCB, and the AMARC. Pacifica, Barlow (1992) argued, is "the forerunner of all these organizations" (p. 1). Here, as in other instances in communications history, the earliest experiment was in many respects the boldest. Today, many mainstream public broadcasters seek to disassociate themselves from Pacifica's strident and rough edges, unaware of their debt to Lewis Hill and the organization he founded.

In the 1990s, Pacifica Radio continues to function as an integrated alternative radio network. Its core consists of five stations in Berkeley, Los Angeles, New York, Houston, and Washington, D.C.—collectively capable of reaching 20% of the American population. Pacifica's stations draw about 1 million listeners a week and 70,000 paid subscribers. A tape library of over forty thousand programs reflects Pacifica's unique role in airing the controversies in American life for nearly half a century. Pacifica's bureau in

Washington, D.C., produces daily news broadcasts and public affairs specials that are received by approximately 100 community and public radio stations (Land, 1994). Pacifica has also made an impact by virtue of the many thousands of media professionals and activists first trained as volunteers at its stations before embarking on careers elsewhere in community, public and commercial broadcasting.

Of even greater importance than these quantitative criteria is Pacifica's continuing role as a model of an institution fostering political discourse and cultural expression independent of both the state and the corporation. Pacifica Radio, which sparked a heterogeneous public broadcasting movement after World War II, remains unique in its commitment to sustain an independent, critical, and oppositional public sphere on the broadcast spectrum.

CHAPTER 6

National Public Radio
The Vision of
William H. Siemering

During the quarter-century following World War II, a metamorphosis occurred in which "educational" radio was transformed into a federal form of
"public" radio. This process was distinct from the development of Pacifica
and community radio in the same period. Although the Pacifica project
synthesized elements of the pre-World War II broadcast reform movement,
it represented a significant departure in American broadcasting history as an
alternative form of local, listener-sponsored radio. Educational radio—dating back to the origins of broadcasting, rooted in colleges and universities
and their instructional mission—had greater institutional continuity.

The activity of the NAEB, the leading professional organization of
educational broadcasters, spanned the eras before and after World War II.
The NAEB had been instrumental in lobbying for the reservation of channels
on the FM band for noncommercial use, which led to a renaissance in the
number of educational radio stations on the air after World War II. However,
these stations, plagued by weak signals, poor financing, and lack of inter-

connection, struggled to constitute a significant presence on the airwaves. Educational radio addressed its problems with limited success for two decades until passage of the Public Broadcasting Act of 1967. This legislation launched—both conceptually and organizationally—"public" as distinct from "educational" radio. National Public Radio emerged as the institutional expression of this shift. Public radio would advance a distinctly different concept of its mission and relationship with listeners and with the state.

After World War II, the NAEB led the effort to create the noncommercial radio network on the FM band that broadcast reformers had failed to establish on the AM band during the interwar years. The NAEB's origins can be traced back to Herbert Hoover's fourth national radio conference in 1925, when representatives of educational stations, primarily from land-grant state universities in the Midwest, formed the Association of College and University Broadcasting Stations. At its first national convention in 1930, it issued the earliest formal call for a noncommercial network. In 1934, following the defeat of the Wagner-Hatfield Bill, the organization's name was changed to the NAEB to signal its ambition to mobilize educational broadcasters nationally. Because educational broadcasters had been virtually eliminated from the AM spectrum, the NAEB began lobbying the FCC for the reservation of educational channels on what became the FM band. The FCC's announcement in 1938 that special educational licenses would be given to noncommercial educational stations above the AM frequency, followed in 1940 by the reservation of five channels on the new FM band, reflected the NAEB's successful lobbying efforts prior to the wartime freeze on the further development of FM.

After World War II, the NAEB had two principal objectives for educational radio: gaining additional channel reservations and creating a network. In 1945, the NAEB together with the U.S. Office of Education successfully petitioned the FCC to set aside 20 of the 100 FM channels exclusively for noncommercial educational stations from 88 to 92 megahertz on the FM dial, which have continued to be designated for noncommercial use throughout the country. How can this apparent triumph be explained after decades of opposition of government regulators and the broadcast industry to the reservation of channels? In the immediate postwar period, the broadcast industry, preeminent in radio on AM, had little interest in FM, an undeveloped system that required listeners to purchase new radios. Perhaps most important, the 1950s witnessed a television boom comparable to the radio boom of the

1920s, and the broadcast industry concentrated its resources on the new medium.

Despite the guaranteed spectrum space, educational broadcasters faced considerable obstacles. FM was still an obscure broadcast medium with an uncharted future. The scarcity of FM receivers restricted educational radio's potential reach. Educational broadcasters had limited resources for inaugurating new FM stations. In response to their financial plight, the FCC in 1948 eased rules to permit low-power 10-watt stations, serving a radius of two or three miles, instead of the normal 250-watt requirement. In 1950, the FCC also reduced the minimal qualifications of operators of noncommercial FM stations. The majority of the new educational stations on the FM band were marginal operations desperately in need of the resources an educational radio network might provide.

In calling for an educational radio system in 1930, the ACUBS, forerunner of the NAEB, had noted the need to "compete on a more even basis with commercial broadcasters" (cited in Haney, 1981, p. 20). Experiments in program exchanges took place in the latter part of the 1930s, but improvements in tape-recording technology made such ventures more feasible following the war. A plan for a tape distribution network emerged as a result of the meetings of educational broadcasters from the United States, Canada, and Great Britain funded by the Rockefeller Foundation and held in the Allerton House Conference Center of the University of Illinois in the summers of 1949 and 1950. A seed grant from the Kellogg Foundation enabled the NAEB to inaugurate a national noncommercial tape network for a five-year period, after which it was supposed to become self-sustaining.

Program tapes from U.S. educational stations and production centers as well as from the British and Canadian broadcast systems were "bicycled"— that is, mailed rather than transmitted instantaneously—to more than 50 NAEB member stations coast to coast. The network increased the pool of programming and fostered a higher level of communication and collective consciousness among educational stations, prompting early regional experiments with direct interconnection. Wisconsin was the first to form a statewide FM network, a simple repeater system that included eight stations by 1952. The short-lived Eastern Educational Radio Network, funded in part by the Ford Foundation, linked about a dozen stations via telephone lines. During the 1960s, countless NAEB meetings were devoted to considering various networking schemes. One study funded by the U.S. Office of Education explored the feasibility of electronic interconnection linking the library, computer, and radio stations of U.S. colleges and universities. In 1965, the NAEB linked some 70 stations for three hours for live coverage of the German national elections, the first national live interconnect in the history of educational broadcasting.

Despite the growth in number of educational stations on FM from 46 in 1948 to 292 in 1966, and the networking efforts of the NAEB, the postwar renaissance in educational radio was more apparent than real. The majority of the stations were weak 10-watt stations with annual budgets of under $10,000 and irregular hours of broadcasting. One third had no full-time professional paid staff. Frequently, stations were off the air on weekends and during the summer months and other school holidays. Much of the programming was limited to instructional and training purposes. Broadcasts aimed at a general audience were frequently amateurish. The level of programs distributed by the NAEB exchange program was highly uneven as was the technical quality of the tapes, which were sometimes received in shreds. In general, the bicycle network could not be considered a substitute for an established mechanism for live interconnection.

Indeed, in the period 1948-1966 the prospects for educational FM radio appeared to deteriorate as the major foundations concentrated their resources on the development of educational television. The focus of educational broadcasters shifted to the reservation of educational television channels during the FCC freeze on TV licenses from 1948 to 1952. After 1948, "radio was relegated to the back burner and would remain there for nearly twenty years" (Avery & Pepper, 1980, p. 127). In 1952, the FAE of the Ford Foundation established the National Educational Television and Radio Center to strengthen the programming of educational broadcasting. Despite the word "radio" in its title, a former official of the FAE stressed that the Center's "operating objective was almost solely to give program service to educational television stations" (Blakely, 1979, p. 103). The Ford Foundation eventually ceased funding networking experiments such as the Eastern Educational Radio Network so as to concentrate its efforts on educational TV.

Educational radio even became a secondary concern within the NAEB. Radio was excluded from the Educational Television Facilities Act of 1962, legislation resulting from concerted lobbying by the NAEB and its foundation allies. The Act gave $32 million to fund the construction of new noncommercial television stations and technical improvement of existing stations over a five-year period. In 1963, the importance of the NAEB's radio division was further diminished in a reorganization of the NAEB in conjunction with the Ford Foundation's creation of the National Educational Television (NET) network to replace the National Educational Television and Radio Center. The NAEB was restructured into two semiautonomous radio and television divisions, in effect segregating educational radio from what had become the organization's principal focus: the advancement of educational television. The NAEB, which had been founded by radio broadcasters, had come under the post-World War II spell of television.

In a critical period from 1964 to 1967, educational radio faced the threat of being excluded from a movement to provide federal funding for educational television in a new public broadcasting system. In 1964, plans were set in motion by the educational TV division of the NAEB to establish a blue-ribbon national commission on educational television. In 1965, the Carnegie Commission on Educational Television was established under the auspices of the Carnegie Corporation of New York in close consultation with the Johnson administration, which viewed federal support of noncommercial television as a component of its Great Society program. The Carnegie Commission's 1967 report, *Public Television: A Program for Action,* provided a blueprint for federal legislation to establish a public TV system. The report invested the proposed public television system with a broader mission than traditional educational broadcasting, characterizing it as a cultural and social instrument to affirm American pluralism. The Carnegie Commission on Educational Television—its genesis, membership, and findings—is examined in greater detail in Chapter 8 on the origins of public television. Suffice it to say that radio was neither considered by the Carnegie Commission nor meant to be included in proposed legislation on public broadcasting. Proponents of noncommercial television apparently feared that "the radio system's long history of weakness would drag the entire Carnegie effort into oblivion" (Witherspoon & Kovitz, 1987, p. 16). Public broadcasting legislation initially introduced in Congress in 1967, following publication of the Carnegie report, was limited to television.

Facing the prospect of exclusion of radio from the new public broadcasting initiative, the National Educational Radio (NER) division of the NAEB waged a counteroffensive. In 1966, as the Carnegie Commission deliberated, NER convened a conference on "Educational Radio as a National Resource" in Racine, Wisconsin. The conference commissioned a study that would provide the basis for an appeal to Congress for radio's inclusion in proposed public broadcasting legislation. The NER board of directors hired Herman W. Land, a former commercial broadcasting executive and editor of a broadcasting trade journal, to document educational radio's current status and future potential. Land's study, *The Hidden Medium,* was published and widely distributed in April 1967, three months after the Carnegie Commission's report, just as hearings on the Public Broadcasting Act were beginning in Congress. Land provided a detailed survey of educational radio's neglect and lack of resources, its considerable achievements despite these conditions, and its untapped potential as a national resource. He did not go so far as to revive the populist protest of the NCER in the 1930s, instead faulting educational administrators rather than the commercial system for the sorry plight of noncommercial radio. Frantic lobbying and congressional testimony by NER based on Land's book resulted in the inclusion of radio in the Public Broadcasting Act of 1967.

Passage of this Act signaled a new financial as well as programming orientation for noncommercial broadcasting. The Carnegie Commission had advocated a switch from the old system of financing educational broadcasting—primarily local, based on the support of educational institutions and state legislatures, supplemented by grants from private foundations—to a national system of public allocations. It recommended that the new system be funded by an excise tax on TV sets, the procedures from which would be placed in a trust fund to ensure independence from government control. However, legislators rejected this proposal in favor of congressional appropriations. The 1967 Act created the Corporation for Public Broadcasting—a nonprofit, nongovernmental entity—to disburse funds for the development of public radio and television. The CPB was designed to provide both political insulation and funds for public radio and TV. The legislation required that the 15-member board of the CPB, appointed by the president with the concurrence of the Senate, be politically balanced, with no more than 8 members from either party. The Act barred the CPB from owning or operating any radio or television stations to preclude the creation of a government network. Hence, although one of its primary tasks was to fund programs, the law prohibited the CPB from producing or distributing programs or operating any interconnection system. Instead, separate agencies were subsequently created as networking arms of the public broadcasting system: National Public Radio and the Public Broadcasting Service.

Despite the report of the Carnegie Commission, passage of the Public Broadcasting Act of 1967, and establishment of the CPB, public broadcasting remained, in the words of Les Brown, "a name without a concept" (cited in Blakely, 1979, p. 178). *The Hidden Medium* was a lobbying document establishing the need—but not a vision or structure—for an expanded non-commercial radio system. In 1969, the CPB and the Ford Foundation jointly funded Samuel Holt's *The Public Radio Study,* which stressed that most of the 384 noncommercial FM stations not only lacked adequate resources and power but a collective identity and sense of purpose. It concluded that strong measures were needed, especially the establishment of a national program service and a station expansion program, to build a strong public radio system. At the NAEB's annual convention in 1969, the CPB announced its intention to build the nation's first noncommercial radio network and established the Radio Advisory Council as recommended in the 1969 Holt study. One of its leading members was William H. Siemering, then general manager of WBFO-FM, an innovative educational radio station in Buffalo, New York. The Council, made up primarily of station managers long active in the NAEB, began a series of meetings under CPB auspices that led to the establishment of NPR in 1970. The structure of NPR, the first national noncommercial radio network, broadly paralleled that of PBS, the public television network established a year earlier in 1969.

William Siemering's (1970) "National Public Radio Purposes" was adopted by the NPR board as the new system's statement of mission. This document represented a synthesis of the views of participants in the CPB-sponsored planning sessions in 1969 but contained Siemering's imprimatur, reflecting his considerable experience and record of innovation in noncommercial radio. Siemering grew up in the 1940s and early 1950s in the Midwest near the transmitter of WHA, the leading educational radio station of the land-grant universities. The station at the University of Wisconsin exercised a profound influence on Siemering's interest in radio and his view of its potential. He recalls that farmers listened to the special agricultural broadcasts at noon, and he notes the impact on his family of the station's goal of taking culture to the people. Siemering financed his education at the University of Wisconsin by working long hours at WHA, managed since the 1930s by the legendary H. B. McCarty. WHA, whose lobby was adorned by a mural charting radio's development, heightened Siemering's awareness of the medium's historic roots and its potential as a populist medium (personal communication, July 25, 1995). Looker (1995) emphasized that the origins of public radio were not elitist: "In fact, NPR's roots are *populist,* growing out of the same rural, self-reliant, self-improving soil as the Chautauqua Movement or the Grange" (p. 15).

In 1962, Siemering became the general manager of WBFO-FM, the State University of New York station in Buffalo, New York, which became a laboratory for bold experimentation. Buffalo had a more heterogeneous population than Madison, Wisconsin. A porch-to-porch survey of minorities led to a storefront satellite broadcast facility from which African American and Hispanic residents produced 25 hours of programming a week. Here Siemering (1991b) explored radio's potential for "speaking with many voices and many dialects" (p. 1), and anticipated the movement for community-based radio. WBFO provided graphic coverage of all facets of a student strike and police occupation of the campus, reflecting Siemering's view of radio as an ideal medium for primary sources. According to Ira Flatow, who worked at WBFO, Siemering believed "that it empowered people to get on the radio, and that everyone should have access to it" (personal communication, January 1, 1995). Under Siemering, WBFO bridged the gap between "town and gown" listeners and acquired a large campus and regional listenership. Influenced in part by the programing of the Canadian Broadcast Corporation (CBC), which reached both Wisconsin and upstate New York, Siemering rejected traditional news and arts formats for more creative uses of radio as a means of personal expression and in-depth reporting. In 1968, Siemering won the Broadcast Preceptor Award of San Francisco State College for "remarkable guidance in bringing a renaissance in radio" to WBFO (Kirkish, 1980, p. 68). Under Siemering's leadership from 1962 to 1970, the station provided new paradigms and a cadre of innovators for the future of noncommercial radio. In retrospect, Siemering said, "I view those years in Buffalo as the formative ones for NPR" (personal communication, July 25, 1995).

Siemering (1969) believed that public broadcasting needed to distinguish itself from educational and commercial models, from both an outdated Victorian concept of cultural uplift and a market-driven system directed toward the lowest common denominator. In "National Public Radio Purposes," Siemering (1970) asserted that, unlike commercial broadcasting, public radio would not view its audience as a mass market:

> National public radio will serve the individual: it will promote personal growth; it will regard the individual differences among men with respect and joy rather than derision and hate; it will celebrate the human experience as infinitely varied rather than vacuous and banal; it will encourage a sense of active constructive participation, rather than apathetic helplessness. (p. 248)

Siemering proposed new uses of the medium of radio in public affairs and the arts that would be instrumental in shaping the character of NPR. He provided a bold blueprint for a daily news magazine, titled *All Things Considered,* that would become NPR's flagship program and give substance to the nebulous concept of public radio. As a journalistic instrument, the program aspired to create a new form of in-depth news and public affairs programming for broadcasting to "enable the individual to better understand himself, his government . . . and his natural and social environment so he can intelligently participate in effecting the process of change" (p. 248).

Siemering (1970) stressed the importance of offering investigative and interpretive reporting on national and international affairs hitherto absent from the airwaves but also cultural reportage of the world of ideas and the arts. NPR would provide a venue for the full range of the culture—both popular and high—of American society. The airwaves of public radio could provide recognition and legitimacy for the aspirations of ethnic and racial minorities. All regions of American society could receive national exposure through NPR. Siemering shared the Carnegie Commission's conception of public broadcasting as a social instrument to reaffirm and to strengthen American democracy politically and culturally. NPR's public affairs and cultural programming could, at once, highlight American pluralism and help reintegrate a fragmented society. In cultural as well as public affairs programming, Siemering envisaged a decentralized system reflecting the diversity of the nation: a system of local audio laboratories to train radio producers, submission of programs to the network by affiliates, and reciprocal trade of material among stations. By fulfilling this mission, Siemering believed that NPR would revitalize the medium of radio.

Responsible for both implementing Siemering's programming plan and the interconnection of stations, NPR amassed considerably more authority over its domain than did PBS, its television counterpart. According to its articles of incorporation, PBS was prohibited from producing programs. It would provide interconnection by selecting and distributing public television programming but would leave the creation of programs to production centers at local stations. This separation of church and state, of interconnection and production, was not applied to NPR's sweeping mandate:

> To propose, plan and develop, to acquire, purchase and lease, to prepare, produce and record, and to distribute, license and otherwise make available radio programs to be broadcast over noncommercial educational radio broad-

cast stations, networks and systems. (cited in Witherspoon & Kovitz, 1987, p. 35)

NPR's articles of incorporation specified that it would both produce and distribute programming, in effect placing the "direction of public radio's future into the hands of the NPR founders" (Doyle, 1990, p. 22).

The sorry state of educational radio provided the rationale for investing NPR with so much power. An argument can be made that a powerful NPR was needed to transform the marginal world of educational radio into a viable public radio system. Yet it should be noted that the weakness of educational broadcasting was in part the outgrowth of policies of the government, foundations, and educational broadcasters in the period from 1945 to 1967. The exclusion of radio from the Educational Television Facilities Act of 1962 and from consideration by the Carnegie Commission reflected the desire of Ford and Carnegie and even of some within the NAEB itself to concentrate virtually all resources on noncommercial television. Hence, the argument for the necessity of a centralized NPR combining interconnection and production was made by the same forces whose policies had kept educational radio in its weakened state.

Besides creating NPR, the CPB established the foundation for a public radio network through a six-year-plan for identifying and supporting a core group of stronger affiliates. This was achieved by establishing criteria to determine which stations would be "CPB qualified"—that is, eligible for federal funds disbursed by the CPB. The standards were set by the CPB in consultation with its Radio Advisory Council and with the NER division of the NAEB. Programming had to be designed primarily for the general public. The CPB also set minimum quantitative requirements for eligibility: Stations were originally required to broadcast at least 8 hours a day, 6 days a week, 48 weeks per year, with a paid staff consisting of no less than one full-time and four half-time paid staff members. Standards would be increased over a six-year period. A CPB-commissioned historical overview of public broadcasting said of the station qualification requirements, "It is probably not too much to say that this policy more than any other has helped build a strong public radio system for the United States" (Witherspoon & Kovitz, 1987, p. 34).

Only 73 stations—just 17% of existing educational radio stations— qualified for the initial infusion of federal funds in 1970. The number increased to 103 by the time NPR went on the air in 1971. The CPB requirements were meant to encourage marginal stations to expand, but the practical effect was to subsidize the strongest stations. Many managers of smaller radio stations bitterly opposed the standards. Robert C. Hinz, a member of CPB's Radio Advisory Council and the manager of an Oregon station, recalled "fist pounding arguments" and bitterness because most educational stations would not qualify for federal funds and would have to change their operations and become answerable to a central authority to qualify for full participation in the public radio system (cited in Haney, 1981, p. 57). John Gregory, who chaired a NAEB committee on the needs of the nonqualified stations that issued a report in 1973, later conceded that his committee was formed to obscure the fact that smaller stations were being abandoned: The purpose was "to show that NAEB and NER were not abandoning them; but in a sense we were. . . . I think on paper it looked good that we showed some concern" (cited in Haney, 1981, p. 108).

The transition from educational to public radio was not painless. Haney (1981), who studied the advent of NPR and public radio in the decade from 1967 to 1977, stressed three factors in the troubled relations between local stations and the new national public radio leadership. First, the CPB requirements came as a shock and seemed unfair to many smaller stations. Second, despite the nominally democratic structure in which decisions about the future of public radio were being made, a small group of insiders seemed to have multiple appointments on all the key deliberative bodies of the NAEB, the CPB, and NPR. Finally, no structure for regular communication between the NPR board and the stations had been established. Meanwhile, NPR absorbed the principal functions of the radio division of the NAEB, the most important of which was its program service. Initially, NAEB continued to function as noncommercial radio's representative before the government and public, but that role would be diminished in 1973 with the establishment of the Association of Public Radio Stations (APRS) as the Washington lobby and public relations arm of CPB-qualified radio stations.

The fact that NPR's top officials had a television background also contributed to tension between educational radio veterans and the new public radio leadership. Donald Quayle, NPR's first president from 1970 to 1973, had been an administrator with the NET network before working at the CPB. His top lieutenants for the task of network building came from the ranks of educational TV, as educational radio had not developed a national system comparable to NET. For example, Lee Frischknecht, former head of station relations at NET, became assistant to the president and director of network affairs at NPR—and ultimately Quayle's successor as NPR president. Nevertheless, NPR management appointed a radio hand as the network's program director: William Siemering. NPR, carried by 90 stations in 32 states, went on the air April 1, 1971. A tape of concerts by the Los Angeles Philharmonic constituted the first offering to member stations. Hearings of the Senate Foreign Relations Committee on ending the war in Vietnam inaugurated live programming. A watershed had been reached: noncommercial radio's first full-time, national, live interconnection system.

Approximately one month after NPR's debut, on May 3, 1971, member stations—now numbering 104 affiliates in 34 states and Puerto Rico—carried the inaugural broadcast of *All Things Considered (ATC)*. Various precedents are said to have influenced its format—among them, Al Hulsen's former show *Kaleidoscope* on the Eastern Educational Network, a program called *This Is Radio* broadcast by WBFO/Buffalo during Siemering's tenure as station manager, the CBC's early-morning offering *America as It Happens,* and the public and cultural affairs programming of the BBC, which influenced Jack Mitchell, another veteran of WHA/Madison who helped create *ATC*. Nonetheless, it was Siemering (1970) who expanded such precedents into a comprehensive vision of a new program contained in NPR's original statement of mission:

> This may contain some hard news, but the primary emphasis would be on interpretation, investigative reporting on public affairs, the world of ideas and the arts. The program will be well paced, flexible. . . . It would not, however, substitute superficial blandness for genuine diversity of regions, values, and cultural and ethnic minorities which comprise American society; it would speak with many voices and many dialects. The editorial attitude would be that of inquiry, curiosity, concern for the quality of life, critical, problem-solving, and life loving. (pp. 250-251)

Siemering believed that a flexible magazine format would permit a montage of hard news, short documentaries on issues and people tangential to the news, and cultural reportage, linked by hosts in an informal setting. Stringers from the BBC, Reuters, and *Christian Science Monitor* would contribute to international reports, but member stations would provide the lion's share of American material. Siemering envisaged less reading of the news and more talking about the news with a wide spectrum of officials and citizens. Time allotments would be based on the requirements of individual stories, not on uniform slots. Several years after the inauguration of *ATC,*

Siemering (1979) spelled out his desire to break with the practice of grounding news in statements by authorities:

> We can share first-person narratives and conversations about the process of living: of parenting, aging, loving, dying. We can help form a vision for the future with listeners sharing thoughts on the kind of society they want. This also gives a structured approach for direct people-to-people communication, eliminating some of the middle information brokers.
>
> We would no longer just report events, but would explore and make news, facilitate connections of ideas and form networks of unions of common interest. . . . It would be a context journalism, a reflective journalism. (p. 36)

Siemering believed that the voices of the citizen and the poet were as important as the voice of the Secretary of State. Structured to receive reports from every corner of the nation through local public radio stations, *ATC* was designed to address the need for a decentralization of political and cultural power exercised by mainstream mass media.

For Siemering, lack of a concrete visual dimension freed radio to be a medium of the imagination. *ATC* would capture the sound of the American experience along with the voices of its citizens. This would be achieved through innovative aural collages and essays. Siemering wished to take the listener out of the studio and into society. A senior producer of *ATC* testified to the desire "to hear a farmer out on his tractor and the sound of a twister coming across the prairie, a dog barking somewhere—things coming from the other side of the brain" (cited in Porter, 1990, pp. 26-27). Looker (1995) wrote of the staff assembled by Siemering that they

> did not come to Washington from "alternative institutions" associated with the counterculture of the period, but neither did they espouse establishment thinking when it came to the broadcast media. They were innovators—even revolutionaries—not because of their politics but because of their aesthetics. . . . They were guerrillas fighting in the media wasteland created by television against the tyranny of the visual. They were subversives who were asking Americans to close their eyes and open their ears. (pp. 115-116)

Larson's (1985) content analysis of *ATC* confirmed the importance of sound in the program's reportage. She noted, for example, the evocative use of the sounds of canoe paddles and birds chirping in a story about a cleanup of the Mississippi River, of a menacing crowd in a story about busing in Norfolk, and of cries of distress in a story of unemployment on the iron range in

Minnesota (pp. 94-95). Siemering envisaged radio as an electronic tool for capturing the diverse voices and experiences of Americans. This vision echoed Walt Whitman's hopes a century earlier that the telegraph would capture "the filaments of the news of the wars, deaths, losses, gains, passions of my race" (cited in Czitrom, 1982, p. 188). In the 20th century, Marshall McLuhan wrote of radio's subliminal depths, "its power to turn the psyche and society into a single echo chamber" (cited in Josephson, 1979, p. 13).

Siemering intended *ATC* to air in the morning, but the realization that many public radio stations still did not broadcast before noon led to a 5 p.m. airtime. Debate over a 1- or 2-hour program led to a 90-minute compromise, still an unheard-of length for a national newscast. Siemering initially assumed the position of director of *ATC* in addition to his overall responsibility for programming at NPR. Stamberg (1982) recalled the original sessions conducted by Siemering analyzing tapes sitting on the floor in makeshift offices: "He taught us to listen, so we could speak" (p. ix). Jack Mitchell, *ATC*'s first producer, helped craft the program's format. The heterogeneous staff ranged from reporters from *The New York Times* and CBS radio to veterans of WBFO/Buffalo and other nonmainstream media and included significant representation of women. The early days of *ATC* were characterized by a great degree of personal creative freedom with the framework of a collective enterprise. The newly assembled *ATC* personnel lacked the clear job descriptions of other NPR departments. Siemering planned to use an unknown anchor or group of hosts to signal *ATC*'s intention of representing a new departure in broadcast journalism.

Tension developed over what NPR's top officials considered Siemering's eagerness to put *ATC* on the air and lack of clarity about the program's structure. Ira Flatow, who moved with Siemering from WBFO to NPR, recalled that Siemering "encouraged you to develop ideas and work out problems yourself, which allowed you to make mistakes but also to find your voice and to grow" (personal communication, January 30, 1995). NPR President Quayle, responding to questions from the CPB, the NPR board, and member stations, pressed Siemering for details about the show's format. An unhappy exchange of memoranda revealed that Quayle and his lieutenants found Siemering's written responses to be vague and frustrating. Siemering did not provide *ATC* with a fixed formula but with a conceptual framework within which a creative staff would function and the program could develop and evolve. According to a study of NPR's early history, Siemering was "confused by Quayle's apparent lack of faith in his ability to operate intuitively rather than from a schematic diagram" (Kirkish, 1980, p. 70). Perhaps the problem was rooted in the inevitable frustration of a creative person operating in an increasingly complex bureaucratic environment.

The maiden broadcast of *ATC* on May 3, 1971 reflected the social conflicts of the period. The lead piece consisted of a report nearly a half-hour in length on the May Day weekend demonstrations in Washington, D.C., led by Vietnam Veterans Against the War. A team of NPR reporters and stringers vividly captured the sounds of physical confrontation, tear-gas canisters, stalled traffic, and surveillance helicopters. Interviews offered a multiplicity of perspectives on the weekend's events. A related segment on the theme of war featured antiwar poetry and ballads of World War I produced by the CBC. An anchor in the studio reported on national and international news in mid-program. Other features included a profile of a troubled black nurse, a droll piece on barbers in Ames, Iowa coping with the popularity of long hair, and a conversation between beat poet Allan Ginsberg and his father on narrowing the generation gap, which ended the show on an upbeat note.

The broadcast contained the inevitable glitches of a new program, but nonetheless established the foundation of a national broadcast news program that would win a Peabody award within its first 18 months of operation. *ATC*'s pioneering use of women included the appointment of Susan Stamberg as the first female anchor of a national news broadcast. As the unique montage of hard news and investigative reporting, public affairs and arts features, in-depth interviews, and sound collages became polished, *ATC* acquired a considerable national audience and reputation. Doyle's (1990) study of *ATC*'s early history emphasized how the program virtually "redirected the programming of non-commercial radio in the 1970s" (p. iv). The program provided an alternative to both the "rip and read" practices of commercial radio news and the "classical music jukebox" and "classroom of the air" character of educational broadcasting. *ATC* also offered a more polished and varied, less strident, and more ideologically committed approach to news and public affairs than Pacifica Radio provided. Moreover, as Siemering had suggested in "National Public Radio Purposes," the daily news magazine gave the new public radio network its programmatic and institutional identity.

Years later, Siemering (1991a) objected to a characterization of *ATC* in the early period as an "alternative" news program:

> The full-time staff came to NPR with experience at UPI, CBS, NBC, and *The New York Times,* and a few from public radio stations. We wanted to demonstrate that radio is a powerful, personal, imaginative medium and to take a broader, more inclusive editorial approach with a harder, more questioning attitude than the commercial network news of the hour.
>
> We did not regard NPR as "an experimental alternative to commercial broadcasting." We ceded nothing to commercial broadcasting. That's why *All Things Considered* starts at 5:00 p.m. Although we had little money, we were willing to take risks to find new ways to tell stories, often using location sound to make them more engaging. We wanted to set new standards for broadcast journalism. (p. 60)

Siemering resisted defining the original conception of *ATC* as "alternative," a term which since the 1960s signified underground and oppositional media such as Pacifica Radio. Although *ATC*'s maiden broadcast gave sympathetic coverage to an antiwar demonstration, the program was not designed to duplicate Pacifica's approach to news and public affairs. In NPR's mission statement, Siemering had envisaged the news magazine as a means of fostering understanding of how the legislative process could be used to effect change and generally of how citizens could become more enlightened participants in a democratic society. He envisaged minorities affirming both their separate identity and their participation in a pluralistic society through access to the airwaves rather than through confrontation. Siemering's (1970) desire to capture the "joy in the human experience" (p. 252) also set him apart from the more adversarial posture of the new left and of Pacifica Radio. *ATC* host Linda Wertheimer reiterated the desire to avoid an overall tone of anger or despair in reporting the day's news: "It's sane, not hyped. We don't talk down, we don't get freaked. Call it an island of calm discourse" (cited in Fox, 1991, p. 35). CBS network reporter Charles Kuralt, who first heard *ATC* in a country store in rural Virginia in 1971, emphasized the program's uplifting quality:

> Its words are well chosen and the voices that speak them are calm. The program has an air of reason and good humor about it, and hopefulness. . . . I bet that man and his daughter in the store where I bought the cheese and apples listen to *All Things Considered* not only because it informs them but also because it makes them feel better. It makes me feel better, too.
>
> It makes me feel better about the world by confirming, from time to time, that there is cause for cautious optimism or even for celebration. (cited in Stamberg, 1982, pp. xi-xii)

Siemering had no desire to duplicate the approach to news of either Pacifica or commercial radio but aspired instead to offer a new model for broadcast journalism.

Siemering relinquished direct supervision of *ATC* to concentrate on developing NPR's other public affairs and cultural programming. This ranged from seeking programs from member stations, airing special live events, and developing a documentary unit. During the first phase of NPR's development from 1970 to 1977, under the presidencies of Donald Quayle and Lee Frischknecht public radio established its institutional foundation. *ATC* became more structured and polished as it moved from a cramped space to a more spacious and modern facility. Liberal and conservative pundits were added to offer commentary and political balance. NPR's news and public affairs department received accolades for its live coverage of the final six months of the Senate and House Watergate proceedings that led to the resignation of Richard Nixon. A group of talented producers created a series of outstanding documentaries. The follow-up Carnegie Commission on the Future of Public Broadcasting (1979), established in 1977 at the end of the Quayle-Frischknecht era, paid tribute to NPR's programming initiatives:

> In small towns and major cities, public radio has become the vehicle for the communication and preservation of uniquely American art forms: jazz, blues, and bluegrass. Even more than public television, public radio has created for itself a strong journalistic voice in its daily news magazine, *All Things Considered*. Public radio has revived radio drama, told stories to children, and has become the broadcast medium of record in its coverage of important congressional proceedings and other national events. (p. 54)

Nonetheless, despite the promising debut of NPR's programming, NPR President Donald Quayle fired William Siemering at the close of 1972, ending his 25-month tenure as program director. The dismissal of Siemering—author of NPR's statement of mission, charter member of CPB's Radio Advisory Committee, and originator of *ATC*—reportedly "shook the network." It was said that the chemistry between Quayle and Siemering was poor, that Siemering was not a "good administrator" (Kirkish, 1980, p. 35). Perhaps NPR's leadership felt that Siemering, the visionary instrumental in defining NPR's mission in its embryonic form, did not have the political and bureaucratic qualities suited for the next stage of NPR's institutional development. According to Siemering, his management style made Quayle uncomfortable: "I was more consensus building, I was more collegial. Everyone knew I was the boss, but I also believed in empowering the staff as much as possible" (personal communication, July 25, 1995). Siemering, surprised and devastated by the firing, considered quitting public radio altogether before accepting a position in 1973 at KCCM-FM in Moorhead, Minnesota.

According to Haney's (1981) study of NPR's growth, at the time of Siemering's dismissal four major issues were unresolved: NPR's capacity to fulfill its mandate to create a national public radio system, the problem of NPR's relations with member stations, the lack of long-term funding, and the question of NPR's independence from political pressure. Moreover, NPR would have to address these formidable problems at a time when public broadcasting came under direct attack from the Nixon administration. In 1972, the same year in which Siemering was dismissed as program director, President Nixon vetoed a two-year authorization bill for the CPB, the source of funds for public radio and television. As a result of the veto, the president of CPB and his top aides resigned, and the Nixon administration appointees gained control of the CPB board.

In 1976, a reorganization at NPR precipitated concern about its journalistic independence. Departments of public information, station relations, and development comprised a new division: corporate relations. The news division, formerly an independent entity, merged with NPR's cultural affairs department and special audience unit. According to a report published in the *Washington Post,* many staff members interpreted the plan as an attempt by NPR "to move away from potentially 'controversial' public affairs programming and . . . to discourage a union organizing effort currently underway at the news bureau" (cited in Haney, 1981, p. 130). At the same time, outside NPR headquarters in Washington, D.C., member stations expressed dissatisfaction over program policies. *ATC* aired few feeds from local stations, whose attempts to contribute or propose other programs for the NPR schedule were also often ignored. Critics like Bill Kling of Minnesota Public Radio felt that too much of CPB money available for programming went to NPR instead of to the stations.

Despite internal problems, NPR's consolidation of authority proceeded apace in 1977 with the merger of NPR and the APRS, which had been established in 1973 to replace the educational radio division of the NAEB as the lobbying arm of public radio. The APRS was created to separate lobbying and programming functions, to avoid conflicts of interest between representing the interests of public radio before government bodies and covering those same bodies on the news. However, NPR and the APRS had engaged in bureaucratic rivalry, which hampered public radio's efforts to compete with the single public TV entity, PBS, for CPB funds. Negotiations to merge NPR and the APRS brought to the surface a host of differences. APRS representatives voiced the grievance of public radio managers that NPR was generally unresponsive to member stations. There was disagreement over whether NPR should compete with commercial radio as a fourth network or provide a more decentralized alternative system. On a host of issues the board was at odds with management, which in turn was at odds with the staff. "At times," Avery and Pepper (1979a) note, "the whole organization seemed out of control" (p. 24). Some felt that the demise of the APRS represented an opportunity to restructure public radio with less centralization and more public participation and called for the creation of a wholly new organization with a different name to replace NPR.

The merger, accomplished in 1977, collapsed the responsibilities of the two public radio organizations for programming, representation, distribution, station relations, promotion, and research into a single national membership organization for radio. The principal purpose of the merger was to create a more powerful organization that would represent public radio with a single voice. After weighing a change in name, National Public Radio was retained to maintain continuity for public radio's listeners. As a concession to local stations, negotiators committed themselves to strengthening the role of local stations in policymaking and programming. Membership dues henceforth paid for NPR's representational duties and for the salaries of the president and head of station relations, restricting federal funds to programming-related activities. On a new 25-member board, 12 public representatives had parity with 12 station manager delegates. The other board member would be NPR's chief executive officer, who would serve as president of NPR and vice president of its board (Avery & Pepper, 1979a, p. 26). Attempts to address the concerns of local stations notwithstanding, the network model for public radio remained largely intact, indeed strengthened, after the 1977 reorganization.

NPR was reconstituted in a new political climate, that of the Carter administration. NPR's new board chairman, Edward Elson, had been a former business partner of Bert Lance and Senator Herman Talmadge of Georgia, and it was hoped that his ties with the Carter administration would benefit public radio. As part of the merger agreement, the former heads of the APRS and NPR became senior vice presidents under a new NPR president. Elson recommended the longtime Democratic Party political operative Frank Mankiewicz, who became NPR's new CEO. The selection of Mankiewicz, a former journalist and press secretary in the presidential campaigns of Robert Kennedy and George McGovern, disappointed the old guard of noncommercial broadcasting officials, who had been passed over for the post. It was rumored that Mankiewicz's name had appeared on a list of potential appointees for the new Carter administration, and that he had not heard of NPR when he was first approached by Elson. Mankiewicz and Elson seemed well positioned politically to preside over the next stage of growth of the nominally nonpolitical NPR.

The Mankiewicz regime began on a high note. The new NPR president negotiated a settlement with the staff union, agreeing to pay raises of more than 70% over a two-year period. The appointment of a new NPR president with a journalistic background was well received in the news division. Mankiewicz took a major step forward in expanding NPR's news coverage in 1979 by launching *Morning Edition,* a weekday morning counterpart to *All Things Considered.* In 1980, NPR completed a nationwide satellite system in which all CPB-qualified stations could receive four program signals from the WESTAR I transponder. To decentralize transmission capabilities, 15 stations across the nation gained the ability to uplink programs to the satellite for national distribution. NPR established the Satellite Program Development Fund to fund creative use of the new satellite system. Larry Josephson, who in 1977 began organizing a series of Arlie Conferences on the Art of Radio that brought together many of the most talented public radio practitioners in the United States and abroad, characterized the period as one of radio renaissance. Besides his starting up *Morning Edition* and the satellite system, it was Mankiewicz's "enthusiastic stumping for public radio in Washington and around the country that helped . . . make it a major player in the news business" (Porter, 1990, p. 31).

However, the high hopes of the Mankiewicz regime were aborted by a financial crisis linked to the election of Ronald Reagan in 1980. A year earlier, the second Carnegie Commission on the Future of Public Broadcasting had warned that public radio was the poor stepchild of the public broadcasting system. The 1980 election meant that suddenly the Mankiewicz-Elson regime, so well connected during the Carter administration, found itself in an inhospitable political environment in which deregulation and privatization were the buzzwords of federal communications policy. Many conservatives viewed public broadcasting as a classic liberal program. On the Reagan administration's recommendation, Congress cut back federal funds for public broadcasting by 20% for the next funding period beginning in 1983.

In response to these cuts and emphasis on the private sector, NPR launched an ambitious—and, in retrospect, quixotic—program to insure its economic independence. The NPR board endorsed a plan of action to eliminate NPR's dependency on federal funds from the CPB within five years. The Public Broadcasting Amendments Act of 1981, which called for reductions in federal support, had also established the Temporary Commission on Alternative Financing. The NPR plan drew on the trend toward increased corporate underwriting in public broadcasting and included creating a profit-making subsidiary, marketing NPR's program services, and participating in technology-related ventures. But in 1983, before the plan could be implemented, a major deficit emerged that threatened to bankrupt NPR. Mankiewicz resigned amid congressional inquiries. NPR's interim head, Ronald Bornstein, a former CPB vice president, fired 84 staff members and negotiated a $7 million loan from the CPB, guaranteed by member stations and by NPR's satellite interconnection system.

In 1983, Mankiewicz's successor Douglas Bennet assumed the presidency of NPR, a position he would hold for a decade. Bennet, like Mankiewicz, had links to the Democratic Party, serving as assistant secretary of state for congressional relations and head of the U.S. Agency for International Development during the Carter administration prior to his appointment as NPR president. Yet Bennet was more of a centrist and a bureaucrat than his liberal and crusading predecessor. Instituting stricter management practices and retiring NPR's loan from the CPB on schedule, he restored NPR's financial stability and directed its further growth. In 1985, Bennet and the NPR board instituted a far-reaching business plan that decentralized the basic funding mechanism for public radio. Instead of providing support directly to NPR, the CPB would send all radio funds directly to the stations, which would then pay NPR through a formula based on each station's revenue. In effect, member stations were buying NPR's services. This was proposed despite fears that stations could choose to go elsewhere with the money, could quit NPR and obtain programming from other sources such as Pacifica Radio or American Public Radio, which had been established in 1981. Bennet argued that the business plan refashioned NPR as a member-driven organization by tying the network's fortunes to local station support of its programming services. Some speculated that Bennet's scheme to end direct funding aimed to insulate NPR from political pressure from Capitol Hill. NPR's membership adopted the plan with one addition: the separate CPB Radio Fund that would support innovative national programming, especially by minorities and independent producers.

In 1986, after NPR had made the final payment on the CPB loan, Bennet was quoted as saying, "Now the sky's the limit. If we handle ourselves right, we're going to wind up as the leading radio network in the country" (cited in Barnes, 1986, p. 17). Bennet gave priority to NPR's news division. *Weekend Edition,* an addition to *Morning Edition* and *ATC* that extended NPR's news report to a full 7 days, represented the first new program since the fiscal crisis. Another important public affairs program launched later in Bennet's tenure was *Talk of the Nation,* a popular, nationwide, 2-hour afternoon talk show with call-ins on current affairs. The program grew out of the success of a series of call-in specials during the American invasion of Panama and the war in the Persian Gulf. Its success reflected the need for a more interactive and spontaneous public affairs programming to supplement the trio of highly produced NPR news magazines. The format of *Talk of the Nation* gave its hosts and listeners greater freedom to express opinions on topical issues. The advent of the show led to a more news-intensive format for some NPR stations. One notable episode dealt with the aftermath of the Los Angeles riots; another featured hunted author Salman Rushdie responding to calls from an undisclosed warehouse near Dulles airport.

Despite Bennet's apparent success in strengthening NPR's finances and news division, his efforts drew criticism from the NPR board and the news staff. In 1989, NPR boardmember Richard Salant, a former president of CBS news and NBC vice chairman, publicly expressed concern over the way that underwriting affected news decisions. Nearly one third of NPR's news budget at the time came from approximately 30 companies and foundations for specific kinds of programming—for example, the John D. and Catherine T. MacArthur Foundation funding coverage of national security issues, the Lilly Endowment coverage of issues connected with youths, and the United States-Japan Foundation coverage of Japanese affairs and American-Japanese relations. Salant expressed concern that the financially hard-pressed NPR would opt to cover subjects on the basis of availability of funding, compromising independent news judgments. *Morning Edition* host Bob Edwards echoed Salant's concern that NPR was offering news for sale. Bennet denied that underwriting was skewing NPR news, noting that NPR editors frequently initiated funding applications based on what they wished to cover. Unconvinced, Salant resigned from the NPR board in protest: "You can't say 'I'm going to be unethical just because it costs me too much to be ethical' " (cited in Porter, 1990, p. 32).

Bennet also drew criticism from NPR's news staff. One factor was his selection of Adam Clayton Powell III in 1987 as news director. A headhunter firm's search resulted in the hire of Powell, who had a background in commercial radio. Powell had numerous confrontations with the staff, which questioned his news judgment and personnel decisions. For example, Powell overruled a decision to send only two reporters and an editor to cover the Reagan-Gorbachev summit in Moscow in 1988. Instead, 10 newspeople were sent at considerable expense to a largely ceremonial event that produced little hard news (Porter, 1990). A supervisor hired by Powell was said to spend her time watching soap operas in her office. Bennet's own relations with the news staff were tense and reached a boiling point just before the Salant affair became public. In December 1989, a meeting between Bennet and news personnel to address problems of finances and poor morale degenerated into a shouting match, which included a nasty exchange between legal affairs correspondent Nina Totenberg and the NPR president. The meeting apparently helped clear the air. Powell resigned shortly thereafter, and Bennet's choice of Powell's successor, Bill Buzenberg, an NPR staff member for 12 years, was popular with the staff (Porter, 1990). Nonetheless, concern about the direction of news during the Bennet regime persisted among some of NPR's old hands. According to independent producer Steve Rathe,

> As NPR attained real recognition, some key staff people seemed defensive—
> more concerned with holding on to insider status than pursuing the kind of
> aggressive journalism and catalytic cultural role that some of us who were at
> NPR in its early years had envisioned. (cited in Wilner, 1993b, p. 16)

In general, many in public radio viewed Bennet's achievement with ambivalence. He was clearly an excellent manager and skilled Washington bureaucrat who put NPR's finances and government relations in order following the 1983 fiscal crisis. He expanded NPR's news programming. Yet Bennet lacked a creative vision and thus moved the culture of NPR in a more traditional direction. Some senior staff members missed the more informal, freewheeling aspects of the old NPR, and contrasted Bennet's Ivy League and State Department style with the leadership of the more gregarious and informal Frank Mankiewicz. The change was reflected in a less skeptic and iconoclastic tone in NPR's programs. Steve Rathe characterized Bennet as "a pragmatic Washington insider," adding that "I don't think he saw NPR from outside the Beltway. On his watch, NPR's audience, its congressional relations and representation functions improved a lot, but its D.C. insularity became more ingrained." In responding to such criticism, Bennet argued that under his watch what used to be a "self-indulgent, isolated" entity became a professional mainstream organization (cited in Wilner, 1993b, p. 16).

CHAPTER  7

Public Radio

*From Supplemental
to Primary Service*

During the period from the mid-1980s into the 1990s, NPR became a more visible and influential part of the national press corps. Its president, Douglas Bennet, a Washington apparatchik, emphasized that NPR, despite its inauspicious origins, entered "the big leagues, the very big leagues," which entailed "a whole new accountability" in its news programming (cited in Porter, 1990, p. 27). NPR's growth transformed its relationship with the political forces in the nation's capital and led to changes in its approach to news reporting. Both the political right and the political left subjected *ATC* and *Morning Edition* to rigorous criticism. In addition, financial pressures led NPR to seek underwriting for its programming, requiring audience research and marketing practices employed by commercial broadcasters. Competition for limited resources also unleashed centrifugal forces within the public radio system. The emergence of a second public radio network, American Public Radio, compounded NPR's difficulties. During Douglas

Bennet's tenure, NPR was forced to engage in soul searching about its mission and future.

Morning Edition, whose listenership exceeded *ATC*'s by the end of the 1980s, represented a shift in news values at NPR. The morning report was faster paced and more tightly structured, with segments allotted to local stations for local news and traffic and weather reports. The program, tied to the clock like a commercial broadcast, imposed shorter time limits on individual reports. Looker (1995) wrote that "the great success of *Morning Edition* had ripple effects throughout National Public Radio. NPR began to devote a larger share of its resources to hard news and provided less support for creative radio production" (p. 126). Combined listenership for *ATC* and *Morning Edition* grew dramatically, with the programs reaching a combined audience of approximately 7 million at the time of its 20th anniversary in 1990. That milestone prompted an article in the *Columbia Journalism Review* that posed the question, "Has Success Spoiled NPR?" The article, written by journalism professor Bruce Porter (1990), suggested that *ATC* had moved away from William Siemering's vision as NPR became part of the Washington establishment. Despite its commitment to inclusiveness, nonpartisanship, rationality, and optimism, *ATC* received criticism both within and outside the public broadcasting system. At the outset, member stations had taken to heart Siemering's original intention that a significant portion of *ATC*'s reports would originate at local stations. During the first six months, nearly half of affiliate submissions were rejected. NPR was disappointed in the technical quality and content of much of the submitted material; conversely, local producers whose work was rejected complained about what they felt was insensitivity and arrogance on the part of NPR staff. *ATC* met its quota of one third of material from outside sources only with a significant number of stories from the BBC.

The former station manager of a public radio station in Knoxsville, Tennessee complained that "as the NPR staff grew in size and expertise, fewer and fewer station submissions were used. NPR began sending field reporters into the back doors of local stations to cover breaking news stories" (cited in Doyle, 1990, p. 93). NPR subsequently opened news bureaus in major cities and established a worldwide network of staff and freelance reporters. Local stations, disappointed by the realization that their contributions to *ATC* would be negligible, nonetheless profited from the growing awareness of public radio and increase in listenership resulting from *ATC*'s success. Paradoxically, *ATC* had a negative impact on the news operations of some local stations, whose limited revenues would go to NPR rather than to coverage of their own communities. Such stations heralded *ATC* as their principal news offering while providing minimal or no local news. Doyle (1990) linked the dilemma over *ATC*'s centralization to an institutional paradox NPR faced in its formative years. NPR staff members and affiliates were instructed to refer to NPR as a "system" rather than a "network," signifying a diversified program entity based on contributions from member stations. Yet, Doyle (1990) emphasized, "NPR could not have become an identity for public radio without being allowed to centralize its programming—to be a network" (p. 93).

As NPR emerged as a public radio network and *ATC* as a radio network broadcast, the program became the target of political criticisms from both the right and the left. Because the Nixon administration's attack on public broadcasting focused on television, public radio developed during the 1970s largely outside the political limelight. However, the election of Ronald Reagan in 1980 marked the triumph of a media-savvy new right and heightened scrutiny of public radio programming. By mid-decade, the Heritage Foundation, which had close links with the Reagan administration, issued a critical report by Mark Huber titled "The Static at Public Radio." The report accused NPR's news coverage of a liberal bias and an inherent conflict of interest in covering Congress, the source of its funding: "There is little chance that NPR will run a negative story on Rep. John Dingell (D-MI), chairman of the House Energy and Commerce Committee anytime soon, because Dingell's committee controls NPR funding" (cited in Werden, 1985, p. 3). In the same period, *AIM Report,* a publication of the arch conservative media watchdog organization Accuracy in Media (AIM), devoted an entire issue to criticizing *ATC* and called for a letter-writing campaign to defund NPR's news programs.

The Heritage and AIM reports prompted editorial responses in major newspapers. For example, the *Atlanta Journal Constitution* defended NPR, but papers in Denver, Durham, and Detroit issued attacks, with a *Detroit News* editorial titled "National Public Rathole." NPR news director Robert Siegel appeared on call-in shows on WHA-FM/Madison and WBEZ-FM/Chicago to respond to the national campaign of criticism from the right. Accusations of bias had repercussions on the local level: For example, management of KUSC-FM, Los Angeles, decided to stop carrying NPR news because it considered the program too liberal for its audience. In 1986, the *New Republic* reinforced and extended the criticisms made by the radical right in an article by Fred Barnes (1986) titled "All Things Distorted." NPR was accused of using its news magazine format to advance a liberal agenda in both foreign and domestic affairs. Barnes, for example, accused *ATC* of providing more sympathetic coverage of the Sandinistas than the Contras in Nicaragua and more sympathetic coverage of radical feminism and homosexual rights than of the conservative resurgence in the United States. Barnes indicated he could live more comfortably with the bias of Pacifica Radio than with NPR, which then received about half of its funds from the federal government: "Who complains about the small, left-wing Pacifica radio network? It relies on listener-contributions and is unabashed about its political tilt" (p. 17).

Criticism of NPR from conservatives reached a fever pitch during the Reagan administration and persisted thereafter. The political right continued the campaign of the Heritage Foundation and Accuracy in Media during the 1990s in the pages of *COMINT,* a conservative journal of media criticism devoted exclusively to public broadcasting and edited by David Horowitz and Peter Collier. *COMINT* worked closely with conservative members of the CPB board like Victor Gold and with public broadcasting's most powerful conservative critic, Republican Senate leader Robert Dole of Kansas. It was Dole's concern with "left-wing ideology" in public broadcasting that led to an amendment to the CPB's three-year $1.2 billion authorization bill in 1992 requiring that the CPB ensure "strict adherence to objectivity and balance" on public radio and television. During the presidency of Douglas Bennet, NPR sought to cultivate and reassure conservative congressional critics like Dole, who was invited to make the keynote address at the opening session of the annual Public Radio Conference in Washington, D.C., in 1993.

If NPR felt the heat of conservative attack, its news programs were criticized from the left as well. In 1985, the same year in which the Heritage Foundation and Accuracy in Media issued their critical reports, *In These Times* published media critic Pat Aufderheide's article, "NPR: Drifting Rightward or Simply Adrift?," which weighed the impact of conservative pressure. In 1987, an essay by Laurence Zuckerman in *Mother Jones* magazine suggested that NPR's news programming had become less free-wheeling and innovative and more safe and attuned to political pressures. For example, when State Department officials complained about an *ATC* story that was critical of the Nicaraguan Contras, NPR news director Robert Siegel agreed and invited them to lunch to discuss the piece with the news staff. During the U.S. invasion of Grenada, Siegel barred from the air the reports of Paul McIsaac, an NPR freelancer who was one of the few journalists to evade the U.S. blockade of press coverage of the military action. Siegel, charged with bringing more balance to NPR, had assumed the mantle of news director in 1983 asking, "Are we describing the country that elected Ronald Reagan?" (cited in Fox, 1991, p. 35).

The issues raised in *Mother Jones* and *In These Times* were examined in a more detailed study by Charlotte Ryan, whose findings were published in 1993 in *Extra!,* a publication of the left-of-center media watchdog organization, Fairness and Accuracy in Reporting (FAIR). Ryan, a professor of sociology at Simmons College and codirector of the Boston College Media Research and Action Project, directed the content analysis of all weekday broadcasts of *ATC* and *Morning Edition* from September to December of 1991. The FAIR report concluded that, despite some notable exceptions, NPR failed to provide the in-depth reports and analysis and the wide range of perspectives originally envisaged by William Siemering (1970) in "National Public Radio's Purposes." Ryan's (1993) study concluded that, although the length of *ATC* and *Morning Edition* permitted more detailed reports, conceptually NPR's approach to the news by the 1990s increasingly mirrored that of commercial broadcasting:

> NPR stories focus on the same Washington-centered events and public figures as the commercial news, with the White House and Congress setting much of the political agenda. NPR's sources often paralleled those of Nightline and other network public affairs shows, with a similar tilt toward government sources and politically centrist or conservative think tanks and publications. While NPR's special series and cultural reporting reflected considerable diversity, its day-to-day coverage of politics, economics and social issues, as well as its regular commentaries, did not come close to reflecting the ethnic, gender or class composition of the American public. (p. 18)

The FAIR report noted that in contrast to commercial and public television, *ATC* and *Morning Edition* did frequently include reactions of a broad spectrum of the public. This was the case, for example, during the confirmation hearings of Supreme Court Justice Clarence Thomas. NPR reporters interviewed representatives of demographic groups such as workers, youths, and the elderly. Some excellent segments highlighted concerns of minorities during the period under review. Yet Ryan contended that a preponderance of government officials and other authorities drowned out other voices. During the period under study, over 25% of NPR's quoted sources were government officials, more than any other category. At the lower end of the source spectrum, ordinary citizens constituted 10% and public interest and citizen groups a mere 7%. NPR made negligible attempts to air the views of leaders of racial and ethnic communities, organized labor, and the women's movement. Instead, Ryan found, NPR relied heavily on the practice of evenly balancing the views of the Democratic and Republican leadership.

Domestic news focused on developments in the nation's capital; international coverage centered on Europe. At times, NPR did break with commercial news conventions in coverage of the third world—for example, the coup in Haiti that deposed President Aristide—but in general, reports on the non-Western world came in response to American foreign policy initiatives. As for news analysis, the study found that nearly 75% of long interviews came from representatives of establishment think tanks such as the centrist Brookings Institution and Carnegie Endowment, the hawkish Center for Strategic and International Studies, and the conservative American Enterprise Institute. However, NPR did not solicit the views of associates of the Institute for Policy Analysis, the leading think tank of the left.

According to Ryan (1993), NPR rarely gave substantial attention to dissident points of view contrary to government policy, even when shared by a critical mass of the public. Ryan speculated about factors that have redirected NPR news along more conventional grounds: the chilling effect of conservative attacks, self-censorship caused by concern about congressional appropriations, and the desire to be perceived as professional by mainstream journalists. She suggested that NPR needed to address fundamental questions about its approach to news:

> Should news report primarily what groups in power do or say? Or should it, in the tradition of investigative journalism, cast a critical eye on groups in power? In the interest of democracy, should it report what groups not in power do or say? (p. 26)

In response to the FAIR critique, Bill Buzenberg, NPR vice president for news and information, made a spirited defense of the news division's record of hiring minority and women reporters and commentators in a letter to Jeff Cohen, director of FAIR, that was also distributed throughout the public radio network (see Buzenberg, 1993; Cohen, 1993). Buzenberg also addressed the accusation about NPR's mainstream orientation, saying that

NPR was proud to be in the tradition of high-quality American journalism: "It appears that FAIR has some other mission in mind for us, presumably as an outlet for viewpoints from the left, but that is not NPR's purpose. Our intent is to air a broad spectrum of views from many different political perspectives" (cited in Wilner, 1993c, p. 3). Buzenberg, reflecting NPR's growing preoccupation with audience size and demographics, ended by citing Arbitron data documenting that between spring 1991 and fall 1992 combined listenership of *ATC* and *Morning Edition* had increased 35% and that every week over 7 million listeners tuned into *Morning Edition* and over 6.5 million tuned into *ATC*.

Although William Siemering did not conceive of *ATC* as a left-wing or alternative news program, many public radio veterans agreed with Ryan that NPR's news program had become more cautious and less apt to challenge the conventions of mainstream journalism. *ATC*'s early iconoclasm was a function of the golden opportunity to become a laboratory for Siemering's inspired concept, the youthfulness of the staff, and the journalistic culture inspired by the Watergate story. Science Editor Anne Gudenkauf, who joined NPR in the late 1970s, observed in 1990 that "we stay too close to the news and are less adventurous these days" (cited in Porter, 1990, p. 27). This was reflected in the paucity of sound montages, of the "movies of the air" once created by radio artists like Joe Frank, Josh Darsa, and Robert Montiegel. The trade-off has been a greater adeptness at interacting with and covering the Washington establishment. The well-connectedness of its reporters is typified by the insider ties of NPR's famous trio of outstanding female correspondents. NPR's outstanding legal affairs correspondent Nina Totenberg is married to Floyd Haskell, the former senator from Colorado. The spouse of Linda Wertheimer, NPR's chief political reporter before becoming *ATC* host, is president of Common Cause. Congressional correspondent Cokie Roberts, daughter of the late U.S. representative from Louisiana, Hale Boggs, is married to Steven Roberts, the political and foreign policy editor of *U.S. News & World Report*.

Perhaps the decisive factor distinguishing *ATC*'s development from its origins over two decades earlier was its evolution into a primary news source. Once thought of as a supplement to mainstream news sources, correspondents throughout the nation and world were now heard over a system that expanded to over 400 affiliates. On the 20th anniversary of NPR it was estimated that NPR's weekday morning and evening newscasts together with *Weekend Edition* and *Weekend ATC* constituted more than five hours of news programming a day, with seven additional hours of updates and repeats (Fox, 1991). As of 1993, 7 million people woke up to *Morning Edition* and nearly the same number listened to *ATC* in the evening. NPR filled the vacuum created by the deregulation of commercial broadcasting in the early 1980s, specifically by the FCC's decision to drop the requirement that stations carry news and public affairs. Arbitron figures revealed that NPR was becoming the primary radio news source in major markets. Preeminent in radio news, NPR also challenged its competitors in print. Its news programs had more listeners than the *New York Times* had readers. The trend toward briefer stories in print journalism, typified by *USA Today,* increased NPR's importance as a principal source of news for well-informed citizens.

This status as a primary news source inevitably had a chilling effect on risk taking and placed NPR under more intense scrutiny. Thus, when the Iran-Contra hearings ended on an inconclusive note, there was reluctance within NPR to pursue the story aggressively for fear of appearing too anti-administration. One media watchdog organization criticized NPR's coverage of the Gulf War as excessively pro-Arab; another charged excessive identification with the American war effort. It is not surprising that a news program rooted in liberal humanism, which attained establishment status as a centrist organization, continued to be the object of criticism from both the right and the left. The debate over NPR's objectivity notwithstanding, no one could dispute that NPR's role as a primary news source reached its pinnacle during the Gulf War, prompting NPR management to issue T-shirts proclaiming "air superiority"—an intentionally ironic but nonetheless curious analogy with the triumph of American military forces (Fox, 1991).

As William Siemering anticipated, the institutional growth of NPR paralleled the success of *ATC.* Federal funding resulting from the Public Broadcasting Act of 1967 enabled NPR to provide national interconnection, initially via telephone lines and later via satellite, as well as a core programming service. The number and reach of CPB-qualified stations affiliated with NPR increased significantly in the first two decades of the network's existence. NPR grew to 220 stations in 1980 and reached 253 stations by 1991. These 253 "full" NPR affiliates plus 17 small, non-CPB-qualified "associate" members and 168 "auxiliary" NPR stations repeating the signals of other public radio stations amounted to 438 interconnected stations. A study by the National Telecommunications and Information Administration estimated that by 1989 86% of the U.S. population was able to receive at least one public radio signal. Within a two-decade period, NPR became a formidable network and the primary national force in noncommercial radio. By the end of the Douglas Bennet regime in 1993, plans were under way for NPR to move to enlarged headquarters at an estimated cost of $32 million.

The essence of the federal form of public radio consisted of CPB-qualified radio stations whose identity was based on their affiliation with NPR. Josephson (1979) eloquently suggested the diversity of public radio formats and roles. In areas of Alaska, he noted, a group of public radio stations serves as a primary means of communication, broadcasting in English, Yupik, and other Eskimo languages.

> In Ramah, New Mexico, public radio speaks Navajo (KTDB); in Santa Rosa, California, Spanish (KBBF); in Warrenton, North Carolina it speaks with a rural black accent (WVSP); in Washington, D.C., in the jazz idiom of the urban black experience (WPFW), as well as the Appalachian twang of bluegrass (WAMU) and in the "high church" unction of classical music (WETA-FM). . . .
>
> In northern Minnesota, public radio is reflected off the Iron Range, amplifying the populist voice of community (KAXE). While down in Minneapolis, Garrison Keillor, an authentic voice of the prairie, regularly evokes a dry chuckle from the store of shared Midwestern values (KSJN and other stations of Minnesota Public Radio). (pp. 8-9)

By 1991, 63 independently chartered community radio stations constituted 25% of NPR's full-member stations. In the mid-1980s, NPR had taken steps to broaden its base by giving "auxiliary" status to stations whose staff and budget size had previously disqualified them from membership.

Despite such diversity, the typical NPR station was still licensed to an institution of higher learning, reflecting the historic role of the college station in the development of noncommercial radio. Only a handful of NPR stations was licensed to states or local authorities such as municipalities or boards of education, whereas by 1991, institutions of higher learning operated about two thirds of the full-member NPR stations. Pacifica Radio together with most community stations associated with the NFCB remained outside a public radio system rooted in NPR affiliation. The follow-up report of the second Carnegie Commission in 1979 expressed concern that the preeminence of stations licensed to institutions of higher learning would prevent public radio from reaching all strata of American society and becoming a vehicle for extending democracy and pluralism: "Diversity is not completely served by classical music or university licensees alone, no matter how laudable either may be" (p. 193). In 1989, Congress required the CPB to engage in a station grant review with the goal of extending greater support to minority audiences, isolated rural communities, and other underserved areas. Three years later, Gibbs Kinderman (1992), general manager of WVMR-AM, Dunmore, West Virginia, asked,

> Will the public radio system remain a "country club" of privileged stations, jealously guarding its portals against undesirables who share neither its style or its high-culture purpose? Or is it willing to share the CPB wealth with a variety of smaller, poorer stations who have a different mission and serve less affluent audiences? (p. 17)

The university base of many NPR stations was a key factor in shaping the identity and listenership of the network. Josephson (1979) noted that research in the late 1970s showed that public radio stations reached a relatively small percentage of potential listeners in large cities, that with the exception of Boston, Washington, D.C., Minneapolis, and Los Angeles, public radio remained primarily a small-town college phenomenon. More recent audience research indicated the high demographic profile of public radio's audience. The Simmons Market Research Bureau found that the 35-54 age bracket predominated, with over a third of listeners earning more than $50,000 a year (Fox, 1991). Research commissioned by NPR in 1989-1990 found that its audience had twice the concentration of college graduates compared to the U.S. population as a whole; two thirds attended college at some point; and one in six possessed a graduate degree. Well over half were employed in white-collar occupations, a third in professional managerial positions. NPR's listenership was considered "highly business influential," an important category in marketing NPR's listenership to corporate under-writers (spokesperson for NPR's Department of Audience Research, personal communication, October 18, 1991). Such statistics led former NPR correspondent and editor William J. Drummond (1993) to characterize public broadcasting as "an entitlement program for the middle class," adding, "I am hearing a steady din of upscaleboomer blues. You know: the angst of choosing the correct oat bran, the painful decision on what to do with investments in the post-CD world, the ticking of the biological clock" (p. 13).

Underwriting credits aimed at public radio's well-heeled audience sounded increasingly like commercials. This was especially true after 1984 when the FCC approved "enhanced underwriting" so that acknowledgment was no longer limited to the corporate name but could include identification of a company's products and services. The FCC sought to maintain a distinction between underwriting and advertising by banning salesmanship and price information, ignoring the fact that a major form of modern advertising involved enhancing a company's image rather than a hard sell of its products and that even some underwriting credits were obviously plugs. Corporate contributions to NPR, which were $2.7 million in 1983, increased nearly fourfold to $10.6 million by 1988 (Lee & Solomon, 1990). Both the indirect and direct forms of promotion were in evidence, for example, during the broadcast of *ATC* on September 20, 1993. Among those identified as contributors to NPR's News and Information Fund were "Valvoline Oil and Valvoline Instant Oil Change and its franchisees, environmentally conscious providers of motor oil and oil change services." Another underwriter, presumably drawn to NPR by its upscale listener demographics, was SkyTel, "providing comprehensive nationwide messaging services to business travelers." A more standard plug was made in acknowledging the contribution of the producers of *The Age of Innocence,* "a Martin Scorsese picture now playing at selected theaters." The FCC, responding to complaints from commercial broadcasters about competition from public broadcasting for advertising dollars, threatened to crack down on underwriting credits that went beyond even the expanded boundaries of enhanced underwriting.

NPR fund-raisers seeking corporate underwriting of programs capitalized upon—and reinforced—the high demographic profile of public radio's largely college-educated audience. Stavitsky (1990) emphasized how CPB audience research, originally initiated in the 1970s to document public radio listenership for Congress, increasingly resembled the quantitative and qualitative criteria of commercial broadcasters:

> The focus of CPB's research effort shifted in 1977 when Tom Church began directing the operation. He viewed research as a tool for audience building; "up your cume" became his slogan. Church . . . began to send out national rankings of stations in terms of cumulative audience. . . . As research became more accepted and expected in public radio, more sophisticated techniques were used, some borrowed from commercial broadcasting, such as "Audigraphics," focus groups and auditorium testing of proposed programs. (pp. 172-173)

Stavitsky (1995, p. 185) also noted that D. Giovannoni conducted two influential studies for the CPB in 1985 and 1988 using demographic and lifestyle segmentation to analyze who supports public radio and why. Such data became especially valuable to NPR and to public radio stations in their efforts to woo underwriters by indicating the resources and influence of the audience hearing their financial support acknowledged on the air.

The focus group, another commercial marketing tool, was employed to assist on-air fund-raising. In 1993, for example, focus groups were used with the Electronic Attitude Response System to test the best strategies for a national pledge drive—part of a public radio research partnership, with headquarters at NPR financed by a $470,000 grant from the CPB. The direction taken by audience research signaled two trends in public radio at odds with its original statement of mission: an emphasis on mass marketing and the cultivation of an elite membership base. An advertisement in 1993 in *Current,* the public broadcasting trade newspaper, reflected the extent to which public radio adopted the language of commercial broadcasting. Stations were advised to "prop up your schedule with NPR's *Talk of the Nation*" if their audience dipped between *Morning Edition* and *ATC*; with "aggressive forward and cross-promotion," the show promised to lure listeners being lost to other talk and call-in shows in "your market" (NPR, 1993, p. 2). The advertisement indicated that *Talk of the Nation,* whose name is a registered trademark, was purchasable as a service separate from the NPR news magazines in fiscal year 1994 by members and nonmembers.

North Carolina community radio activist David Kirsh (1993) described the emphasis on marketing as part of a process of "professionalization" that was eroding the differences between public and commercial radio:

> A wave of ambitious managers in nonprofit radio has sought to centralize control over broadcasts; emphasize "production values," often at the expense of program content; maximize revenues by courting corporations and using high-paid consultants; and oust long-time volunteers who disagree with the new policies. (p. 27)

Kirsh noted that in 1989 dissident NPR board member Richard Salant was appalled to hear about "product testing" for NPR: "In my shop," he said of his tenure as head of CBS news, "if you called news 'product,' you had to wash your mouth out with soap" (cited in Kirsh, 1993, p. 27). "Professionalization" often involved replacing independent local programs with blander fare available from NPR or its competitor, the APR network. For example, management's 1987 attempt to eliminate free-form programming at KUNM-FM/Albuquerque precipitated a struggle that led to the firing of 60 paid and unpaid staff members and a $6 million civil suit by volunteers. A similar crisis developed at Seattle's KCMU-FM in 1992 when the station was restructured, volunteers were fired, and innovative music programming was dropped in favor of APR's *World Cafe,* which played songs from the American and international pop charts.

For critics of programming trends, *World Cafe* became a symbol of misdirection. Josephson (1993) criticized the policies of the CPB Radio Fund, the successor to NPR's more innovative Satellite Program Development Fund:

> The CPB Radio Fund claims to support innovation and to take risks, but it does neither. It is a temple of numbers, absolutely controlled by one person who is more into systems analysis than actual content. CPB gives grants to just enough independents and minorities to cover themselves politically, but the lion's share . . . has gone to six-and seven-figure projects that do produce numbers, but not much love from listeners. . . . The $1.1 million *World Cafe* grant is a scandal, a thoroughly misbegotten attempt to buy young demographics with a service that is, in essence, a commercial radio music format. (p. 31)

Ruth Hirschman, station manager of Santa Monica, California's KCRW-FM, protested that for 1993 the CPB Radio Fund would award *World Cafe* $1.1 million but eliminate $300,000 for William Siemering's *Soundprint,* public radio's only general-interest national documentary program and one of the most respected sources of radio journalism.

As documented by Stavitsky (1990), the changing culture of public radio had ramifications within some of the most venerable noncommercial radio stations. During the 1980s, audience research conducted by D. Giovannoni and George Bailey, a former consultant to CBS radio, led to a restructuring of programming at the University of Wisconsin's WHA (Stavitsky, pp. 121-123). The evolution of WNYC in New York City was illustrative. WNYC, a municipally owned AM, FM, and TV system, began as an AM station in the 1920s with a public service orientation rooted in the Progressive movement. It had been used by Mayor Fiorello LaGuardia in the 1930s to rally the city's citizens during the Depression. Prior to 1975, WNYC had engaged in no fund-raising other than program-guide subscriptions. New York's fiscal problems led to the establishment of the WNYC Foundation, made up of prominent civic and business leaders, to develop new entrepreneurial ventures and programs for corporate and foundation support. By the end of the 1980s, the Foundation, chaired by Billie Tisch, wife of CBS Chairman Lawrence Tisch, had helped reduce the city's support of

WNYC substantially. WNYC tailored its programming and development toward the most educated, affluent residents of New York. A 1989 survey revealed that 86% of respondents had undergraduate degrees and 65% had graduate degrees. That year WNYC's 65th anniversary was celebrated at a gala dinner at Lincoln Center for New York's business, legal, and cultural elite (Stavitsky, pp. 78-80, 85). By the 1990s, New York City relinquished ownership of WNYC's public AM, FM and TV stations.

Despite achieving "air superiority" as a primary news source in a 400-plus station affiliate system with many features of a commercial network, NPR faced a growing host of internal and external challenges. Within NPR, the status of its staff posed dilemmas. A relatively small group of broadcasters had a stranglehold on what many considered the most desirable positions in radio journalism, limiting the capacity of NPR to nourish fresh talent. Yet, at the same time, the options for professional growth was limited compared to their counterparts in the primary state broadcasting systems in Britain, Canada, and Western Europe. Some of NPR's most talented staff members gravitated to commercial television. Jay Kernis, Barbara Cohen, Robert Krulwich, and Ira Flatow left for CBS in the 1980s, although Krulwich and Flatow continued to do work in public broadcasting on the side. Other top NPR reporters became cross-over successes. Scott Simon took a leave of absence to become a cohost of NBC's weekend *Today* show. Nina Totenberg doubled as a roving reporter for NBC. Cokie Roberts, NPR's chief political reporter, cut back her work for public radio and began making regular appearances on ABC's *World News Tonight, Nightline,* and *This Week with David Brinkley.* Deborah Wang, Jackie Judd, and David Ensor left NPR for full-time positions at ABC.

ABC-TV also recruited John Hockenberry, NPR's former Middle East correspondent and host of *Talk of the Nation,* who observed that the transition was less extreme than might be assumed: "You can turn on a public radio station and hear the [General Electric] theme just as easily as you can on [ABC's] *This Week with David Brinkley*" (cited in Wilner, 1992a, p. 23). If Pacifica served as a training ground for NPR, the public radio network became a farm team for the networks. In late 1992, NPR issued a memorandum discouraging moonlighting and requiring news staff also employed by the commercial networks to offer exclusive information to NPR first, to always be identified as affiliated with NPR, and to maintain impartiality. Some viewed the success of Hockenberry and other NPR veterans in landing high-profile positions in commercial broadcasting as an indication of public radio's big-league status. However, the cross-fertilization of personnel, like underwriting credits, blurred the distinction between public and commercial broadcasting in the eyes of the public.

NPR weathered criticism from noncommercial radio professionals outside the system along with malaise among staff members within. Minorities struggled for greater representation. The original master plan for NPR did not include a blueprint for supporting minority stations. Although there were over 40 black noncommercial radio stations by 1990, only 7 were CPB-qualified and eligible for the CPB community grants so critical to upgrading a station. Adam Clayton Powell III said of his appointment as vice president for news at NPR: "When I walked in here in July 1987, NPR had no—zero—minority hosts, correspondents, newscasters, directors, executive producers, or senior editors" (cited in Dates & Barlow, 1990, pp. 240-241). Minority organizations inside and outside public radio exerted pressure to make NPR's personnel and programming more diverse. In response to such pressure, the CPB Radio Fund took steps to support minority programing: For example, in 1993 a three-year $460,000 grant was earmarked for the 24-station American Indian Radio on Satellite system, and $220,000 was awarded to *Latino USA,* a weekly Hispanic news and cultural journal produced at the University of Texas in Austin. NPR's Hothouse Project was created in 1992 to foster "mission driven" programs promoting cross-cultural understanding. Nonetheless, critics complained that programs on public radio continued to reflect inordinately its traditionally white, affluent, college-educated audience.

Independent producers, who are not salaried staff members of NPR or member stations, constituted another vital, heterogeneous but struggling constituency in public radio. Freelancers make substantial contributions to NPR's news broadcasts, sometimes more than half of what the national news desk puts on the air. However, in the early 1990s, the paltry pay of $55 for each minute of airtime for a labor-intensive and technology-intensive undertaking, made the financial position of independents untenable (Mahler, 1993). David Isay, an independent radio producer based in New York, linked the plight of independents to the dearth of radio documentaries. Characterizing radio as an art form with almost limitless potential, Isay (1992) lamented the fact that "highly produced radio has been effectively edged out of the NPR equation by the monumental task of covering a world's worth of news on a limited budget" (p. 20). The CPB Radio Program Fund, conceived in large measure to support the work of minorities and independent producers, received widespread criticism as an unrepresentative and arbitrary body. Independent producers played an even lesser role in public radio than in public television. "Words like 'diversity' and 'innovation,'" independent producer Jay Allison (1992) wrote bitterly, "are the inflated paper currency of public radio" (p. 14).

Their outsider status led independent producers to band together in advocacy organizations—for example, in Audio Independents during NPR's early years and more recently in the Association of Independents in Radio (AIR), which in 1992 organized the first national conclave of radio "indies" in nearly a decade. At the meeting, William Siemering (1992b) spoke of the need to reassert the imaginative possibilities of radio and "to guard against a nay-saying orthodoxy which precludes innovation, creativity and risk taking" (p. 2). In 1993, AIR representatives met with CPB President Richard Carlson and Vice President Bob Coonrod to propose an office of producer relations within the CPB to ameliorate the history of feuding between the CPB Radio Fund and independents. The CPB may prove receptive to such entreaties so as to avoid the kind of conflict with public TV independents that led to the creation of the Independent Television Service (ITVS). In 1993, the CPB System Development Fund announced support of the AIR's next public radio producers' conference. Despite significant obstacles, some resourceful independents have been able to gain entry into the public radio system. Yet isolated success stories are no substitute for a more systematic involvement of independents in public radio. In response to critics, the CPB Radio Fund, the largest single source of funds for public radio programs, allocated nearly 50% of its funds for fiscal year 1993 to independent and minority programs, including the creation of a national Hispanic network.

Besides the pressure from minorities and independents, a related challenge to NPR's control of satellite distribution was mounted by a group of community broadcasters protesting NPR's fees for the service. In 1992, the NFCB, Pacifica Radio, Native American broadcasters, and Philadelphia's WXPN began exploring the possibility of using a separate satellite system, despite protestations from NPR that such an undertaking might bifurcate the public radio system and undermine congressional funding for NPR's administration of satellite interconnection. Although the proposal faced serious obstacles, it reflected dissatisfaction with NPR's control of interconnection for noncommercial radio.

The impetus toward democratization within public radio was provided by the Radio Expansion Task Force in 1988-1989 and a station grant review in 1991-1992. Symptomatic of the breakdown of NPR's hegemony was the testimony of the AIR, the National Association of Blacks in Public Radio, and Hispanics in Public Radio before Congress in 1991 in connection with the reauthorization of funding for the CPB. These groups joined the NFCB to issue a common statement recommending changes in allocation of community service grants, in assignments of funds for national programming and independent production, and in NPR's management of the satellite system. The growing assertiveness of interest groups within the world of public radio included the revival of regional organizations, among them the Alaska Public Radio Network, Rocky Mountain Public Radio, and Southern Public Radio.

Besides minorities, independent producers, and community broadcasters, NPR has been forced to deal with growing discontent among its own member stations. To make governance more democratic, public radio stations voted in 1992 to amend NPR's by-laws to permit the removal of board members by a two-thirds-majority vote of the membership. That was the same year in which conflict over membership dues, an annual ritual, came to a head when the NPR board voted a 9.7% increase. The dilemma facing Tom Godell, general manager of WSIU-FM in Carbondale, Illinois, was typical. A painful reduction in staff size could not offset the increased transfer of resources from the local to the national level: "If it comes down to the choice between *All Things Considered* and maintaining our existing staff, we will go with the staff" (cited in Behrens, 1992, p. 1). Fourteen stations circulated a petition recommending a systemwide vote on the increase and an amendment to NPR's bylaws requiring a majority of stations to approve future increases, measures that would have weakened the authority of the NPR board. The petition threatened to precipitate a floor fight at the 1992 Public Radio Conference. It was reluctantly withdrawn at NPR's request out of fear that the resolution would jeopardize a bond issue for NPR's new headquarters by diminishing the fiscal authority of the NPR board in the eyes of the banks. However, the board agreed in principle to change network membership fees, program access dues, and programming bundles, and elected as chair Carl Matthusen of KJZZ-FM/Phoenix, a critic of public radio's status quo. In another acknowledgment of internal problems, NPR hired Conflict Management Inc., a consulting firm based in Cambridge, Massachusetts, to address conflicts between the network and its member stations.

Pressures from member stations led to partial "unbundling" of NPR's programming. This represented a reversal of a policy of offering a package

124

of programs for a single price, which had required stations wishing to receive *Morning Edition* and *ATC* to pay for other programs irregardless of whether they were aired. The changed policy permitted stations to select segments or in some cases individual programs at a lower fee. Cultural programming became unbundled, although a popular show like *Car Talk* cost nearly as much as the entire cultural package. A related challenge to NPR's original role as the virtually exclusive supplier of national programming was represented by APR, whose origins can be traced back to the early 1980s when NPR had the capacity to send out only one program at a time. Producers at local stations, led by William H. Kling of Minnesota Public Radio, the licensee for seven stations with headquarters in St. Paul, saw a conflict of interest in NPR's task of determining whether its own in-house productions or program submissions from local stations would receive national distribution. One precipitating factor was NPR's rejection of a request to distribute nationally Garrison Keillor's *A Prairie Home Companion,* originated by Minnesota Public Radio and ultimately a great national success. The inauguration of satellite distribution by NPR meant that stations would be able to receive a selection of up to 12 national public radio programs. This led four major public radio stations—WNYC/New York, WGUC/Cincinnati, KQED/San Francisco, and KUSC/Los Angeles—to join Minnesota Public Radio in establishing a second national program service, which was incorporated as American Public Radio in 1983.

APR was structured in a way that permitted it to avoid some of NPR's financial problems. APR offered its programs individually at a time when NPR's entire program service came at a single price. APR also did not combine the functions of distribution and production like NPR, thus avoiding the costly role of program producer by acquiring finished shows and helping fund new shows made by local stations and independent producers, but eschewing any direct role in production management. Initially, APR specialized in cultural programming rather than more expensive news programming. This proved to be a bonanza after 1983 when NPR nearly went bankrupt and eliminated a great deal of cultural programming so as to funnel limited resources to *Morning Edition* and *ATC.* In 1985, the year Garrison Keillor appeared on the cover of *Time* magazine, APR became public radio's leading supplier of cultural programming—nearly 200 hours a week. 1985 marked the approval of NPR's new business plan requiring that about 80% of federal funds for public radio would be channeled by the CPB through local stations, which would therefore have discretion in buying programs from NPR or APR.

APR-NPR competition became more intense by the end of the 1980s, as APR began to distribute an array of news programming. There is disagreement over whether APR promised not to compete with NPR's news programming at the time of its establishment in 1983. APR offered both the BBC World Service, which previously had only been available to listeners on shortwave, and the news and public affairs programming of the CBC. These highly regarded foreign sources of news were further supplemented by *Monitor Radio,* produced by the *Christian Science Monitor* company, a relatively inexpensive undertaking subsidized by the newspaper's worldwide news operation. In keeping with APR's role as a distributor but not a producer of programming, it was able to offer news programming from the BBC, the CBC, and the *Christian Science Monitor* without incurring the high cost of its own news operation. APR, seeking to expand business and economics reporting, sought alliances with other institutions. For a period, CBC Radio produced *Business Update.* In 1989 came the premiere of *Marketplace,* launched with $500,000 in seed money from APR and produced by KUSC-FM at the University of Southern California. *Marketplace,* with 10 domestic bureaus at public radio stations and overseas bureaus in London and Tokyo, was heard daily over approximately 200 stations, with 2 million listeners weekly, after four years. A conflict developed over approximately 100 stations using a *Marketplace* module in a 10-minute slot of *Morning Edition* and over the possibility of other APR inserts. NPR complained about confusion over the source of the program-within-a-program and over two sets of funding credits. In 1992, a revolt of member stations aborted an attempted NPR ban on such inserts.

In his discussion of "Public Radio's Air Wars," Fox (1992) observed that APR's news offerings, originally timed to supplement *Morning Edition* and *ATC,* came into direct competition with NPR's flagship programs. In 1992, APR hired its first vice president for news. *Monitor Radio Early Edition,* carried by 90 NPR stations in 1992, went up against NPR's *Morning Edition.* Conversely, NPR decided to expand ATC to two hours and schedule it to contend with *Monitor Radio*'s time slot. Many public radio stations chose to combine the news offerings of NPR and APR. However, there were a number of defections from NPR in the early 1990s, with unsettling implications for the network. For example, KUMD in Duluth, Minnesota, left NPR, whose full news package for a station its size came to $47,000, relying instead on the combined offerings of APR, the Associated Press, and the Pacifica News Service at a lower cost (Fox, 1992). Pacifica Radio entered the fray in 1992, embarking on a plan to establish an expanded national news program to air both morning and evening. That year WXPN/Philadelphia dropped NPR's news service while considering whether to disaffiliate completely, and WBGO in Newark, New Jersey indicated its intention to drop *ATC* and NPR membership because of the burden of its dues: $144,000 out of a $1.6 million budget (Behrens, 1992). Competition between APR and NPR increasingly resembled the combat over affiliates and ratings waged by the commercial networks. There was a danger that NPR, which received nearly two thirds of its funds from member station payments, could become caught in a vicious cycle of shrinking membership and rising dues.

APR was a success story: by its 10th anniversary in 1993, it had surpassed NPR in number of affiliated stations and hours of programming distributed each week. APR offered 18,000 hours of programming in 1992, although NPR still supplied a greater percentage of public radio programming actually broadcast. To be sure, the existence of a second major program service injected a greater element of choice and competition in national programming in public radio. However, APR did not represent a solution to many of the problems posed by NPR's development and in some respects represented a narrower form of public radio than its competitor. Privately operated with an independent board of directors, APR was not structured as the at least nominally more democratic NPR, which was theoretically owned by member stations and governed by an elected board (Salyer, 1993).

In news and public affairs, APR made available to American listeners the BBC World Service and radio reports from the *Christian Science Monitor,* both established and establishment news organizations. These programs, like Garrison Keillor's *A Prairie Home Companion,* were noncontroversial and unlikely to ruffle feathers in Washington, D.C. APR lacked any counterpart to William Siemering's innovative and comprehensive vision for public radio, his desire to break new ground. APR, a very market-oriented player in public radio, did not develop an institutional identity based on a programming concept as NPR or Pacifica had. NPR took some steps to reach out to diverse audiences through its cultural programming despite the increased emphasis on demographics in public radio. The thrust of APR's programming was more unapologetically upscale. APR's emphasis on classical music contrasted with NPR's greater effort to present jazz, blues, gospel, and Latin music. APR's most important initiative in news and public affairs, *Market-*

place, targeted professional strata interested in business and economics reporting. APR showed itself less concerned than NPR about conflicts of interest in program underwriting. For example, NPR returned a restricted grant for coverage of Japan from the Japan Foundation's Center for Global Partnership when it learned that it was funded by the Japanese Foreign Ministry, whereas APR saw no conflict. APR, which earned about a sixth of its budget from underwriting in 1991, proudly noted that *Marketplace* attracted "a prestigious group of underwriters led by General Electric" (Salyer, 1993, p. 181).

APR has as much compounded as relieved the problem of centralization of programming in public radio. As APR President Stephen L. Salyer (1993) observed, the most dramatic shift in public radio programming patterns in the five-year period from 1987 to 1992 consisted of increased use of nationally produced and distributed shows by local stations. Whereas in 1987 60% of programs heard on public radio were locally produced, by 1991 the ratio was in favor of national shows, a trend that showed no sign of abating. The financial crunch experienced by many public radio stations, which utilize a remarkably inexpensive and flexible medium compared to TV, was in part self-inflicted, the result of heavy fees for NPR and APR that precluded providing greater resources for local service. Indeed, the federal system of public radio stations consists largely of CPB-qualified stations whose identity is based primarily on national programming provided by NPR and APR in contrast to community radio whose priorities are independent and local service. James C. King (1992), general manager of WYXU-FM/Cincinnati and a 16-year veteran of public broadcasting, complained in 1992 that

> our industry is turning into a pale replica of what has already taken root in commercial radio. Our reserved tiny space on the FM dial is rapidly becoming little more than two or three (forgive me) 'tent pole' NPR/APR programs buffered by classical and/or jazz programs. (p. 30)

At a time when it was buffeted by centrifugal forces—from discontent on the part of minorities, independent producers, and member stations to the challenge posed by APR—NPR embarked on a bold new venture: the internationalization of public radio. In 1993, CPB President Richard Carlson circulated a memorandum recommending that in the post-cold-war environment the U.S. government's foreign broadcasting services, including the Voice of America and Radio Free Europe/Radio Liberty, be reorganized into a unified international network administered by the CPB. Carlson stressed that a unified radio and TV network operated by the CPB "could transform disparate foreign affairs tools into an 'electronic Peace Corps' " (cited in Wilner, 1993a, p. 1). He suggested that by shifting supervision from an official government agency, the USIA, to the "nongovernmental" CPB, news and information broadcast without the taint of propaganda would have the credibility of a BBC. John Wallach, foreign editor of Hearst newspapers, speculated that if the Voice of America became NPR's foreign service "it could give the BBC a hell of a run." NPR President Douglas Bennet, a former official of the U.S. Agency for International Development, commented that NPR would be "happy to become an international broadcasting entity," adding that in the noncommercial radio field NPR "has the capacity to do it and no one else does" (cited in Wilner, 1993a, p. 12). Nonetheless, APR indicated its intention to market its programs aggressively overseas by changing its name to Public Radio International in 1994.

Richard Carlson's memorandum was a bold, if highly problematic trial balloon. In 1993, NPR took a concrete step in the direction of internationalization by offering public radio programming overseas, initially in Europe, with plans to expand broadcasts to other continents. Noting concerns on the part of independent producers and community broadcasters that NPR would dominate an international satellite system as it had domestic satellite interconnection, CPB officials acknowledged the unlikelihood that offerings by non-NPR sources such as Pacifica network news would be carried internationally. Those officials viewed NPR's plans as a means of expanding public radio's mission and of strengthening CPB's case to take over the government's overseas broadcasting operations (Wilner, 1993d, p. 16). In summer 1993, NPR began broadcasting to Europe its flagship newsmagazines *Morning Edition, ATC,* and *Weekend Edition.*

NPR also set in motion plans to broadcast abroad the topical call-in program *Talk of the Nation,* with European as well as American listeners participating by telephone. NPR also entered into negotiations to become the largest contributor to a radio channel available to the 15 million European households that receive satellite signals and to listeners as far east as Moscow and as far south as Turkey. NPR explored arrangements with European cable operators and radio stations to allow terrestrial rebroadcasts. This venture was launched with an understanding that start-up costs would not affect the new NPR dues structure so as to avoid another member station revolt. Instead, initial costs were underwritten by the Wellington Management

Company of Boston, and NPR considered developing "sponsorship credits" for U.S., European, and Japanese companies as a source of future funding. It appeared that public radio would be underwritten by private corporations internationally as well as domestically (Wilner, 1993d). NPR, already considered too centralized a network by many in noncommercial radio, stood on the brink of becoming a vastly expanded public multinational corporation.

* * *

The imperatives of the state and the market impinged on the independence of NPR, which was chartered as a nongovernmental, noncommercial entity. American public broadcasting did not attain the degree of independence enjoyed by the BBC. NPR's reliance on appropriations from Congress, a body it covered in its news reports, as well as public radio's dependency on a CPB board made up of presidential appointees confirmed by the Senate, compromised its insulation from the federal government and the political process. No wonder that seasoned political operatives such as Frank Mankiewicz and Douglas Bennet presided over the critical period in NPR's development. The noncommercial and nongovernmental character of NPR became blurred as public radio increasingly spoke the language of the advertising-supported networks rather than the rhetoric of public service.

Yet the problems posed by NPR's development were linked to its considerable achievements. In the half-century prior to the establishment of NPR in 1970, noncommercial radio developed into decentralized, locally autonomous entities lacking the resources to establish network interconnection. NPR established that interconnection, first via telephone lines and subsequently via satellite. In presiding over the transformation of "educational" into "public" radio, NPR established a noncommercial network, hitherto the unrealized goal of generations of noncommercial broadcasters and their allies. After World War II, noncommercial radio was in a lamentable state; by the early 1990s, 9 of 10 Americans could tune in to a public radio station. By inaugurating and administering satellite interconnection, NPR made the success of its competitor, APR, possible.

As conceived by William Siemering, NPR's flagship programs gave public radio a national character and legitimacy. The evolution of *ATC* and *Morning Edition* from a supplemental to a primary news source imposed on NPR's news magazines increased scrutiny and caution. Here, too, success created new pressures and dilemmas. And if NPR was too structured along the lines of a commercial network, it was also true that it created the means by which minorities and independents could at the very least struggle to reach a national audience.

NPR's difficulties can also be understood in terms of the contradictions arising from the sheer breadth of its functions, in part as a democratically conceived membership organization, in part as a trade and professional association with lobbying and fund-raising responsibilities, in part as a market-oriented producer, and in part as a program distributor for both its own programs and those of other producers. NPR assumed these myriad responsibilities in the process of virtually inventing public radio, a federal form of noncommercial radio distinct—conceptually and organizationally— from both educational and community radio. The university rather than the federal government represented the primary force in educational broadcasting. Unlike community radio, highly local in character, public radio in its federal form was conceived as a national system from the outset.

NPR origins, as the outgrowth of federal legislation and funds, inevitably resulted in greater interdependence with government. It became part of a Byzantine "nongovernmental" bureaucratic structure headed by political appointees located in the nation's capital. Despite these contradictions and many obstacles, NPR realized, however imperfectly, the aspiration of radio reformers reaching back to the 1920s to establish a national noncommercial radio system.

The odyssey of William Siemering is illustrative of the contradictions in NPR's development. He remains proud of the institution he helped conceive and launch and is revered by its first generation of programmers. Yet Siemering also experienced a kind of exile from the center of NPR's affairs when, after being fired as program director in 1972, he considered quitting public radio completely. His tenure as manager of WHYY in Philadelphia, where he expanded Fresh Air from a local to a national program, ended unhappily. In 1987, Siemering became the first executive producer of *Soundprint,* a Baltimore-based series distributed by APR to about 125 stations. The series featured half-hour documentaries by independent producers whose vivid sound essays recalled an earlier era of *ATC.* Subjects included, for example, personal stories on the process of going blind and life within a prison.

Although many came to consider *Soundprint* the soul of public radio, by the early 1990s its funding was in jeopardy. A documentary series like

Soundprint faced difficulty getting corporate funding because, lacking a single thematic focus, specifics about its content and controversial elements could not be anticipated. The program was also at a disadvantage because it did not serve public radio management's growing emphasis on building large audiences. A threatened cut in funding by the CPB Radio Fund prompted a petition at the 1992 Public Radio Conference. Siemering (1992a) wrote that this initiative was part of a larger struggle "about preserving the mission that is the identity of public radio" (p. 14). Ironically, on the eve of its possible demise, *Soundprint* together with the late Robert Montiegel, a gifted reporter and producer, were honored by the conference. Independent radio producer Jay Allison (1992) argued that Montiegel's brand of creative radio was no longer supported by NPR, adding that

> *Soundprint,* too, is largely unsustained by the system that claims to value its achievements. At the Public Radio Conference, over half of those present signed a petition to preserve the program, yet both CPB and the majority of stations are unwilling to put forward the actual money to do so—further dissonance between words and action. If we allow *Soundprint* to go off the air, public radio will be left with no regular, general-interest, national documentary program. We will lose our weekly opportunity to consider any issue or idea for more than a few minutes. No award can compensate for that loss. (p. 14)

A petition circulated at the 1992 Public Radio Conference failed to get the CPB Radio Program Fund to reconsider its decision to cease funding *Soundprint.* After five years as the program's guiding force, worn out by the struggle for funding, William Siemering resigned as *Soundprint*'s executive producer. In a letter to colleagues, he wrote that his "professional future is uncertain" and that he would keep his hand in public radio as a consultant (cited in Wilner, 1992b, p. 8). In reviewing his career in public radio, Siemering reflected that he had miscalculated the resistance to his humanistic approach and "how the idea of multiculturalism would become a pejorative instead of an affirmation of what is America." He added, "In some ways we haven't moved very far from the white male voice of authority" (personal communication, July 25, 1995). Siemering received belated recognition for his contribution to public radio in 1993 when the John D. and Catherine T. MacArthur Foundation awarded him one of its "genius" fellowships. Siemering used the proceeds of his award to further the development of community radio—not in the United States but in the new democracies of Eastern

Europe and newly multiracial state of South Africa. Siemering's efforts through the Open Society Foundation of South Africa to help establish community public radio systems linking towns and rural areas, in some instances for the first time, were in the tradition of the Wisconsin idea and radio station WHA.

In 1992, Josephson wrote of mainstream public radio, "We've become a mature industry. It's time to reinvent ourselves" (p. 34). Renewal of public radio and as a news and public affairs instrument, Looker (1995) suggested, hinged on the resolution of the conflict between two cultures within public radio. Should radio journalism be rooted in traditions of oral storytelling and aural experience, or should it be perceived as an extension of print media? Should it be animated by a populist or Washington, D.C. sensibility, or by audience building or a desire to challenge listeners with alternative programming? "Should NPR strive," in the words of Looker, "to be a primary news source for its audience or should it provide a range of insights and experiences for listeners that they cannot get through television or print?" (p. 405). For Jim Russell, a former executive producer of *ATC* and public radio manager, NPR paid a price for its success by compromising the principles contained in William Siemering's original statement of its mission. Russell (1992) bemoaned the impact of underwriting, audience research, and the marketing approach to programming:

> The late '80s and early '90s weren't good years for programming. Inventive and strange programs like *Heat* died on the launching pad, cancelled before it could mature. Now, *Soundprint* and *Fresh Air* may be on the chopping block. During all the hoopla about *Morning Edition*'s 10th anniversary, I couldn't help wondering why it had been a decade since a major program like that had been invented. Where are the new ones? (p. 29)

Russell criticized the intolerance for risk-taking, a prerequisite for creative success, suggesting that NPR's creative crisis was a "silent killer" as threatening to its existence as its fiscal crisis a decade earlier: "If permitted to continue, it will devour our core and leave us with a hollow shell" (p. 29).

PART III

Public Television

CHAPTER 8

The Foundation Years

The Ford Foundation and the Carnegie Corporation of New York wrote the book, chapter and verse, on noncommercial television in both its incarnation as educational TV prior to 1967 and as public TV thereafter. Noncommercial television in the United States first emerged as the carefully nurtured offspring of the Ford Foundation and later as the adolescent stepchild of the Carnegie Corporation. Both foundations controlled—indeed orchestrated—the rise of public television at each stage of its development up until passage of the Public Broadcasting Act of 1967. Without the patronage of these two powerful private philanthropic institutions, a noncommercial television system would not have assumed its present form and might not have come into existence at all. We have seen how during the 1920s and 1930s private foundations helped shape broadcast policy and practices—for example, support of the broadcast reform movement by the Payne Fund and of the Cooperation movement by the Carnegie Corporation of New York and the Rockefeller Foundation. The private foundations, often working behind the scenes, made an even more critical contribution to the emergence of noncommercial television. The role of the private foundations, especially the

135

Ford Foundation, warrants closer scrutiny. The orientation of the major philanthropic foundations—institutions engaged in social engineering, strategically situated between the public and the private sectors of society—left an indelible mark on public television. The Ford Foundation's role posed the problem from the outset of the public's participation in public television and the ambiguous relationship of the new institution to the public sphere. The role of foundations of the eastern establishment also provides the background for the attacks on public television by the political right, beginning at the end of the 1960s and reaching a crescendo by the 1990s.

Following World War II, prior to the intervention of the Ford Foundation, it appeared that noncommercial broadcasters would not seek the reservation of TV channels as they had for radio channels during the 1930s. No educators accepted the FCC's invitation to make the case for reservations at hearings prior to the FCC's freeze on new TV licenses in 1948. In 1949, the FCC proposed a TV allocation system with no reservations for noncommercial stations—over the objections of Commissioner Frieda Hennock, who became a leading champion of noncommercial TV. Still, educational broadcasters, with their roots in radio technology, showed little interest in television. Only a small group of educational broadcasters expressed interest in TV, among them Richard B. Hull, president of the NAEB from 1947 to 1949. Hull was director of WOI, a major noncommercial radio station since 1922 at Iowa State College, which successfully applied for a commercial TV license and became the only TV station run by an educational institution during the FCC freeze. Hull encouraged NAEB members to see TV as part of its mission at the Allerton House Seminars, which were held at the University of Illinois in 1949 and 1950, and funded by the Rockefeller Foundation. However, the small group of educational broadcasters interested in television lacked the resources to mount a successful campaign to reserve channels in the short time remaining before the FCC established a structure for TV's development and ended the freeze on new licenses.

The Ford Foundation provided those resources. *The Fourth Network,* a monograph produced by the Network Project (1971), a media research organization based at Columbia University, termed the first phase of non-commercial television's history the "foundation years." The report revealed the finesse with which the Ford Foundation virtually invented noncommercial television by marshaling forces for the allocation of spectrum space and for the creation of an institutional infrastructure for noncommercial television. Toward this end, in 1951 the Ford Foundation charged two of its agencies with distinct but related tasks. The Fund for the Advancement of Education became its tactical arm, laying the political and institutional foundation for a noncommercial television system. It is noteworthy that when the Ford Foundation entered the picture not a single noncommercial television station was on the air. (Iowa State College's WOI operated on a commercial license.) Furthermore, educational broadcasters, who had failed to establish a significant presence on AM radio, had little clout. Television was a new communications technology. The public was generally unaware of and indifferent to its educational potential. Against this background the Ford Foundation waged a brilliant campaign on a series of fronts.

The Fund for the Advancement of Education sponsored a series of key studies with broad implications. Some explored in-school use of TV on the primary, secondary, and college levels. The Chelsea Closed-Circuit Television Project pioneered the first experimental use of educational television for the urban poor in a Spanish-speaking neighborhood in New York City. The Fund's own evaluation of the project concluded that educational TV could meet the special needs of ghettos with "hard core educational or cultural problems" and that, moreover, it could serve "as a form of psychotherapy" and "as an instrument for the development of community leaders" (Network Project, 1971, pp. 15-16). This study anticipated the development of the Children's Television Network and *Sesame Street*. More broadly, it suggested the potential of noncommercial television as a powerful social instrument beyond the classroom. Thus, an ambitious social agenda for educational television, more "public" than "instructional" in the traditional sense, was already at play in the 1950s. The second entity employed by the Ford Foundation in 1951 was the Fund for Adult Education. Its task was nothing less than to put together from scratch a rudimentary educational broadcasting system in the United States. The most pressing task, without which prospects for such a system were dim, was to get the FCC to reserve television channels for noncommercial use. The failure of the Communications Act of 1934 to set aside noncommercial channels for radio permitted commercial interests to eliminate educational broadcasters as a force on the AM spectrum. The Ford Foundation was determined that this chapter of broadcasting history not repeat itself.

A look at the alphabet soup of early educational television organizations reveals the deftness with which the Ford Foundation's FAE laid the political groundwork for a favorable FCC decision. At its very first meeting in spring 1951, the FAE awarded strategic grants to two rickety organizations: the

NAEB and the Joint Committee on Educational Television (JCET). Ford money enabled the NAEB, historically important but nearly defunct by the end of World War II, to become educational TV's principal trade association and Washington lobbyist. The reconstituted JCET supplemented the NAEB's lobbying efforts by parading an elite group of educators, labor leaders, and politicians before the FCC and congressional committees to testify on behalf of educational TV. The FAE also drew up plans for the National Citizens' Committee for Educational Television (NCCET) to spread the gospel of educational television to the American public as a whole.

The JCET, representing seven national educational agencies, advocated noncommercial allocations at critical FCC hearings in late 1950 and early 1951. The JCET was acutely aware of how educational broadcasters had suffered from a lack of strategic planning and political clout in FCC hearings in 1934. It hired as legal counsel Telford Taylor, former chief counsel at the FCC and U.S. prosecutor at Nuremberg, and prepared its case with meticulous care. Witnesses drew on the historical experience of educational broadcasters. A representative of the association of state universities encouraged the FCC to draw upon the principles of the Morrill Act that had established land-grant colleges in reserving TV channels for public, noncommercial use. Witnesses documented the failure of promises made by the commercial networks before the FCC in 1934 to engage in educational programming on their radio stations, and a study prepared by the JCET documented the informational, educational, and cultural deficiencies on commercial television. Commercial interests represented by the National Association of Broadcasters, CBS, and NBC were overwhelmed at the hearings by the JCET's presentation, in which the coordinated testimony of over 70 witnesses—among them U.S. senators, governors, rural, municipal, and labor officials, and representatives of all levels of education—was supplemented by more than 60 exhibits. The flurry of Ford-inspired and Ford-financed activity paid off. In 1952, the FCC's Sixth Order and Report ended the four-year freeze on TV licenses by establishing parameters for television's development, including the reservation of 242 channels—80 in the VHF band and 162 in the UHF band—for noncommercial use. This measure marked the birth of noncommercial television in the United States, the opportunity to gain a foothold on the television dial.

Robert J. Blakely (1979), an officer of the FAE from 1951 to 1961, noted the "general climate of fear and suspicion" when the Ford Foundation became a partisan of noncommercial television (p. 85). In 1950, the publication of *Red Channels: The Report of Communist Influence in Radio and Television* marked the application of the blacklist to television. Blakely recalled that Congress established the House Select Committee to Investigate Tax-Exempt Foundations and Comparable Organizations in 1952 specifically to investigate the loyalty of the Ford Foundation and that the committee chairman, B. Carroll Reece (R-Tenn.), was a long-time ally of commercial broadcasters. The political climate of the 1950s was certainly a factor in the Ford Foundation's modus operandi of advancing its agenda indirectly through entities with their own boards and staffs, like the FAE, which was dissolved in 1961 when John F. Kennedy became president and the Foundation's support for educational TV more overt. If the Ford Foundation's early support of noncommercial TV was indirect, it nonetheless exercised a high degree of control over the initiatives it funded. The FAE, a Ford Foundation satellite, refashioned independent organizations like the NAEB and the JCET to serve the Foundation's policies. Seybold (1978) discussed the process by which this occurred:

> Any organization seeking support from the Foundation needed to discern the foundation's current line on a particular problem area and gradually tailor its grant requests to fit this orientation. This often involved a rather extensive period of instruction by the Foundation regarding the appropriate ways to conceptualize a problem followed by a period of negotiation in which the grantee demonstrated that it had learned its lessons well and understood completely the Foundation's requirements in order to obtain support. The end result . . . entailed an almost unilateral shift of the perspective of the organization to one which matched the foundation's interests in an area. (pp. 378-379)

Interviews conducted by James Robertson with James Armsey (1981) and Robert Hudson (1982)—part of an oral history of educational TV—revealed how key operatives of Ford's educational television program initiated grant proposals and maintained the liaison between the Foundation and its satellite organizations.

In 1952, the FAE embarked on the next stage of its program: to make the provisional reservation of educational channels permanent. It stimulated license applications through the JCET and the NCCET. The JCET sponsored conferences and publications promoting educational TV and offered legal and engineering expertise to communities interesting in launching stations. The 106-member NCCET Advisory Council, which included representatives of the AFL-CIO, the National Council of Churches, the NAACP, and the League of Women Voters, mobilized public support for activating and supporting new stations. The FAE gave matching grants to stations: From 1953 to 1961, 33 stations received nearly $4 million for equipment. Sixteen educational television stations were in existence by 1956; the number would increase to 76 by 1962, when the federal government assumed the FAE's program of grants-in-aid through the Educational Television Facilities Act of 1962.

The Ford Foundation also recognized a need for a national center to link stations through the exchange of information and programs. The failure in the 1950s to keep on the air *Omnibus*—a much praised, Ford-supported experimental program on commercial TV, a throwback to the cooperation doctrine of the 1930s—reinforced the Ford Foundation's determination to build a noncommercial television system. The Educational Television and Radio Center (ETRC) was established in 1952 by the FAE, whose head, C. Scott Fletcher, became the Center's first acting president. This program service, based in Ann Arbor, Michigan, received grants from the FAE to support the production and exchange of programming in four areas: international, national, and economic affairs, and the humanities. The program service began in early 1952 for the two stations then on the air. Programs were "bicycled," that is, sent through the mail, as the Center's network lacked direct interconnection. By 1955, the ETRC supplied about five hours of programs to its affiliates weekly but still had no mechanism for direct interconnection. All educational stations were ETRC affiliates, as affiliation was a prerequisite for FAE grants-in-aid. The ETRC would expand to become National Educational Television, noncommercial TV's first bona fide network with headquarters in New York City. Today's PBS can be considered a descendant of the ETRC, the embryo of a public television network.

What is remarkable about the Ford Foundation's creation of a regulatory and institutional infrastructure for a noncommercial television system is that it antedated the existence of a single educational TV station. (The first, KUHT in Houston, began broadcasting in May 1953.) A networking arm for a noncommercial system was established when nary a station could join it. The Ford Foundation had initiated key research, mobilized public opinion, influenced the FCC's 1952 ruling, and set up the Educational Television and Radio Center prior to KUHT's maiden broadcast. After 1952, the FAE focused on station origination and activation. The FCC's reservation of noncommercial channels was contingent upon their use, and the Ford Foundation successfully ensured that the programs and stations would be in place so that the reservation of 242 channels would become permanent. The Network Project (1971) noted the paradoxical nature of the Ford Foundation's role: "A supposedly educational or public system of television was wholly the progeny of a private economic institution" (p. 8).

The educational television movement went into high gear after 1958, when John F. White, a protégé of Ford Foundation President Henry Heald (1956-1966), became head of the ETRC. White had been a university administrator and general manager of WQED in Pittsburgh, one of the ETRC's leading affiliates. Robert Hudson, television consultant to the FAE, would later recall that White brought to educational TV "dynamism, a sense of motion, and sense of mission that infected the entire movement" (cited in Frederickson, 1972, p. 62). In 1959, White moved the ETRC's main offices from Ann Arbor to New York City and added "National" to its name. That year White applied for, and received, an addition $5 million grant from the Ford Foundation. The NETRC assisted the incorporation of new stations as well as circulating, by 1962, a 10-hour weekly package of programs that embraced the arts, public affairs, and children's shows. Most programs were produced by the affiliate stations because the NETRC had no production staff or facilities of its own. NETRC also contracted programs from independent producers and acquired material from foreign sources. The improvement of programming so that educational television would be transformed into a major national network of information and culture was one of White's two major objectives. The second was diversification of funding sources to lessen dependency on the Ford Foundation. Ford Foundation officials restructured the NETRC on the basis of a meeting of affiliates and a study by Ford's staff member James Armsey in which White's participation was excluded. White was never able to obtain a copy of the study that led to a far-reaching reorientation of the office he headed. The message to White was unmistakable: The Ford Foundation made policy, his job was to carry it out (personal communication, October 14, 1982).

In 1964, Henry Heald, on the basis of the study, redefined the NETRC's function. For the time being, he announced, the Ford Foundation would remain educational television's principal financial supporter. Now that a network infrastructure was in place, Ford would apply its resources to the development of quality programming. Heald announced the first of a series of $6 million annual grants to transform the NETRC into a program production center. The new plan meant that the NETRC would cease to exist and its functions would be assumed by other entities. Its development office was closed down, and it ceased receiving grants for instructional television; the NAEB would take over station origination and support services; and radio development would end, after which the network would be rechristened National Educational Television. The origination of improved programming was clearly the next task for establishing the legitimacy and permanency of noncommercial television in the United States. Under the new system, independent producers and programmers at affiliates lost final editorial control over programs funded by the Ford Foundation. Armsey required that half of NET's shows be devoted to public affairs and, in general, watched NET like a hawk. To appease White, Armsey was transferred to another division of the Ford Foundation, but Fred Friendly would soon assert the Foundation's prerogatives in programming in a more far-reaching way than Armsey ever did.

The Ford Foundation was not quite ready to loosen its control over a movement it had built, block by block, since the early 1950s. The last block, a programming model to establish once and for all the great potential of noncommercial television, was not yet in place. As programming experimentation progressed, however, it became increasingly apparent that the foundation years would come to an end. This, too, was part of the game plan. Private foundations wield their influence largely as initiators; new programs or institutions are designed to attain eventual permanency independent of their original patrons. If educational television was the well-nurtured offspring of the Ford Foundation, it was not meant to be its permanent ward. But this raised a new set of questions about the future of noncommercial television. What would be the primary source of its funds? And how would it be permanently structured?

Enter the Carnegie Corporation of New York, another private foundation, one with a long history of educational and broadcasting policymaking. In 1965, it established the Carnegie Commission on Educational Television. Its 1967 report, *Public Television: A Program for Action,* gave currency to the expanded concept of *public* television that had been implicit in the Ford Foundation's support of educational TV. The report laid out an ambitious plan to make public television a major national institution supported by the taxpayer. It called for the creation of additional national production centers and for more sophisticated network interconnection based on satellite technology then being developed. The centerpiece of this plan was a federally chartered, nonprofit, nongovernmental agency that would administer public television's funds and ensure its orderly growth. From this idea would spring the Corporation for Public Broadcasting. Congress did modify certain features of the Carnegie master plan. For example, the proposal to finance public TV through a tax on the sale of television sets was set aside in favor of appropriations by Congress. Nonetheless, the report constituted a not-so-rough draft of the Public Broadcasting Act of 1967. The thrust of the study and a remarkable number of its specific recommendations became law. The institutional framework for public television as we know it today is in large measure attributable to the groundwork of the Ford Foundation, capped by the report of the Carnegie Commission on Educational Television.

As the Ford Foundation before it, the Carnegie Corporation of New York showed itself adept at setting an agenda and then implementing it in the political arena. The Carnegie Commission presided over the critical task of facilitating the transition from the foundation years to the federal years of noncommercial television. What are we to make of the extraordinary role of these two foundations in the establishment of public television in the United States? A closer look at both institutions reveals the ideological underpinnings of the public broadcasting system they created.

Silk and Silk (1980) linked these two New York City-based foundations to the eastern establishment and its approach to public policy. They trace the roots of the establishment back to a network of clans and institutions in colonial America. The families of the great industrial empire builders of the 19th and early 20th centuries—Andrew Carnegie, John D. Rockefeller, and Henry Ford, among others—added the privately endowed foundations to the roster of establishment institutions like the Episcopalian Church and Harvard University. Andrew Carnegie articulated the ethos behind 19th-century philanthropy in his essay "The Gospel of Wealth." Carnegie maintained that a third force was needed to mediate between the disruptive forces of popular democracy and industrial capitalism. Those who profit most from the laissez-faire system were advised to temper its inequities so that, in Carnegie's words, "the ties of brotherhood may still bind together the rich and poor in harmonious relationship" (cited in Silk & Silk, 1980, p. 106). Carnegie updated the Protestant ethic so that the good works of the elect were carried out by an array of nonprofit agencies ranging from libraries and educational institutions to museums and endowments. Such bodies could help maintain the nation's social fabric independent of the twin evils of unruly popular movements from below or state control from above.

In modern times, the Calvinist terminology and spirit of noblesse oblige has occasionally appeared—for example, in 1975 in official documents of the Ford Foundation, in which its mission was defined as "working against evils" and the "redress of inequity" (cited in Silk & Silk, 1980, pp. 125, 136). In the more characteristic modern idiom of social science, moral exhortation has given way to public policy in which a technocratic orientation is evident. The premise was that social problems can be solved through the enlightened application of expertise. Social science and technology were seen as means to bridge the gap between rich and poor that troubled Andrew Carnegie a century earlier. Third-force institutions such as public broadcasting, which were engaged in the enlightened application of behavioral science and technology, were meant to strengthen American democracy. Silk and Silk (1980) stressed that inclusivity was the hallmark of the modern establishment, that by demonstrating its openness and responsiveness it aspired to remain "the only game in town" (pp. 10-11). Social engineering could not be left to the vagaries of the political process; an enlightened elite needed to exert leadership to assure stability and progress.

The language of the Carnegie Commission on Educational Television (1967) suggested how much public television owed to the ethos of the liberal establishment. The report stressed the potential of television as a broad vehicle for public enlightenment and social amelioration. Public broadcasting could go beyond traditional educational television and compensate for the inadequacies of the American educational system. It could also, in a more general sense, help Americans understand themselves and their times. Improved programming in public affairs would make us better citizens of the world. Then, too, public television could facilitate experimentation in drama, music, film, and other forms of artistic endeavor. Avant-garde American artists would be recognized and nurtured rather than ignored. Public TV's overriding goal was defined as strengthening a society "proud to be open and pluralistic" (p. 14). It could become a platform for "the unheard" (p. 14), a "forum for debate and controversy" (p. 92), and "the clearest expression of American diversity" (p. 18). By celebrating our diversity we would reaffirm our unity; by examining our problems we would rediscover "the far reach of our possibilities" (p. 93). The report pleaded for the use of "a great technology for great purposes" (p. 14).

The Carnegie Commission's objective of fostering a sense of community among all strata was rooted in the gospel of wealth of its namesake, Andrew Carnegie. The desire to exploit the "great technology" of television reflected the technocratic perspective grafted on to the old faith. Characteristically, despite strictures against commercial television, the Carnegie Commission sought to supplement the existing system, not dismantle it. The emphasis on pluralism expressed the goal of inclusivity. Situated between unchecked commercialism sanctioned by the state and popular discontent over unmet needs, public television was designed to function as a third force in American broadcasting.

Transition to the Federal Years

The Public Broadcasting Act of 1967 represented more than the triumph of an idea backed by the private foundations of the liberal establishment. It was enacted as a result of the political ascendency of that establishment during the administrations of John F. Kennedy and Lyndon B. Johnson. Public television came into its own thanks to the New Frontier and the Great Society and to officially neutral political entities like the Ford and Carnegie foundations. The election of Kennedy as president in 1960 marked the emergence of a new administration drawing many of its ideas and personnel from the eastern establishment. Silk and Silk (1980) characterized JFK as the "perfect emblem" of the new order because of his Harvard education, his activism and appeal for service, and his reliance on academia, think tanks, and foundations (pp. 51-52). The Kennedy administration, acutely aware of the political importance of television, committed itself to media reform and to the expansion of what was still called educational television. During Kennedy's presidency, the majority of Americans began to rely on television rather than newspapers for the news as the commercial networks expanded their evening newscasts from 15 to 30 minutes. For the first time, television carried presidential news conferences live. Indeed, the great events of the Kennedy years—from the inauguration to the assassination—are intimately linked to television in the popular consciousness.

Newton Minow, JFK's appointee as chairman of the FCC, emerged as both a critic of the "vast wasteland" of commercial television and an aggressive champion of noncommercial television. At the time of his appointment, educational TV was still dependent on the Ford Foundation and lacked sufficient funds and equipment for the creation of a viable network. Minow promoted the Educational TV Facilities Act of 1962, which earmarked $32 million for upgrading the equipment of educational television stations and represented "the first explicit expression of federal responsibility for non-commercial broadcasting" (Head, 1972, p. 379). The process of federaliza-tion, the shift from foundation to government patronage, was under way. Minow also played a direct role in acquiring an educational television station in the New York City metropolitan area.

In the early 1960s, the NET network was stymied by a lack of outlets in such key cities as New York City, Los Angeles, and Washington, D.C. In 1961, Minow, through a series of maneuvers, arranged the transfer of Chan-nel 13/WNTA, a Newark station with studios in New York City, from commercial to noncommercial hands. Minow's role in the transfer, as de-scribed by Barnouw (1970), demonstrated the aggressiveness with which the Kennedy administration supported the cause of educational TV. As a result of Minow's extraordinary efforts, Channel 13 became the 65th noncommer-cial station in operation in 29 states. It represented more than simply an additional outlet: New York was the nation's communications capital, and its metropolitan area contained the largest concentrated television audience in the United States. Channel 13's debut as a noncommercial station was celebrated by Minow himself on September 16, 1962 in the Sunday *New York Times Magazine.* His article read like a manifesto on behalf of educational television. As for the acquisition of Channel 13, Minow (1962) stressed that NET had turned an important corner: "The base of the 'fourth network' is firmly set" (p. 39).

Besides the appointment of Newton Minow, the Kennedy administra-tion's ambitious space program had a profound impact on noncommercial television. Communication satellites were developed in the context of the U.S.-Soviet space race. 1962 saw the launching of Telstar I and the creation of the Communications Satellite Corporation (COMSAT). The stage was set for the development of domestic communication satellites, which would revolutionize both commercial and noncommercial broadcasting. Several years later, the Ford Foundation would seize upon this technological break-through with a bold plan to tie the future of public television to the develop-ment of domestic communication satellites. During the Kennedy years, which saw a growing interest in the social ramifications of broadcasting, Marshall McLuhan emerged as the prophet of a new communication era that he believed would reintegrate modern society. During the heady days of Camelot, a far-reaching political and technological transformation of broadcasting took place that gave enormous impetus to noncommercial television.

The short-lived Kennedy administration prepared the groundwork for the Public Broadcasting Act of 1967. However, changes in the political climate affected the further development of noncommercial television during Johnson's presidency. The liberal optimism of the Kennedy years gave way to the sharp divisions of the mid- and late 1960s over civil rights, urban disorders, the war in Vietnam, and the emergence of a radical counterculture. The establishment came under attack. The upheavals of the Johnson years led to growing criticism, especially on the country's college campuses, of the nation's dominant institutions and elites. Educational television itself, formerly a sacred cow, also came in for criticism. At the outset of the 1960s, when commercial television was tainted by the quiz show scandals, virtually all press coverage of noncommercial television was favorable. The title of an article on San Francisco's educational station, KQED-TV, in the February 16, 1960 issue of *Look* magazine was characteristic: "No Sponsors, No Censors, No Scandals." However, after NET expanded with great fanfare during the Kennedy administration, expectations began to rise.

During the Johnson administration, rumblings of discontent became audible. Blakely (1979), former vice president of the FAE, recalled how during this period local stations resented their powerlessness over national programming. He wrote that interconnection was clearly necessary to create a national educational television system: "But interconnection raises to an unavoidable position the always latent question: Who's in charge?" (p. 164). Critics began to raise troubling questions about the programming and structure of the emerging noncommercial television system. Some of the sharpest criticisms emanated from "The Air," the television column in *The New Yorker* written by Michael J. Arlen. Arlen (1967a) complained about the sacrosanct and stifling atmosphere pervading programming on educational television and the lack of controversy and creativity. One of the most searching critiques, written by Richard M. Elman, a former employee of NET, appeared in 1965 in *The Nation* magazine. He objected to NET's near monopoly on the distribution of noncommercial television programming in the United States. It was a question that would bedevil both educational and public television.

In his *Nation* article, Elman charged that John White, and educational television in general, were beholden to powerful interests and institutions, chief among them the Ford Foundation. Elman noted that "White's chief responsibility is to the Ford Foundation which subsidized and created NET, chose White as its executive, and reserves the right to inspect every NET program produced with Ford money" (p. 217). Elman added that, although the Ford Foundation's role was preeminent, other foundations, corporations, and government agencies like the Atomic Energy Commission also wielded influence by funding specific projects. Important programming decisions were made by phantom experts and committees behind the scenes. A program, say, on "Why Johnny Can't Read" called for a consultant from the Department of Health, Education, and Welfare; an advisor from the State Department would be brought in for a program on Southeast Asia. Elman argued that the powerful, well-connected groups controlling NET's purse strings inhibited controversial programming. In 1965, for example, NET officials felt that Benjamin DeMott had gone too far when he asked pointed questions about nuclear arms outside a facility of the Atomic Energy Commission while filming an episode for the *Pathfinders* series. Stanley Kauffmann's weekly *The Art of Film* broadcast on Channel 13 was not syndicated by NET because the show was deemed too urbane, too irreverent, and too unpredictable. The avoidance of controversy was surely a factor in educational television's minuscule audiences.

Elman discerned a political bias in programming reflecting the eastern establishment's control of educational television. As an illustration he pointed to the NET series on the presidential nominating conventions and elections in 1964. Elman had worked on the series *Of People and Politics,* subtitled "21 Programs on the Way Americans Perpetuate the System under which They Live." The programs prior to the Republican National Convention stressed that consensus, not ideological conflict, lay at the heart of the American political system. From this it followed that the nomination of arch-conservative Barry Goldwater was unthinkable. One entire preconvention episode consisted of an idealized portrait of a middle-of-the-road Scranton delegate from Wisconsin. NET's coverage had missed the boat. As Elman (1965) observed, "The Establishment had been crossed up by Goldwater's nomination, and so had its mouthpiece—NET" (p. 218).

Elman closed his article by calling on educational television to cut its ties with the establishment, lest it become "a domestic version of the Voice of America" (p. 221). By becoming an instrument of social change instead of the status quo, he suggested, noncommercial TV could acquire a significant mission and audience. Elman failed to indicate how this noncommercial broadcasting system cut loose from its establishment moorings would be funded. Nonetheless, his article raised hard questions about the structure and goals of the noncommercial television, and about the troubled state of its soul. Nor was its body well: Individual stations felt increasingly hard-pressed after the Ford Foundation shifted its emphasis from general station support to network programming. The plight of Channel 13 in New York City was illustrative. By 1965, the year Elman's article appeared in *The Nation*, Channel 13 faced the possibility of going off the air for lack of funds. It cut back dramatically on program production, relying instead on repeats and NET programs. Massive layoffs were made. In search of other sources of revenue, Channel 13 accepted a Shell Oil grant for newscasts that would carry two institutional acknowledgments of the company's support. NET's John White, among others, criticized the acceptance of the grant as a form of advertising. The controversy over corporate underwriting of noncommercial television was under way.

Despite the boost given by the Kennedy administration, at mid-decade noncommercial television's identity was not fixed, its financial health and future development not assured. At this critical point, a new regime took over at the Ford Foundation committed both to ensuring noncommercial television's future and to freeing the Foundation from primary responsibility for the fourth network. In 1966, McGeorge Bundy became president of the Ford Foundation after six years in the White House as national security advisor to Kennedy and Johnson. At about the same time, Fred Friendly resigned after a 16-year career at CBS, following a bitter conflict with network head William Paley. Bundy wished to take a fresh look at the Ford Foundation's involvement in noncommercial television; Walter Lippmann suggested that Friendly conduct the review. The first call that Friendly took the morning after his resignation from CBS was from Bundy, who offered him the post of television consultant to the Foundation. Bundy and Friendly, who together would change the face of educational television, were an odd couple, a study in contrasts. Bundy, the former Harvard dean, had impeccable establishment credentials. Brilliant and arrogant, supremely sure of himself, he kept his emotions at bay. As Edward R. Murrow's collaborator and subsequently as head of CBS news, Friendly showed himself to be a perfectionistic and highly emotional television producer. In addition, both men viewed the burning issue of the day—the war in Vietnam—from different perspectives. Bundy was an architect of the war, Friendly a critic, quitting CBS over its refusal to preempt a rerun of *I Love Lucy* to carry live coverage of George Kennan's testimony on the war before the Senate Foreign Relations Committee.

Despite their differences, Bundy and Friendly became an effective team. They came up with two bold initiatives: one to resolve noncommercial TV's funding problems once and for all, the other to invigorate programming along the lines advocated by critics like Michael Arlen and Richard Elman. The first initiative reflected the global outlook of the new president of the Ford Foundation. Bundy and Friendly proposed that a nonprofit corporation be created to develop a domestic satellite system similar to the international system already in existence. Four domestic satellites, instead of AT&T's telephone lines, could transmit the programs of the three commercial networks at sharply reduced rates. The corporation's profits would be earmarked for noncommercial television. Hence, the proposed domestic satellite system would bankroll educational broadcasting by providing an independent and permanent source of revenue. Moreover, NET would get free satellite transmission, replacing the "bicycling" of programs via parcel post with live interconnection, making the fourth network a reality. Bundy referred to the proposed system as "a people's dividend, earned by the American nation from its enormous investment in space" ("People's Satellite," 1967, p. 76).

Kinsley (1976) recalled the stir caused by the Ford Foundation satellite plan:

> Aided by a major publicity drive in honor of McGeorge Bundy's first major project as the foundation's new president, the satellite plan was greeted with attention rarely paid to briefs filed in obscure regulatory proceedings. Editorial writers and television columnists wrote about turning points and breakthroughs. Senator Pastore held hearings. (p. 131)

The 80-page Ford proposal ran up against a barrage of opposition from the telecommunications industry during the hearings of the Senate Communications Subcommittee held in summer 1966. Leading the pack of critics was AT&T, whose spokesman exchanged harsh words with Bundy. Officials of COMSAT, the corporation chartered by Congress in 1962, claimed it had a monopoly on domestic satellite service. The networks opposed the plan on the grounds that they would be forced to subsidize a competing television network in the name of public service. As *Newsweek* reported, Bundy and Friendly were "able to generate heat within the liberal establishment with the argument that the real issue is not private vs. public ownership, but the opportunity satellite technology presents 'for greatness' in American life" ("People's Satellite," 1967, p. 77). The Ford Foundation satellite plan was a perfect expression of the technocratic approach to public policy. However, the proposal threatened too many vested interests and raised too many questions to gain quick acceptance in Congress or by the FCC. Bundy and Friendly were ahead of their time in realizing the central role that satellite communication would play in the future. In the aftermath, Bundy and Friendly were praised for an unsuccessful initiative that put the twin issues of domestic communication satellites and the permanent funding of noncommercial television on the national agenda.

The second Bundy-Friendly initiative was no less controversial, but its impact on the American broadcasting scene was more immediate. They launched a unique experiment, a ground-breaking program called the *Public Broadcasting Laboratory (PBL)*. It represented a bold step forward in the Ford Foundation's commitment to upgrade programming, intensified by Fred Friendly's determination to outdo and shame commercial television. The Ford Foundation earmarked $10 million for the project late in 1966. *PBL* was designed to be an innovative and controversial national television magazine covering public affairs and the arts. The two-hour Sunday night program would be carried live on the fourth network. *PBL*'s avowed purpose was to create a new form of public affairs programming and to prove beyond a doubt the great promise of public television. As noted by Barnouw (1970), an atmosphere of political and cultural crisis in the United States gave the *PBL* experiment added significance. By 1967, the focus of the civil rights movement had shifted from integration to black power. The escalation of the war in Vietnam produced a growing antiwar movement and bitter divisions in the nation's political life. Political breakdown contributed to cultural breakdown, to a generational revolt and a multifaceted counterculture. The dominant culture was challenged through love-ins and teach-ins, underground films and the alternate press, and off-Broadway and street theater. Television, more than anything else, epitomized the staid, conservative, commercial culture against which the rebellion was directed. Barnouw (1970) cited a 1967 Louis Harris poll indicating that the college-educated, by virtue of their viewing habits, were in effect engaged in a growing boycott of commercial television.

PBL was designed to give expression to the political and cultural revolt of the period. Av Westin, the 38-year-old former CBS producer hired as executive director of *PBL*, spoke of his intention "to stir things up, to challenge the status quo of both commercial and educational television" (cited in Tebbel, 1967, p. 87). It was announced, for example, that "truth commercials," a regular feature, would expose misleading advertising and consumer fraud. An aggressive talent search was mounted. *PBL* executives raided commercial television, luring chief correspondent Edward P. Morgan away from ABC and reporters Robert MacNeil and Tom Petit from NBC. Others came from the world of print journalism: *PBL*'s foreign affairs editor Robert McCabe had worked for *Newsweek,* its science editor for *Look,* and national affairs editor John Wicklein for the *New York Times.* A coast-to-coast network of stringers included representatives of the counterculture and alternative media. A 60-person editorial staff worked out of *PBL*'s headquarters on Madison Avenue in New York City, preparing for the program's debut in November 1967.

Expectations generated by the widely publicized preparations became a factor in noncommercial television's quest to achieve a permanent place in American broadcasting. 1967 would clearly be a critical year, a possible turning point, for the fourth network. In January 1967, President Johnson, in his State of the Union message, called for the transformation of educational broadcasting into a major public resource. The speech was carried live on 70 noncommercial television stations through a NET hookup financed by a special Ford Foundation grant. A month later, the Carnegie Commission on Educational Television published its report. Congressional hearings on the question of federal aid were to follow. *PBL* was in a position to influence— positively or adversely—the drive to establish a public broadcasting system in the United States. Tebbel (1967) wrote in *The Saturday Review* that *PBL* "may be the most significant step in television's brief, cluttered history" (p. 85). The institutions and individuals involved in the experiment all suffered from the jitters. Initially, *PBL* was to operate as a program of Columbia University's School of Journalism. Both the school and Friendly apparently had second thoughts about assuming responsibility for *PBL* and shifted course: *PBL* would function as a semiautonomous department of NET, and Friendly was relieved of direct control. An editorial policy board, chaired by the dean of the School of Journalism, met weekly in New York to supervise *PBL.* The distinguished body of educators, policymakers, and artists included Princeton's provost and William P. Rogers, former U.S. attorney general. The board was reported to be highly critical of *PBL*'s dry runs. As *PBL*'s first broadcast approached, chief correspondent Edward P. Morgan acknowledged the pressure: "I don't mind saying I'm scared to death at this point" (cited in *"PBL* on the Brink," 1967, p. 104).

According to Barnouw (1970), *PBL*'s debut pulled no punches. Racial conflict was the theme of the first *PBL* program broadcast on November 5, 1967. The opening segment contained reports on the racially charged mayoral elections in Gary, Cleveland, and Boston. Here the format did not depart markedly from commercial television. However, a report on race relations in Chicago did. It began with a tour of black Chicago, filmed and narrated by a local black nationalist named Russ Meeks. The filmed tour was followed by a heated verbal exchange between Meeks, a moderate black minister, and white liberals, which was broadcast live from the studios of Chicago's educational television station. *PBL* made no attempt to balance or interpret the viewpoints. The confrontation, raw and gripping, had an authentic, unedited, and unmediated quality unknown to conventional television, commercial or educational. Finally, the main and most controversial segment of the premiere was the presentation of an off-Broadway play called *Day of Absence*. In the drama, blacks disappear from a Southern town, which is thereby rendered helpless. What offended many sensibilities was the fact that the whites were caricatured by blacks in "whiteface."

The official reaction to *PBL*'s debut can best be described as squeamish. Reviews were largely negative. Critics and the broadcast industry seemed eager to cut down to size the much heralded experiment. Members of *PBL*'s editorial board were unhappy. Fred Friendly was quoted terming the debut "disappointing." This prompted Arlen (1967b) to observe that only recently Friendly had expressed the same disappointment with CBS, "and right now I don't know what there is for any of us to do except just get back to study hall and work a whole lot harder for the rest of the term" (p. 143). Arlen became a champion of *PBL* as an important and exciting—if admittedly uneven—experiment in expanding the frontiers of television. At the end of the year, Arlen (1967c) wrote that *PBL* was "the most consistently interesting and substantial public-affairs program right now in American broadcasting" (p. 54).

PBL continued to take chances. And what would be riskier, as the war in Vietnam reached a crescendo of intensity, than a sympathetic look at the other side? In January 1968, *PBL* aired Felix Greene's *Inside North Vietnam*. His documentary was a clearly partisan and sympathetic portrayal of the enemy that, through powerful images, undermined the official notion of a fanatic, enslaved, inhuman foe. The film contained evidence contradicting Defense Department claims that no antipersonnel bombs were being employed by the United States. Thirty-three congressmen wrote a letter addressed to Jack White of NET protesting the film as communist propaganda and implying that a purge of top personnel in educational television was in order. Despite such attacks, Barnouw (1970) noted, *PBL* did not temper its radicalism: "Mindful of its function as an alternative voice, it dipped into work of fringe theaters, cabarets, and underground films, and inevitably reflected the angry subculture. The thrust of the message was anti-war, anti-racist, anti-establishment" (p. 294).

Here we confront the seemingly contradictory nature of public television on the eve of passage of the Public Broadcasting Act of 1967. How could it come to pass that noncommercial television, which owed its growth to establishment support, would develop an anti-establishment emphasis by the late 1960s? The Ford Foundation's sponsorship of *PBL* highlighted the issue. *PBL* was launched with the support of the foundation's new president, McGeorge Bundy, who had impeccable establishment credentials. Why would Bundy, an architect of the war in Vietnam, support a TV program that would feature antiwar perspectives such as Felix Greene's film? Perhaps it reflected the establishment's own sense of crisis and disenchantment with the war. More generally, *PBL* could be understood in relation to noncommercial television's status as a third force, seeking to acknowledge and remedy problems independent of both government and citizenry. The establishment, facing mounting criticism, reaffirmed its openness and legitimacy by offering the counterculture and the antiwar movement a piece of the action. The revolt of the 1960s could thereby be recognized, brought into the mainstream, tamed. The *PBL* experience was an illustration of the principle of inclusivity. By covering all the bases, by mounting the war in Vietnam and also providing a platform for the antiwar movement, the establishment could remain, as Silk and Silk (1980) put it, "the only game in town" (pp. 10-11). *PBL* reflected a remarkable tolerance for dissent and faith in the social system's adaptability and potential for peaceful reform. This outlook provided the ideological foundation for the development of public television. Yet the radicalism of *PBL* also suggested that public TV could assume a life of its own and go beyond the confines of its establishment sponsors. Had the establishment been hoisted by its own petard, or had it co-opted the opposition?

PBL, conceived with great fanfare, ended on an anticlimactic note. It would come and go like a brilliant meteor, without an enduring impact as a programming model for public TV, as *All Things Considered* became for public radio. (*PBL*'s television magazine format was later used by CBS's *60 Minutes*.) *PBL* would constitute the last hurrah of Ford domination of noncommercial television, the swan song of the foundation years. Bundy had other plans for the Ford Foundation. And Friendly, the angry refugee from CBS news, may have been interested in *PBL* more as a personal project than as a means to strengthen noncommercial television as a whole. Some speculated that Friendly wanted to shame CBS by having *PBL* do for the war in Vietnam what *See It Now* had done for McCarthyism. *PBL* was never a bona fide NET operation; as such it eroded the strength of noncommercial TV's core institution at a time when plans were being laid to phase out NET and to transform the character of the fourth network. In part, *PBL* obscured the reorientation of noncommercial broadcasting already under way that would cast off the old guard of public television represented by John White and NET. As a result, White (1982) reserved for Fred Friendly one of the "blackest pages" in the history of public television (personal communication, October 14, 1982).

In 1967, public television ceased being primarily a Ford Foundation operation and entered the federal era of its history. This came about as the result of a series of maneuvers by a new set of leading players in high places. These developments were obscured by the mythology surrounding the Carnegie Commission on Educational Television. According to the legend, an independent study group made up of a broad cross section of distinguished private citizens convened by the Carnegie Corporation of New York—that is, a decidedly unofficial, apolitical, nongovernmental panel—prepared the groundwork for the Public Broadcasting Act. However, one must look behind the facade of the Carnegie Commission on Educational Television to observe the machinations that led to the federalization of public broadcasting. Two important resources in this regard are the monograph by J. E. Burke (1979) on the Carnegie Commission and the Public Broadcasting Act of 1967 and the 55 interviews in the educational broadcasting oral history project conducted by James Robertson (1979-1982). On the surface, the makeup of the Carnegie Commission appeared diverse enough: Its membership included black novelist Ralph Ellison, concert pianist Rudolf Serkin, and labor leader Leonard Woodcock. Or were they window dressing? The Commission's composition deserves further scrutiny. As Rovere (1962) observed, "Committee rosters serve Establishmentologists in the same way that May Day photographs of the reviewing stand above Lenin's tomb serve the Kremlinologists" (p. 10).

The key member of the Carnegie Commission was its chairman, James R. Killian, Jr., the corporation head of MIT. The core membership and staff of the Commission were made up of close associates of Killian. His outlook would have a profound impact on the Commission's report and on the future of public television. Killian, the nation's first White House adviser on science, had a distinguished record of presidential appointments for key government programs involving technology development and national security in the period following World War II. Truman appointed him to the Science Advisory Committee of the Office of Defense Mobilization, Eisenhower to his Surprise Attack Panel. After Sputnik, Eisenhower named him "missile czar"; Killian helped establish the U.S. space program and NASA. Under Kennedy, he chaired the President's Foreign Intelligence Advisory Board and the Institute of Defense Analyses. Killian was a prominent representative of the Cambridge-Washington axis which fed high-level personnel back and forth between MIT and Harvard and the federal government. It is noteworthy that the seat of the Carnegie Commission was in Cambridge: Some saw a deliberate attempt to distance the Commission from NET's base in New York City. Public television—body and soul—would be spirited away from New York to Washington, D.C. by way of Cambridge, Massachusetts.

Indeed it was a distinguished Boston Brahmin, Ralph Lowell, an associate of Killian's and scion of the Boston Lowells, who provided the impetus that led to the creation of the Carnegie Commission. He headed the Lowell Institute, which had provided series of free lectures for over a century. As chronicled by Weeks (1966), Ralph Lowell brought the Institute into the electronic age in the 1950s by founding noncommercial radio and television stations WGBH-FM and WGBH-TV in conjunction with the major universities and cultural institutions in the Boston area. Ralph Lowell was the first president of the governing body of the two stations, the WGBH Foundation, which became and remains a major force in public broadcasting. The first manager of WGBH-FM recalled his awe in first encountering this scion of the Boston wing of the eastern establishment: "There sat this magnificent old man. . . . He looked . . . like a sea captain. He had a beautifully cropped mustache, a perfectly tailored suit" (cited in Robertson, 1992, p. 101). The origin of the Carnegie Commission can be traced to a proposal that Ralph Lowell brought to a conference of the Educational Television Station (ETS) division of the NAEB held in 1964 in Washington, D.C. ETS had been established to assume station service activities dropped by NET in its reorganization of 1963-1964 in order to focus on programming. The creation of ETS also reflected growing station hostility toward the Ford Foundation's leadership and NET's control over Ford funds for educational television. One of the principal purposes of the NAEB-ETS meeting in the nation's capital, which was funded in part by a grant from the U.S. Office of Education, was to explore alternatives for long-term funding.

The item that received most attention at the ETS meeting was a proposal for a White House conference presented by Ralph Lowell and prepared by Hartford Gunn, Jr., then general manager of WGBH-FM and WGBH-TV and about to come into his own as a public television power broker. The meeting resolved that Lowell head a committee to interest President Johnson in either a White House or citizens' commission on the future of noncommercial television. After meeting with Lowell and consulting with his advisors, Johnson opted for an unofficial, privately financed commission—perhaps because LBJ's family broadcasting interests made him vulnerable to conflict-of-interest charges. More important, the findings of a politically "independent" panel would carry more weight and give the administration room to maneuver by modifying, if necessary, the Carnegie Commission's final recommendations for legislation. Hartford Gunn, Jr., who had a strong preference for a White House commission, nonetheless continued to play a central role in the creation and proceedings of the Carnegie Commission. Gunn had worked closely with James Killian, one of the original trustees of WGBH; the two men lived in the same apartment building in Cambridge. Gunn belonged to the core group that recommended Killian as chairman of the Carnegie Commission and that convinced him to accept the position (Gunn, 1981). The Cambridge/Boston locale made an imprint on the character of public television just as Berkeley, California did on Pacifica Radio.

Despite its nominal independence, the Carnegie Commission on Educational Television was largely controlled by the White House—a fact that emerged through James Robertson's oral history project, undertaken approximately a decade and a half after the appearance of its report and passage of the Public Broadcasting Act. The key behind-the-scene players were Leonard Marks and Douglass Cater. Marks, a communications lawyer and longtime counsel to the NAEB, represented the Johnson family broadcasting interests and was a member of LBJ's inner circle. During the Johnson administration, he headed the United States Information Agency (USIA). Cater was a White House special assistant, who specialized in domestic affairs and educational policy. On occasion, he was also involved in national security issues and made a trip to Vietnam in 1966 as part of a White House task force. A former journalist, Cater (1964) had written a book titled *Power in Washington* in which he took issue with C. Wright Mills's critique of the nation's power elite: "To elevate the art of governing must require the existence of a power elite, not of the cynical or sinister sort, but comprising those who by distant vision and capacity to see things whole came to play a superior role" (p. 247). Cater's basement office in the White House served as the command center for the creation of the Carnegie Commission and for passage of the Public Broadcasting Act of 1967.

Leonard Marks and Douglass Cater were instrumental in naming and approving appointees to the Carnegie Commission. They made sure that the Commission was made up of both dependable members of the Cambridge/Washington axis and close personal and political associates of President Johnson. One such Johnson confidant was J. C. Kellam, president of the Texas Broadcasting Corporation, and manager of Lady Bird's radio and TV properties; another was Mrs. Oveta Culp Hobby, board chair of the *Houston Post* Company. The funding of the Carnegie Commission was arranged by another Johnson political ally, John Gardner, then president of the Carnegie Corporation of New York and soon to join the Johnson administration as Secretary of Health, Education, and Welfare. Unlike the Ford Foundation, which had its own agenda for educational television and had exercised direct control over its growth, the Carnegie Corporation of New York acted more as a broker for the forces effecting a transition from the foundation to the federal years of noncommercial television.

To flesh out the Carnegie Commission, Killian turned to colleagues similarly committed to using science and technology in the national interest. Appointed as members were three scientists with whom Killian had worked closely on government assignments since the Truman administration: Edwin Lamb, president of Polaroid, Lee A. DuBridge, president of the California Institute of Technology, and Harvard's president, James B. Conant. DuBridge was a physicist who headed the radiation laboratory established at MIT by the government to develop radar for the military, a model for collaboration between scientists and government later employed for the Manhattan Project to develop the atomic bomb. Conant, a leader of the Manhattan Project, like Killian moved in the Cambridge-Washington, D.C., orbit of science and national security policymakers during the cold war era. Stephen White, the Carnegie Commission's first staff member and author of its final report, had worked at MIT. Hartford Gunn, general manager of WGBH radio and television, remained actively involved in the work of the Commission in an unofficial capacity.

Thus, the Carnegie Commission was in its personnel and geographical center of operations essentially a Cambridge, Massachusetts operation, outside the purview of the New York-based NET network. The Commission deliberately kept itself at arm's length from educational television's old guard. John White of NET was asked to make only a perfunctory presentation to the Carnegie Commission during one of its busy stops in New York. Nothing would slow down the Carnegie Commission bandwagon as it moved swiftly toward the legislative arena. Its report, subtitled "A Program for Action," appeared in January 1967. The Public Broadcasting Act was signed by President Johnson in November of that year. The Carnegie Commission on Educational Television was a catalyst for the federalization of public television, and its recommendations provided the basis for the 1967 Act. The legislation established a federally chartered, nonprofit, nongovernmental agency to support stations, programming, and interconnection and thereby foster a national system of public broadcasting. The CPB assumed responsibility for disbursing funds and insulating public broadcasting from political interference.

Two features of the Public Broadcasting Act—the funding mechanism and the composition of the CPB board—would complicate the implementation of the CPB's mandate to create a regular source of revenue independent of the political process. One significant departure from Commission recommendations in the final legislation concerned funding. In retrospect, Lee DuBridge (1981), the Caltech president who served on the Carnegie Commission, conceded that he and others had been naive in proposing a 2% excise tax on the sale of television sets—the recommendation could never have withstood the lobbying efforts of the television industry. Instead, the system would be funded by Congress. (The revised bill was supported by the commercial networks, including a pledge of $1 million from CBS to the CPB, reflecting the view of the networks that public broadcasting would provide quality arts and information programming they considered too costly and unprofitable.) Because annual congressional appropriations for public broadcasting could be affected by shifting political winds, consideration was given to devising a long-term funding mechanism. However, the provision for multiyear funding was deleted as a result of the budgetary constraints resulting from the Vietnam War.

Another political factor was the appointment of the CPB's board of directors. According to the 1967 Act, the board was barred from involvement in political activity, and its composition was required to be culturally, professionally, and regionally diverse. However, the Public Broadcasting Act required that the president of the United States appoint the 15-member CPB board, with the advice and consent of Congress and with no more than a bare majority drawn from one political party. Lashley (1992) noted the complex governmental jurisdictions impinging upon public broadcasting under the 1967 Act: Four congressional committees concerned with communications and appropriations, the National Telecommunications and Information Administration, the Office of Education of the Department of Health, Education, and Welfare, and the National Endowment for the Humanities, among others. It remained to be seen whether a new public broadcasting system, its very creation the outgrowth of a highly political process, funded by Congress, governed by presidential appointees, and enmeshed in the bureaucratic intricacies of the nation's capital, could remain insulated from politics.

The CPB was authorized to create an entity to interconnect public stations, distribute programming, and provide other services. NET, the administrator of the old educational network, proposed that its affiliate council administer the interconnection of the new system. As Witherspoon and Kovitz (1987) observed,

> NET was the primary source of national programming and had the most obvious administrative mechanism to manage the forthcoming system. On the other hand, the most cursory reading of the Carnegie Commission report and the legislative history of the Public Broadcasting Act revealed that the corporation's mandate was to diversify the system, and specifically to reduce the relative power of NET. (p. 29)

Under the leadership of Ward Chamberlin, functioning as the agent of CPB Chairman Frank Pace, Jr., a plan was developed to create a new entity to operate the public television network. In 1969, the new mechanism was chartered as the Public Broadcasting Service, designed as a membership organization to provide interconnection services for member stations. Its board consisted of representatives of member stations, national program centers, the CPB, and the public. PBS, like the CPB, was chartered as a nonprofit, nongovernmental organization based in Washington, D.C.

After 1967, the top administrative echelon of public broadcasting had a new profile. Whereas educational broadcasters once predominated, the new leadership was more closely linked to government service. Killian became vice chairman of the original CPB board. WGBH's Hartford Gunn, Jr., Killian's close associate, became the first president of PBS, which subsequently replaced NET as public television's networking arm. No one typified the changing of the guard better than Frank Pace, Jr., who was named the first chairman of the CPB board by President Johnson. Pace, a southerner, had been something of a Democratic Party *wunderkind*. President Truman appointed him Director of the Budget and later Secretary of the Army, when Pace was still in his 30s. He gained a reputation as a crack modernizer and pioneered in nuclear weapon technology. During the Eisenhower administration, Pace joined General Dynamics, the nation's largest defense contractor, where he became CEO and chairman of the board. Pace and Killian had collaborated on a variety of enterprises: For example, they had served together on Eisenhower's Commission on National Goals and Kennedy's Foreign Intelligence Advisory Board. Pace, in accepting the position as chairman of the CPB board, expressed interest in public television's potential for riot control (Barnouw, 1970).

A number of prominent figures in the CPB's genesis had ties to Frank Pace, Jr., dating back to his tenure as Secretary of the Army. For example, John Macy, Jr., the first president of the CPB, had been an assistant to the Secretary of the Army under Pace; Macy had been director of the U.S. Civil Service Commission and President Johnson's chief headhunter for federal appointments before going to the CPB. A second person with long-standing links to Pace was Ward Chamberlin, the CPB's first vice president and general manager, one of the creators of PBS, and subsequently president and general manager of WETA-TV and WETA-FM in Washington, D.C. Chamberlin worked as associate counsel at General Dynamics and served on various advisory boards alongside Pace. A third was Douglass Cater of the Johnson White House, who had been a special assistant to Secretary of the Army Pace in 1951. Besides the involvement of a network of associates of James Killian, Jr., and Frank Pace, Jr., many of public broadcasting's new guard had government backgrounds.

The Carnegie Corporation of New York helped establish another key institution in this period of public broadcasting's federalization: Joan Ganz Cooney's Children's Television Workshop (CTW), the producer of *Sesame Street*. In 1966, the Carnegie Corporation funded a study of the use of television in preschool education conducted by Cooney, a former staff member of the USIA. Two years later, she became the president of CTW. Heavily funded by the U.S. Department of Education, CTW also entered the international arena. Its first director of international development was Jack ·Hood Vaughn, the former director of the Peace Corps.

The reorganization of noncommercial television carried out under the auspices of the Carnegie Commission on Educational Television led to a public television system more directly tied to the state than policymakers at the Ford Foundation would have had it. This is not to say that the reorientation of 1967 represented a repudiation of the agenda for a third force in broadcasting. Rather, it represented a shift in emphasis, reflecting different strategies within the ranks of the establishment. Hence, during the critical period of 1966-1967 an element of rivalry had developed between the Ford and Carnegie programs for public television. The Ford Foundation's proposal to base funding on a nonprofit satellite system, along with its sponsorship of *PBL*, coincided with the deliberations of the Carnegie Commission. Both of these Ford initiatives and its support for NET reflected a desire to distance public TV more from government. Hartford Gunn (1981) later recalled that Killian was furious when he learned of the Ford satellite proposal, "so angry that he was ready to chew nails and spit them out at Bundy and Friendly" (p. 55).

The Ford Foundation would not be able to counter the Carnegie Commission/Johnson administration onslaught. AT&T had blocked the satellite proposal. McGeorge Bundy had little interest in a protracted struggle as he was eager to move the Ford Foundation into new areas and to relinquish its role as public TV's chief sponsor. A common front was forged: Bundy minimized Ford-Carnegie differences and testified in favor of the Public Broadcasting Act before Congress. As Killian (1981) recalled, Fred Friendly was deeply disappointed by the shift in fortunes of the Ford Foundation's programs and agenda for public television. Nonetheless, after creation of the CPB, Friendly's assistant at the Ford Foundation, David Davis, played a major behind-the-scenes role in the creation of PBS, the new system's networking mechanism, with headquarters in official Washington instead of liberal New York.

What about NET? John White had muted his reservations and testified on behalf of the Carnegie plan. After all, the Ford Foundation was withdrawing as public TV's chief financial angel, and the future of the noncommercial television system that White helped build would be threatened without passage of federal legislation. Nonetheless, White did indicate before Congress his fear that the new system, without adequate financial and political safeguards, could become a domestic USIA. NET's affiliate stations were less preoccupied with such structural questions. They anticipated an infusion of federal funds passing directly from the CPB to individual stations without

Ford-sponsored, New York-based entities like NET and *PBL* positioned as intermediaries. On the part of the stations there was an understandable desire to take the money and run. As White (1982) later recalled, "We at NET were sitting out in the cold with our pants inside" (personal communication, October 14, 1982). He made one last appeal to Friendly and Bundy: Would Ford continue to support NET as the new system's principal production center, if not its networking arm? They said no. In 1969, after 11 years at NET, Jack White resigned to become president of Cooper Union in New York.

How CPB carried out its mandate to assist in establishing a system of interconnection had significant implications for the future of public television. The detailed account by Avery and Pepper (1979b) of negotiations, which took place at the time when Richard Nixon was elected president, revealed deep divisions. James Killian, Jr., wanted the CPB to operate the interconnection. The stations opposed combining production and distribution responsibilities in one entity. NET thought it should operate the network by virtue of its history and experience. Foes viewed NET as arrogant in its dealings with stations in the past, and capable of overshadowing the CPB if permitted to administer interconnection. The new Nixon administration cast a shadow: NET was deemed too liberal in its programming and New York a poor choice for the seat of another, albeit noncommercial, network. The Ford Foundation, having invested so much in the creation of a public television system, worked behind the scenes to broker an agreement. A complex compromise was built around the creation of a new agency for the interconnection, PBS, which was called a "service" rather than a "network" to appease the stations. NET became one but not the sole national production center. Avery and Pepper (1979b) concluded that the agreement involved a considerable degree of deception and ambiguity:

> PBS was created by a process of negotiated compromise controlled by CPB—with support from the Ford Foundation—in which NET and the stations erroneously believed that they were having significant input into, and control over, the final decision. (p. 20)

The nature of the agreement establishing PBS guaranteed subsequent confusion over its status. It began operations in 1970 with fundamental differences over whether PBS was a subsidiary of the CPB or an independent agency of the stations. NET, considered too liberal and potentially too strong an entity, was replaced by a flawed entity with headquarters, like the CPB, in the nation's capital.

Despite the practical problems of operating the new system, the Public Broadcasting Act of 1967 was a great milestone. Public television was crowned as a national institution; its future in one form or another seemed assured. True, public TV had been federalized in the sense that it now depended on congressional appropriations, political appointees, and its own Washington bureaucracy. Yet the CPB and PBS were chartered as nonprofit, nongovernmental agencies: The notion of a third force had not been completely abandoned. This contradiction together with the liberal rhetoric of the Carnegie Commission report and the 1967 Act provided an opening for diversity and dissent within the system. The transition from the foundation years to the federal years meant that the politics of public television would be more open to scrutiny.

Thus, public television came of age replete with inner tensions. The Public Broadcasting Act of 1967 pleased a variety of constituencies for a number of reasons. Commercial broadcasters supported it because it would lessen demands on them for greater social accountability. Kennedy liberals applauded the legislation because it was responsive to the technological breakthroughs and idealism of the early 1960s. The establishment saw public television as an instrument for wooing back to the mainstream the nation's disaffected intelligentsia and for promoting America's image abroad. And LBJ's war-torn Great Society would be well served by a liberal institution that remained under the ultimate control of the military-industrial complex. Radicals, conversely, hoped to build on the model of *PBL* and use public television as a tool for protest and social reform. Indeed, the complex left-liberal-conservative crosscurrents gave public television much of its vitality and promise as the CPB and PBS came into being. The balance of power between different visions and interests—a basic institutional equilibrium—was based on the flexible support of the eastern establishment and the liberal administrations of JFK and LBJ. However, that equilibrium would be tested by changes in the American social and political landscape signaled by the election of Richard Nixon as president in 1968.

CHAPTER 9

The Government Years

The Public Broadcasting Act of 1967 marked a transition from educational to public broadcasting and from foundation to federal financing of a noncommercial television network. The legislation represented a culmination of the policies of the Ford Foundation in the 1950s and of the Kennedy and Johnson administrations in the 1960s. During the 1970s, the federal government became the source or focus of public television's development, from expansion of the system to political conflict with the White House and a grassroots campaign for new legislation.

PBS was incorporated in late 1969 as a station membership organization with nine directors—five representatives of stations, one each for NET and the CPB, plus two representatives of the public at large. The appointment of Hartford Gunn, Jr., a former manager of WGBH, as PBS's first president reflected the growing prominence of Boston public broadcasters at the expense of the New York-based NET in the restructuring of noncommercial television. Its architects constituted PBS as a private, nonprofit corporation financed by the CPB but controlled by the stations through a governing board with representatives of the CPB, NET, and the public. PBS would deal with national and regional production centers, make scheduling decisions, and generally administer the interconnection. Unlike NPR, PBS was barred from combining direct program production with distribution. Responsibility for program grants rested with the CPB. Yet the CPB would come to rely on PBS to survey stations on their programming needs and to work with producers at every stage of program planning and production. Overlapping responsibilities in programming and other areas needed to be addressed. The establishment of PBS as an entity with its own board of directors, based in Washington, D.C.—in proximity to the CPB and Congress—increased the danger both of bureaucratic rivalry within public broadcasting and of political pressure without.

Significant growth of a system infrastructure took place from 1969 to 1972. The number of public television stations nourished by federal funds nearly doubled to 233. Important initiatives were taken in programming. In 1969, NET received the CPB's first program production grant for *Black Journal.* NET flourished as a production unit within the New York City public television station, rechristened WNET, under the leadership of Jack Willis, its executive producer from 1971 to 1973. Willis produced two high-water marks in public television history—*The Great American Dream Machine,* an iconoclastic public affairs magazine, and *The 51st State,* which broke new ground in local news in its coverage of New York City's political, cultural, and environmental affairs.

After beginning interconnection in 1970, PBS distributed innovative programs produced by NET and other production centers in political analysis (*Washington Week in Review*), public affairs (*The Great American Dream Machine*), drama (*The Forsyte Saga*), education (*Sesame Street*), and science (*Nova*). In addition to *Black Journal,* plans were laid for other shows serving minority audiences such as *Soul, Realidades, Interface, Black Perspective on the News,* and *Villa Allegre.* On the local level, important experiments in community access to public television took place in the early and mid-1970s with programs like *Catch 44* in Boston, *Take 12* in Philadelphia, *Your Turn* in Detroit, and *Open Studio* in San Francisco (Del Solar, 1976). The National Center for Experiments in Television at KQED in San Francisco and the Television Laboratory at WNET under David Loxton explored new uses of video and TV as artistic and social instruments. During this period, perhaps the most creative in public television history, its audience increased by nearly a third.

At the outset, central program review did not take place because block grants sent to NET and six other production centers were not tied to specific program proposals. However, as the CPB became involved in long-term program planning and PBS instituted "standards and practices" guidelines for national programming and the practice of "flagging" controversial programs, conflict with the production centers escalated. PBS asserted the right to censor its offering to the system but tolerated "off-schedule" broadcasts by individual stations of shows it deemed unacceptable. To weaken the power of the production centers, their number was reduced in favor of a program fund to which all public television producers might apply. During PBS's second season, beginning in 1971, several censorship controversies developed. For example, PBS caused an uproar by eliminating a segment of *The Great American Dream Machine* broadcast October 6, 1971, which dealt with the use of agents provocateurs by the FBI. It also removed from its national schedule *The Relay,* a dance program with nudity, and *The Politics of Woody Allen,* which included satirical caricatures of Henry Kissinger and other figures in the Nixon administration. In a widely quoted and published speech in 1971, Arthur L. Singer, Jr., one of the organizers of the Carnegie Commission on Educational Television, charged that the new system was at odds with its recommendations: "The present system is not pluralistic. It is dominated structurally by the Corporation for Public Broadcasting, the Public Broadcasting Service and the Ford Foundation" (cited in Avery & Pepper, 1979a, p. 30).

Already in PBS's first season, the controversy in 1970 over *The Banks and the Poor* suggested that public television faced political trouble on the horizon. The NET documentary dealt with bank discrimination against the poor and minorities through redlining and ended with a long list of members of Congress with ties to the banking industry, including Senator John Pastore, chairman of the Communications Subcommittee of the Senate Commerce Committee. The program also singled out Michael A. Gammino, Jr., president of a Rhode Island bank and a member of the CPB board. The show received favorable reviews in the *New York Times* and the *Wall Street Journal* but upset official Washington. Nixon White House aide Peter Flanagan sent a clipping about the program with a note to CPB board member Albert Cole: "Herewith another example of NET activity that is clearly inappropriate for a government-sponsored organization" (cited in Witherspoon & Kovitz, 1987, p. 40). The CPB and PBS, designed to insulate public television from such pressure, reacted defensively. Some CPB board members challenged the legality of advocacy programming. Public broadcasting officials questioned its fairness. CPB President John Macy, while defending the system's right to broadcast *Banks and the Poor,* said the program had hurt public television at a delicate moment in its development. The controversy led to new guidelines permitting PBS to review programs on behalf of the stations. In 1971, PBS identified 25 programs as problematic. Nonetheless, PBS's attempts to placate the Nixon administration proved futile.

Nixon believed that public television had a liberal/left agenda hostile to his administration. He was infuriated by the assignment of perceived enemies Sander Vanocur and Robert MacNeil to anchor a political program under the auspices of the National Public Affairs Center for Television (NPACT) in Washington. The White House railed against programmers like Bill Moyers and Elizabeth Drew. In attacking public television, the Nixon administration was also acting in response to resistance from the commercial networks and from the CPB itself to the possibility that PBS—its temporizing notwithstanding—could become too strong and independent a force in national programming. Memoranda acquired through the Freedom of Information Act revealed that Nixon would have liked to dismantle the newly established public broadcasting system. Clay T. Whitehead, head of the Office of Telecommunications Policy in the White House, convinced Nixon that this was impractical but initiated a series of measures to exert control over the content and structure of public television. For example, he worked behind the scenes to discourage the CPB from funding NET and other objectionable sources of programming. An internal White House memorandum declared that, besides a purge of public affairs programming on public TV, "we need eight loyalists to control the present CPB board and fire the current staff who make the grants" (cited in Wicklein, 1986, p. 28). Aufderheide (1991b) wrote that White House staff memos betrayed "a canny understanding of public television's limitations as a public medium" (p. 175). Public participation was limited to viewing programs, especially children's and cultural fare, so that isolating public affairs programming for attack became a viable strategy.

The Nixon administration formally launched its offensive against public television in late 1971 when Clay Whitehead addressed the annual meeting of the NAEB in Miami. Whitehead accused the CPB and PBS of creating a centralized fourth network. He criticized the political orientation of the newly created NPACT and the ability of the Ford Foundation in effect to purchase millions of dollars worth of public affairs programming for the noncommercial TV system. Whitehead called for a reorganization of public television in which national entities such as the CPB, PBS, and NET would be weakened and the power of local stations increased. The Nixon administration expressed special concern about the potential impact of public affairs programming, which grew to about one third of the PBS network schedule. The White House wanted to end public television's capacity to function as a strong national network. The rallying cry of a "return to localism" and decentralization masked an attempt at a political takeover.

The White House sought to cripple public television by exploiting tensions within the system. PBS's first two years were punctuated by disputes over programming involving PBS and NET as national entities and local stations opposed to controversial public affairs programming. Whitehead sought to alter the balance of power in favor of more conservative local stations, thereby rendering a more decentralized system less capable of creating a national platform for public policy debates. In the aftermath of Whitehead's speech, the Nixon White House mounted a surreptitious campaign to destabilize public broadcasting, which included attempts to discredit journalists Sander Vanocur and Robert MacNeil of NPACT. In early 1972, the CPB board voted against funding news, news analysis, and political commentary. One board member even proposed a ban on controversial programming altogether.

The CPB's tactical retreat was of no avail. The assault on public television came to a head later in 1972, when Nixon vetoed a two-year authorization bill for the CPB that had been passed by large margins in both houses of Congress. Future funding was contingent upon the restructuring of public broadcasting. As a result of the veto, CPB President John Macy, Jr., and his chief aides resigned. CPB Chairman Frank Pace, Jr., was replaced by Thomas B. Curtis, a former Republican congressman. Nixon was able to appoint or reappoint 11 of the 15 members of the CPB board. Henry Loomis became its new president. Loomis was a close associate of James Killian, Jr., chairman of the Carnegie Commission on Educational Television, and had a long record of government service in the fields of defense and communications. A former director of the broadcasting service of the Voice of America, Loomis had served for three years as deputy director of the USIA prior to his appointment as president of the CPB. With new leadership in place, the Nixon administration recommended a $45 million authorization for the CPB for 1973.

The Nixon veto had an impact on programming as well as personnel. The new CPB board rescinded a commitment for multiyear funding of the

NPACT, and voted to discontinue funding all public affairs programming except *Black Journal*. Virtually all the programs the Nixon administration found objectionable—with the exception of *Washington Week in Review*—disappeared from the air after exhausting their funding. The upheaval also upset the delicate balance between the CPB and PBS, precipitating a bitter conflict between the two agencies, especially in regard to responsibility for programming. In early 1973, the CPB board voted unanimously to take away from PBS a wide range of responsibilities, including final authority for financing program acquisition and production. The board also declared its intention to assume "pre-broadcast acceptance and post-broadcast review of programs to determine strict adherence to objectivity and balance in all programs or series of programs of a controversial nature" (cited in Witherspoon & Kovitz, 1987, p. 45). The intention was to reduce PBS's role to a narrowly technical one of operating the interconnection. In response, Hartford Gunn, Jr., took steps to broaden PBS's political base by establishing a dual board. A board of governors made up of prominent citizens with influence in the domains of politics and business exercised legal authority; a professional board of station managers represented the stations. PBS thus sought with some success to establish itself as a membership organization independent of the CPB, putting its parent organization on the defensive.

CPB Chairman Thomas Curtis sought to negotiate a truce and restore a working relationship with PBS but resigned when his overtures were thwarted by administration hardliners on the CPB board. The selection of James Killian, Jr., as his successor marked a shift in power to more moderate elements on the CPB board opposed to continued confrontation. Killian and the new PBS chairman, Ralph B. Rogers, negotiated the so-called partnership agreement of 1973 defining the relationship between the CPB and PBS. The preamble of the document asserted the desirability of strengthening the autonomy of local stations, a goal of the Nixon administration. Yet it also affirmed the importance of public affairs programming and the desirability of a long-term financing plan to protect public broadcasting from the political pressure of annual appropriations. The agreement permitted PBS to continue operating the interconnection under the authority of its station-controlled board. A substantial portion of the CPB's discretionary funds would go directly to stations, reducing its authority over funding. As a result, stations would receive nearly one third of the CPB's funds in 1974, compared with about a seventh in 1973. PBS established the Station Program Cooperative, which enabled stations to pool their increased funds and to make their own decisions in regard to national programming. As for the respective roles of the CPB and PBS in funding programs, the agreement was ambiguous. The CPB retained final authority for programs it financed but was required to consult with PBS's programming staff.

The partnership agreement provided the basis for passage of a new two-year $110 million authorization bill for the CPB, which was signed by President Nixon. The Nixon veto had precipitated a major reorganization of public broadcasting, although the CPB's power play at the expense of PBS had not been fully successful. Satisfied with the partnership agreement and increasingly preoccupied by the growing Watergate crisis, White House pressure on public television diminished. Indeed, PBS's live coverage of the Senate Watergate hearings helped restore public affairs programming on PBS and bring new audiences to public television.

However, Rowland (1976) has stressed the debilitating effect of the partnership agreement, which ended the Nixon assault on public television, especially insofar as programming was concerned. In a sense, both the CPB and PBS emerged as weakened entities: the CPB as more of a purely administrative apparatus for channeling tax dollars and PBS as more of a technical service for coordinating program selection and operating the inter-connection. The CPB nonetheless gained significant if indirect leverage shaping national programming. For the first time, it received a formal programming role by initiating programs through the funding of pilots. True, this was to be done in consultation with PBS, which exercised final responsibility for scheduling specific programs. It was also true that stations could make their own programming decisions through the Station Programming Cooperative. Yet Rowland (1976), a former researcher at PBS, stressed how the arrangement enabled the CPB to shape future programming options and exercise a high degree of bureaucratic control over program development:

> That is, aspects of the national programming service now require the kind of complex, inter-institutional bureaucratic negotiation process that can thoroughly sap the vitality, imagination and daring that otherwise might have become the hallmarks of contemporary public television.
>
> The second implication of the [partnership] agreement is that CPB's control of program pilot and development funds ultimately gives it the upper hand in defining the eventual scope, character and content of the national public television service. (p. 131)

The CPB/PBS partnership agreement was a Pyrrhic victory for public television. As Auferderheide (1991b) observed, "The failure of the frontal attack to destroy public television had little to do with public mobilization" (p. 175). Despite the reprieve for public TV resulting from Watergate and the spirit of compromise shaping the partnership agreement, much of the Nixon agenda was realized. The CPB's takeover attempt had been only partially thwarted. A more overtly politicized CPB board continued to exercise greater authority over the development of public television. Programming development for the network at PBS was constrained by pressures from the CPB above and member stations below. Public television's leadership became ever more wary of bold or controversial initiatives. The brief period of innovation in the late 1960s and beginning of the 1970s gave way to a high degree of cautiousness in public affairs programming. Jack Willis (1979), WNET veteran, emphasized the great divide separating programming in the pre- and post-1972 epoch. In a heated exchange between independent producers and CPB officials at the end of the 1970s, Willis (1979) said:

> People from the networks, people coming out of school were attracted to [public television] because there was the promise of a certain kind of freedom, a certain kind of experimentation, a certain kind of risk taking. It ended in the 1970s with the Nixon purge and the fragmentation of the system. Today what we have is a series of stations that with few exceptions are nothing more than minor bureaucracies, who represent only a small part of the public, who have very high overhead, who do not see their job as producing programs, nor fostering talent, nor representing the diversity in our society. (p. 3)

The denouement of the Nixon assault provided important general lessons about the public broadcasting system established in 1967. The failure of the Public Broadcasting Act to address the problem of long-term financing as recommended by the Carnegie Commission clearly made public television vulnerable to political pressure. The CPB had failed abjectly in its mission to provide insulation and ensure independence for the system. Indeed, a second Carnegie Commission on the Future of Public Broadcasting (1979) noted that "many stations have come to lose respect for CPB leadership and to regard the corporation as a government agency" (p. 49).

The Public Broadcasting Financing Act of 1975 appeared, on the surface, to address the need for long-term financing. Significant increases were authorized over a five-year period. In 1978, the CPB received a twentyfold increase in funds from its original allocation less than a decade earlier. CPB funding was based on a matching formula of $1 in federal support for every $2.50 in nonfederal support so as to base congressional appropriations on community support of public broadcasting irrespective of political considerations in Washington, D.C. The CPB passed along half of its funds as unrestricted grants directly to stations, using a formula similar to that in the partnership agreement. The 1975 Act, hailed as an important step forward, afforded public broadcasting breathing space and an opportunity for expansion. However, as Rowland (1976) observed, the legislation contained inherent limitations. Congress undermined the principle of long-term financing by eliminating the combined multiyear authorization and appropriation provision, requiring annual appropriation bills providing funding only two years in advance. Certain funds required separate, annual appropriations. The uncoupling of authorizations and appropriations was one of a number of measures rendering the status of public broadcasting similar to that of other government programs. The CPB had to file an annual report for the president. The bill also mandated that CPB board members and officers be available each year to testify before congressional committees, a requirement characterized by Rowland (1976) as "ominously similar to the oversight proceedings imposed on governmental agencies" (p. 128). The basic flaw of the Public Broadcasting Act of 1967 remained: Allocations for public TV still did not come from a dedicated tax but from general treasury funds that could more easily be subject to political considerations and rescinded. Thus, the Public Broadcasting Financing Act of 1975 did not provide a structure for public television conducive to controversial programming in news and public affairs.

During the Ford and Carter administrations, from 1974 to 1980, the size of the public television system and audience expanded significantly. By 1978, 280 stations had the capability of reaching 80% of American homes. The number of Americans tuning in at least once a month increased to nearly two thirds of American households. According to Lashley (1992), President Ford was "benignly indifferent" (p. 55) to public broadcasting, whereas President Carter was more supportive. The CPB board, with a majority of Carter appointees, voted in 1979 to stop making specific program recommendations by establishing the semiautonomous Program Fund to commission national programming in news, public affairs, and the arts. The fund also instituted an open solicitation process seeking proposals from independent producers and member stations for hour-long documentaries to be shown as PBS specials. According to its charter, the Program Fund protected the program selection process from outside influences, including CPB board members. Its early successes included commissioning an award-winning 10-part documentary series, *Crisis to Crisis,* in which independent producers addressed controversial issues.

Although the Carter years provided a more favorable environment for public TV's development, censorship pressures nonetheless emanated from the White House and Congress. One controversy concerned *Death of a Princess,* scheduled for broadcast in 1980 as part of the *World* series produced by David Fanning at WGBH in Boston. The program dramatized the true story of the execution of a Saudi princess for having had a love affair with a commoner. The Saudi government applied pressure to the U.S. government to prevent the broadcast at a time when the Carter administration was seeking improved ties with oil-producing countries. Acting Secretary of State Warren Christopher forwarded the protest of the Saudi government to Larry Grossman, head of PBS, along with a cover letter implying that the program should be canceled. Mobil Oil, a major underwriter of public television programming, also brought pressure to bear on PBS. Some within PBS supported cancellation, but after wavering, Larry Grossman ordered the program broadcast as planned, with provisions for a rebuttal. Nonetheless, 19 public television stations refused to carry the program, including KUHT/Houston, located in the heart of the oil industry.

Another controversy involving *World* executive producer David Fanning concerned *Blacks Britannica,* a radical analysis of racism and black resistance in England. To temper the program, Fanning reedited the program in consultation with PBS, leading to charges of censorship and a lawsuit by David Koff, one of the documentary's producers. Koff characterized *World*'s board of advisers as a group with ties to the White House and the State Department, led by representatives of the "Charles River Gang" who shuttle between academia in Boston and government service in Washington. The uncut version, eventually aired in Boston, was never carried nationally by PBS. Bogart (1980) described a pattern in which controversial documentaries about international affairs were rejected by the public television system for lack of balance, adding that "pervasive, loose contact between the government and public TV obviates the need for more overt strong-arm tactics by the State Department or other agencies concerned about a program's international repercussions" (p. 21).

World's executive producer was subjected to cross-pressures characteristic of the public television system as a whole, ranging from the "Charles

Street Gang" and angry independent producers to station managers wary of controversial programming, who were prepared to vote to discontinue the *World* series. As Berkman (1980) noted, only a little more than a quarter of public TV stations were licensed to private, nonprofit community organizations, whereas the overwhelming majority were controlled by state commissions, state-supported educational institutions, and local school boards. The Nixon administration's empowerment of state and local public TV systems, affirmed in the CPB-PBS partnership agreement and in the Public Financing Act of 1975, meant that pressures against controversial public affairs programming were exerted from the stations below as well as from the central public TV bureaucracy above.

Besides the conflict within the system over programming and authority, public television faced a growing external challenge. The concept of public broadcasting was advanced in 1967 to distinguish the new federally funded system from the stodgy notion of educational broadcasting and to legitimate the expenditures of tax revenues. Neither those who created the new system in the 1960s nor those who administered it in the 1970s addressed the issues of governance, accountability, and access inherent in the notion of a democratic public system—until they were forced to do so as the result of a revolt by the very constituencies that public television claimed to serve. Challenges to the public television system took myriad forms. The Network Project, a student media research and action collective based at Columbia University, sued CPB and PBS in federal court on the grounds that the CPB's board was unrepresentative and that PBS inhibited diversity and freedom of expression. Although the suit was ultimately unsuccessful, it generated national publicity about grievances against the public television system.

The revolt by media activists in the latter half of the 1970s drew attention to the problem of representation and participation in public broadcasting discussed by Rowland (1976). Local stations' boards, as well as those of CPB and PBS, were drawn from a narrow circle of prominent representatives of business, commercial mass media, and politics. In most cases, local social, economic, and political elites controlled the boards of stations licensed to university trustees, state commissions, or nonprofit community organizations. Public television executives were reluctant to mobilize members of their audiences except for specific supportive tasks such as fund-raising campaigns. The pattern held for national representation as well. Following the Nixon assault, the reorganization of PBS into parallel boards of station managers and prominent citizens limited representation to an elite component of the public. As for the CPB, a study as early as 1971 concluded that the circumscribed membership of its board and conflicts of interest violated the intent of the Public Broadcasting Act of 1967. Looming behind the problem of representation was a larger question of how public TV's leadership envisaged its audience. Rowland (1976) faulted an approach to measuring viewers in mass terms, like commercial broadcasters, and failing to see them as a diverse body of active partners:

> For, in finding themselves perceived as mere aggregates on the one hand, yet in also lacking any sense of unity as local or nationally participating public broadcast audiences on the other, such publics fail to develop a significant sense of responsibility. . . . Scattered as audiences, and ignored as potentially active, creative partners in a public communications endeavor, noncommercial broadcasting publics have been and remain unaware of their rights and potentialities in the formulation of policy for the control and funding of the enterprise. (p. 113)

Following the recommendation of the Carnegie Commission in 1967 to create a national advisory citizens council, the CPB established the Advisory Council of National Organizations (ACNO), an umbrella for 78 national organizations, among them the American Bar Association, the United States Jaycees, the NAACP, and the AFL-CIO. The ACNO was meant to cultivate support for the CPB before the public and Congress. As Lashley (1992) observed, CPB executives sought to control the nature and extent of public participation in public television as much as their counterparts in commercial broadcasting did. However, in 1973, the AFL-CIO, the National Organization of Women, and the NAACP broke with the ACNO over increased imports of foreign productions, low wages, and a poor employment record for women and minorities in public television. Also in 1973, FCC Commissioner Benjamin Hooks and representatives of the National Black Media Coalition testified before Congress that the CPB had violated the civil rights acts. During 1975 oversight hearings, members of Congress pressed the CPB—which itself employed only two minorities on the managerial level— to respond to its critics and to address its problems. At the CPB reauthorization hearings in 1976, an array of groups testified to the CPB's repeated failure to fulfill its mandate for diversity in employment and programming.

"By 1976," according to Lashley (1992), "strident advocates and critics unequivocally concluded that 'public involvement' in public television was a myth" (p. 25). A year later, ACNO, perceived as a tool of the CPB rather than a true public interest group, was dissolved. The CPB was compelled to establish the Task Force on Minorities in Public Broadcasting. Its 1978 report, *A Formula for Change,* documented "what appears to be a vicious cycle designed to exclude minorities from public broadcasting" (p. xiv). Programming by and about minorities was seriously deficient. Not one primary decision maker at the CPB or PBS came from the ranks of minority communities, whose representatives were excluded from decision-making positions throughout the system. Only one minority-controlled public television station existed in the continental United States. Concluding that "the public broadcast system is asleep at the transmitter" (p. xiii), the report called on minority groups to build multiethnic coalitions to forge a place for themselves within public broadcasting.

In the same period, media activists expressed concern about popular access and control of communication satellites, whose tremendous impact on public and commercial broadcasting loomed on the horizon. The United States launched the first domestic communications satellite in 1974. The Public Interest Satellite Association (PISA), formed in 1975 by the Network Project's Andrew Horowitz and Bert Cowlan, led a grassroots movement to forge a public stake in communication satellites independent of government and business exploitation. After the failure in court of the Network Project's challenge to public television, Horowitz and Cowlan decided to move from the legal to the political arena to try to create public space on what promised to be "one of the most dominant and controlling technologies of our time" (McGraw, 1977, preface). The PISA, like the Ford Foundation a decade earlier, called for a public dividend for satellite technology, which was developed with taxpayers' money. However, unlike Fred Friendly and McGeorge Bundy, the PISA and its allies—among them the Community Video Satellite Project, the Consumers Union, the Women's Action Alliance, and a host of other organizations—championed direct public use of satellites. The PISA played a critical role in providing information to public interest and social action groups about the history and potential of communication satellites, in developing proposals for their public use on an experimental basis, and in testifying before the FCC, Congress, and other official bodies. In McGraw (1977), the PISA noted in 1977 that AT&T and other companies were vying for approval of applications for communication satellites: "If action is not taken soon by the public, led by the nonprofit sector, this is only one of many 'windows' that will be closed to us forever" (p. 31). Would public television, and the public itself, be able to take advantage of communication satellite technology?

Organizations with a national focus, like the PISA, the NAACP, and the AFL-CIO, were joined by media reformers, independent producers, and citizens' groups that targeted individual public TV stations for reform on the local level. Stations large and small were pressured by media activists who combined local actions with appeals to federal authorities during the second half of the 1970s. For example, in the late 1970s, KLRU/Austin and its affiliate KLRN/San Antonio were criticized for mismanagement by local media activists, prompting two investigations by the FCC. The first involved a questionable transfer of control of the station licenses. In the second, a 1979 program on KLRU/KLRN in response to station critics, was deemed a violation of the Fairness Doctrine by the FCC. In 1978, the D.C. Media Task Force mounted a challenge to the license of WETA/Washington, D.C., as a tactic to make the PBS affiliate in the nation's capital more responsive to its largely minority local population.

In Boston, the Committee to Make Public Broadcasting Public filed a complaint to the U.S. Commission on Civil Rights in 1980 alleging that the WGBH Educational Foundation violated equal opportunity and affirmative action regulations in programming and in training and employment. The group questioned the propriety of a single entity, WGBH, dominating public broadcasting in the Boston area by virtue of holding licenses for a public radio and two public television stations. WGBH was accused of pursuing corporate funding of national series at the expense of programming fashioned by and for the local community. The multiethnic Boston coalition, embracing independent radio and video producers and local citizens, pointed to the "very narrow stratum of society" represented on the WGBH Board, and called for its diversification (Committee to Make Public Broadcasting Public, 1980, p. 7). A community advisory panel established by KCET/Los Angeles came to a similar conclusion in 1980 after an 11-month study: Both the station board and its programming needed to become more reflective of the city's extremely diverse, multiethnic population. The report recommended more local programming, investigative reporting, documentaries, and live drama so that the station would become "an outlet for the controversial, the unconventional, the unpopular, the voiceless" (Margulies, 1980, p. 14).

In St. Louis, the Media Access Group, a coalition of 44 community and public interest groups, lobbied management of KETC/St. Louis to enlarge its board and increase citizen participation. The head of the coalition, Evonne Ianacone (1980), chastised CPB for failing to create adequate mechanisms for public involvement either at the local or the national level, despite the lofty objectives of the Public Telecommunications Financing Act of 1978: "In large measure, CPB has continued to perpetuate a passive medium for entertainment and information to be programed for people without the participation of the people themselves" (p. 5).

In New York City, the Coalition to Make Public Television Public included black, Puerto Rican, Asian American, feminist, and gay media organizations along with Third World Newsreel and the Association of Independent Video and Filmmakers. It mounted a campaign demanding that WNET (Channel 13), the richest station in the public television system, implement the recommendations of the CPB Task Force on Minorities in Public Broadcasting. Bob Brewin (1982) wrote in the *Soho Weekly News* that WNET ignored New York City and skewed its programming to the suburbs where its contributors lived: "New York City—its people, its problems, and its excitement—has received less and less attention from WNET over the years" (p. 16). Goldstein (1980) observed that because WNET drew more than a quarter of its revenue from state and federal taxes "in effect, the poor are helping to subsidize television for the upper middle class" (p. 33). Corporate underwriters funded about a fourth of WNET's programming for its target audience of upscale viewers.

The New York Coalition focused on the dearth of local programming, and the censorship of four films for the *Independent Focus* series. Activity reached a peak with two events in 1980. Questions about programming and station finances were raised in a presentation before WNET's board of advisors. And Coalition members protested WNET's policies at a black-tie WNET gala at the Metropolitan Opera House. On the picket line, Jack Willis, the former program director at WNET and three-time Emmy award-winner, accused NET of turning its back on the city: "Look at the programs they've dropped: *51st State, The Great American Dream Machine, Realidades, Black Journal*" (cited in Brewin, 1980, p. 8). Among the protesters were Crane Davis, former producer and host of *The 51st State,* and George Stoney, the distinguished documentary filmmaker who had contributed to the discontinued landmark program. Stoney said at the protest that WNET should serve the community in which it is based by providing programming "that helps people to deal with living in that community. What relevance does a schedule like 13's—filled with Shakespeare, BBC imports, opera, ballet . . . —have for diverse cultures of New York?" (cited in Brewin, 1980, p. 8).

One of the oldest and most active of the citizens' groups, the Committee to Save KQED, grew out of a staff strike and censorship charges in 1974-1975 at San Francisco's PBS affiliate. Led by media activist Laurence S. Hall, the committee became involved in a protracted conflict with management over public participation in the affairs in the station, resulting in a license challenge and in the eventual election of insurgents to the KQED board. Critics of public television on the west and east coasts joined forces to coordinate activities as the insurgent forces began to develop a national focus. Hall teamed up with DeeDee Halleck, the driving force behind the New York-based Association of Independent Video and Filmmakers (AIVF), to establish the National Task Force for Public Broadcasting as a clearing house and resource center for the movement to democratize public television. Halleck was instrumental, through the AIVF, in making independent producers a political force within public television, and she became an important catalyst in the community television movement.

Independent producers occupied a special place in the communications field. The heterogeneous community of independent film and video artists was not, by definition, employed by film studios, the commercial networks, or public television stations. Independents prized control over every phase of production—from selection of topics to final editorial control of the finished work. Largely excluded from commercial media, independents saw in public television the potential for what Zimmerman (1982) termed a "participatory public sphere":

> Diversity, then, for these independents, infers a democratization of the public airwaves, a redistribution of media production, access, and distribution in order to represent the heterogeneity of American life, rather than the homogeneous representation offered by the networks. (p. 11)

Zimmerman (1982) and Fox (1994) have outlined the history of the struggle of independents within public television to realize that promise. NET, lacking its own production facilities, had given independent producers an important role in programming on its network. Independents, often with NET support, made a major contribution to local stations as well. In 1961, for example, KQED/San Francisco broadcast *The Rejected,* a ground-breaking documentary about gay men. Frederick Wiseman's cinema vérité documentaries about social problems and public institutions were carried in the early years of PBS. DeeDee Halleck believed that independents, organized as a professional and political force, could make public television a more democratic institution.

Halleck's involvement with media developed somewhat outside the orbit of the new left: She had taught children art and animation and worked at Henry Street Settlement House in Manhattan before raising a family on a farm in upstate New York in the late 1960s. "I was raising goats and chickens and kids in 1968-69," she recalled, "which explains why I was energized instead of burnt out in the 1970s" (personal communication, June 5, 1986). As a filmmaker in contact with the underground cinema movement, which admired her film *Children Make Movies,* she became interested in problems of funding and distribution and in the role of independents in public broadcasting. One of the AIVF's founders and first presidents, Halleck defined its mission in 1979 at a seminar on "Independent Television-Makers and Public Communications Policy" sponsored by the Rockefeller Foundation. She observed that activity over the past two years marked a departure from the tradition in which independent media producers limited their political involvement to documenting the struggles of other groups. Halleck (1979a) noted that now independents were advancing their own agenda: "These demands, however, are not just for access or more grant money. They are addressing the issue of control of the system as a whole" (p. 109). Halleck stressed that the AIVF was engaged in making alliances with a wide range of grassroots organizations and was committed to using their knowledge as media professionals to spearhead the movement for the reform of mass media in general and public television in particular. Noting that the demand for increased media accountability was part of a global movement, Halleck concluded:

> Imaginative regulatory structures can be responsive to humanity's needs— both for justice and for unconstrained creative expression. These discussions are the cultural aspect of the demands for conservation and the just allocation and development of the world's resources. The crucial resource at issue here is not the spectrum, it is the human mind. (p. 114)

The National Task Force on Public Broadcasting, headed by Hall and Halleck, developed a broad critique of the structure and practice of public television and served as a clearing house and resource center for local initiatives. Hall (1979) characterized public television as essentially a closed system dominated by the bureaucracies of the CPB, PBS, and member stations, which all lacked mechanisms for community accountability. These bureaucratic entities operated in an atmosphere in which

> management considers the questioner his enemy. Creative staff persons are dismissed or driven to resignation. Community input is discouraged. . . . Outsiders, such an independent production groups, are competitors. Equal opportunity employment interferes with obtaining the most efficient staff. Sunshine regulations are harassment and anathema. (p. 193)

AIVF emphasized and documented the growing reliance of public television on corporate sponsorship, and the inevitable impact on programming. "We're tired," Halleck testified at a public hearing, "of the repeated and overused network formats tailored to attract corporate sponsors. Public funds underwrite tax-free corporate advertising, and we give them their market with matching funds to boot. Tax-free corporate advertising and developing innovative work don't seem compatible" (AIVF, 1977, p. 3). The task force questioned both the public and noncommercial character of the public broadcasting system.

The National Task Force for Public Broadcasting led the reform movement to make a strategic shift to a federal legislative emphasis in response to the more favorable political climate during the Carter administration. For example, in 1977, groups affiliated with the task force testified at the oversight hearings on public broadcasting and on the proposed rewrite of the Communications Act of 1934 held by the House Subcommittee on Communications. Representatives of the task force met with White House staff, the National Telecommunications Information Agency, and the FCC to draft legislation aimed at creating a more democratic structure for public television. The proposed legislation included provisions for sunshine legislation opening community advisory boards, and the full application of federal race and sex discrimination laws. Special facilities grants would be earmarked to increase the control and operation of stations by minorities and women. The initiative also included provisions guaranteeing levels of support for independent producers, peer review in programming and funding decisions, and wide access to PBS's satellite system for national distribution.

A broad constellation of forces, comparable in scope to the coalition that campaigned for the Wagner-Hatfield Bill in 1934, provided input and support for the proposed legislation. The AFL-CIO Executive Committee and the American Federation of Television and Radio Artists—angered by PBS's reliance on BBC imports, lack of labor-oriented programs and anti-union bias—provided leadership and considerable resources for the campaign. If the AFL-CIO revived the tradition of labor broadcast pioneer Edward Nockels, Everett Parker of the communications office of the United Church of Christ walked in the footsteps of John Harney, the Paulist Father who operated WLWL in the 1920s and 1930s. The Consumers Federation of America, the National Citizens Communication Lobby, the National Black Media Coalition, and the National Organization of Women, among others, joined forces with the labor and religious groups.

As in the 1934 campaign, the coalition of the 1970s mass-mailed manifestos and organized conferences to rally public opinion for what became—with most proposed provisions intact—the Public Telecommunications Financing Act of 1978. The AIVF (1978) rejoiced, "A year ago, we were the 'lunatic fringe'; today we're the Horatio Algers of the media world and in the eyes of policy makers are recognized as an energetic and creative constituency" (p. 1). The Public Telecommunications Financing Act of 1978 took major steps to open up the system to women, minorities, independent producers, and to increase public accountability. The CPB was mandated to distribute program grants directly to independent producers, local stations, and production centers. The legislation recognized the principle of public access to satellite technology, the rallying cry of the PISA. Laurence Hall (n.d.), who together with DeeDee Halleck served as national coordinator of the campaign, later characterized the 1978 Act as a legislative landmark:

> Its amendments to the Communications Act of 1934 are of a different quality—arguably beyond that of any other communications legislation in nearly 50 years since passage of the original act. PUBLIC rights in telecommunications were reinforced; the 1978 bill recognized the rights of citizens to be involved in communications and communications policy. (p. 1)

The decade of the 1970s was tumultuous for the officialdom of public broadcasting. Reeling from the Nixon assault from the right in the early 1970s, public broadcasting was subjected to attacks from a coalition of media reformers on the left later in the decade. The reformers were successful in establishing provisions in the Public Telecommunications Financing Act of 1978 requiring enforcement of equal opportunity employment, the establishment of a task force on women and minorities, and open board meetings. The Program Fund was established in 1979 to diversify funding of programming. However, the coalition forged by independent producers weakened after 1978, making possible the subsequent erosion of the gains of 1978. As Hall (n.d.) observed, "When the promise of money arrived, by and large the independents scattered in its quest" (p. 7). In time, independents felt betrayed by the level of support they received. Halleck (1980) expressed the growing bitterness and radicalism of independent producers seeking to overcome tokenism and to realize the 1978 Act in their dealings with public television officials. Halleck wrote that "the set-up feeds on keeping us angry and frustrated. The madder we get, the more reasonable they sound," adding, "Like the poverty programs of the Sixties, their gestures at reform need to fail" (p. 3). So citizen protests continued in the late 1970s and early 1980s but without the earlier coherence and force, suggesting that the fundamental questions posed by the protests had not been fully resolved:

> Posed in the context of 1960s and 1970s debates about the redistribution of power throughout U.S. society and institutions . . . noncommercial broadcasting found it could not claim to be public and yet avoid scrutiny about its responsibilities to that public. To accept more tax-generated funding . . . was to invite inquiry into its criteria and mechanisms for choosing governing boards and managements, for determining necessary services, and generally providing participation for diverse interests, particularly for those that had historically been underrepresented in U.S. broadcasting. Long accustomed to the benefit of the doubt about such matters—to a presumption of inherent goodwill and progressivism—public broadcasting was not well-prepared for charges of discrimination, elitism, and fiscal irresponsibility. (Rowland, 1986, p. 261)

A reflection of the continuing malaise afflicting public television during the 1970s was the establishment of a second Carnegie Commission on the Future of Public Broadcasting (Carnegie II) in 1977, a decade after the original Carnegie Commission on Educational Television (Carnegie I). A sense of institutional crisis led both public broadcasting officials and critics to pin their hopes on a deus ex machina for renewal. The Carnegie Corporation of New York attributed the creation of the new commission to the failure of public broadcasting to fulfill the mission enunciated in 1967. Joan Ganz Cooney, president of Children's Television Workshop, underscored the importance of the proposed study. Suggesting that *Sesame Street* could not have been launched in the current chaotic state of public broadcasting and bemoaning the growing importance of corporate underwriters, Cooney referred to the new Carnegie Commission as "our last best hope" (cited in Brown, 1977, p. 67).

Carnegie II was chaired by William J. McGill, president of Columbia University, and included former government officials (Walter Heller, John Gardner), CEOs from the business world (Eli N. Evans, Kenneth Mason), public broadcasters (Bill Moyers, Josie Johnson), media reformers (Red Burns, Peggy Charren), and artists (Tomas Rivera). The scope of the issues addressed by the Commission was broad, ranging from the fiscal and structural problems of the current system and CPB/PBS/NPR jurisdictional conflicts to questions of citizen participation and the very mission of public broadcasting. Considerable attention was given to programming-related problems: the need to foster greater creativity, service to minority audiences, and the dilemma of excessive dependency on corporate underwriting and foreign imports. Finally, the Commission sought to address the impact of new communication technologies, especially communication satellites, which were scheduled to link the public broadcasting system by 1979, when the Commission's report was due to be completed.

The authors of Carnegie II's 1979 report, *A Public Trust,* wrote, "We find public broadcasting's financial, organizational and creative structure fundamentally flawed" (p. 11). They recommended the abolition of the CPB and PBS and their replacement by new and more independent entities, the Public Telecommunications Trust and the Program Services Endowment. The report called for substantial increases in funding, with federal appropriations supplemented by a spectrum fee for commercial broadcasters. Steps were proposed to ensure greater public accountability through improved access for minorities, citizen involvement in governance, and increased financial disclosure. Alluding to the chilling effect of the Nixon assault, *A Public Trust* underscored the need for a renewal of hard-hitting public affairs programming:

Without this strong editorial purpose expressed in diverse, even controversial ways, and without an ability to construct a context for understanding the events that occur around us and the meaning of history, public broadcasting will never be taken seriously. (pp. 29-30)

Looking ahead, reaffirming public broadcasting's potential to be an instrument of national renewal, Carnegie II asserted that public broadcasting could become "indispensable during the next decade as our fragmented and troubled nation attempts . . . to heal its wounds, and to discover the strength that emerges in the wake of a shared ordeal" (p. 32).

An exchange at the press conference issuing the Carnegie report was an omen that the divisions within public television would not be easily resolved:

> Its chairman, William J. McGill, was fielding questions with no little wit, when Dee Dee [*sic*] Halleck, president of the 1,000-member Association of Independent Video and Filmmakers, arose. "It's a Band-Aid," she announced. McGill's expression grew darker. "Then you haven't read the report," he snapped. "Read on, Ms. Halleck. Read on." McGill jabbed a finger to indicate his next questioner with enough force to poke an eye out. (Pierce, 1979, p. 39)

Despite the call for a substantial reorganization of public broadcasting, *A Public Trust* exerted little impact on either media reformers or legislators. Laurence Hall and DeeDee Halleck, coordinators of the National Task Force on Public Broadcasting, criticized *A Public Trust* for emphasizing increased funding but failing to address the question of governance. "Trust isn't the answer," Halleck (1979b) wrote, "CONTROL is. Public television will only begin to change when it is in the public's control, through open board elections,and community participation in programming decisions and program making" (p. 4). The recommendations of Carnegie II did not have an impact on public policy comparable to that of its predecessor. When Carnegie II was established, it received the endorsement of President Carter. However, it was not a quasi-governmental commission like Carnegie I with close ties to the White House but a more independent body answerable to the divided house of public broadcasting. Moreover, the political climate had changed since the Johnson administration, despite the fact that a Democratic president was in office. Deregulation was the watchword of communications policy in an environment in which the need for government regulation and for public broadcasting itself was questioned in the light of the abundance of channels afforded by cable television, communication satellites, and other developing technologies. By the end of the 1970s, a growing conservative mood in favor of marketplace solutions resulted in the election of Ronald Reagan as president. Prospects for public television in the 1980s were not promising if Carnegie II represented its last best hope.

The government years of public television, during the 1960s and 1970s, were framed by Carnegie Commission reports aimed at Congress. In that interval, the infrastructure of a public television system came into being supported by federal funds. That system was the target of a political attack mounted by the Nixon administration from the right and of a campaign for democratization from the left. Both attempts to redefine public television faltered and left it resting on a narrow base in a weakened state on the eve of the Reagan administration. Yet, as Hoynes (1994) emphasized, public television remained an important site of struggle for democratization of communication: "Although public television may not have been the direct result of a demand for the democratization of mass media, its early proponents were certainly influenced by the broader movement for the democratization of American institutions" (p. 167). Public TV was at least *partially* independent of the state and the market. Maintaining and expanding its independence would be a long-term struggle. "Rather than focusing solely on the building of new institutions," Hoynes concluded, "those concerned with constructing a more democratic media need to see the 1967 creation of public television as a significant early step in an ongoing process" (p. 167).

CHAPTER 10

The Corporate Years

The election of Ronald Reagan in 1980 marked the return to the White House, less than a decade after the Nixon administration, of a president openly hostile to public television. Whereas the focus of Nixon's opposition was political, Reagan's was more broadly ideological, involving a wholesale attack on the public sphere in the name of privatization. The Reagan administration accelerated the trend toward increased corporate underwriting and influence in public television. Emphasis on market solutions fostered the transition from the government to the corporate era of public television's development. DeeDee Halleck (1981) wrote at the time that "although liberal-dominated government agencies may have found 'alternative' and 'independent' expression necessary to their co-optive system, with the installation of Ronald Reagan and his legions, the very term 'alternative' becomes 'oppositional'" (p. 6).

As part of the Reagan administration's program to streamline government, the CPB's board was reduced from 15 to 10 members, with a limit of 6 to be appointed from the same party as the president. Reagan followed Nixon's lead in appointing highly partisan board members. For example,

Richard Brookhiser, a senior editor at *National Review,* and R. Kenneth Towery, a conservative and former deputy director of the USIA, received appointments to the CPB board. Sonia Landau, the 1981 appointee to the CPB board and head of Women for Reagan-Bush in 1984, joined the board in 1981 and became its chair in 1984. The actions of the CPB board reflected administration policy. Bylaw changes made key CPB officers such as the general counsel, the congressional liaison, and the head of the Program Fund more directly accountable to the board. The Reagan majority on the CPB board also became more directly involved in programming. As Wicklein (1986) noted, Landau ignored the CPB's own guidelines in pressing her views about the kind of programs the Program Fund should support and in sitting in on a Program Fund open solicitation panel. She called for more programming of a historical nature on topics such as the American Revolution and fewer documentaries on current affairs. R. Kenneth Towery recommended that the Program Fund defund *Frontline,* the topical documentary series. Board interference included its vote in 1985 to cancel a trip by CPB President Edward J. Pfister to Moscow, part of a series of trips organized by the CPB International Affairs Department and approved by the State Department, to exchange and sell programs abroad. Landau opposed the trip on the grounds that "an institution that operates on federal money is dealing with the Soviet government" (cited in Wicklein, 1986, p. 31). Pfister resigned in protest, stating that the CPB was not a government agency and that its independence had been compromised.

Reagan, like previous presidents, basked in the nonpartisan glow of *In Performance at the White House.* But the Reagan administration went a step further in using the public broadcasting system for political purposes. In 1982, *Let Poland Be Poland,* a program produced by the USIA, was transmitted to 36 countries and made available to public television over PBS's satellite system. In the program, a group of show business celebrities and Western leaders made statements criticizing the Polish government and the Soviet Union for suppressing the Solidarity movement. Distribution of the program coincided with Reagan's proclamation of "Solidarity Day." A vote in Congress waived a law preventing USIA productions from being shown at home, which was enacted to prevent the agency from becoming a domestic propaganda apparatus. Critics, among them Howard Rosenberg (1982) in the *Los Angeles Times,* denounced the decision to "usurp public TV for propaganda purposes" and to make it "a tool of Administration policy" (p. 1).

The administration employed public TV for a domestic issue in 1983 when Nancy Reagan appeared as the host of *The Chemical People,* a two-part series produced by WQED/Pittsburgh and shown on 300 public television stations. Metropolitan Life was the program's principal underwriter. It was announced that 10,000 community meetings would accompany the broadcasts. The program and a book produced as a spinoff, part of Nancy Reagan's antidrug crusade, emphasized private and voluntary rather than government initiatives to address the problem, in accordance with administration policy. Besides these direct White House initiatives, the conservative Scaife family, Smith Richardson, and John M. Olin foundations funded programs in line with the prevailing ideology and policies of the Reagan administration, featuring individuals like free-market economist Milton Friedman and neo-conservative Ben Wattenberg.

Despite the actions on the CPB board and political uses of PBS, the Reagan attack on public broadcasting was primarily fiscal in nature. Initially, an attempt was made by the newly elected Reagan administration to defund public broadcasting. Its first budget proposal contained no funds for public broadcasting; a subsequent version phased out all funding over five years. In his first year in office, Reagan rocked public broadcasting by getting Congress to rescind $35 million of the $172 million already appropriated for public broadcasting for 1983. As a result, the CPB was forced to cut community service grants to stations by 20%, causing several smaller stations to collapse and threatening the existence of some larger ones. Reagan vetoed subsequent attempts to restore the cut funds and extend long-range funding. Furthermore, the Omnibus Budget Reconciliation Act of 1981 specified how certain funds were to be disbursed. It stipulated, for example, that the Program Fund receive a quarter of the entire allocation for public television. The CPB was also required to allocate program distribution funds directly to licensees instead of through PBS. As a result, public broadcasting officials had less discretion over diminished funds.

Unable to get Congress to eliminate all funding, the Reagan administration embarked on a plan to put public broadcasting on a more commercial footing. Steps were taken in accordance with the emphasis of "Reaganomics" on deregulation, privatization, and market-based remedies. Legislation in 1981, calling for reductions in federal support for public broadcasting, established the Temporary Commission on Alternative Financing for Public Telecommunications to explore new fund-raising stratagems and enterprises. The commission, made up of the chairman of the FCC, members of Congress, and a representative of the Reagan administration from the National Tele-communications and Information Administration (NTIA), included the presidents of PBS and the CPB. An 18-month pilot project for increased corporate underwriting authorized 10 public television stations to circum-vent past restrictions on the identification of corporations and the display of their logos. The messages were limited to two minutes and could not interrupt programs. Key stations in New York, Philadelphia, Chicago, Pittsburgh, Miami, New Orleans, and Louisville participated in the experiment in "lim-ited advertising." Seven of the stations carried standard advertisements identifying products in 60-second, 30-second, and 10-second slots; the other participants limited themselves to "enhanced" underwriting credits.

The Temporary Commission also encouraged stations to explore a host of ancillary revenue-producing enterprises ranging from leasing facilities and providing teletext and teleconferencing services to program sales and joint ventures with cable TV and direct broadcast satellite companies. One of the supporters of the commercial experiments was John Jay Iselin, presi-dent of WNET/New York. The *New York Times* reported in 1982 that the advertising director of Chemical Bank jumped at the opportunity to support Louis Rukeyser's investment program on WNET: "We're delighted that *Wall Street Week* is ours. Its audience suits us to a T" (Dougherty, 1982, p. D15). A full-page advertisement a day later in the December 13, 1982, issue of the *Times* promoted WNET's magazine, *The Dial,* as "the hot book for the hot medium," offering potential advertisers an opportunity to reach the "affluent, educated, discriminating viewers of public television" (p. C24).

Public broadcasters were divided about the new initiatives. If some public television executives were enthusiastic, others were opposed, includ-ing the presidents of PBS and the CPB, who feared that commercialization would ultimately blur public broadcasting's identity and noncommercial character. As with so many controversies in the history of public TV, the outcome was inconclusive. To the chagrin of the Reagan administration, the Temporary Commission on Alternative Financing concluded that although advertising and auxiliary business ventures might provide supplemental revenues they would be insufficient to represent an alternative to continued federal funding. Its report recommended against continuing to expand per-missible limits for advertising on air. Yet a dissenting opinion was registered by the minority in the name of the NTIA, and the majority declined to recommend federal spending levels. The Temporary Commission ended in a stalemate that satisfied none of the contending parties. The Reagan administration's attempt to defund public television and make it self-supporting in the commercial marketplace had been blunted. However, the victory against commercialization was hardly definitive—morally or pragmatically. As Rowland (1986) noted, the Temporary Commission rejected advertising and auxiliary enterprises as a panacea on pragmatic grounds:

> It provided no ringing objection of principle to continuing commercialization of public broadcasting and, indeed, it recommended further steps toward "enhanced underwriting," provisions that the FCC has since adopted . . . and, which as implemented in 1985 and 1986, were resulting in numerous public radio and television stations underwriting messages that struck many observers, including the FCC itself, as commercials. (p. 267)

The question of corporate underwriting had a long history in noncommercial television dating back to the 1950s, when corporations funded programs at KTCA in St. Paul and at NET, which in 1961 issued a formal appeal of support to 2,000 major businesses (Barnouw, 1978). The FCC had limited the way in which such support could be indicated on the air. Commercial announcements or corporate logos were not permitted; credits could not interrupt programming; and underwriters could not support a program directly related to their products. The arrangement was similar to the discrete, indirect form of advertising based on general trade-name publicity, characteristic of the earliest phase of commercial broadcasting in the 1920s. PBS guidelines banned underwriters from exercising editorial control of programs but added that "a program funder's participation in the *generation* of program ideas or proposals shall not be considered an aspect of editorial control" (cited in Zimmerman, 1982, p. 17).

The convergence of Nixon's veto of the CPB appropriations bill in 1972 and the oil crisis of 1972-1975 provided conditions for a quantum leap in the role of corporate underwriting. Major oil companies were subjected to public criticism and government scrutiny in the aftermath of the oil embargo, windfall profits, and revelations of bribery and illegal gifts to high officials. To prop up their image with the public and promote goodwill among customers, the major oil companies became generous and highly visible sponsors of public television programming. For example, Mobil supported *Masterpiece Theater,* Exxon *Theater in America* and *Dance in America,* Arco *In Performance at Wolf Trap,* and Gulf a series of National Geographic specials. By 1981 the oil companies underwrote in full or part over 70% of prime-time

PBS programs in a typical week (Lee & Solomon, 1990). Critics dubbed PBS the Petroleum Broadcasting Network. Barnouw (1978) noted that there were precedents in commercial TV for such support: DuPont's sponsorship of *Cavalcade of America* and Alcoa's of *See It Now* were prompted by public relations problems resulting from federal investigations.

Appeals for corporate underwriting in the past emphasized the high demographics of public television's audience, so it was natural that companies engaged in damage control would now see public television as an effective tool to reach a well-heeled and influential audience. Corporate underwriting could redirect the thrust of programming on public television by determining what type of programs would air. The infusion of oil money came at the very moment when public broadcasters were reeling from the Nixon attack. The retreat from news and public affairs programming was compounded by the preference of the oil companies for noncontroversial high culture as an effective vehicle for corporate public relations. Finely produced classical dance and musical programming and British period theatrical productions fulfilled a need not met by the commercial networks. Yet the growing importance of the cultural programming sponsored by corporations on public television was at odds with the vision contained in Carnegie I of a public system dedicated to public affairs and cultural programming reflecting the diversity of contemporary American society.

The Reagan administration intensified the process of commercialization already under way. The Temporary Commission on Alternative Financing balked at recommending the reduction of federal financing and outright commercials but legitimated the trend toward increased reliance on corporate support and auxiliary enterprises. In 1984, the FCC officially approved "enhanced underwriting," permitting public broadcasters to acknowledge underwriters by using brand names, logos, slogans, and brief institutional messages. The FCC sought to make a distinction between identification, which was permissible, and promotion, which was not. Descriptions of a product line or service were supposed to be neutral. The distinction between underwriting and advertising was becoming increasingly blurred. As reported by Morgan (1986), the new guidelines apparently permitted, for example, a program on Texas history on KERA/Dallas to end with the chairman of the Texas American Bank extolling the virtues of his company. And a tagline after a WNET/New York production indicated that "*Nature* is made possible by public television stations, your gas company and the

American Gas Industry, developing new sources of gas energy and ways to use gas more efficiently for more than 160 million people across America" (p. C26).

Herb Schmertz, Mobil Oil's vice president for public affairs, demonstrated how a corporate underwriter could use public television not only to promote goodwill but as a vehicle to advance a political agenda. Mobil's use of public television was part of a multifaceted media offensive to loosen government controls on the oil industry and, more generally, to counter a supposed antibusiness bias in the media. Schmertz became a vocal critic of print and broadcast journalism. He fought with the networks over their refusal to sell Mobil airtime for public policy statements and then established the Mobil Showcase network, consisting of local network affiliates that sold Mobil time to broadcast opinions in a pseudo-news format, with an anchor behind a desk and a reporter in the field. As for print media, the first Mobil "advertorial," which would become a staple of the Op-Ed page of the *New York Times,* appeared in 1970, a month after the advent of the Op-Ed page itself. Mobil played hardball with newspapers containing critical articles about the company and its executives, leading to an information and advertising boycott of the *Wall Street Journal* and a libel suit against the *Washington Post.*

Schmertz's active involvement in public TV began in 1970 when the president of WGBH/Boston approached Mobil with a proposal that it underwrite for PBS 39 hours of BBC television drama for only $10,000 an hour. The initiative led Mobil to commit over $1 million in 1970-1971 for the establishment of Masterpiece Theater. The amount of funding, the popularity of productions of British serials such as *I, Claudius, Tom Brown's School Days,* and *Upstairs, Downstairs* together with Mobil's extensive promotion of *Masterpiece Theater* placed corporate underwriting of public TV on a new plane. Mobil also sponsored highly acclaimed documentaries like David Attenborough's *Life on Earth* series and Jacob Bronowski's *The Ascent of Man.* Public television became increasingly associated with corporate underwriting and with oil and Mobil support in particular.

Herb Schmertz's involvement in public television seemed to defy PBS guidelines prohibiting underwriters from exercising editorial control. In theory, WGBH/Boston had final say over selections for *Masterpiece Theater.* However, an associate of Schmertz at Mobil asserted that in fact

> Schmertz makes the first judgment and the final judgment. He selects the program or Mobil won't put up the money, and WGBH knows it. He goes to England to look for product and also has others looking for him. (cited in Charlton, 1981, p. 30)

In one instance—*The Way It Was,* a sports show produced by KCET/Los Angeles and sponsored by Mobil—credits indicated that the show was conceived by Schmertz. Mobil underwrote and shaped public affairs programs as well as entertainment. For example, Mobil gave substantial funding in the late 1970s to *In Search of the Real America,* hosted by the neoconservative Ben Wattenberg, a former Mobil consultant. The series aired programs like *There's No Business Like Big Business* to oppose criticism of large corporations. In 1987, Mobil funded and promoted the PBS program, *Hollywood's Favorite Heavy: Businessmen on Prime Time TV,* and was also accused of using its clout to attempt to censor programs like *The Nader Report* and *Death of a Princess.*

Mobil demonstrated how the financial and political vulnerability of public television could be exploited by private corporations for their own ends. Schmertz conceded that

> it would be naive to deny that there is a link between the popular acclaim for *Masterpiece Theater* and our other profitable operations of our business. As a commercial company, we are concerned not only with day-to-day money-making but with the climate of opinion in which we can continue to operate successfully. (cited in Barnouw, 1978, p. 193)

Sponsorship of public television programs was a critical part of a sophisticated and successful media campaign. Dodge (1981) noted that Mobil traded in ideas as well as products, seeking freedom from government restraints and popular criticism to ensure its long-term profitability. He quoted a member of Schmertz's staff, Raymond D'Argenio, suggesting that programs like *Masterpiece Theater* "build enough acceptance to allow us to get tough on substantive issues. Public broadcasting is the keystone" (p. 31).

Mobil was only the most prominent example of a company underwriting programs to advance its interests and provide a business perspective on public television. Despite guidelines to the contrary, many firms and trade associations underwrote program categories in which they had a vested interest and could target an audience of potential customers. For that reason, former FCC Commissioner Nicholas Johnson criticized a program produced by WHA/Madison on consumer electronics, *High Tech Times,* for being sponsored by the Electronics Industry Association. Programs on health and medicine are often funded by pharmaceutical firms such as Eli Lilly, Squibb, and Bristol-Meyers.

The financial industry underwrote a number of prominent business-related programs on PBS: The brokerage firm A. G. Edwards & Sons, Inc. supported the *Nightly Business Report,* and Metropolitan Life underwrote *Adam Smith's Money World. Wall $treet Week With Louis Rukeyser,* attracting the largest audience in the history of financial broadcast journalism since 1970, was "underwritten nationally by Prudential-Bache Securities, The Travelers, and MFS: The First Name in Mutual Funds Since 1924" (*The New Yorker,* February 7, 1994, p. 43). Corporations and corporate-supported think tanks funded public affairs programs on PBS with a conservative orientation such as William F. Buckley's *Firing Line* and *American Interests,* a weekly look at foreign policy sponsored by the American Enterprise Institute. General Electric, a major military contractor and owner of the NBC network, sponsored *The McLaughlin Group,* a weekly panel of rightist and centrist views hosted by an archconservative, with an average audience of 4 million in 1994, its 13th season on the air. GE's exclusive sponsorship of *The McLaughlin Group* since 1984 permitted the weekly program to be carried at no cost by over 300 public television stations and by 4 commercial stations in Washington, D.C., New York, Boston, and Los Angeles.

PBS was less receptive to underwriting from the labor movement than from corporate America. In the mid-1970s, labor unions offered independent producer Elsa Rassbach seed money for *Made in U.S.A,* a series of docudramas based on American labor history for public television. However, PBS objected to the labor movement's funding of a series in which it had an interest, limiting such support to $50,000, a fraction of the $15 million budgeted for the series. Critics accused PBS of a double standard that permitted Wall Street firms to underwrite business programming or the Bechtel Corporation to sponsor Milton Friedman's PBS series, *Free to Choose,* which extolled the virtues of free-market economics. PBS President Lawrence Grossman sought to distinguish between underwriters with a general interest and a specific interest in a program. After mounting criticism, Grossman relented, permitting union contributions up to half the costs for the pilot program of the series. *The Killing Floor,* which portrayed black laborers in the Chicago stockyards, aired in 1984 to critical acclaim on PBS's *American Playhouse* drama series. An initial commitment of $400,000 from

American Playhouse for a second installment, *Lost Eden,* about union organizing at the Lowell textile mills in Massachusetts, was reversed. (James Lowell, chairman of WGBH/Boston, the parent station of *American Playhouse,* was the heir of the textile company.)

Despite favorable reviews for *The Killing Floor,* Elsa Rassbach was unable to get subsequent episodes produced for public television. The media watch group FAIR posed the question "No Place for Labor on PBS?" in the summer 1990 issue of *Extra!* During the controversy over *Made in U.S.A.,* Steelworker President Lynn Williams expressed to PBS reservations about a list of purportedly labor-oriented programs: "Not a single one of the films you list focuses on the workplace. None are about the labor movement, unions or labor history. Not one is about working women. . . . We remain totally unconvinced of public television's responsiveness to our concerns" (FAIR, 1990, p. 13). A study by the City University of New York Committee for Cultural Studies of PBS programs devoted to labor and workers over a two-year period in 1988-1989 found that fewer than 10 hours were specifically devoted to the lives and concerns of workers as workers. Henwood (1990) underscored the contrast between labor and business-oriented programming:

> The *Public Broadcasting Service,* which was launched to offer a voice to the voiceless, offers no regular programming from a consumer rights or labor standpoint. It does, however, offer several regular platforms for business, a constituency not normally thought of as voiceless. (p. 13)

The double standard was similar to the distinction made by Herbert Hoover and the FRC in the 1920s between the "general interest" programming of commercial broadcasters and the "special interest" status of noncommercial broadcasters.

Elsa Rassbach's frustrating experience was characteristic of the experience of independent producers during the Reagan era, when gains achieved in the late 1970s were rolled back. The CPB canceled two series for independent work, *Matters of Life and Death* and *Crisis to Crisis,* and phased out the Independent Documentary Fund. As Fox (1994) noted, PBS favored "independents" tethered to larger entities like WGBH/Boston's *Frontline* documentary series or the CTW. The Program Fund's support of independents declined as an increasing percentage of its funds went to station productions and coproductions such as *Great Performances* and *American*

Playhouse. Increasing reliance on corporate sources further limited resources available for controversial perspectives.

In 1984, the National Coalition of Independent Public Broadcasting Producers lobbied Congress for an autonomous programming service within public broadcasting separate from the CPB Program Fund and exempt from restraints by the CPB and PBS in general. In 1988, Congress established the Independent Television Service as a separate production unit within the CPB and mandated increases in funds for minority producers. ITVS's mission statement contained a commitment to bring to public television "innovative programming that involves creative risks and which addresses the needs of unserved or underserved audiences" as well as "diverse programming of excellence that is insulated from political pressure and marketplace forces" (cited in Fox, 1994, p. 16). Aufderheide (1991b) observed that the legislation represented a tacit admission that public television was not fulfilling its mission. The CPB and the National Coalition of Independent Public Television Producers concluded contentious negotiations over the governance and financial accountability of ITVS in 1991. In a conundrum characteristic of public broadcasting, Fox (1994) wrote that "both ITVS and independents argued that ITVS is ultimately accountable to CPB, yet at the same time autonomous" (p. 17). In 1991, 21 projects from a large pool of proposals received funding. ITVS may represent a victory of limited scope, embroiling independents in competition for limited funds while systemwide issues of diversity and public participation remain unaddressed.

Instead of focusing on funding mechanisms for unrelated independent projects like ITVS, Globalvision offered another approach—an issue-specific magazine format—for independent producers to open up public television to more diverse and participatory forms of public affairs programming. Globalvision, a small independent production unit based in New York City that produced two series, *South Africa Now* (1988-1990) and *Rights & Wrongs* (1993-), demonstrated both the possibilities and problems facing enterprising independents seeking to break new ground in public television.

It started *South Africa Now* to fill a void in television reporting from South Africa caused by media censorship and lack of network attention. The weekly program began with a small multiracial team on a paltry budget in a cramped studio located in a loft in downtown Manhattan. The program used materials and video footage smuggled out of South Africa, supplemented by material from African and European broadcasts. The show's format combined a news report, a background or investigative report, and a cultural segment. Reports ranged from nightlife in the beer halls of the black townships to South Africa's development of a nuclear capability. Although clearly sympathetic to the anti-apartheid movement, the program let all sides speak. In 1989, Senator Paul Simon (D-Ill.), chairman of the African Subcommittee of the Senate Foreign Relations Committee, held a special screening of a program documenting the execution of 20 Namibian prisoners, which was denied by South African authorities. The program also served as a journalism laboratory, analyzing coverage of South Africa in the American press and training black South African exiles to produce and to anchor the program. As executive producer Danny Schechter (1989) wrote, "We aspire to be a model for another type of TV programming that deals with international issues of importance in a popular and accessible manner" (p. 2).

South Africa Now was seen nationwide on 72 public television stations and worldwide via satellite in 82 countries in the Caribbean, Africa, and Japan, in part through CNN's *World Report.* The program received widespread praise from mainstream media, including *Time* magazine and the *New York Times,* and garnered an Emmy and the George Polk Award. *South Africa Now* was financed on a shoestring, with a budget of $20,000 a week for a staff of 22 people and a 52-week season; its annual budget was roughly comparable to what the networks spent on a single hour-long news magazine show. Globalvision had to scramble continuously for funding. Corporate backers, many of whom did business with South Africa, did not support the program: According to one PBS station manager, "It's not perceived as corporate friendly" (cited in Cohn, 1990, p. 34). Seed money was provided by the United Nations for *South Africa Now,* which thereafter subsisted on short-term grants from private foundations and donations from sympathetic show business performers.

South Africa Now appeared on public television without support from the CPB or PBS. The former gave it no funds, the latter did not distribute the program as part of its national program service. That meant the lack of the substantial advantages of the PBS imprimatur in terms of better time slots, promotion, and audience size. Instead, Globalvision had to appeal to individual stations to run the program, which was usually aired during non-prime-time hours. PBS was loath to carry controversial programs like *South Africa Now,* which was attacked as "hard-line Marxist propaganda posing as news" by conservative public broadcasting watchdog David Horowitz's Committee on Media Integrity (cited in Cohn, 1990, p. 33). In late 1990, two major stations, KCET/Los Angeles and WGBH/Boston announced plans to drop the program. KCET's station manager claimed the program was an unbalanced advocacy program with an African National Congress bias. KCET reversed itself after strong protests by blacks in Los Angeles and reinstated the program for several months. WGBH also reversed its decision, resuming broadcast on WGBX, its UHF channel. Schechter (1994) observed that the public pressure that forced the two stations to keep *South Africa Now* on the air was bitterly resented: "It seems like the last thing the public stations want is to hear from the public!" (p. 2).

Globalvision faced similar obstacles in launching and sustaining *Rights & Wrongs,* a weekly human rights news magazine hosted by Charlayne Hunter-Gault that first aired in 1993. The program covered human rights stories around the world, often using lightweight video equipment for unobtrusive reporting. Hoyt (1993) wrote of the program, "Faraway issues and dramas were presented on a human scale, with clarity and a sense of place, thus making them fascinating—and not so far away" (p. 30). The program aired on about 85 public television stations and in 35 foreign countries but, like *South Africa Now,* failed to receive PBS support. Instead, *Rights & Wrongs* was distributed through the alternative American Program Service and carried at irregular hours by fewer than a quarter of public television stations. Ironically, the show had more prime-time viewers in Europe and the former Soviet Union, where it reached 50 million homes via the Super Channel. Globalvision had to lobby individual stations for carriage while desperately raising money to keep *Rights & Wrongs* on the air.

Jennifer Lawson, PBS's executive vice president for national programming and promotion services, repeatedly denied the program support, arguing that human rights issues were already being addressed on other PBS news and public affairs programs such as *Frontline* and that additional programs on the topic should take the form of specials rather than a series. Hoyt (1993) reported that Lawson deemed human rights an "insufficient organizing principle" for a prime-time PBS series, to which the producers of *Rights & Wrongs* countered with references to existing PBS programs: "What *is* a sufficient organizing principle? Cooking? The stock market? Rebuilding a house?" (p. 30). Schechter (1994) wrote of PBS's decision,

> A credible weekly series on human rights, they say, is not "appropriate" at a time when human rights is the universal post-Cold War challenge. It this a political judgment? You bet. Does it reflect an agenda? No question. Are

those issues ever raised and debated within public television in these terms? Never. (p. 3)

Globalvision's *South Africa Now* and *Rights & Wrongs* reflected both the possibility and the difficulty that independent producers faced in mounting a hard-hitting public affairs series on public television. These two programs aired in the United States in spite of the public broadcasting system and by virtue of its existence. Foundation executive Eli N. Evans wrote of public television: "Every success story in the past twenty-five years is a saga of personal courage, often by a remarkable individual with a special vision who succeeded in spite of the politics of the system" (Twentieth Century Fund Task Force, 1993, p. 62).

Frontline, PBS's flagship documentary series, was the more representative public affairs program on public television than *South Africa Now* and *Rights & Wrongs.* The topics and perspectives contained in its documentaries seemed to defy the political limits of public television during the Reagan era. David Fanning, its executive producer, founded the program at WGBH in Boston at a low point in the history of television documentaries. The commercial network news divisions had virtually abandoned single subject long-form documentary series such as NBC's *White Paper* and *CBS Reports,* and public TV was under attack from the Reagan administration. *Frontline* was established "to uphold and enlarge a tradition of broadcast journalism that stretches back to Edward R. Murrow and the birth of the television documentary" (*Frontline,* n.d., p. 2).

Frontline flourished under the direction of Fanning, a native of South Africa with experience at the BBC prior to his tenure as executive producer of the international documentary series *World* at WGBH for five years beginning in 1977. Fanning designed *Frontline* with no single reporter or anchor as host to avoid being formulaic or stylistically homogeneous and to allow a personal voice and perspective. He assembled what he characterized as a repertory company of filmmakers and journalists, mixing unknowns with distinguished names like Roger Wilkins, Bill Moyers, Gary Wills, and Seymour Hersh. Documentaries ranged from investigative pieces on, for example, ties between Nazi war criminal Klaus Barbie and U.S. intelligence agencies or reflective essays such as Ofra Bikel's program on African American responses to the Clarence Thomas/Anita Hill controversy to topical programs on fast-breaking stories like the Gulf War. The format expanded to a miniseries for subjects like the *Crisis in Central America* or *The Decade of Destruction,* which was about the Amazon rain forest.

Many *Frontline* programs provoked controversy, and some raised searching questions about American domestic and foreign policies. Disclaiming any political agenda, Fanning responded to suggestions of a liberal bias by stating, "It is, at heart, a conservative country, and we ask hard questions about social issues that have always been uncomfortable issues and that have in a large part been the territory of the left" (cited in Endrst, 1991, p. B1). *Frontline* nearly cornered the market on documentary television awards, winning a score of Emmys and the DuPont-Columbia, George Polk, Peabody, and Robert F. Kennedy journalism awards. After a decade of offering 26 programs a season, *Frontline* reached between 5 and 7 million viewers on 290 public television stations, the largest audience for public affairs on PBS. The *Cleveland Plain-Dealer* termed *Frontline* "the most consistently important weekly hour on television, the crown jewel and standard-bearer for the mission of public television" (cited in Frontline, n.d., p. 3).

How did *Frontline,* PBS's top public affairs program, succeed against the odds in becoming a venue for serious and often controversial programming on public television? The answer is rooted in the political astuteness of David Fanning, veteran of the *Blacks Brittanicus* and *Death of a Princess* controversies. Fanning realized that *Frontline* reaped advantages from being based at blue-chip public TV station WGBH in Boston—outside both the Washington, D.C., beltway and the world of New York journalism—where executive producers of national programming were able to create small fiefdoms with a great deal of independence. *Frontline*'s base was strengthened by structuring it as a consortium made up of WGBH and major public stations in New York City, Seattle, Miami, and Detroit. A *Frontline* board of directors consisting of representatives from the five stations reviewed budgets and other administrative matters but did not prescreen or otherwise review programming. The setup provided Fanning with insulation from programming interference from his own board, itself a buffer against PBS, which exercised no editorial control over programs. As for funding, *Frontline* avoided the pitfall of corporate underwriting. All money was channeled through the public television system—via the CPB, PBS stations, and the PBS National Program Service. (*Frontline*'s $11 million annual budget for 1991 was slightly less than the combined budget of the annual salary of the three network anchors.) Some documentaries were collaborative efforts made by, for example, the BBC's *Panorama,* Columbia University's Seminars on Media and Society, and the Center for Investigative Reporting in San Francisco. Fanning, carefully creating a mix of serious and popular programs from a variety of political perspectives, generally avoided charges of bias.

From the outset, *Frontline*'s relationship with independent producers was no less complex than its position within the public television system. The CPB originally launched *Frontline* with a $5 million Program Fund grant, the largest such grant to date, in the same period it ceased funding the *Crisis to Crisis* series for documentaries by independents. As executive producer, Fanning wielded absolute control over programs for which *Frontline* held the copyright. He and his staff were involved in production every step of the way, from the original idea to writing and editing, unlike *P.O.V.*, a series more on the fringes of public television, which acquired completed works by independents. The AIVF took the position that *Frontline* would not fulfill the CPB's mandate to fund independents on the basis of peer review as required by the Public Telecommunications Financing Act of 1978. The centralized authority of Fanning was contrasted with the freedom for producers at the pioneering WNET TV Lab under David Loxton. *Frontline* was also criticized for the lack of minorities among its top staff.

Some have gone so far as to question *Frontline*'s status as a venue for independents because Fanning relied on a core group of producers and hence filmmakers were not free from external control to propose and develop their ideas. Many independents vying to get their work on *Frontline* viewed Fanning as another gatekeeper for the limited funds and exposure offered them by public television. Fanning has said, "I am not the Czar of Documentaries" (cited in Unger, 1991, p. 40), but as Boston filmmaker Jay Anania observed, the mandate to support independents has largely been relegated to one series based at WGBH:

> The problem is that these people are the sole dischargers of that mandate: decision-making is centralized in one room. The task is just too large for one show and the machinery wasn't there to do an equitable job. They couldn't answer to all the independents in America. The mandate to help independents has been usurped—it's gone. Now CPB can say it's done its job. (cited in Linfield, 1983, p. 11)

Hoynes (1994) observed that *Frontline* has achieved mythical status as a symbol of purity: "As long as there is a *Frontline* around to provide an example of programming that is not tainted by private interests, the overall integrity of the system cannot be questioned" (p. 109). The objections of the independent community notwithstanding, *Frontline* has provided many of the most thought-provoking documentaries on public television since 1983. The general lesson of *Frontline*'s success was that it depended on a consummate bureaucratic politician successfully negotiating a complex system that normally inhibited controversial public affairs programming. To achieve that success, Fanning had to engage in an exquisite balancing act in which he kept both public broadcasting executives and independent producers at bay.

If *Frontline* was public television's representative public affairs documentary program in the 1980s and 1990s, the *MacNeil/Lehrer NewsHour* emerged as its flagship news broadcast. The five-day-a-week show originated in 1975 as a half-hour report devoted to a single leading story. The talking-heads format featured interviews with officials and experts conducted by coanchors Robert MacNeil in New York and Jim Lehrer in the nation's capital. Two months later, PBS began national distribution. In 1983, the same year *Frontline* went on the air, *MacNeil/Lehrer* expanded to become the first and sole hour-long national news broadcast on public *or* commercial television. Local stations, which were required to foot part of the bill, had offered some resistance to expansion to an hour-long format within the public television system. Creating a 60-minute slot in the early evening posed scheduling problems. It was feared that the show would not be a good magnet for local underwriters. According to Boyer (1987), many stations viewed the program's expansion as "a fanciful flight of arrogance on the part of the journalists themselves as well as their home stations, WNET in New York and WETA in Washington" (p. C26). Some station managers announced their intention to refuse to carry the program. Having created their own production unit in 1982, MacNeil and Lehrer threatened to take the program elsewhere if stations rejected the expanded version.

The first years of the hour-long format were rocky. At a public television convention at Seattle in 1984, one station manager received the majority of "yes" hands when he called for a vote on canceling the show in the presence of MacNeil, who later observed, "We know what real hell is from the public television system" (cited in Boyer, 1987, p. C26). Some, applying commercial news standards, criticized the length, pace, and initial low ratings of the show along with the lack of banter and trendier hairstyles for the anchors. Critics at the other end of the spectrum found the *MacNeil/Lehrer* approach to news too "establishment" and mainstream. A group of public broadcasters from Maryland and New Jersey tried to launch an alternative half-hour newscast called *America Tonight,* but the project did not get off the ground because it failed to get a name anchor necessary to attract underwriting.

Conversely, the *MacNeil/Lehrer NewsHour* attracted substantial corporate support, especially from AT&T, which initially committed $10 million, with an additional $2-$3 million promised for promotion. (The rest of the budget came from the CPB's Program Fund and directly from stations.) From 1980 to 1988, AT&T insisted on being the sole corporate underwriter of *MacNeil/Lehrer* at a time of telecommunication deregulation and new ventures by the company in information transfer at home and abroad. As part of its public relations strategy, AT&T wished to be associated with *MacNeil/Lehrer* the way Mobil was associated with *Masterpiece Theater.* As Wicklein (1986) noted, "AT&T chose to sponsor 'the nation's first hour-long news program' because this would help position it, in the public's mind, for its planned emergence as electronic information provider to the nation" (pp. 32-33). The "public" represented by the *NewsHour*'s audience was upscale and worthy of AT&T's interest, with 40% of viewers holding college degrees and half with an income of $40,000 or more. Besides its on-air credits, AT&T aggressively promoted its link to the *NewsHour* in leading publications and on billboards.

In 1988, MacNeil/Lehrer Productions announced a five-year, $57-million package of support, the largest financial commitment to a single program in the history of public broadcasting. AT&T, which offered $36 million while relinquishing sole corporate sponsorship, was joined by Pepsi-Co and the John D. and Catherine T. MacArthur Foundation. The underwriters required public TV stations and the CPB to increase their share of support to $62 million over the five-year period. Building on the foundation of corporate support, the *NewsHour* gained what the public television system as a whole had failed to achieve: long-term funding. MacNeil/Lehrer Productions also sought ties to the world of commercial communications, entering into a five-year partnership with Gannett, a communication conglomerate with the largest chain of newspapers in the United States. In 1988, MacNeil/Lehrer Productions also began producing programs for commercial and cable television.

The association between Robert MacNeil and Jim Lehrer on public television reached back to their involvement during the early 1970s in the National Public Affairs Center for Television. The center and MacNeil personally were attacked for liberal bias by the Nixon administration. MacNeil and Lehrer first teamed up to anchor public TV's coverage of the Senate

Watergate hearings. The direct antecedent of the *NewsHour* was the *Robert MacNeil Report,* which began broadcasting in 1975. MacNeil, executive editor of the *NewsHour,* was a native of Canada who had worked as a reporter for Reuters and the BBC's *Panorama* series and for NBC-TV before coming to public television.

Despite the accusations of the Nixon administration, MacNeil eschewed adversarial forms of journalism in favor of purportedly dispassionate analysis. In 1985, MacNeil spelled out his journalistic ethos in *The Mass Media and the Public Trust,* title of his inaugural address delivered at the March 13 formal opening of the Gannett Center for Media Studies at Columbia University. The speech consisted largely of an attack on post-Watergate, post-Vietnam advocacy journalism "which regards fairness as effete and unmanly, and thinks telling both sides of the story and letting the public decide the merits is wimpy and even irresponsible" (p. 6). MacNeil criticized the sanctimoniousness and negativism of much of the Fourth Estate, noting that many institutions discredited in the decade from 1965 to 1975, including the presidency, had been rehabilitated in the public mind. He chided those journalists with a ritualistic hostility to authority, including aggressive investigative reporters and documentary filmmakers, "the macho arm of American journalism, the commandos of the Fourth Estate" (p. 7). It is noteworthy that MacNeil's speech was given during the Reagan administration when public television was under attack and when the press, as noted by Hertsgaard (1988), had largely capitulated to the dictates of a popular president.

MacNeil envisaged the *NewsHour* as an alternative to the headlinelike network news reports and to the sensationalism of the news magazines. The program's format—which included a news summary, taped features, and a focus segment with live studio interviews—permitted substantial attention to a limited number of stories. The anchors strove to provide context and analysis—especially in their interviews with newsmakers and experts. "And I think there's an aesthetic on our program," MacNeil stated, "of a quieter, more thoughtful, more civil atmosphere in the questioning" ("The *NewsHour* Format," 1993, p. 1). *New York Times* television critic John Corry (1985) wrote that

> a topic can be beaten to death. In part, this is because Mr. MacNeil and Mr. Lehrer, in their passion to avoid adversarial or advocacy journalism, do not draw conclusions. They only ask questions. . . . Still, the idea of searching

for truth, rather than just handing it down, is something to be recommended for television. (p. C18)

However, a number of critics questioned the neutrality and inclusivity of the perspectives presented on the *NewsHour.* Hoynes and Croteau (1990), who examined the backgrounds of guests interviewed on the program over a six-month period, found a high percentage of present or former government officials, corporate representatives, and authorities from top universities and think tanks. They concluded that 89% represented elite opinion, whereas only 6% represented public interest, labor, or minority organizations. This was true particularly of environment-related stories, in which government and corporate representatives overwhelmed environmentalists. Jim Lehrer was said to dislike interviewing people from peace and public interest groups, whom he considered "moaners" and "whiners." In general, Hoynes and Croteau noted that broadcast time was devoted largely to events and officials centered in Washington, D.C. Women, people of color, consumer rights advocates, and labor representatives were often missing from programs on economic trends:

> Just as the media tend to equate the nation with the federal government, they also equate the "economy" with corporate management and government officials, to the exclusion of the workers and consumers who make up the bulk of the economy. (p. 8)

Frequently, opposing views were limited to those of the two major political parties with common underlying assumptions. Hence, a debate in 1987 on nuclear arms featured two hawks, Republican Defense Secretary Caspar Weinberger and Democratic Senator Sam Nunn. As noted by Kopkind (1986), the fashion in which issues were defined was critical: A program examining fighting in Nicaragua, for example, explored the more narrow question "Can the Contras win?" instead of "Should the Contras win?" The explosion of the space shuttle *Challenger* was treated as a scientific problem without regard for broader questions about the American space program. Hoynes and Croteau (1990) suggested that *NewsHour* coverage of U.S. military involvement in Grenada, Panama, and the Persian Gulf focused on the implementation of American diplomatic and combat objectives, with virtually no opportunity to debate decisions to enter into conflict. Instead, *NewsHour* anchors and correspondents implicitly identified with American policy, using the collective "we" in interviews with present and former U.S. officials about the details of U.S. military interventions. In such instances, the *NewsHour* engaged no less than the commercial networks in what Herman and Chomsky (1988) termed "manufacturing consent."

Kopkind (1986) emphasized that, despite the aura of neutrality and an open marketplace of ideas, the program was structured in a "style guaranteed to narrow the field of vision and rid the discussion of genuine controversy," limiting "the ideological frame in which debate can be conducted" (p. 51). Public policy issues were presented as technical rather than political problems. In the search for civil dialogue, burning issues were de-emotionalized, removed from the public arena, and transposed to the realm of expertise. Carefully juxtaposing the perspectives of Democratic and Republican policy-makers supplemented by established authorities, the *NewsHour* was ranked as "the most balanced network news show" by a conservative political action poll (Lee & Solomon, 1991, p. 87).

The *MacNeil/Lehrer NewsHour* was emblematic of the strengths and weaknesses of news and public affairs programming on public television. Its achievements were considerable. Since its inception in its half-hour format, it provided a unique weekday forum for the discussion of breaking news stories. In 1983, it became the sole hour-long national news broadcast in the United States. Ten years later, the *NewsHour* was carried by approximately 300 public stations with the potential of reaching 96% of American households. By 1993 about 4.6 million viewers watched the program each weeknight and 12.4 million at least once a week—roughly one third of the viewership of NBC and CBS nightly news programs and nearly double that of CNN's. The *NewsHour* was also carried worldwide—in Asia, Europe, Latin America and Africa—via the USIA's WORLDNET satellite. Singled out by a *Times-Mirror*/Gallup poll as the "most believed" news program on American television, the *NewsHour* won more than 30 major journalism awards, among them six Emmys, five Peabodys, and one each from the Television Critics Circle and the Association for Continuing Higher Education. The national audience for the *MacNeil/Lehrer NewsHour* could not have been realized without the CPB/PBS infrastructure resulting from federal legislation in 1967 that marked the transition from educational to public television. Indeed, the report of the original Carnegie Commission on Educational Television (1967), which provided the foundation for the 1967 Act, had called for programs like the *NewsHour* as the hallmark of a new public television system:

> Its programming of the news should grow to encompass both facts and meaning, both information and interpretation. . . . Its programs should call upon the intellectual resources of the nation to give perspective and depth to interpretation of the news, in addition to coverage of news day by day. (p. 95)

In other respects, *MacNeil/Lehrer* was less responsive to the mission for public television articulated by the Carnegie Commission, especially the goal of providing a platform for the "unheard" and for the "expression of American diversity" (pp. 17-18). The Carnegie report had a democratic component, calling for news and public affairs programming in the spirit of town meetings "that demand the engagement of each individual citizen, who must be both informed and moved to act." The report also made reference to "the whole living, meaningful world of civic affairs at something less than the national level" (p. 17). To the contrary, the perspectives offered by the NewsHour emanated from the nation's capital and its political and economic elites, overwhelming the views of civic, labor, and reform organizations. PBS strove to offer in its news and public affairs programming what Englishman Bruce Cumings termed an authoritative synthesis, "an appearance of probity, a semblance of objectivity, a package that would not offend, and a position in the 'middle' of television's fictive consensus" (cited in Hoynes, 1994, p. 112).

The *MacNeil/Lehrer NewsHour* reflected the dynamics of public television's approach to news and public affairs. Its centrist politics and emphasis on expertise in policymaking linked it to the ethos of the private foundations that were instrumental in the origins of public television. Its political cautiousness was reinforced by the structure that linked the CPB board to official Washington, a function of the federalization of public TV during the government years. The program, originating in the 1980s, was dependent on corporate underwriting, a result of the failure of the Public Broadcasting Act of 1967 to establish secure, long-term funding as recommended by the Carnegie Commission on Educational Television. Thus, *MacNeil/Lehrer,* as a promotional tool of AT&T and as business partner of the Gannett Company, was also emblematic of public television's corporate era.

The periodization of public television into foundation, government, and corporate eras is meant to suggest frames of reference, not absolute categories. Foundation, government, and business participation commingle throughout public television's history. During the corporate era, private interests increased their leverage in shaping programming as public television responded to the call for privatization. According to CPB statistics, in the period 1973-1990 total government funding declined from 70% to 47% of public television's income, whereas the percentage of business contributions increased more than threefold. By 1990, corporate support had increased from 4% to 17% of total income, surpassing the percentage of federal money. On the surface, the 17% figure for corporate funding in 1990 did not appear disproportional next to the 22% figure for subscriber income. However, member dollars primarily supported the operations or overhead of local stations and had little direct impact on national or even local programming. CPB community service grants and state government aid also provided general support.

Conversely, corporate funds were targeted almost exclusively for specific programs. By fiscal year 1992, corporate support, the largest single source of funds for national programming, reached $89.5 million, nearly 30% of total funding (Twentieth Century Fund Task Force, 1993).

Programs for PBS's national schedule received funding from a variety of sources, but corporate underwriting was often the critical ingredient in their genesis. Producers were keenly aware of the necessity of pitching—and tailoring—proposals for the consideration of corporate underwriters. Corporate interests rarely engaged in direct censorship; their role in shaping programming content was more indirect and insidious. Private underwriters wielded influence primarily in the proposal stage, determining the kinds of programs that aired on PBS rather than in something as crass and untenable as monitoring the production stage. Because corporate underwriters had the resources for promotion of their largesse outside the public television system, their programs received greater attention and larger audiences. Indeed, PBS itself increasingly viewed promotion as a means of addressing its problems. As Hoynes (1994) observed, public television accepted the ideology of the market along with the underwriting dollars of corporate America:

> The growing sense that more aggressive promotion, rather than increased public participation, is a key to the future of public television indicates that public and network television operate within the same market-oriented paradigm. The contrast between *promotion* and *participation* is emblematic of the difference between a television system that relates to an *audience* and one that relates to a *public*. (p. 134)

By the mid-1990s, the components of the corporate years were coming apart. Public television viewership was declining as public TV's upscale audience turned to cable television for arts and other types of programming that had once been PBS's exclusive province. Mobil Oil and other corporations had originally supported—and exploited—public television in a contentious social environment, the residue of the protests of the 1960s, the war in Vietnam, and Watergate. By the 1990s, these events and an antibusiness climate were receding into the past. In a weaker and more competitive economy characterized by downsizing, many leading corporations cut back on their support of the arts. *Current,* public television's trade publication, reported in 1994 that "corporate underwriting for PBS programs was down 13 percent between fiscal 1992 and 1993, and after a series of stunning underwriter departures, development officers suggest that the past year will show a decline as well" (Behrens, 1994, p. 1). Jensen (1994) reported in the *Wall Street Journal* that the number of blockbuster underwriters providing exclusive funding of specific programs declined from 20 PBS programs in 1991, for a total of $17 million, to only 14 programs by 1993, for a total of $6.3 million. In a desperation measure, PBS officials indicated they were considering further loosening corporate underwriting restrictions.

Once again, the example of the *MacNeil/Lehrer NewsHour* was instructive. It lost AT&T, its long-time major underwriter, and then PepsiCo, replacing them with Archer Daniels Midland and New York Life, which offered a diminished level of corporate support. (Cockburn, 1995c, noted that the sensational charges by a government mole of price fixing at Archer Midland received brief mention on *MacNeil/Lehrer,* which for the period 1993-1998 will receive $6.9 million a year, representing 27% of its funds from the company.) Furthermore, a financial crisis at WNET/New York forced the shutdown of some of its New York studios, including that of the *NewsHour,* requiring it to rent space elsewhere. In 1994, Robert MacNeil announced that he would retire as New York coanchor in a year, and that a streamlined broadcast would originate exclusively from WETA in Washington, D.C., with Jim Lehrer as sole anchor. MacNeil said, "We needed to make some economies if we were going to survive" (cited in Carter, 1994, p. C15). The seriousness of public television's crisis was underscored by the impact on its flagship news program and its New York station.

Prospects were hardly promising that the drop in corporate support would be made up through additional federal funding. The renewed attack on public television in the early 1990s—spearheaded by Laurence Jarvik of the Heritage Foundation and David Horowitz of the journal *COMINT* and disseminated in the press by columnist George Will—made substantial inroads in Congress. This was especially true of Horowitz's accusation of left-wing bias and a call for Congress to monitor programming, a proposal enthusiastically endorsed by Senator Robert Dole, who would move from Senate minority to majority leader in 1994. Dole supported the provision contained in the federal funding bill for fiscal years 1994-1996 that required the CPB board to review the objectivity and balance of programming and submit its findings annually to Congress and the president. Hence, despite the general cautiousness of PBS, critics zeroed in on the relatively few examples of disputatious programming. Complaints about specific programs increased on Capitol Hill. During hearings to reauthorize the CPB for 1997-1999, Senator Ted Stevens of Alaska, a longtime supporter of public broadcasting, warned its top officials that concerns about programming put the future of the entire system at risk: "My point to you is that the confidence of the elected representatives is not with this system. We are going to have just one trip to Hades on the floor with this bill this year" (cited in Bedford, 1994, p. 1). In the Republican-controlled Congress elected in 1994, the political right shifted its agenda for public television from privatization to elimination.

The decline of government and private support represented a crisis but also an opportunity for public television. To be sure, there is reason for public television officials to experience anxiety—if not panic—as the supports of both the federal years and the corporate years crumble. Public television can respond to this challenge by turning inward or outward, either by making more frantic attempts to curry favor with government officials and private underwriters, or by welcoming greater public participation and support. The current crisis might force noncommercial television to reverse its historic failure to reflect and to involve the American public more fully—a failure in theory and practice dating back to the foundation years, Carnegie I, and the Public Broadcasting Act of 1967.

Despite all the constraints, programs such as *PBL, The American Dream Machine,* broadcasts of the Senate Watergate hearings, *Frontline, South Africa Now,* and *P.O.V.* (the showcase for independent productions), among others, demonstrated public TV's capacity to break new ground in news and public affairs programming on American television. A base exists for broadening public support. Hoynes (1994) noted that despite the emphasis on upscale demographics to woo underwriters, public television has the potential to reach a surprisingly large and diverse audience. In 1992, over 80% of households with TVs tuned into public television at least once in a four-week period. Seventeen percent of *Frontline*'s viewers have not completed high school, and nearly 25% have an annual family income under $20,000; a comparable percentage of this population also watches the *MacNeil/Lehrer NewsHour.* Subscriber support for public TV, only 7% of total income in 1973, reached 22% in 1990.

Contemporary models exist for expanded community involvement, created in some cases by veterans of the early period of public television. For example, WYBE-TV was established in 1983 and began broadcasting in 1990 as an alternative to WHYY-TV, Philadelphia's principal public television station (DiGiacomo, 1995). WYBE-TV's 1995 mission statement promised

> to encourage the democratic use of public telecommunications and to serve communities and audiences currently unserved or underserved by existing area television broadcasters. WYBE-TV seeks to use broadcast TV as an active medium for positive social change, the empowerment of communities and individuals, and for innovation in public communications.

Toward that end, the station resolved to represent the diverse public of the Philadelphia region in its governing and advisory bodies as well as in its staffing and programming. Daniel del Solar became one of the station's chief architects and its general manager from 1992 to 1995. In shaping the station, he drew on his experience at Pacifica Radio, NPR, KQED-TV in San Francisco, and the CPB, where he managed a training program for minorities and women. WYBE's signature annual series, *Through the Lens*—a kind of locally produced *P.O.V.*, a festival of work by independents and community representatives—explored themes of urban life and cultural identity. "Tell Me a Story in a Different Voice," the theme of the series in 1995, provided a framework for diverse personal, social, and cultural testimony (Storm, 1995). Demonstrating that localism does not necessarily entail provincialism, WYBE also broadcast World News Television, three consecutive half-hour shows from France, Germany, and Japan. WYBE's signal reaches 19 counties in Pennsylvania, Delaware, and New Jersey.

Besides alternative stations like WYBE, some major public television systems redoubled their commitment to local service. A case in point is KTCA/KTCI, Twin Cities Public Television in Minnesota, whose president is Jack Willis, former producer of *The American Dream Machine* and program director at WNET. Although it produced programming for the national schedule like the science show *Newton's Apple,* Willis (1995a) committed Twin Cities Public Television to "changing the definition of what it means to be a local broadcaster" (p. 2). His orientation harked back to an earlier era of public television and even further back to the first generation of radio broadcasters at the land-grant state universities in the Midwest: "We believe we must go beyond the tube to impact the community, to help improve the quality of life statewide for all Minnesotans" (p. 2). Toward this end, KTCA/KTCI produced a series of documentaries that focused on telling the Minnesota story and became a major venue for local artists. Steps were taken to further diversify the staff, and a community affairs unit gave exposure to people of color and trained inner-city youths to produce their own show *Don't Believe the Hype.* Willis (1995a) explained the rationale for *NewsNight Minnesota,* a four-night-a-week statewide newscast with the goal "to create citizens, not consumers":

> We are fed bits of information that lead to alienation instead of wisdom. Alienation because we are never given the content or analysis of follow-up to see the significance to our daily life. . . . *NewsNight Minnesota* will help right that imbalance by supplying thoughtful, serious analysis of the major events affecting Minnesotans. At the same time, it will be a program reflecting the needs and concerns of ordinary people as seen from the community level. (p. 3)

Willis (1995b) emerged as a leader of efforts to defend public television from representatives of the right in Congress, declaring, "We're in the fight of our lives, but our cause is just and vital to the well-being of America" (p. 2).

Some public television stations have pooled resources to do innovative programs addressing the needs of their local communities. For example, the Nitty Gritty City Group, formed in 1989 and consisting of 15 stations, shared their resources to produce programs like *Street Watch,* a series comparing the way different cities deal with inner-city problems like homelessness, gangs, and drugs. The programs were accompanied by closed-circuit tele-conferences. The prime mover of the Nitty Gritty City Group, which included Twin Cities Public Television, was Robert F. Larson of WTVS/Detroit. The report of the Twentieth Century Fund Task Force on Public Television (1993) commended the example of the Nitty Gritty City Group in its recommendation that all public television stations be refashioned into an "instrument to the service of the community" (p. 171) as part of a broad program of structural change. The report, titled *Quality Time?*, reflected a growing awareness of the depth of public television's crisis among elite policymakers. It recommended that individual station operations rely on local community support, that commercialization be resisted, and that federal funds be limited to national programming.

In the report, Markle Foundation executive Lloyd Morrisett suggested consideration of the wholesale abandonment of federal funding—never as important as state and local government support—as a means of making public television a freer and more vital force. The task force suggested changes in the makeup and role of the CPB to foster more independent and controversial programming. Most important, aware of the need for financial independence, and harking back to the concerns of the 1967 Carnegie Commission, the 1993 report declared, "National funding of public television should come from new nontaxpayer sources of funding such as possible spectrum auctions or spectrum usage fees" (p. 5). As Eli N. Evans commented in the report, "Spectrum space belongs to the American people and just as ranchers must pay a free for grazing their cattle on public lands, so should those broadcasters and other services pay who 'graze' on the public airwaves" (p. 61). This proposal may become the only viable alternative to funding a national public television system.

The ferment within public television, from experimentation with community broadcasting by WYBE in Philadelphia and by the Nitty Gritty City Group to the report of the Twentieth Century Fund Task Force, is a healthy antidote to the crisis facing public television in the mid-1990s. A fundamental reorientation is required to create the sense of collective identity among viewers that would be a prerequisite for mobilizing a new level of support—political and financial—from the public. It would entail a greater degree of diversity in the form and content of programming, transcending establishment visions of public TV as a demonstration project of American pluralism and as a consensus builder, so that a full spectrum of issues and perspectives in contemporary public life could be aired. Such a reorientation would mean reversing the process of privatization and reviving the notion of social ownership. This could only be achieved by building on experiments with new forms of public participation and interaction.

A reconstitution of the broad popular coalition that sought to reform public television in the 1970s, heirs of the campaign for the Wagner-Hatfield Bill in 1934, could energize and democratize public television. The eclipse of the federal and corporate years makes it possible for public television to become a more genuine site of public communication, independent of the state and the corporation. Eli N. Evans was a staff member of the original Carnegie Commission of 1967, which concluded that public television should "see America whole, in all its diversity . . . to help us look at our achievements and difficulties, at our conflicts and agreements, at our problems, and at the far reach of our possibilities" (pp. 92-93). Evans, a participant on both the second Carnegie Commission and the Twentieth Century Fund Task Force, wrote in *Quality Time?* that the principles of 1967 were never put in force, that the structure created by the Public Broadcasting Act of 1967 had failed to fulfill its mission. In 1993, more than a quarter-century later, Evans wrote, "It is time to begin again, to sweep away this history and create a new national entity that will lead the system into a new world" (Twentieth Century Fund, 1993, p. 60).

PART IV

Community Television

CHAPTER 11

Public Access

The Vision of
George Stoney

The stations represented by PBS, the outgrowth of Ford Foundation support and the Public Broadcasting Act of 1967, do not represent the sole form of public television in the United States. Public access programming on cable television emerged as a new form of journalism and of noncommercial television in North America in the late 1960s and early 1970s. At issue during this period was the reservation of cable TV channels for noncommercial use, comparable to the struggle for the reservation of a portion of the AM radio spectrum in the 1930s and of the broadcast television spectrum in the 1950s. These channels, conceived as free of charge and available on a nondiscriminatory basis, were meant to provide programming controlled by the general public and public institutions rather than by the cable operator. The drive for access stations was part of a larger community television movement, which aspired to use TV as a means of communication and empowerment without interference from professional middlemen such as journalists, directors, and producers. Community television embodied the approach to journalism advanced by Mitchell Stephens, one rooted in the verbal news systems of common people, conceived as a social practice basic to the human condition. Stephens (1988) used the term journalism "to refer to more than just the production of printed 'journals'; it is the most succinct term we have for the activity of gathering and disseminating news" (p. 3). The community form of public television—in its origins, theory and practice—differed markedly from the federal form established in 1967.

Public access was rooted in both the high technology of contemporary mass communication and traditional forms of oral communication. The introduction of cable television and portable video technology provided the means to make television a more open medium—more decentralized, more diverse, and more accessible to ordinary citizens. The abundance of cable channels and introduction of portable video cameras made it possible to set aside channels for public use. Community TV represented an attempt to break with mainstream forms of both commercial and public television by permitting broad participation in the most pervasive mass medium of con-temporary American culture. "Access" became the rallying cry for a new conception of television as a means for fostering a more responsive govern-ment and a more democratic culture. Sue Miller Buske (1986) together with other public access pioneers considered the emancipatory potential of com-munity television, with its potential to democratize modern communications, comparable to the introduction of the printing press.

Community television offered a vehicle to realize the aspirations of proponents of the access school of the First Amendment. In the 1960s, Professor Jerome A. Barron led efforts to assert the right of citizens to gain access to the press—print and electronic—to present their views. His cele-brated article, "Access to the Press: A New Concept of the First Amendment," originally appeared in the *Harvard Law Review* in 1967 when community television existed only in embryonic form. Barron thought that in the context of concentration in the communication industry a right of access to mass media was implicit in the First Amendment. He warned that the nation's marketplace of ideas was threatened by the trend toward monopoly in the communication industry. Barron (1972) suggested that the communication modes of the protest movement of the 1960s—the sit-ins, the teach-ins, the underground press—"bear tragic witness to the unwillingness of existing mass communications to present unpopular and controversial ideas" (p. 17). However, the access school made little headway vis-à-vis mainstream media. The U.S. Supreme Court's 1974 decision in *Miami Herald v. Tornillo* "sounded the death knell for this access theory for print media" (Pember, 1987, p. 53). Proponents of access fared little better in the broadcasting field. The Supreme Court and the FCC repeatedly held that citizens without licenses possess no inherent First Amendment right of access to the airwaves. Broadcasters, like newspaper publishers, could refuse to do business with anyone. Thus, the access movement was forced to look beyond broadcast television to realize its aspirations.

The access movement crystallized during a period in which the emancipatory impulse within public broadcasting peaked and faded. By the time of the Nixon appropriations veto in 1972, public television was in disarray. The crisis of public television in the late 1960s and early 1970s and the advent of new communication technologies led a group of media activists to advance a new concept of community television. The Sony Corporation's introduction in 1968 of the "Portapak," the first portable video camera and recorder unit, represented a critical technological breakthrough. Early experimentation in the use of new equipment and in outreach to citizens took place on the margins of public television in the TV laboratories housed at WGBH-TV in Boston, KQED-TV in San Francisco, and WNET-TV in New York. For example, John Godfrey, an engineer at WNET's TV Lab, succeeded in developing half-inch video for broadcast quality.

In 1971, the WGBH Foundation established a regular half-hour program called *Catch 44* that gave any local group the opportunity to air its views free of charge. In the words of its producer, Henry Becton, Jr. (1971-1972), the show was the "one place on the North American continent where a large metropolitan community is given open access to prime time, broadcast television" (p. 23). Groups taking advantage of the live, nightly, half-hour slot ranged from the Socialist Workers' Party to the Neponset Valley Young Republicans, from the South End Tenants' Action Council to the Komitas Armenian Choral Society and the Great Boston Kite Festival.

Participants were encouraged to experiment with half-inch video equipment to preproduce segments of the shows. The WGBH staff noted the ease with which people learned to use the video camera and their excitement at instantaneously viewing the results on a monitor. Becton observed that the experience of creating programs for *Catch 44* "has helped to pull groups together and directed their energies toward more effective action, or in some cases has created ongoing groups to fill some void in the community involved" (p. 23). *Catch 44* was an important precedent in public access television, and similar pilot projects in access programming took place at other public TV stations in the early and mid-1970s. Such programs, how-ever, proved to be a transient, marginal factor in the public television system developed by the CPB and by PBS, which in key respects accepted the network model of broadcasting.

A Canadian experiment, one not rooted in broadcast television, provided a more viable and influential model for community television in North America than *Catch 44*. American filmmaker George Stoney, considered the father of public access in the United States, worked as guest executive director at Challenge for Change of the National Film Board of Canada from 1968 to 1970. He subsequently founded the Alternate Media Center at New York University, which was instrumental in the spread of community televi-sion throughout the United States. Stoney's experiences as a journalist, New Deal official, and educational filmmaker prepared him for the leadership role he played in the community television movement. A native of North Caro-lina, he had worked as a young man as a journalist and as a researcher on Gunnar Myrdal's classic study of American racism, *An American Dilemma.* An associate of Myles Horton and the Highlander Folk School in Tennessee, the great center of southern progressivism, Stoney had strong ties to the labor movement, especially organizers for the textile workers and the CIO.

During the New Deal, he worked as associate regional information director of the Farm Security Administration in the Southeast, an important experience for his subsequent development. In that capacity, he worked to gain acceptance of Farm Security Administration programs by publicizing their impact on the poor via newspaper articles, photographs, radio, and public meetings. Using media to foster dialogue across class and racial lines, Stoney recalled, "I learned the importance of writing and producing material so it could be shown in the community in which it was made" (personal communication, August 24, 1995). After World War II, Stoney became interested in filmmaking through a former college classmate, Nicholas Read, who had worked with John Grierson, founder of the National Film Board of Canada. Stoney subsequently worked in the Southern Educational Film Production Service and made instructional films, among them the 1953 classic *All My Babies,* a training film for midwives featuring a legendary black midwife who directs a natural childbirth in a sharecropper's shack. A common ideal linked all of Stoney's work, from the Farm Security Admini-stration and his instructional films to Challenge for Change and the Alternate Media Center: "Allowing people to speak for themselves" (personal commu-nication, August 24, 1995).

Stoney's career and outlook suited him ideally for Challenge for Change, originally established in 1966 by the National Film Board of Canada to use film in Canada's war on poverty. The program was designed as a collaborative effort between the National Film Board and a consortium of federal agencies and departments, including Agriculture, National Health and Welfare, Indian Affairs and Northern Development, and Labour. As the English section of the National Film Board launched Challenge for Change, the French unit developed its parallel Société Nouvelle. The fundamental idea underlying Challenge for Change was the use of film to foster citizen-government dialogue. Stoney characterized the program as

> a social contract between the people who were in charge of a government program—an agency or social service—and the people who were the recipients of that program or service, designed to find out how they felt about what was being done and what would they would like to see changed. (cited in Bednarczyk, 1986, p. 20)

In a report written for the National Film Board, Boyce Richardson identified the priorities of Challenge for Change:

> the concern for inarticulate or underprivileged groups; the idea of establishing a more adequate method for people to communicate with the authorities; . . . the importance of the process of making the film, as distinct from the end-product of the film itself; the idea of filming with, rather than about people; the concept of the filmmaker as an organizer, activist, stimulator, catalyst, or whatever he might choose to call himself, as distinct from his usual role. (cited in Francis Spiller Associates, 1983, p. 5)

Richardson added that this approach entailed a rejection of the mass media and the mass audience as vehicles of social change: "This represented a turning away from the macro scale of politics (which was seen to be largely fraudulent), and towards consciousness raising among local people working together" (cited in Francis Spiller Associates, 1983, p. 6).

Although Challenge for Change eventually developed a model for community television in the United States and the rest of the world, it needs to be understood in its Canadian context. As noted by Czitrom (1982), by the time Challenge for Change was established, Harold Innis and Marshall McLuhan had established a specifically Canadian tradition of communication theory. Innis, the renowned historian of Canadian social and economic development, had criticized his fellow academicians for failing to study the role of communication in world history. His pioneering work posited a central relationship between mass media and economic development in Canada and in modern society in general. Innis viewed Canada as an embattled island on the margin of Western civilization exploited by a succession of empires—French, British, and American. He saw Canada's cultural identity rooted in an oral tradition undermined by the penetration of mass media linked to international market forces. "My bias," Innis (1971) wrote, "is with the oral tradition, particularly as reflected in Greek civilization, and with the necessity of recapturing something of its spirit" (pp. 190-191). He juxtaposed the personal interaction of oral communication with what he considered the cruelty of mechanized communication. Innis saw oral communication as inherently democratic but mechanical communication as an agent of uniformity and empire. He sought a revival of the oral tradition of classical Greece—central to the democracy and humanism of the Greek city-state—in modern society.

McLuhan at once extended and redirected the thrust of Innis's work. McLuhan (1964) advanced the thesis that electronic media would propel civilization to a higher—rather than a more oppressive—stage of development in the form of a global village. McLuhan accepted Innis's premise about the impact of communication systems on human consciousness and social change, but he reversed Innis's critical approach to modern communication technology and his fear that American advertising and broadcasting threatened Canadian cultural autonomy. Challenge for Change was established two years after the 1964 publication of McLuhan's *Understanding Media: The Extensions of Man,* a work that generated heated debate (Rosenthal, 1968) and helped McLuhan attain worldwide renown as a communication guru. In the same period, Canada was approaching its centennial celebration at Expo, including a major National Film Board presentation coproduced by Colin Law, a key participant in Challenge for Change. Challenge for Change reflected the special historic role of mass communication for a widely dispersed population in the large Canadian geographical expanse.

Challenge for Change also drew on the tradition of the social documentary pioneered by Robert Flaherty and John Grierson. Flaherty's 1922 masterpiece, *Nanook of the North,* was revolutionary in its portrayal of social reality without a studio, a story, or professional actors and with the participation of the subject himself in production decisions. Grierson, a British filmmaker influenced by the work of Pudovkin and Eisenstein, stressed the social rather than the aesthetic nature of documentary film. Grierson advocated examining the drama of everyday life to heighten people's awareness of their own predicament. In the 1930s, Grierson was invited by the Canadian government to examine the communication needs of the vast nation and its uneven population distribution. The National Film Board was established on the basis of his recommendations, and he became the first government film commissioner. Grierson said the National Film Board "will be the eyes of Canada. It will, through a national use of cinema, see Canada and see its whole . . . its people and its purpose" (cited in National Film Board of Canada, n.d., p. 2). Shortly before his death, Grierson affirmed that the approach of Challenge for Change was rooted in the cinema verité tradition reaching back to the portrayal of England's *Housing Problems* three decades earlier in 1935: "With that film there was talk of 'breaking the goldfish bowl' and of making films 'not about people but with them'" (cited in Gillespie, 1975, p. 43).

Challenge for Change extended the Flaherty/Grierson tradition by involving the subjects of its films more systematically in their production. Problems with the program's 1966 maiden film *The Things I Cannot Change* accelerated this process. The film was commissioned by the Privy Council to help the Canadian people understand the human dimension of poverty. The filmmaker lived for three weeks with a poor Montreal family with 10 children. Her film, sympathetically portraying the hardships of the family's everyday life, was broadcast on Canadian television. The broadcast had a devastating impact on the family: The children were ridiculed at school, and the parents felt humiliated in their neighborhood. The family had received neither an opportunity to see the film prior to its release nor advance warning of its broadcast date (Watson, 1970).

The discrepancy between the high intentions of the film and its impact on the family it portrayed led to soul searching at the National Film Board and a quest for a higher level of communication and collaboration between filmmaker and subject. That same year Fernand Danserau established a different procedure for his film on the impact of social change and government policies in the town of St. Jacques in Quebec province. Danserau was a Montreal filmmaker working with Société Nouvelle, the French branch of Challenge for Change. He periodically invited participants to screen rushes and permitted them to censor anything they found objectionable. This procedure minimized the danger that subjects would be surprised or offended by the outcome. Moreover, the process had a considerable impact on both the film and its subjects, who gained a heightened awareness of their own situation through their involvement in its portrayal on film (Gillespie, 1975).

The Fogo Island project of Challenge for Change forged a new relationship between filmmaker and subject. The locale was chosen because its problems were characteristic of many small, isolated, rural communities. Fogo Island, located 10 miles off Canada's northeast coast, faced staggering problems. More than half of the approximately 5,000 people there lived on welfare because of the decline of the fishing industry. Despite a 300-year history, the government was considering relocating the entire population. Fogo itself was divided into 10 isolated and antagonistic settlements, without either active unions or cooperatives. This was to be the site for Challenge for Change's first major experiment with the use of film as a social catalyst.

Colin Low, a distinguished senior producer at the National Film Board, headed the film crew that went to Fogo Island in 1967. Intending to produce traditional social documentaries, the team found that the islanders were more responsive when short films were made based on a single interview or event. Instead of being edited and interwoven with other footage and narrative, these shorts, 28 in all, were left largely intact. Regional Projects Director Dorothy Todd Hénaut (1971-1972) referred to them as "linear chunks of reality" (p. 4). In the six hours of footage, subjects such as *Fishermen's Meeting, The Songs of Chris Cobb, The Children of Fogo Island,* and *Billy Crane Moves Away* offered a panorama of the people and problems of Fogo.

Colin Low relinquished the artistic prerogatives of the documentary maker in offering film as a tool for the people of Fogo Island. He worked in tandem with Newfoundland's Memorial University, community organizers, and the inhabitants of Fogo. Members of the island community helped select topics and sites, were filmed only with their permission, and were the first to view and to edit the rushes. Their consent was also required before a film could be shown outside a village or outside the island itself. The process by which the films were made and screened was central to their impact on the lives of the islanders. Group viewings organized throughout the island fostered dialogue for an isolated, divided population. The films and discussions heightened the inhabitants' awareness that they shared common problems and strengthened their collective identity as Fogo Islanders. As a result, the planned relocation of the community of Fogo Island was abandoned.

The Fogo films had a direct impact on the island's negotiations with government officials on the mainland. For example, past efforts to convince authorities to establish a cooperative fish processing plant had failed. Now the Fogo films were sent to the provincial government to make the case for the cooperative. Through film, fishermen were talking to cabinet ministers. This led to meetings with the Minister of Fisheries and provincial cabinet members and to the creation of the plant with official support. The film project resulted in other collaborative ventures on the island such as a boat-building collective and a consolidated high school.

The Specialists at Memorial Discuss the Fogo Films (1969) documented the impact of the films on academics and government officials. Thus, film served the Fogo Islanders as a catalyst for both internal communication and external communication with outside authorities. A number of media historians and activists have traced a new concept of public access to mass media and the seeds of community television to the Fogo project. Watson (1970) wrote,

> Perhaps the first [National Film Board] films to really involve a community in practical decisions about the contents and style of films about their lives were the Fogo Island films that Colin Low showed us during the Expo summer—the first that elaborated clearly the principal of taking equipment and film and technical skill to a people whose problem was at least in part communication with each other and communication with those that governed them. (p. 16)

The passive subjects of the film *The Things I Cannot Change* were transformed into active participants on Fogo Island. At the root of the Fogo experiment was the process of filming and playback. Anthony Marcus, a Canadian psychiatrist, indicated the psychosocial implications:

> The simple device of reflecting an image magnifies the individual's self-image. The emotional dilemma induced by the gap between the image on the screen and the subjective feeling of the viewers, produces a crisis in which the person attempts to bring the two aspects into harmony, thus increasing his self-knowledge. (cited in Gwyn, 1975, p. 409)

The Fogo experience represented a significant departure for the documentary filmmaker, who traditionally maintained absolute control over film production. The classic documentary in the Flaherty-Grierson tradition reflected a filmmaker's personal vision of social reality. Colin Low and his team gave up the traditional prerogatives of documentary filmmakers so as to function, in the language of Challenge for Change, as communication catalysts and social animators. They took the Grierson tradition one step further: Documentary films would be made *by* the people depicted instead of merely *with* them.

The fortuitous introduction of portable videotape recorders and expansion of cable television in Canada in the early years of Challenge for Change permitted the Fogo experiment to be applied on a new scale. Film, an expensive and cumbersome medium, had serious drawbacks. Professionally trained directors and camera and sound personnel were needed to operate bulky and costly equipment. Lab expenses for developing and synchronizing 16mm film were high, and the time lapse between filming and screening slowed down the communication process. Although the Fogo Island model represented an important breakthrough in public communication, the expense of the film process precluded its broad application. The staff of Challenge for Change began to experiment with automated slide and sound systems.

Advances in videotape technology gave Challenge for Change a viable alternative to film. The portable video camera and recorder unit, or Portapak, introduced by Sony in 1968, weighed less than 20 pounds and had distinct advantages over the documentary filmmaker's standard 16mm movie camera. One person could carry the Portapak without a sound person and heavy equipment trailing behind. As a result, the camera became a less obtrusive and intimidating factor in the work of Challenge for Change. Anyone could be trained to operate the Portapak; a professional crew was not needed. No lab work was required to develop videotape or to synchronize picture and sound. Improved models of the Portapak introduced in the 1970s permitted in-camera playback, so videotape could be viewed instantaneously. By erasing and rerecording material, mistakes would be remedied, initiating the editing process inside the camera. Thus, the Portapak made videotape a more accessible and flexible medium than film for community organizing.

At Challenge for Change, Dorothy Todd Hénaut and Bonnie Klein, a former student of George Stoney's at Stanford University, recognized the potential of portable video technology. George Stoney (1971-1972) wrote of them,

> The two women who persuaded us to launch our first community videotape projects were no ordinary filmmakers. Dorothy Hénaut and Bonnie Klein brought to the task a philosophy about democratic participation that shaped

every aspect of their work, from the way to run training classes to the way editorial decisions are made. It is largely their concept, their way of working, which guides social animators, teachers and community leaders generally who are now applying *Challenge for Change* techniques across Canada. (p. 10)

Hénaut and Klein initiated the early videotape projects despite considerable skepticism within the National Film Board. The use of videotape posed a number of problems. It was incompatible with the 16mm projectors that the National Film Board had labored to make standard equipment at schools and village halls throughout Canada. Nor was television considered an alternate means of distribution because the technical means did not yet exist to transfer half-inch videotape to two-inch broadcast tape. Also, some filmmakers opposed the use of half-inch videotape because of its lack of high resolution, which confined it to a small screen. Others, Watson (1970) noted, felt threatened by the loss of control over the final product: "Ceding authority over the edit is revolutionary; it requires a curious submission of the director's ego" (p. 19).

Despite reservations within the National Film Board, a number of pilot projects demonstrated how the Portapak—by virtue of its inexpensiveness, simplicity of operation, and potential for immediate playback to small groups—could serve the objectives of Challenge for Change. The portable video recorder permitted the Fogo concept to be applied in a series of projects in different regions of Canada.

One such project, cosponsored by the School of Social Welfare at the University of Calgary and Challenge for Change, took place in 1969-1970 in the Drumheller Valley, a depressed mining area in Alberta. The village of Rosedale lacked local government, water, sewers, and gas. A community organizer, Anton Karch, trained the Rosedale Citizens' Action Committee to tape interviews with residents about local problems. Those interviewed were given the opportunity to edit their comments. Committee members then compiled the interviews into a one-hour videotape, which was viewed at a community center by more than half of Rosedale's residents. At the end of the meeting, subcommittees were established to address specific problems, which led to a series of local initiatives and productive negotiations with government and industry. The tangible results of this activity included the installation of gas and water lines and the establishment of a new factory. The Portapak was used by Challenge for Change as a tool for communication and organization in a variety of isolated, neglected, problem-ridden communities in the Canadian countryside (Hénaut, 1971-1972).

The Portapak was employed in urban settings as well. In 1968, Hénaut and Klein had organized the first video production assistance team of Challenge for Change in Montreal. Klein knew of a militant organization of poor people in a Montreal slum, the Saint Jacques Citizens' Committee, which had founded a citizen-operated medical clinic where her husband worked as a doctor. Committee members, trained to use the Portapak, took to the streets to interview residents and analyzed their taped discussions and actions at public meetings. In 1970, the Parallel Institute in Montreal, assisted by Challenge for Change, began using video equipment as a means of mobilizing grassroots organizations for confrontations with authorities. The Parallel Institute provided technical and informational services to the Greater Montreal Anti-Poverty Coordinating Committee, an umbrella organization for 16 welfare rights groups. For example, a neighborhood video wagon was outfitted to organize the poor in Pointe St. Charles, Quebec.

The wagon was used to interview people in the streets and to show them tapes of meetings of welfare rights groups. Video permitted their views to enter the public domain and to find political expression in local organizations. Furthermore, the Portapak became a factor in dealings with officials. Monitors were used to show people outside what was happening at a meeting inside. The video recorder was deliberately used to intimidate government representatives and establish a record of promises made. Another member of the Parallel Institute team stressed how

> video helps equalize the bargaining power of poor people when they confront welfare and government officials and, for once, the people have a means of controlling records of their own experiences. Tapes are also shown to people who are not yet involved in citizens' groups. . . . They do get excited when they see other people taking on the welfare office, and discover that they don't have to be afraid of the police coming in and beating them up. (cited in Prinn, 1971-1972, pp. 14-15)

The growth in Canada of cable television—with its multiplicity of channels—offered new possibilities for the communication visionaries at Challenge for Change. Cable television developed earlier in Canada than in the United States. 1968, the year Sony's Portapak was introduced, was also a watershed in the development of cable television in Canada. Penetration of cable TV in Canadian households approached the 25% mark. This was a period of jurisdictional dispute in Canada as policymakers sought to define a medium that was a hybrid of common carrier and broadcaster. The government established a new body, the Canadian Radio-Television Commission (CRTC), to regulate cable and establish an integrated national broadcasting policy (Caron & Taylor, 1985). The synergy of video and cable meant that the concept of community film and video could be extended to television. Following their first experiment with video in 1968, Hénaut and Klein had expressed the hope that community groups using video would get access to television outlets.

An early experiment in community television supported by Challenge for Change took place two years later in Thunder Bay, Ontario. In 1970, Town Talk, a civic organization, developed a plan to run one cable channel on behalf of the local community at a time when the local cable license was up for renewal. Challenge for Change supplied equipment and trained members of Town Talk in the use of film and video. At Thunder Bay, the concept of a charter board became the foundation of citizen participation in community television. Jim Hyder (1971-1972), in a short manifesto on community TV based on the Thunder Bay experience, stressed that free access and control by citizens were prerequisites for community television to address the local population's lack of participation in the decision-making process.

As a result of the Town Talk proposal and technical assistance from Challenge for Change, Thunder Bay community programs received four hours of time on the cable system for locally produced programming. An important precedent was set by cablecasting inexpensive half-inch videotape. Locally produced videotapes were supplemented by live studio segments and phone-ins. The programs won a substantial following. Nonetheless, the experiment lasted less than a year. Local authorities opposed the presence of video crews at certain meetings. Government officials in Ottawa charged that the project was controlled by radicals. The local cable company, backed by the national trade association of the Canadian cable industry, resisted giving up control of programming and finances to a citizens organization. The company asserted greater control by requiring submission of programs three weeks in advance and an end to phone-ins. According to Stoney (1971-1972), "the [CRTC], despite considerable public pressure from all over Canada to set a different precedent for community cable use, sided with the industry" (p. 10).

Despite its brief history, the Thunder Bay project was a milestone in the application of the Fogo process and of videotape to a new form of community television. Other initiatives supported by Challenge for Change in public access programming on cable television drew on the abortive Thunder Bay model. One of the most successful took place in Normandin, located in the Lake St. John area of Quebec. The community television project there profited from a more receptive cable operator and local power structure; the school system assumed considerable responsibility for the access channel. Ten percent of the population of an area comprising three villages became actively involved in the community television system. An important feature of the Normandin operation was group viewing of community television at assembly points instead of in the isolation of individual homes. The coordinator from Challenge for Change stressed that "community television is a process—not a product—and it works better with a group" (cited in Gillespie, 1975, p. 48).

The experiments at Thunder Bay and Normandin helped set the agenda for discussion of the future of public access at public hearings in 1971 of the CRTC. The result of these deliberations, the CRTC's Policy Statement on Cable Television of July 16, 1971, required that access channels be an integral part of the development of cable television. The CRTC recognized two principal forms of citizen participation in programming. The first, known as local origination, involved coverage of local activities by coordinators trained and supervised by the cable company staff. The second consisted of a mechanism for direct access by a large number of individuals and groups.

Hence, after 1971 the concept of community television became institutionalized in Canada, the culmination of a succession of pilot projects of Challenge for Change, from Fogo Island and the slums of Montreal to Thunder Bay and Normandin. Nonetheless, some observers questioned whether community television represented a viable extension of the experiments in citizen use of film and video pioneered by Challenge for Change. Thunder Bay revealed how opposition of the cable industry could cripple community television. Where public access did take hold, the very nature of cable television posed problems for community organizers. Challenge for Change had been developed to serve the needs of poor people, whereas the cost of subscribing to cable TV made it less of a universal medium for the entire social spectrum than over-the-air television. Gwyn (1975) suggested that television itself could undermine the interactive communication that Challenge for Change sought to foster:

> Sitting alone in a living room watching a small screen can isolate viewers more than it brings them together. As several groups have discovered, tapes and films made by a community are often more effective when shown in church basements or village halls. (p. 419)

It remained to be seen if methods such as group viewing in Normandin could overcome the private character of television viewership.

Gwyn noted another shift in emphasis from public to private expression in some enterprises supported by Challenge for Change, especially in urban centers. For example, at Vidéographe, a Montreal media resource center, and at Vancouver Metro Media, a new generation of video artists worked side by side with video activists. It was inevitable that interest would grow in the formal qualities of the new communication hardware. This led to increased emphasis on production values for video—on product rather than process. Gwyn (1975) observed, "At the same time as they strengthen personal identity, film and videotape also strengthen ego, and the goal of community development can be lost in a rush to make personal rather than collective statements" (p. 417).

The original purpose of Challenge for Change was to first use film and then video and cable television to foster a government-citizen dialogue to address social ills. Enhanced communication, it was thought, would improve the mechanisms by which the Canadian government provided social programs and services. Some went beyond this pragmatic approach to embrace a far-reaching vision of how new channels of communication could transform contemporary life. Impressed by the magic of video and cable technology and influenced by the writings of Marshall McLuhan, they viewed new communication technologies as tools for reintegrating a fragmented society, for resolving the social and spiritual ills of the modern age. Boyce Richardson, in a preliminary evaluation of Challenge for Change, argued that such expectations could work against the interests of the very people the program was designed to help:

> The premise of all this work was that the underlying problem of our society was a lack of communications. It is one of the favorite myths of the establishment. Nothing is wrong with our socio-political structures, it is just that

there is a lack of communication between groups. (cited in Francis Spiller
Associates, 1983, p. 6)

Many of the community organizers associated with Challenge for Change
took issue with the belief that community television represented a substitute
for traditional forms of popular mobilization and that new electronic media
could strengthen the bonds of modern society without fundamental changes
in social structure. Bonnie Klein cautioned, "Video equipment does not
create dynamism where none is latent; it does not create action or ideas; these
depend upon the people who use it" (cited in Gillespie, 1975, p. 151). Some
activists—for example, the Parallel Institute, organizing the Montreal poor
with its television wagon—used the Portapak as a tool of social protest and
confrontation, as a means of challenging rather than strengthening the
welfare state. In many areas in Canada, militant groups demanded the right
of direct access to the community cable channel and, in some instances,
exclusive responsibility for its operation.

Various tendencies and tensions existed within Challenge for Change,
which would also surface in the public access movement in the United States.
The history of Challenge for Change, from *The Things I Cannot Change* to
the film-versus-video debate and the emergence of video art, suggested that
the conflict between individual and collective forms of expression had not
been resolved. Incompatible agendas—liberal, McLuhanesque, and leftist—
coexisted uneasily in a program with government funding that would end in
1975. The experiment in community television as a public forum in Canada
was far from secure. Hénaut (1971-1972) wrote early in 1972, "The questions
about who controls the programming, who will guarantee that all segments
of the community will have access to the media and how they will be financed
are yet to be resolved" (p. 7).

The same could be said about public access in the United States, where
George Stoney assumed a leadership role in the movement for community
television. The social ills that Challenge for Change sought to address were
hardly limited to Canada. Gillespie (1975), an early advocate and historian
of community television, observed that Fogo Island could be considered a
microcosm of pockets of isolation and privation throughout the North American continent: "This condition has its counterparts, certainly, in Appalachia,
in the innumerable ghettos, in the sharecropping South, and in the migratory
worker camps" (p. 25). Could the innovations of Challenge for Change in

Canada be applied in the context of political traditions and communication systems unique to the United States?

The Alternate Media Center and Guerrilla Television

George Stoney returned to the United States in 1970 to become chair of the undergraduate Department of Film and Television in the School of the Arts at New York University. In 1971, he founded the Alternate Media Center at NYU with the goal of ensuring a public stake in new communication technologies. Stoney established the Alternate Media Center together with Red Burns, a Canadian who had worked as a secretary at the National Film Board before marrying a successful communication entrepreneur. If Stoney excelled as an organizer of public communication, Burns was adept at dealing with cable and foundation executives. She initiated contact with the John and Mary R. Markle Foundation, which provided a three-year grant of $250,000 in seed money. A brochure later published by the Alternate Media Center (n.d.) stated its commitment

> to inform and educate people who are becoming increasingly confused by the integration of new technologies into their lives; to provide a basis upon which people can control these vital information resources; . . . and to increase communication among diverse groups of people. (p. 2)

The Center's original project was to promote use of cable technology by local, nonprofessional communicators, namely, the general public. For a six-year period, the Alternate Media Center remained the focal point of the community television movement for the disparate constituencies interested in public access in the United States. Its office in New York City—above a movie theater on Bleeker Street in Greenwich Village—became an assembly point for public access pioneers, members of experimental video collectives, educators, city planners, and federal policymakers from around the nation. Here experiences and tapes were shared and strategies developed for a public foothold in the development of cable TV.

The Alternate Media Center took major initiatives on various fronts. Demonstration tapes were circulated nationally. Center interns subsequently helped establish access centers throughout the nation. Besides providing production and technical support, the Alternate Media Center entered the policymaking arena. Locally, as early as 1971, the Center became involved in the struggle over the cable franchising process and the introduction of community channels in New York City—which many considered a bell-wether for the future of public access cable television in the United States. On the national level, Stoney and Burns collaborated with Nicholas Johnson, the maverick FCC commissioner, in the campaign to create federal require-ments for access channels. In leading the movement for public access, the Alternate Media Center could not replicate Challenge for Change, which had developed in the context of cultural and communication conditions unique to Canada. The absence of an Anglo-Canadian tradition of state-operated public communication systems in the United States meant that its community television movement would be more dependent on two nongovernmental sources of support. First, community television, like public television, de-pended on Markle and other private foundations to fund experimental pro-grams and public policy initiatives. Second, the ultimate fate of community television hinged to a greater degree on its relationship with the cable television industry. Hence, Burns became codirector of the Alternate Media Center because of her background in the entertainment industry and acquain-tance with key executives of multiple systems operators, which were increas-ingly dominating the growth of cable television.

A variety of factors led to cable industry support of community televi-sion in the early 1970s. The historical overview of the growth of cable TV in the United States by Sparkes (1985) reveals "an evolution involving many different players and constantly shifting alliances" (p. 16). In 1948, coaxial cable began to be used to transmit broadcast signals in small communities lacking a television station in the area or suffering from poor reception due to interference from mountains or other geographical obstacles. Cable tele-vision owed its origins to local entrepreneurs, often hardware or electronic dealers, who erected towers that received broadcast signals. Coaxial cable linked these towers or "community antenna" to local households for a modest fee. This was the inauspicious birth of Community Antenna Television (CATV). By 1952, some 70 systems served about 14,000 customers; a decade later, 800 systems had 850,000 subscribers. During the 1960s, cable spread to cities like New York and San Francisco that had special reception prob-lems. During this first period, CATV could be viewed as a common carrier selling a transmission service with no control over content.

Broadcasters initially welcomed the new medium as a means of extending their markets. However, a second phase of development pitted CATV against the broadcast networks. Microwave transmission made it possible for cable systems to carry the programs of independent TV stations across the country. Also, cable operators developed the capability to originate their own programs. Channel capacity increased. CATV, evolving from an auxiliary service to a distinct medium, became "cable television." The three major networks feared an eventual loss of audiences and advertising revenue. There was already speculation about a third phase in which the cable technology would integrate TV, satellite, and computer technologies and provide an array of programming, information, and telecommunication services unprecedented in the history of television. Concerned that cable television could undermine the television status quo, the networks used the NAB to lobby for federal protection. Would the three networks be able to maintain their preeminence? Despite the fact that the Radio Act of 1927 and the Communications Act of 1934 defined broadcast stations as local media, radio had come under the control of the national broadcast networks. Sobel (1986) emphasized how broadcast television—despite being an outgrowth of the press and of film as well as of radio—was captured by the radio network structure:

> There was no early period of trial and error among a group of pioneers, as there had been in the other media. Instead, from the first, television was an arena for giants. Nor was there a period of relatively free enterprise, for the government was there at creation. Each of the other media experienced some of this; there was little in the evolution of the television industry. (p. 334)

Television's old guard—NBC, CBS, and ABC—was based in New York and had strong ties with the eastern establishment and with the liberal wings of both the Democratic and Republican parties. For example, Lyndon B. Johnson, president from 1963 to 1968, an important period in cable TV's development, had controlling interests in nine CBS affiliates. During his administration, cable's growing penetration of urban markets and the lobbying efforts of broadcasters led the FCC to reverse its original hands-off policy and assert broad jurisdiction for cable television. DeLuc (1973) demonstrated how federal regulatory policy in this period defended the broadcasting marketplace status quo against the threat posed by cable TV. In 1966, in a major ruling, the FCC extended its jurisdiction over cable TV and banned further distant signal importation into the nation's 100 largest markets. It represented a de facto halt to the growth of cable in the country's major cities, where 87% of the television audience resided (Hollins, 1984). Furthermore, the networks argued that the unauthorized cable transmission of broadcast signals constituted an infringement of copyright. AT&T and the film industry joined the campaign against the new medium.

Early support of public access by the cable industry took place in the context of the bitter struggle between broadcasters and cablecasters over the future of commercial television in the United States. The 1966 FCC ruling caused a virtual freeze in the expansion of cable TV that would last until 1972. The cable industry hoped that the election of the Nixon administration would result in a more favorable political climate for its growth. During the period from 1968 from 1972, the FCC reviewed existing broadcast policies and proposals for a comprehensive plan for cable regulation.

The vested interests of the networks notwithstanding, significant questions about the nature of cable television needed to be addressed. The tendency of electromagnetic waves to interfere with one another limited the number of separate broadcast signals in a given area. Cable television, transmitted through a bundle of wires, was not subject to such restrictions. In comparison, cable TV potentially offered an abundance of channels and services. The essential quandary was posed by Caron and Taylor (1985), policy analysts in Canada, where cable television had expanded earlier than in the United States: "How does one define a system that is neither common carrier nor broadcaster but a hybrid with some of the characteristics of each?" (p. 50). Cable exercised broadcasting functions by originating and cablecasting its own programs. Yet cable also had some characteristics of a telecommunication service: It redistributed signals it did not originate, could transmit both private information and general entertainment, and collected fees from subscribers rather than advertisers. Caron and Taylor emphasized that

> the broadcasting versus telecommunications dichotomy is not merely a conceptual conundrum; from it flows important practical implications. Broadcasting depends on an exceedingly costly production system: as such it limits access to production facilities. . . . Telecommunication (telegraph, telephone) is cheap to access and receive. (p. 50)

Other policy analysts suggested analogies with print media rather than with telecommunication. Schmidt (1976), for example, wrote, "Indeed, the contrast between cable and traditional broadcasting, in physical, economic and legal terms, is so striking that cable seems more akin to newspapers when one is considering access" (p. 200).

In the perilous period from the mid-1960s to the early 1970s, the cable industry struggled to define its status and to chart its future growth against the formidable opposition of the broadcast networks. The NAB characterized cable as a mercenary threat to "free" television, to the leading instrument of mass culture available without any direct fee. In response, the cable industry could point to a precedent of its own in public service. The Junior Chamber of Commerce of Dale City, Virginia operated a full-time public access channel from 1968 to 1970. It carried no advertising. Its advisory board consisted of representatives from 13 community organizations. A RAND report on the venture for the Ford Foundation indicated that it "appears to be the first community-operated closed circuit television channel in the United States" (cited in Gillespie, 1975, p. 36).

Such public access channels could make cable television appear to be a more socially responsible medium. Might not the public access movement serve as a useful ally in the cable industry's quest for legitimacy? The support of public access by key leaders of the cable industry such as Irving Kahn of Teleprompter reflected enlightened self-interest as well as altruism. The Alternate Media Center and the cable industry were natural partners at a time when the very future of cable TV was at stake. The Center had been established in 1971 when the FCC was entering the final phase of its review of television policy and preparing a new set of long-awaited rules for cable TV. Hence, the work of the Alternate Media Center was facilitated by the fact that at a critical moment the interests of the cable industry and the community television movement seemed to coincide.

Another force that impinged on the development of public access originated outside the cable industry and established institutions—namely, the radical video collectives of the late 1960s and early 1970s. Groups such as Raindance, Videofreeks, People's Communication Network, Video Free America, Ant Farm, Global Village, and the May Day Collective added a utopian thrust to the community television movement. The collectives were an outgrowth of the free speech, civil rights, and antiwar movements of the 1960s. They sought to extend to new communication technologies the role of the underground press in developing an adversary culture. At the time of the introduction of the Sony Portapak, approximately 500 underground newspapers had a 2-million circulation. These products of off-set technology were supplemented by the new left's own press agency, Liberation News Service; a film collective, Newsreel; and periodic national alternate media conferences. The underground press served as the chief educational and organizational tool of the new left (Peck, 1985).

Radical Software, the leading publication of the video collectives, was itself a product of the underground press. The journal, which appeared irregularly from 1970 to 1974, was published by the Raindance Corporation, founded in 1969 by a group of video enthusiasts including Paul Ryan, formerly Marshall McLuhan's student and research assistant at Fordham University. The group's name, suggesting an affinity with the ecology movement, was also a play on R&D, or research and development, from which the RAND Corporation took its name. "The original purpose and idea for Raindance . . . ," according to cofounder Michael Shamberg (1971), "was to explore the possibilities of portable videotape, which was then less than a year old, and generally to function as a sort of alternate culture think-tank concentrating on media" (p. 37). The large-format pages of *Radical Software,* filled with graphics, embraced the whole range of political and cultural tendencies of the alternate media movement. On a practical level, it contained articles about the uses of video as a political instrument, reports on Challenge for Change, and accounts of community video projects across the United States. One issue reproduced an appeal for video equipment from Black Panther leader-in-exile Eldridge Cleaver in Algeria to record his upcoming trip to China.

On a more theoretical level, *Radical Software* drew on the writings of Marshall McLuhan, Buckminster Fuller, and Gregory Bateson to explore the potential significance of new video technology. Attempts were made, for example, to relate cybernetics to Eastern philosophy, to promote the use of video in electronic kindergartens and dance and biofeedback therapies and to extend the drug and rock subculture to high communication technology. Thus, an issue of *Radical Software* might embrace a highly technical article on modifying the Sony Portapak, information about access networks, and Paul Ryan's ruminations on the process of self-discovery through video that he termed "infolding." Linking the disparate perspectives was a belief that revolutionary uses of new communication technologies (i.e., radical software) could transform human consciousness and social relations.

At its core, *Radical Software* expressed the program of "video freaks" who wished to extend the counterculture to a countertechnology. Its ethos was captured in an unsigned article, "Revolutionary Engineering: Towards a Counter-Technology," in the summer 1971 issue, which criticized the new left for its anti-technological bias and called instead for a revolutionary appropriation of present technology and science. Renegades from bourgeois science and technology could play a key role in the creation of a new social order by organizing technologically advanced communes. The author revealed the utopian vision that inspired many of the video collectives when writing that such communes would reveal "the possibilities of the re-formation and redeployment of the physical plant of society, of decentralization and de-urbanization, resulting in knowledge which will be crucial to a society undergoing a radical social revolution, such as the U.S. may be within the next decade or so" (p. 12).

Michael Shamberg, a former Time-Life correspondent and one of the founders of Raindance, spelled out an approach to social change through communications technology in *Guerrilla Television,* a special issue of *Radical Software* published in book form in 1971. Shamberg's work, a classic of the alternate media movement, was a remarkable synthesis of the experience and philosophy of the video collectives. This "meta-manual," as Shamberg termed it, served at once as a practical guide to video technology, as a political program, and as a speculative exercise in futurology.

Guerrilla Television posited that technology, especially communications technology, determined the character of a society. The West had evolved from a print to a nonprint culture. The 27-year-old Shamberg testified to his childhood addiction to television, the medium which in his view was the primary influence in his generation's development. TV was central to a revolution in communication technology since World War II that now included computers, communication satellites, and video. This revolution ushered in a new epoch in the history of the United States, which Shamberg termed "Media-America." Anticipating the notion of an "information society," Shamberg claimed that a fundamental shift "from product to process" had occurred, resulting in the primacy of electronic information transfer in all spheres of American life. It followed that social change could occur through the appropriation of the means of communication.

Shamberg (1971) wrote that the purpose of his "meta-manual" was to suggest the infinite promise of the contemporary information environment in general and of portable video systems in particular to "enhance survival and generate power in Media-America" (p. 2). Shamberg linked the destiny of the United States to the future of television. He criticized broadcast TV—in both its commercial and public forms—as inherently one-dimensional and authoritarian. Portable videotape and cable TV permitted more decentralized and participatory forms of television and the restoration of a "media-ecological balance" between commercial and public uses of television (p. 9). Shamberg proposed that the marriage of video and cable technology could result in a new emancipatory form of "guerrilla television." He contrasted cable with broadcast television, especially the former's greater channel capacity and interactive features.

Shamberg hailed cable's potential to be a great public utility, a two-way lifeline of information. For the first time, the possibility existed that television would become a popular instrument. Local programming could provide video pioneers with a larger audience and permit ordinary citizens to express a wide range of perspectives and sensibilities. Shamberg enumerated a variety of scenarios for electronic town meetings, information exchange systems, and video data banks proposed by Paul Ryan and by George Stoney and Red Burns, among others. Moreover, cable systems could be linked by microwave or satellite to create a refashioned "wired nation," a term popularized by Ralph Lee Smith (1970). Shamberg (1971) called upon media activists to get involved in the struggle to secure public channels on cable systems and proposed a number of strategies and tactics toward that end. Shamberg suggested that video expertise was the trump card of media activists in gaining both popular and industry support. The video collectives could educate cable executives, conceptually bound by broadcasting tradition, about new programming modes for cable television. "The contribution of Guerrilla Television to a developing cable set-up," Shamberg wrote, "is in an attitude towards assessing and using the technology" (p. 79).

Despite the radical rhetoric of "guerrilla television," Shamberg distanced himself from the new left. He warned that his book would disappoint hard-core revolutionaries because it championed the open use of information technologies rather than clandestine and violent actions: "True cybernetic guerrilla warfare means re-structuring communication channels, not capturing existing ones" (p. 29). Shamberg made critical asides about the confrontational tactics of the Black Panthers and Students for a Democratic Society. Characterizing the present information environment as "inherently post-political," he chastised the new left for its antitechnological orientation (p. 29). "In a cybernetic culture," he wrote, "power grows from computer print-outs, not the barrel of a gun" (p. 2). The historic task of the video collectives and the alternate media movement was to design "radical software" for advanced communication systems in Media-America. Shamberg underscored his belief that "the inherent potential of information technology can restore democracy in America if people will become skilled with information tools" (p. 30). As Armstrong (1981) observed,

> Lacking a politically radical tradition—indeed, lacking any tradition—video attracted media activists who followed McLuhan rather than Eisenstein or Godard. Instead of viewing media as tools with which one class would overthrow another, video activists saw media as means of bringing people together. That was consistent with McLuhan's belief that . . . one joins in the communion induced by the flowing, unifying, fusing nature of the electronic media themselves. (p. 70)

Guerrilla Television owed a considerable debt to the thoughts of Marshall McLuhan. Paul Ryan had worked under McLuhan at Fordham University. Michael Shamberg absorbed McLuhan's worldview from Ryan and from a cultural climate in which the slogan "the medium is the message" was common currency. The development of the Portapak and the subsequent establishment of Raindance and other video collectives occurred at a time when McLuhan's prestige and popularity were enormous. McLuhan's ideas penetrated his native Canada in the same period. Some participants in Challenge for Change criticized the tendency fostered by McLuhan to view new communication technologies as a substitute—rather than a tool—for political mobilization and social change.

McLuhan, unlike Harold Innis, ultimately found a more receptive environment for his work in the United States than in his native Canada. As Czitrom (1982) noted, American support was important for McLuhan's career as a communication theorist. From 1953 to 1955, the Ford Foundation sponsored the interdisciplinary seminar on culture and communication at the University of Toronto chaired by McLuhan. *Understanding Media: The Extensions of Man,* the 1964 book that made McLuhan a household name, was originally commissioned by the U.S. Office of Education as a guide to teaching the effects of mass media. McLuhan broke with Innis's critical approach to the growing domination of the American continent by the technology and the communication industries of the United States. Indeed, the very notion of critical thinking was linked in McLuhan's thought to an excessively rational, divisive, and now obsolete print culture.

McLuhan juxtaposed print with "cool" or low-definition electronic media epitomized by television. The latter require greater involvement of all the senses of the audience. McLuhan claimed that this higher level of

participation promised to end the alienation of modern humanity, to retribal-
ize and reintegrate contemporary civilization. In the words of Carey (1968),
McLuhan became "a poet of technology," extolling the redemptive powers
of electronic media (p. 303). His biological rather than social approach led
him to minimize the political and economic factors in the development of
communication technologies. In his chapter on television in *Understanding
Media,* a virtual paean to American commercial television, McLuhan wrote
of "the power of the TV mosaic to transform American innocence into depth
sophistication" (p. 282). Czitrom (1982) emphasized how "his glorification
of television slid very easily into an apology for the corporate interests that
controlled the medium" (pp. 181-182). Despite McLuhan's salutary encouragement of greater media awareness, "his enduring legacy may well be his
role in legitimating the status quo of American communications industries
and their advertisers" (p. 148).

Thus, Michael Shamberg's *Guerrilla Television* undertook the seemingly impossible task of grafting onto McLuhan's thought the radicalism of
the 1960s. Armstrong (1981) observed that Shamberg and other video artists
enamored of the new technologies were not as reductionist as McLuhan; they
did not believe the medium was the entire message. This was reflected in
their use of television on behalf of the Young Lords, American Indians, and
other disenfranchised groups.

> Unlike political radicals, however, video visionaries believed that the impor-
> tance of strikes, sit-ins, marches, and the like was chiefly as raw material for
> the cameras. To video activists, political actions had little value in and of
> themselves; their greatest worth was as symbols for transmission through the
> media—as electric drama, in McLuhan's terms. (p. 73)

Shamberg's relationship to McLuhan and the new left—poles apart in their
attitude toward technology—was complex. Many members of the video
collectives considered student radicals hopeless Luddites. The new left's
antitechnological bias was exemplified during the Berkeley Free Speech
Movement in 1964 when Mario Savio called for the "machine" to be brought
to a grinding halt (Wolin & Schaar, 1970). The "machine" referred to
University of California head Clark Kerr's conception of a technocratic
university serving the needs of industry and the state. Savio's association of
high technology with political and cultural repression and with the military-
industrial complex found fertile ground within the new left during the

Vietnam war era. *Guerrilla Television,* an expression of what may be called Left McLuhanism, was fraught with contradictions. Nonetheless, Michael Shamberg and other members of the video collectives were influential players in the movement for public access on cable television in the early 1970s. *Guerrilla Television* was, in the words of Boyle (1986), "the seminal book that gave the movement a manifesto and a name" (p. 2).

Boyle wrote of Shamberg's desire to unite video and cable,

> The mid-Sixties' advent of half-inch, black-and-white, portable video equipment promised to liberate television from corporate control and rigid studio production and deliver it into the hands of "the people" so that a Whitmanesque democracy of ideas and opinions could be "narrowcast" on cable television. Just as the development of offset printing and photocopying led to the rise of the underground press, the arrival of portable video coupled with the development of cable television heralded a new era of guerrilla television. (p. 2)

Michael Shamberg and George Stoney were strange bedfellows. Stoney's vision for community television derived from his experiences in the New Deal and involvement in Challenge for Change, Shamberg's from a younger generation's embrace of television-related technology as a force for refashioning consciousness and society. The Alternate Media Center was housed at New York University and received blue-chip foundation support, whereas the radical video collectives, a technocratic offshoot of the new left, shared the outlaw spirit of the underground press. Despite significant differences in style and substance, Shamberg and Stoney both envisaged portable video technology and cable television as great potential resources for public communication and social change. This common denominator linked their agendas for public access. Would the original impulse for community television prove a transitory phenomenon, a function of unique conditions and initiatives of the early 1970s, or would it gain a permanent foothold in American telecommunication?

CHAPTER 12

The Struggle Over the Future of Community TV

In the early 1970s, realization of the aspirations of George Stoney at the Alternate Media Center and of Michael Shamberg at the Raindance Corporation depended in large measure on the existence of viable public access channels on cable systems. The early battle over public access in New York City initiated a quarter-century of struggle—involving local and federal officials, the cable industry, and contending forces within the community television movement—to define public access and to determine its role as a public instrument.

The first venture in public access in Dale City, Virginia, received scant attention and ended in early 1970. The awarding of cable franchises with access provisions in Manhattan was expected to provide a model for the development of community television in the rest of the nation. New York City, media capital of the nation and home to the Alternate Media Center, the Raindance Corporation, and the Markle and Ford foundations, was a logical locale for a major experiment in public access. The outcome promised to influence FCC deliberations on whether or not to require cable companies to set aside access channels. Fred Friendly, television advisor to the Ford Foundation and a major force in public television policy, also played an important role in the development of public access in New York City. Friendly served in 1968 as chairman of Mayor John Lindsay's 1968 Advisory Task Force on CATV and Telecommunications. Its report recommended that the cable companies operating in Manhattan give up control of two cable channels, which could be leased for a modest fee by the public. The two channels would in effect function as common carriers in that the cable companies would offer the service on a nondiscriminatory basis and have no control over content.

In 1970, two cable companies, Sterling Information Services and the Teleprompter Corporation, sought 20-year franchises for cable systems in Manhattan that they had operated on an interim basis since 1965. Cable and city officials worked out a draft agreement behind closed doors before being presented for examination by the public. The franchises were criticized by a number of media specialists and community representatives. For example, Sidney W. Dean (1970), a member of the Communications Media Committee of the ACLU and of the City Club of New York, opposed awarding long-term franchises at a time of rapid change in cable-related technology and policy. The debate came to a head on July 23, 1970 at a tumultuous public meeting of the Board of Estimate at City Hall planned just prior to the signing of the franchise agreements. Fred Friendly criticized the secret, private character of the franchising process. Actor Ossie Davis and Cliff Frazer, director of a community film workshop, charged that the agreement did not provide for sufficient participation by minorities in the cable system.

Representatives of the access movement opposed leased access for a fee, arguing that only free use of the noncommercial channels constituted genuine public access. Irving Kahn, president of the Teleprompter Corporation, eager to avoid a last-minute stumbling block, responded by promising to "open our public channels at no charge unless we are precluded from doing so by Federal Communications Commission action" (cited in Ferretti, 1970, p. 63). Thus, the principle was established that access to the two public channels would be free, although this was not written into the final franchise agreement, which only referred to leased channels. Teleprompter agreed to provide community producers free of charge a studio, one camera, a playback deck, and a director. Sterling eventually waived all fees for use of its studio. The cable companies also agreed to provide upon request free cable hookups for public institutions such as churches, day care centers, and schools.

Besides the two channels set aside for the general public, two more were reserved for use by the City of New York for what came to be known as educational and government access.

In July 1971, a year after the signing of the franchise agreements, public access programming began for the 80,000 subscribers to cable television in Manhattan. The maiden production, *A Town Meeting of the Air,* featured official and community leaders discussing the new public access channels. The focus now shifted from securing the channels to developing programming. This involved familiarizing New Yorkers with the existence of the channels and demystifying the medium of television. To facilitate the public access experiment in New York, the Markle Foundation and the Stern Fund awarded grants to Theadora Sklover's Open Channel to provide tape facilities and personnel for groups wishing to use the public access channels. Sklover, then a 33-year-old communication specialist and educator, was an important public access pioneer. She had previously tried to get a cable bill with access provisions through the New York State Legislature. Open Channel was established to produce access programs and to encourage other sources of programming in the community. At the time she established Open Channel, Sklover (1971) wrote in the summer 1971 issue of *Radical Software,* the stakes were high. The New York experiment in public access could establish an important precedent for the growth of community television in the United States:

> However, if it fails, if these channels are not used, or if they carry programming that no one cares about . . . , or if they are utilized for the entertainment of the esoteric few, then we probably will have provided the necessary fuel for those who are fighting against the opening of this medium. (p. 23)

Sklover stressed the need for outreach: identifying constituencies, organizing local cable committees, and training citizens in the use of video equipment. She established a professional talent pool of over 200 TV and film producers, directors, writers, and camera, audio, and lighting technicians who volunteered their time and expertise for public access programming. Determined to nourish diversity, Open Channel arranged airtime for groups ranging from the Boy Scouts to black militants, from the Museum of Modern Art to church choirs. In an interview with *Newsweek,* Sklover stressed that public access must be open to all perspectives: "We're not here to editorialize or make decisions about what people can say over the air" ("Do It Yourself TV," 1972, pp. 49-50).

Open Channel was one of five facilitator groups. The Alternate Media Center, which received $10,000 in equipment from Sterling for access producers, was another. Drawing on George Stoney's experience at Challenge for Change, the Alternate Media Center demonstrated how video could be used in local conflicts with authorities. For example, the Center taped and cablecast a two-hour documentary of a neighborhood protest over the need for a traffic light. Three video collectives funded by the New York State Council on the Arts cablecast their own work and also functioned as access facilitators. John Reilly's Global Village became a leading supplier of documentaries. Raindance Corporation and People's Video Theater captured nontraditional forms of reportage and agitprop on videotape. Eventually, about 200 hours of tape were being cablecast weekly on the two public channels.

In July 1972, a three-day citywide public access celebration commemorated one year of community television in New York City. The purpose of the event was to promote greater awareness of public access. Organizers also sought to "help emerging communities to define their information needs" and to explore "integrating various media into communication nets to create a flexible broad-based public access information system" (Anshien et al., 1971, p. 28). The celebration went beyond documenting accomplishments to date to advancing a model for a citywide system of public communication. The coordinating committee included representatives of video collectives, the local school and library systems, church groups, tenants' and women's organizations, and other groups involved in public access. Print media and radio publicized the event to encourage maximum participation.

Sterling and Teleprompter officials permitted their systems to be interconnected for the first time. Organizers linked special closed-circuit television systems to the access channels. Programs were cablecast from noon until midnight for three days. One channel contained a retrospective of programs of the previous year. Another cablecast live shows and tapes produced during the celebration. A third channel carried live programming from a mobile unit in Central Park transmitted via microwave. Telephone call-ins were employed on each of the channels for live responses from viewers. Radio station WRVR-FM simulcast live programming. To accommodate those who did not receive cable TV at home, 18 viewing centers were mounted throughout

Manhattan, each equipped with monitors and video cameras to demonstrate video production techniques, to record the reactions of bystanders to the cablecasts, and to tape material for cablecasts. The celebration was designed to demonstrate the two-way, interactive potential of video and cable technology.

Teleprompter opened the first video access storefront on 125th Street in Harlem in conjunction with the festival. Benjamin Hooks, just appointed the first black FCC commissioner, said at the opening, "Black people have been largely uninvolved and ignored in the growth of television, and so I'm enthusiastic about the possibilities of using community public access studios for the black people to produce and stage our own programs, to do our own thing in our own way" (cited in Anshien et al., 1971, p. 28). Other constituencies traditionally underrepresented on television also participated, among them Latinos, feminists, labor unions, the elderly, and gay activists. One program on health care originated from Bellevue Hospital, another on education from a public school on the Lower East Side. Several musical performances were taped on the streets of the city. The three-day event, in the words of its organizers, "created a public nervous system throughout Manhattan" (cited in Anshien et al., 1971, p. 70). The celebration represented a remarkable attempt to demonstrate hitherto abstract notions of a "wired" community and "guerrilla television."

The final *Public Access Report* (Anshien et al., 1971) issued by the organizers sought to place the celebration in relation to the history and future of public access. It made clear that the event was designed to be a protest as well as a celebration. The festival documented a year of programming but also created a model for a vastly more developed citywide public access system. The organizers of the celebration stressed the constraints under which public access functioned in New York City: dependency on the cable companies, the lack of community representation in the governance of the system, the need for adequate facilities for training and program origination, and the desirability of viewing centers for people without cable TV. "The present, unplanned, pre-taped system," they wrote, "is not serving the public" (Anshien et al., 1971, p. 69). The report concluded that the city had abdicated its responsibility by allowing the cable companies to determine the nature of public access. Was the New York experience a viable model for a national program of public access?

The experiment in public access in New York City occurred at a time of feverish debate and lobbying during the freeze on new franchises in major metropolitan areas, as the FCC labored to establish a regulatory framework for cable television. The United States lacked a tradition of public film and television comparable to Canada's. What would prevent officials from losing sight of the public interest, from permitting the cable industry to determine policy—which had barely been averted in New York? Once again, as with public television, a group of private foundations and think tanks served as intermediaries to shape public access policy during the FCC freeze on new cable franchises in large cities, a critical juncture comparable to the FCC freeze on television licenses two decades earlier.

In 1969, the Ford Foundation teamed up with the Markle Foundation to fund a series of studies on the future of cable television by the RAND Corporation in response to the FCC's request for policy recommendations. A year later, the Alfred P. Sloan Foundation established a commission to consider the future of cable TV and public access. The Markle Foundation provided seed money for the establishment of the Alternate Media Center and Open Channel in 1971. Some of the same foundation officials who helped launch public television provided strategic support for public access. For example, Lloyd Morrisett, president of the Markle Foundation since 1969, had been vice president of the Carnegie Corporation at the time of its Commission on Educational Television and had helped develop *Sesame Street* with Joan Cooney of the Children's Television Workshop (Daviss, 1986).

The Sloan Commission on Cable Communications became community television's counterpart to the Carnegie Commission on Educational Television. Here was another blue-ribbon committee led by representatives of the Cambridge, Massachusetts-Washington, D.C. axis of policymakers from academia, foundations, the business world, and government. The chairman of the Sloan Commission was Edward S. Mason, a professor of economics at Harvard whose government service included work at the Department of Labor and State Department. Emanuel R. Piore of IBM, Franklin A. Thomas of the Bedford-Stuyvesant Restoration Corporation, and former mayors of Boston and Atlanta were appointed to the commission. Commission members included the presidents of MIT, the Brookings Institution, the Institute for Advanced Study, the Rockefeller University, the University of Chicago, and the RAND Corporation. The function of bodies such as the Sloan Commission was to provide a forum for various interests and broker a consensus. Advocates of community and guerrilla television were given an opportunity to make a presentation. Ralph Lee Smith, then a research

assistant on the Sloan Commission, recalled a decade later the impact made
by representatives of the access movement:

> At the Sloan Commission we had to listen to everybody. But my opinions on
> this matter [public access] were fairly well formed, and they were, I should
> say, quite traditional. These people with the cameras were something new
> that had not penetrated very much into the consciousness even of the people
> who were doing research in the new communications technologies. . . . It was
> an afternoon I never will forget. When I walked out of that room, something
> had happened that could never be reversed. (cited in Bednarczyk, 1986,
> pp. 22-23)

Smith was impressed with the concept advanced by the visitors of a new form
of participatory television serving as a tool of ordinary citizens.

The report of the Sloan Commission on Cable Communications, *On the
Cable: The Television of Abundance,* appeared at the end of 1971. It echoed
the language of the Carnegie Commission on Educational Television but
emphasized the import of public access for local service in contradistinction
to Carnegie's emphasis on a national system of public television. The Sloan
report hailed the capacity of the new television of abundance to revolutionize
American cultural and political life: "If one has any faith at all in the value
of communications, the promise of cable television is awesome" (p. 167).
The report stressed cable's potential use for a multiplicity of services and
perspectives—in the social and political arena as well as in entertainment
and the arts. De Sola Pool and Alexander (1973) wrote in a background paper
prepared for the Sloan Commission, "The abundance of channels may offer
a new opportunity for discussion. . . . The opportunity exists for 'reasoned
argument' to prevail where party, class, and community cues are relaxed"
(p. 78).

In arguing that the growth of cable television was in the public interest,
the Sloan report emphasized the possibilities of noncommercial use of the
medium, spelling out possible uses of cable channels for education, the
delivery of social services by local government, and public access. Public
access received special attention. An appendix was devoted to "Public Access
Channels: The New York Experience." The report stressed the promise of
cable as "an institution within which the separate voices of the community
may be heard," one that addresses a pervasive "need to be seen and heard"
(pp. 123-124). Public access, it was said, could facilitate the expression and
resolution of community grievances and foster local cultural expression as

well. The Sloan Commission concluded that each cable system should have at least two public access channels to serve as "the community voice."

In 1972, the FCC issued its long-awaited Cable Television Report and Order. It endorsed the call of the Sloan Commission for the relatively unfettered growth of the cable industry with limited federal and primarily local regulation. Many of the specific recommendations of the Sloan Commission were accepted. The Report and Order asserted the FCC's authority to regulate cable TV but gave communities wide latitude in drawing up franchise agreements. Provisions were made to protect broadcast television in the 50 largest markets, giving the broadcasting industry more protection than the Sloan Commission thought necessary. The effect of FCC policy was to foster the growth of cable TV from its rural base into the nation's smaller cities. Finally, the FCC required all cable systems in the top 100 markets to reserve three noncommercial "access" channels: educational, governmental, and public. The educational and governmental channels had to be available free of charge for at least five years. The free public access channel was required to be set aside indefinitely. Whereas citizen reformers had a marginal impact on the Public Broadcasting Act of 1967, the community television movement played a significant role in adding a public dimension to cable television.

After 1972, the Alternate Media Center undertook a series of initiatives to carry the torch of public access outside New York City. The Markle Foundation did not renew its original three-year grant for the Center. However, George Stoney convinced the National Endowment for the Arts to fund an apprenticeship program that was critical to the national development of public access. From 1973 to 1977, young public access organizers were dispatched by the Center across the country to provide assistance in establishing access centers. During the first year, for example, the Center's interns initiated programs within schools and cultural groups in Dubuque; a library-based community channel in Bloomington, Indiana; a *Health Line* program in Concord, New Hampshire, which became a model for other health programming; and a taping project of local culture in Appalachia. The interns assembled periodically to share experiences. George Stoney himself made on-site visits. The process was in some respects akin to labor organizing.

The apprenticeship program created the foundation of a national public access infrastructure. On the basis of these field experiences, the Alternate Media Center created a series of seminal access workbooks for the first generation of community television centers. Many key leaders of the public access movement came out of the apprenticeship program. During the mid-1970s, the Alternate Media Center conducted a major experiment in Reading, Pennsylvania in which the concept of community television was applied to the capacity of cable television systems for two-way communication. The pilot project demonstrated how the interactive potential of cable and video technology could be used to facilitate communication among senior citizens, the city council, and social service agencies (Moss, 1978).

In 1976, as the apprenticeship program by the National Endowment for the Arts neared its completion, the Alternate Media Center began to phase out its access programs. That year, participants in the apprenticeship established the National Federation of Local Cable Programmers (NFLCP), which became the chief professional organization of the community television movement. (It was renamed the Alliance for Community Media in 1992.) The NFLCP provided support services and networking mechanisms through its publications, regional workshops, video festivals, and national conferences. It also represented the interests of the public access programmers before the FCC, Congress, and other governmental bodies. The NFLCP's success in building an institutional infrastructure helped the community television movement face major challenges in the late 1970s and early 1980s.

Important programming precedents took place in the period spanning the end of the apprenticeship program and passage of the Cable Communications Policy Act of 1984. One example is *Alternative Views,* which began with an interview format in 1978 at the University of Texas and Austin Community Television. From the outset, many of its programs were political in nature: an interview with an Iranian student who predicted the overthrow of the Shah, a discussion of Sandinista movement before the networks discovered the opposition movement to Somoza in Nicaragua, and in-depth interviews with former Senator Ralph Yarborough, the Texas progressive. The show featured prominent intellectuals and social critics and representatives of peace, environmental, feminist, gay, minority, and labor organizations visiting the University of Texas. At the same time, *Alternative Views* interviewed community members engaged in local struggles, creating a bridge between academics and working people in Austin and revealing the connections between national and local reform efforts.

The organizers of the program began receiving documentaries and expanded its format to integrate video footage and slide shows with interviews. The submissions ranged from pictures of local political actions to footage from war zones in Latin America and the Middle East. These materials became the basis of a news program based on nonmainstream sources. Douglas Kellner (1990), one of the founders of *Alternative Views,* wrote of its programming,

> Most of this material would not have been shown on network television; at the least, it would have been severely cut and censored. Hence it is probably true that the best existing possibility for producing alternative television is through public access/cable television. Obviously, progressive groups who want to carry out access projects must make a sustained commitment to media politics and explore local possibilities for intervention. (p. 210)

Alternative Views eventually aired on access centers in approximately 35 communities and had produced over 500 hour-long shows by the 1990s. Austin Community Television, the home of *Alternative Views* and an important model of public access since 1973, had to defend itself against attacks from conservative forces in Texas, including an attempt to replace it with another system controlled by the local government and cable company (Fuller, 1994).

Whereas *Alternate Views* developed in a university town and state capital, other public access programs emerged in different communities and milieus in the late 1970s and early 1980s. The labor movement, especially its reformist elements, took advantage of public access. For example, *Inside Labor* began its first season in Atlanta, Georgia in 1982. The program developed out of a "concern by local labor people that there was no television programming that truly reflected labor's perspective" (Alverez, 1984, p. 12). *Inside Labor* cablecast a news summary and in-depth reports on single issues like the Greyhound Bus strike or brown lung disease among textile workers. A local member of the United Auto Workers produced a labor show in Fridley, Minnesota; the Labor Film Club produced *The Labor Journal. Mill Hunk Herald,* a newspaper of militant steelworkers in Pittsburgh, made creative use of public access to spoof images of workers in the mass media and to document the historic strikes of the past and the culture of steelworkers through an oral history project. Nationally, the AFL-CIO's Labor Institute of Public Affairs launched a pilot project consisting of a national news magazine and documentaries for use on local cable channels. The labor movement was but one of many constituencies—among them farmers, minorities, and women's groups—that gained direct access to television for the first time.

The FCC requirement of access channels in 1972 represented a milestone, initiating a period of significant innovation in a new community form of public television into the 1980s. However, changes in the communication and political landscape threatened to undermine the public access movement. As early as 1972, critics of the Sloan Commission and of the FCC Report and Order questioned whether the public would be short changed in the commercial cable boom that loomed ahead (Heitler & Kalba, 1972). The public access movement remained highly dependent on the cable industry, but the conditions that fostered their initial marriage of convenience changed as cable began to emerge from the shadow of the networks during the mid- and late 1970s. Furthermore, a shift to the right was taking place in American political life. The student movement of the 1960s and its underground press, which had provided impetus and political focus to the community television movement, went into eclipse. Changes in the political climate and in funding policies threatened, in the words of Paul Ryan (1988), to transform video "from a countercultural gesture to an art genre," from a progressive social instrument to a medium for individual artistic expression (p. 39).

FCC v. Midwest Video Corporation (1979) represented a major legal challenge to public access along jurisdictional lines. This decision rendered by the U.S. Supreme Court stated that the FCC did not have the statutory authority to require public access, forcing the community television movement to scramble for state and local regulatory protection. The cable industry subsequently introduced legislation in Congress prohibiting *any* local, state, or federal requirements for access channels. In 1980, legislation to this end contained in a Senate communication bill was successfully opposed by a coalition of 128 religious, consumer and community organizations. The coalition was led by Everett C. Parker, director of the communications office of the United Church of Christ, and the National League of Cities, which represented 900 municipalities and included minority and labor organizations. This alliance was forced to counter the initiatives of the National Cable Television Association (NCTA), the cable industry's aggressive lobbying arm. The NCTA struck again in 1981, when, at the last minute, provisions were tacked on to a telecommunication deregulation bill just before it reached the floor of the Senate that would have virtually eliminated local governmental authority over cable television, including the right to require public access in franchise agreements. Once again, the public coalition was able to defeat the effort, but the community television movement was clearly on the defensive as the cable industry continued its dramatic growth during the years of the Reagan administration.

The Cable Communications Policy Act of 1984 sought to resolve the conflict between private and public interests within a loose federal deregulatory framework (Aufderheide, 1992). Despite acknowledging public access channels as a citizen tribune, the legislation rejected the FCC position in 1972 requiring the reservation of such channels on cable systems. After the legislation went into effect, cities like Pittsburgh, Milwaukee, and Portland, Oregon ended or altered public access provisions of franchise agreements. By 1990, only 17% of cable systems had public access, 13% educational access, and 11% governmental access. "Since the 1984 Act," Aufderheide (1992) noted, "access cable has been under relentless assault" (p. 60)—by the cable industry and by financially hard-pressed municipalities interested in applying franchise fees to general expenses.

Changing conditions took a toll within institutions of the public access movement like the Alternate Media Center and the NFLCP. After funding stopped for the apprenticeship program in 1977, George Stoney was forced to relinquish his position as codirector of the Alternate Media Center "because I wasn't bringing in the money" (personal communication, May 7, 1990). Foundation support for public access dried up, and Red Burns redirected the Center's focus toward new technological developments in telecommunication, computerization, and international communication. Burns, who served with Eli Revson on the second Carnegie Commission on the Future of Public Broadcasting, received a large grant from the Revson Foundation. Bell Atlantic and AT&T became participants in the Center's work. As Stoney reflected on its early history, he suspected that the original Markle grant had been awarded to focus on the more limited objective of public access as a way to explore the potential of cable technology rather than to launch an American counterpart to Challenge for Change. He regretted, too, the fragmentation of access into separate public, educational, and governmment channels, which opened the door to considerable control by local governmental authorities.

Stoney continued to teach at the Alternate Media Center but felt increasingly estranged from the change in its orientation and that of its students. His estrangement reached an emotional climax in class one day in the mid-1980s, when he played a tape from a Minneapolis public access program, *Video Mailbox*. The show, in which people spoke before a fixed camera, harked back to the earliest and purest form of public access as a popular tribune. Stoney began to show two examples that had moved him deeply. A Native American and a white priest spoke eloquently about their attempt to disarm a nuclear missile, their subsequent imprisonment, and how the experience had transformed their lives. For Stoney, it represented a remarkable example of the exercise of First Amendment rights and of community television: "Here is a public, government-supported medium that allows men who have engaged in sedition, and been in jail, to have their say." Several minutes into the first tape, a student in class was squirming, talking, visibly impatient. Stoney stopped the tape and asked the student for an explanation. She replied, "Why are you showing this? It has no production values. And besides, how will it help me make $60,000 a year?" Stoney, distraught, called for a break before resuming class. In 1987, he stopped teaching at the Center. Several years later, Stoney was appalled to learn that documentation of the Alternate Media Center's original role in the establishment of public access was being discarded in a clean-up of its library (personal communication, May 7, 1990).

The character of the NFLCP, like that of the Alternate Media Center, changed during the 1980s. The NFLCP's focus became its annual national conventions, which relied increasingly on funding from cable companies. According to DeeDee Halleck, these meetings came to resemble trade shows cut off from the public access rank and file, where cable companies displayed their wares and cable access managers and executives jockeyed for better jobs. Halleck faulted the NFLCP for not becoming a more independent and aggressive advocacy organization like the Association of Independent Video and Filmmmakers (personal communication, June 5, 1986).

Speaking in 1985 before the NFLCP's annual national convention in Boston, for which the local Cablevision franchise served as "host system," Halleck reasserted a vision of the public access center as an independent sphere of free speech. She criticized the practice of those cable franchises replacing public access on a first-come, first-served basis with "local origination," in which cable companies administered community programming. The distinction between public and private control of noncommercial television was becoming blurred for community television as well as for public television during the 1980s. Halleck (1985) said,

> Think of public access as a Little House on the Prairie. It's almost midnight and the wolves are at the door. They've been out there all the time. But it's getting darker and they are growing bigger. With the recent mergers of the communications industry they have grown to proportions only imaginable in a George Lucas film. . . . The job of empires is to control and expand. And to eliminate all obstacles that are in the way. And make no doubt about it, public access is in the way. (p. 1)

Halleck argued that true public access programming—not subject to control, rough around the edges, at times critical and oppositional—inevitably conflicted with corporate sensibilities and culture. Halleck (1985) angrily reminded the NFLCP membership that

> local origination is NOT public access. Nor is it a substitute for public access. Who's kidding whom? Public access is first come, first served: open access to the channels of communication. Now that's pretty romantic. So is the First Amendment. But it's there to PROTECT freedom of speech. No abridgments, no compromises, no continuity selection. Romantic? Hell, yes. But the First Amendment's strength IS its romanticism. It is the strength of an idea. That idea cannot be programmed by a cable corporation, or a local cable authority, or a town board. That idea is the cornerstone of any democracy worthy of that name. (pp. 4-5)

Halleck sounded a warning about access managers working in local origination who believed that they knew how to protect themselves from the wolves, or who harbored the hope of becoming wolves themselves someday.

Along with external pressures on institutions like the Alternate Media Center and the NFLCP, the use of existing public access channels as an arena for significant public discourse was hampered by the theory and practice of the access center itself in the United States. The impetus behind Canada's Challenge for Change was to enable citizens to use communication technology to address social problems. In some of the early Canadian experiments, public access centers were run by community-based boards that engaged in outreach and administered the public channel collectively. The general absence in the United States of community-based boards operating access channels gave public access a more individualistic cast. The tension between the authenticity of the individual programmer and the collective nature of broader public constituencies, reflected in Lewis Hill's objectives for Pacifica Radio, also existed within public access. Too often, public access became associated with the kind of vanity video parodied in the film *Wayne's World,* a perception capitalized on by mainstream media to delegitimate public access further. Public access centers were also increasingly used by those wishing to gain experience for careers in the television industry, who replicated the conventions of commercial TV instead of creating alternative forms of discourse.

In 1990, five years after Halleck's critique of local origination, Devine (1991) used the platform provided by one NFLCP national convention to make a searching critique of the practical and theoretical orientation of public access. "Unfortunately," he lamented, "no one is systematically training people to use video as a cultural practice, as a means for critique, for developing 'local vernaculars of analysis' . . . , or as a vehicle for creating and sustaining oppositional culture" (p. 10). The use of public access by individual speakers was grounded in a classic liberal conception of pluralism, which posited that "power is evenly diffused throughout society and citizens rule as consumers with the free marketplace of ideas" (Good, 1989, p. 55). It followed from this premise that to fine-tune democracy all that was needed was to add to the multiplicity of voices that made up public opinion. Such a view of public access, the antithesis of the critical approach to mainstream media as agents of social control, mystified the true role of elite groups and power relationships in American society. As Aufderheide (1992) emphasized, "The public interest is broader than that of consumers, or even protection of the individual speaker" (p. 52).

A distinction needed to be made between the quantity and the impact of public access programming. By the early 1990s, about 2,000 access channels cablecast roughly 15,000 hours a week of original local programming, more than the three commercial networks combined produced in a year (Blau, 1992). Nonetheless, Devine (1991) concluded in his presentation before the NFLCP in 1990 that

> public access has been only marginal in setting a public agenda. As yet we have not consistently nurtured *effective* speech, created a literature of the people or developed a local approach to analysis. In spite of vigorous efforts on the part of access providers to democratize electronic communications, the "marketplace" of ideas remains essentially limited and skewed toward professional commercial speakers. (p. 8)

Blau (1992) stressed the need to reconceptualize public access as a community resource instead of as a television show. Aufderheide's (1992) study of programming at 81 cable access centers found a significant if atypical strain of controversial programming. Yet the local character of public access meant that programmers often worked in isolation, unaware of other media activists engaged in related work elsewhere. In the best of circumstances, public access represented an arena in which dissident voices could occasionally be heard but would rarely reverberate in society in the form of expanded debate or popular mobilization. As Halleck (1984) wrote, "The opportunity that public access provides for wider dissemination of progressive-oriented media is an emancipatory moment yet to be realized" (p. 317).

Paper Tiger TV—the original series as well as its role in the development of *Deep Dish TV* and the *Gulf Crisis TV Project*—provided a model for the transformation of a politically benign showcase of pluralism into an expanded oppositional public sphere. The show began in 1981 as a segment of *Communications Update,* a weekly Manhattan public access show started by independent producers DeeDee Halleck and Liza Bear. *Paper Tiger's* first programs consisted of communication critic Herb Schiller's witty, incisive six-part analysis of the content of *The New York Times.* The program initiated a regular series of critical readings of major newspapers, magazines, and television news and entertainment shows. Issue-oriented programs on topics like the AT&T divestiture, racial stereotyping, and the new world information order followed.

Paper Tiger TV assumed the structure of an open-ended collective of volunteer staff members who assisted producers of specific episodes. Halleck (1984) acknowledged the challenge of functioning in a nonauthoritarian structure: "Achieving unity and strength, while maintaining maximum participation, imagination and humanism is an old structural problem" (p. 316). The well-researched programs, mixing live and pretaped segments, were produced in a deliberately informal, handmade style—with catch-as-catch-can props and credits penned on a cranked scroll—to make viewers feel they too were capable of making such programs. They reflected the influence on Halleck of the "cheap art" of the Bread and Puppet Company, the innovative, participatory, and socially committed theater group based in rural Vermont. Halleck stressed the goal of creating a provocative and engrossing series while avoiding pompous director chairs and slick video effects. Graphics were held in place so that the fingers would show; budgets at the end of the show revealed the cost of magic markers and studio rental. As Halleck (1984) wrote, "If there is a look to the series, it is handmade: a comfortable, nontechnocratic look that says *friendly* and low budget" (p. 315). Gever (1983) noted the affinity of *Paper Tiger's* production strategies—the mock sets, the juxtaposition of text and image, ironic forms of dramatization—with Brecht's concept of didactic theater. *Paper Tiger's* achievement was to provide an alternative model of television in terms of production, content, and distribution.

The name of the program, derived from Chairman Mao's characterization of the United States as a paper tiger, suggested its premise: "The power of mass culture rests on the trust of the public. This legitimacy is a paper tiger" (cited in Hulser, 1985, p. 61). The effect of the series, which produced over 200 programs in a decade, was two-dimensional: "to uncover the political agenda of corporate media, and explore possibilities for a more democratic and open communications system" (Marcus, 1991, p. 31). *Paper Tiger* tapes, produced on a shoestring, received remarkably widespread distribution to other access channels, university communications programs, and museum video installations and libraries. "The brilliance of the *Paper Tiger TV* model," De Michiel (1991) wrote,

> is that it forgets the "mass" part of the media, and looks at video as a field of endeavor that can reach out to audiences in the most unlikely . . . places—from a cablecast to a museum, to a media center to a mall to a labor meeting to a community storefront on VHS to a satellite . . . wherever audience activists can reproduce and take it. This is dissident television—creating new channels, new tunnels, above ground and under. (p. 15)

Still, the issue of how to link the activities of public access programmers—as activists and as programmers—had not yet been addressed. Halleck (1984) wrote of the difficulty of creating a unified political force out of public access producers and audiences:

> Access at its best has been narrow-casting: covering specific local issues and directed to a specific local audience. . . . There have been few programs on access that offer a progressive political perspective to a wider community. With few exceptions, the American Left has ignored the cable potential. (p. 313)

The cumulative effect of *Paper Tiger TV,* a comprehensive critique of the culture industry as a whole, set the stage for the New York collective's second major venture: *Deep Dish TV,* the first national public access satellite network, cablecast in 1986. As George Stoney had emphasized, the community focus of public access was not defined solely by geography but extended to broader areas of identity and interest (Rogoff, 1986). The organizers of the *Deep Dish* satellite network, drawing on the experience of the Washington, D.C.-based Public Interest Video Network, demonstrated the possibility of putting into practice the program for public use of communication satellites proposed by the Public Interest Satellite Association in the late 1970s.

Deep Dish organizers solicited tapes from across the nation, which were received in Halleck's apartment in Manhattan that served at the outset as *Deep Dish*'s office and part-time production facility. The name *Deep Dish* conjured up satellite technology but also an American pie shown coming out of Halleck's oven on the first cablecast, suggesting the homemade and popular character of the new network. From tapes received, the organizers compiled hour-long programs cablecast weekly in 10 installments to cable systems in over 400 cities across the nation. A *Deep Dish* press release stated that "these programs, chosen from over 20,000 hours of locally produced television cablecast each week across the nation, shows that access has . . . become an important forum for community communications" (Deep Dish TV, 1986a). The program themes of the 10 *Deep Dish* cablecasts suggested the scope of public access activity. For example, *This Land Is Our Land* focused on the farm crisis in America as portrayed by the farmers themselves; another, *Labor Produces,* reflected the many union shows on public access across the nation. One program was devoted to minorities, another to children's programming, a link to Halleck's earliest media work.

The series was inaugurated with a general program on public access in which George Stoney reaffirmed the concept of community television he had helped initiate: a new kind of televised news or report in which citizens communicated directly with one another and with their representatives. *Deep Dish TV* captured a wide spectrum of voices, amplifying and linking them via satellite in a noncommercial public access network. The project represented a video equivalent of William Siemering's desire to capture on public radio the sounds of America and the everyday lives of its people. Like Siemering's conception, the *Deep Dish* project sought to transcend the contradiction between the democratic tradition of oral communication and the authoritarian tradition of mechanical communication juxtaposed by Harold Innis.

A manual published by *Deep Dish TV* following the national cablecast cited congressional commentary accompanying the Cable Communications Policy Act of 1984, the first major federal legislation dealing with cable television:

> Public access channels are often the video equivalent of the speaker's soapbox or the electronic parallel to the printed leaflet. They provide groups and individuals who generally have not had access to the electronic media

with the opportunity to become sources of information in the electronic
marketplace of ideas. (cited in Deep Dish TV, 1986b, p. 5)

A year after *Deep Dish TV*'s first cablecast, over 100 people involved in the
experiment from across the nation met to discuss the future of the network.
Besides organizing another series of its own, the *Deep Dish* network distributed programs for such organizations as the United Farm Workers and the
International Women's Day Video Festival. Martha Wallner (1991), one of
its organizers, stressed *Deep Dish*'s desire to "nurture and prime the links
between media centers, activists, artists, teachers, viewers and journalists"
to help build "a network of alternative communication systems in this
country and the world" (p. 34).

If *Paper Tiger TV* represented a critique of mainstream media and *Deep
Dish TV* network cablecasts constituted a national register of community
television, then the *Gulf Crisis TV Project* marked a third step: Public access
took a leap forward as a social instrument through direct political intervention in an international crisis. The project, organized by a group within the
Paper Tiger TV collective, drew on the *Deep Dish* infrastructure; material
was submitted from more than 40 different states. In collaboration with the
peace movement, five hours of footage were assembled from sources both
domestic and foreign to constitute a video teach-in, a multifaceted response
to the mainstream media's role in preparing the American public for the Gulf
War and subsequently in interpreting the conflict. *Operation Dissidence*
examined the marketing of the war in the United States; *Manufacturing the
Enemy* explored anti-Arab racism provoked by the conflict. The series was
presented before, during, and following the conflict on over 100 public
access stations, dozens of PBS channels, and in Canada, Britain, Australia,
and Japan. Two chief objectives of community television—grassroots participation and the presentation of diverse, alternative perspectives—were
achieved in a context in which local video productions were shared on a
national and international level.

*   *   *

The emergence of public access on cable television in the early 1970s
was a historical accident, the result of the confluence of social and technological developments that spawned strategic if transitory alliances. The

Canadian Challenge for Change program took place at a key moment in the development of portable video technology and in the expansion of cable TV. The heyday of the video collectives and guerrilla television coincided with the desire of a nascent cable industry to promote access so as to help establish its legitimacy vis-à-vis the networks. Furthermore, George Stoney had the experience and vision to provide leadership for the community television movement through the Alternative Media Center at New York University. A strong advocate of public access, Nicholas Johnson, sat on the FCC, providing the same critical support that Frieda Hennock had given educational television after World War II. The establishment weighed in with its mechanism to broker a compromise between the disparate forces: the Sloan Commission on Cable Communications. All these factors and forces contributed to the reservation of public access channels in the FCC's Cable Television Report and Order in 1972.

Aufderheide (1992) wrote two decades after the FCC ruling that "access—lacking a national substructure as public television did until 1967—is still in its pre-history" (p. 62). During this 20-year period, the alliance between the community television movement, the cable industry, and local government broke down. Public access suffered a series of legal and legislative defeats. The 1980s were as inhospitable to public access as to public television, when marketplace approaches to public policy issues led authorities to interpret First Amendment rights in favor of private over public interests. Public access could not flourish in a hostile environment. Much of access programming consisted of vanity video or lame attempts to mimic commercial forms of television. Yet given all the obstacles, Aufderheide (1992) emphasized, it is remarkable that public access continued to exist at all, that it produced a body of programming establishing a model for strengthening the public sphere. Moreover, Halleck observed, the original cadre of public access programmers remained a significant force: "You've got an army out there, many people who have had hands-on experience not only with the equipment, but with organizing audiences, making shows, and fighting local officials" (personal communication, July 14, 1986).

Paper Tiger TV, through the *Deep Dish* and *Gulf Crisis* projects, revealed the potential of public access to create a truly oppositional public sphere on a national and even international level. The opening for community television created in the early 1970s has not been closed. But as Halleck (1984) emphasized, "How long this will continue depends on how large a constituency the access activists and programmers can muster" (p. 313).

PART V

Conclusion: Public Radio, Public Television, and the Public Sphere

CHAPTER 13

The Mystification of the Public Sphere in the History of American Broadcasting

The public, the state, and the corporation struggled for control of American radio and television in the earliest days of broadcasting. In the formative years of radio, amateurs and educational broadcasters represented the public interest, the Navy the interests of the state, and American Marconi and RCA the corporate interest. Initially, public forces independent of government and business pioneered the use of radio technology for broadcasting as a means of communication able to create a community of programmers and listeners. These pioneers saw radio as a vehicle for a revitalization of American democracy.

However, radio and television in their noncommercial forms experienced great obstacles and limited success in serving as the basis for an expanded public sphere of communication—independent of the state and the marketplace—in the United States during the 20th century. The marginalized status of independent radio and television, the result of powerful social and economic forces, was reflected in the mystification of the very concept of the public sphere. Distinctions between the interests of the citizenry, the state and commercial interests were increasingly blurred from the 1920s to the present. In 1995, a century after the earliest experiments with wireless telegraphy, conservative forces in control of Congress challenged the very legitimacy of public radio and television. An analysis of the history of noncommercial radio and TV in relation to the problem of the public sphere may help media activists defend and revitalize public radio and television.

As summarized by Douglas (1987), an expanded public sphere was central to the original popular aspirations for the use of radio:

> Wireless in 1900 would allow individuals to communicate with whomever they wanted whenever they wanted. Thus, through wireless, Americans could circumvent hated monopolies such as Western Union; the benefits of modern communication would be made available to all. In the 1920s, radio was again portrayed as a democratic agent, leveling class differences, making politicians more accountable to the people, and spreading education "for free." Radio, then, would do nothing less than resurrect the values of the early Republic and, through the power of technology, restore their primacy in an era of monopolistic capitalism. (pp. 320-321)

Amateur wireless operators and educators linked the inauguration of broadcasting to participatory democracy and public service. True, early ham operators were almost exclusively male and middle class and as hobbyists generally did not conceive their experiments in terms of a larger social project. Nonetheless, the brotherhood of amateurs became politicized by necessity when resisting the attempts of the Navy and private interests to curb ham activity and to appropriate radio for government and commercial use. The movement for a national network of amateurs was led by Hiram Percy Maxim's American Radio Relay League and dramatized by his 1916 coast-to-coast relay experiment. The ham movement had an international component also: The American Radio Relay league was a charter member of the International Amateur Radio Union. A more conscious concept of public service was introduced by the land-grant colleges of the Midwest. This approach, rooted in the mission to meet the needs of the general population through extension programs, was enriched by the ideological impetus of Populism.

The government and the corporations evolved their own agendas as well. After the First World War, the Navy failed in its attempt to gain control of radio because of historic opposition to government ownership of utilities and the political climate of the postwar period. Instead, the American government presided over the creation of a "chosen instrument" against the Marconi interests—i.e., RCA— a joint venture linking AT&T, GE, and Westinghouse. Beginning with the Radio Act of 1912, the state assigned preferred portions of the radio spectrum to commercial interests. This precedent was reinforced by the policies of Secretary of Commerce Herbert Hoover, an advocate of government-industry collaboration, which emerged during the radio conferences of 1922-1925. Out of the conferences emerged the principle that commercial broadcasters served the general interest whereas noncommercial educational, religious, and labor stations represented special interests. This provided the rationale for assigning high-power frequencies to commercial broadcasters and low-power frequencies to noncommercial broadcasters. The Radio Act of 1927 and the Communications Act of 1934 further formalized this policy and established a federal regulatory apparatus to implement it. Thus, from the earliest days of broadcasting, forces were at work to undermine the status of radio as an autonomous public sphere of communication.

During the 1930s, commercial ascendancy was complemented by the "doctrine of cooperation" promoted by Levering Tyson's NACRE, which was funded by the Carnegie Corporation of New York. Tyson and his allies in the foundation and corporate world posited that educational broadcasters should produce programming within the framework of the commercial networks rather than through a separate noncommercial system. The doctrine of Cooperation was opposed by Joy Elmer Morgan's NCER, which mounted a campaign with populist overtones to reserve radio channels for a separate noncommercial system. This crusade peaked with the Wagner-Hatfield Bill of 1934, which was drafted and supported by a broad coalition of educators, agricultural interests, the labor movement, church groups, and civil libertarians. Its defeat represented the last hurrah of the movement for a popular stake in broadcasting during the interwar years. Now the corporatist and paternalistic trusteeship model could reign supreme, to wit: The state sanctioned commercial licensees to broadcast on behalf of the public. This paradigm, which mystified distinctions between state, corporate, and public interests, justified and hastened the virtual liquidation of noncommercial radio stations on the AM band by World War II. Hence, as Leach (1983) noted, " 'The industry' emerged from the war commanding the lion's share, not just of broadcasting's resources but of the power to define the medium's purposes and potentials in the public mind" (p. 16).

Tyson's NACRE and Morgan's NCER represented the twin poles of the American media reform movement from the 1920s to the present. The emphasis of the former was on *public access*—civic use of electronic media operated by commercial or governmental entities. The goal of the latter was *public control*—a greater degree of popular dominion over electronic channels of communication. Lewis Hill resurrected the independent orientation of Morgan when he revived the movement for public broadcasting in the form of community radio after World War II. Pacifica radio exhibited elements of both continuity and discontinuity with the noncommercial pioneers of the interwar years. Having built a crystal radio receiver as a child in the 1920s, Hill had an affinity with the radio amateurs and their ethos of interactive, two-way communication, an ideal lauded by Bertolt Brecht in 1930:

> Radio could be the most wonderful public communications system imaginable, a gigantic system of channels—could be, that is, if it were capable not only of transmitting but of receiving, of making listeners hear but also speak, not of isolating them but connecting them. (cited in Lewis & Booth, 1990, p. 186)

Volunteer trainees and community activists—that is, amateur rather than broadcast professionals—were to play a central role at Pacifica stations.

Lewis Hill also revived the political program of the crusading public radio pioneers and activists of the interwar years. His "Radio Prospectus" synthesized elements of Roger Baldwin's desire to make radio an instrument of the First Amendment and Father John Harney's approach to the medium as a resource to address social inequities. Hill echoed Edward Nockel's desire to provide a platform for the concerns of the working class, and especially Morgan's conviction that radio could be a valuable resource for the resolution of conflict and promotion of world peace.

With the defeat of the Wagner-Hatfield Bill, the dream of a noncommercial system on AM ceased to be a possibility. Hill desired an AM station but was forced to accept an assignment on FM, a new frontier on the electromagnetic spectrum. Hill did not realize that the fact that FM was in its infancy and not of interest to the commercial networks after World War II was of critical importance in making it possible for Pacifica to gain a foothold in

Berkeley and expand to a five-station system. This illustrates a recurrent theme: The boldest experiments in public telecommunication take place when technologies are new and their commercial potential not yet fully apparent. This was true with the first generation of radio amateurs, Hill's use of FM, public television's early interest in communication satellites, and the use of lightweight video equipment by Challenge for Change in Canada and the radical video collectives in the United States. Indeed, noncommercial experimentation often revealed to corporate interests the potential to exploit new forms of communication for commercial ends, beginning a process of privatization in which public participation became increasingly circumscribed. De Michiel (1991), a *Deep Dish TV* associate, lamented that "our visions are always transforming mainstream media, but never in the ways we might like or be able to control" (p. 15).

Unlike his forebears of the 1930s, Hill launched Pacifica when the hegemony of commercial broadcasters could no longer be contested. Pacifica Radio was conceived as a counter or oppositional public sphere. Hill created a comprehensive model for a radical alternative to commercial broadcasting in terms of programming, funding, community participation, and self-management. Pacifica would pay dearly for its independent and often oppositional relationship to the state, in stark contrast to the symbiotic association between the government and commercial broadcasters. Pacifica stations were subjected to witch-hunts by congressional committees, surveillance by the FBI, harassment by the FCC, subpoenas from law enforcement authorities, and bombings by right-wing extremists. And Pacifica frequently stood alone in testing major First Amendment issues in the courts. As Blakely (1979) observed,

> When one listens to the Pacifica stations, one is aware of how comparatively bland are the programs of the stations dependent upon means of support other than the listeners and contributors. When one reviews the ordeals of the Pacifica stations, one understands why the others are cautious. (p. 125)

Pacifica also paid a price for listener sponsorship in the form of minimal and often inadequate funding for equipment and salaries. Independence was costly, materially as well as politically. At times, financial pressures became so great that the Pacifica national board had to stem calls within its most hard-pressed stations to accept corporate underwriting. External political and financial pressure exacerbated internal conflict in an organization dedicated to a significant degree of self-management. Pacifica stations were plagued by conflicts within stations, among stations, and especially between stations and its central office. Pacifica's history of organizational and ideological conflict dated back to its origins, contributing to Lewis Hill's suicide and a succession of internal crises and strikes circumscribing the national impact of Pacifica's strategically located network of stations. In the future, Pacifica will have to temper both the arbitrary initiatives of its national office and the antiauthoritarianism of its local stations if it is to develop a more fully integrated theory and practice of alternative radio.

Pacifica's experience testifies to the fact that the public sphere is not—as conceived by Lewis Hill—a unified expression of an autonomous general will, a neutral domain for rational debate about society. Pacifica's history since the 1960s has revealed a public sphere made up of an aggregate of counterpublics ranging from the radical intelligentsia to the working class, people of color, women, and gays, among others. Spark (1987), a former program director at Pacifica's Los Angeles station, posed the question in the 1980s whether Pacifica was shouldering an impossible burden in its almost singlehanded attempt to provide a platform for the full range of counterpublics:

> Perhaps the obstacles to bucking the whole system of American capitalism and its media institutions are simply insurmountable at this time . . . ; this weakness is undoubtedly due in large measure to the objective situation of left movements, which by necessity consist of coalitions of large numbers of relatively powerless, divided individuals. . . . With oppositional media like KPFK so rare, and so many disenfranchised groups in the world, power struggles are bound to erupt. (p. 580)

Pacifica sought to recognize the heterogeneous nature of the public sphere while avoiding its fragmentation into separate and therefore more easily marginalized constituencies. Pacifica—and other alternative systems of public radio and TV—must continue the struggle to reconstruct a democratic public sphere along the lines suggested by McLaughlin (1994):

> Because so many social and economic inequalities cut across group interests and prevent the realization of a truly democratic public sphere, an effective strategy would seek unity amongst transformation-oriented counterpublics for a collective struggle, to form coalitions that extend beyond micropolitics. (p. 21)

Its problems notwithstanding, Pacifica remains a unique and vital force in noncommercial radio. Its independence, maintained with such difficulty, permits it to continue functioning as a broadcasting gadfly in keeping with the vision of its founder. Nearly half a century after Lewis Hill first conceived it, Pacifica—now five stations in major metropolitan centers, with a news and program service and tape library—has achieved a level of continuity and a promise of permanency, if not stability. Pacifica has a unique potential—partially but not fully realized—to help forge a freer, critical public sphere on the national as well as local level. To its credit, against both external and internal pressure Pacifica has maintained an independent and oppositional character distinct from mainstream public radio.

If Pacifica emerged as a community-based variant of public radio, National Public Radio represented its federal form. NPR, which developed as a result of the Public Broadcasting Act of 1967, absorbed and transformed educational radio. The success of the National Association of Educational Broadcasters in convincing the FCC to set aside for noncommercial purposes a portion of the FM spectrum—then considered of little commercial value—permitted a rebirth of educational radio after World War II. However, weak signals, poor financing, and the lack of interconnection prevented the creation of a viable national noncommercial radio system prior to 1967.

The Public Broadcasting Act of 1967, which effected the transition from educational to a new form of public broadcasting, established the Corporation for Public Broadcasting. The CPB channeled funds to the system's two principal networking mechanisms, National Public Radio and the Public Broadcasting Service. The relationship of the new public broadcasting system to the state was complex, if not paradoxical. The CPB was chartered as a *non*governmental as well as *non*profit agency. Yet it received its funds from congressional appropriations in much the same manner as government programs did. Furthermore, the CPB was designed to provide political insulation for NPR and PBS. Yet its board, which was required to have balanced representation of the two major political parties, was appointed by the president with the advice and consent of the U.S. Senate.

In terms of building a national noncommercial radio system, the Public Broadcasting Act of 1967 succeeded where the NAEB had failed. A quarter of a century after the 1967 Act, NPR presided over a satellite-linked network with over 250 full-member stations and approximately 300 associate stations. Besides providing interconnection, NPR was designed as a production center to provide programming for member stations. NPR's mission statement and programming owed much to the humanistic vision of William Siemering, creator of the news magazine *All Things Considered,* which in large measure established NPR's identity. Siemering saw public radio as a vehicle for affirming American pluralism, encouraging participation in the political process, and reintegrating a fragmented society. He was a radio artist, revealing the medium's potential to capture the voices of ordinary people and the sounds of American life—from the countryside to the factory. Siemering envisaged *ATC* as a clearinghouse of sorts, in which reports from different corners of the country, filtered through local stations, would be aired to the nation as a whole. Here was a Whitmanesque conception of radio in which a public platform would be mounted to capture and celebrate the sounds of a people.

There were common elements in the original formulation of the missions of NPR and of Pacifica Radio linking Siemering's "National Public Radio's Purposes" and Hill's "Radio Prospectus," written a quarter-century earlier. Both manifestos shared a commitment to employ the medium of radio to promote human expression and understanding. The point of departure for the visionaries behind NPR and Pacifica was a rejection of the conventions of commercial radio, especially in regard to coverage of the public affairs and cultural life in a diverse nation. Siemering and Hill were driven by a similar desire to extend radio's use as a cultural and social instrument.

However, there were differences in emphasis in the two projects. Hill's agenda for an alternative radio network was rooted in American radicalism, originally the peace movement, and became associated with the collective struggle of disenfranchised groups. Siemering also saw radio as an agent of social improvement but one that fostered individual enlightenment and participation in the existing political structure. Hill saw radio as a vehicle for social protest; Siemering saw it as a tool for social integration. The differences between Pacifica and NPR would be attributable in large measure to the discrepancy between social radicalism and liberal humanism.

There would also be structural differences in the two noncommercial radio systems. Local listener sponsorship was the foundation of Pacifica's finances and independence, whereas NPR would rely more on federal funding. Pacifica's relationship to the state was more adversarial, NPR's more interdependent. Hill viewed Pacifica Radio as an experiment in self-management, whereas Siemering, preoccupied with the opportunity to put his inspired programming ideas into practice on a national level, was less concerned about the financial and bureaucratic apparatus of public radio. The structure of NPR would exhibit greater centralization and more traditional lines of authority than Pacifica Radio. The original 14-member NPR board consisted of 9 station representatives, 3 public members, and the presidents of the CPB and NPR. In theory, member stations determined the policies of NPR through its representatives on the board. Governance within Pacifica and NPR reflected the difference between participatory and representative democracy. Despite the kinship of Pacifica and NPR within the noncommercial radio family, the conception of the public sphere implicit in the community and the federal form of public radio differed fundamentally: a site of independence and opposition versus a site of social integration.

Some principles enunciated by Siemering at the birth of NPR could not be fully sustained. For example, he had posited that "National Public Radio will not regard its audience as a 'market' or in terms of disposable income." However, the need to justify congressional appropriations and to interest corporate underwriters led to audience research establishing the size and high social profile of NPR's listenership. The preoccupation with "cumes" and demographics came at the expense of the original goal of addressing the diversity of American society. So-called enhanced underwriting, permitted since 1984, had the ring of advertisements. Former CBS broadcast news executive Richard Salant quit the NPR board in protest over underwriting influencing NPR's news coverage. Public radio programmer Josephson (1993) charged,

> In our financial panic we've abandoned the ideals and original purpose of public radio. We've become drunk on numbers, buzzwords and simplistic formulas. And we are well on the way to becoming commercial radio—with commercials—but without ideals. (p. 31)

Siemering's own odyssey within the public radio system was illustrative. While acknowledged as a founding father, he was eased out of his position as NPR's first program director and later struggled to keep his documentary series *Soundprint* alive before resigning as its executive producer in 1992.

Siemering's goals for NPR's acclaimed flagship program, *All Things Considered,* were not completely realized. The conception of a program based on feeds from local stations did not materialize. Instead, the lion's share of the program's report came from NPR staffers in Washington, D.C., or its bureaus. In general, local news programming languished at NPR affiliates; in many cases, the only news report they offered was centrally produced *ATC* and *Morning Edition*, which had been added in 1979. As NPR evolved from a supplemental to a primary radio news report, a diminished number of creative radio montages, off-beat interviews, and hard-hitting investigative pieces were replaced by a greater focus on the agenda of official Washington. The Siemering approach may survive more intact on the new regional news and cultural magazines like *Northwest Journal,* first produced by a consortium of Northwest stations in 1994 and carried by about 30 stations from Alaska to California.

By 1993, *Morning Edition* had 7 million listeners a week, *ATC* 6.5 million. NPR correspondent Cokie Roberts entered the Capitol every day aware that half the members of Congress had heard her on the air that morning. The increased prominence of NPR's correspondents led to positions with the networks, sometimes held concurrently with public radio assignments, further clouding the distinction between the noncommercial and commercial systems. Former NPR President Douglas Bennet, a consummate Washington insider, emphasized that after inauspicious origins NPR entered "the big leagues, the very big leagues," which entailed "a whole new accountability" in its news programming (cited in Porter, 1990, p. 27). According to Ryan (1993), the new accountability meant that NPR news programming "tended to frame political debate as something that occurs within the government, not among the public" (p. 20).

The annual meeting in May 1993 of the Public Radio Conference in Washington, D.C. in the early months of the Clinton administration demonstrated NPR's intimate relationship with the federal government. Conference organizers covered all political bases, inviting public broadcasting critic and Senate minority leader Bob Dole of Kansas to give the keynote address, which included an attack on programming at Pacifica Radio. Participants heard the speeches of three cabinet members: the secretaries of housing and urban development, transportation, and labor. When President Clinton visited the conference, he greeted staff from KUAR-FM in Little Rock and told the audience that he and Hillary were "NPR junkies" who had started the day with *Morning Edition* for a decade. He added that he thought so highly of NPR that he had asked its former president, Douglas Bennet, to join his administration as an assistant secretary of state (Wilner, 1993b).

Although not chartered as a government radio network, NPR neither exhibited the independent and adversarial relationship to the state championed by Pacifica Radio nor the orientation toward local service of the National Federation of Community Broadcasters. How could it have, insofar as it was the product of federal legislation and federal funds, with a parent body governed by a presidentially selected board, and headed by political operatives like Frank Mankiewicz and Douglas Bennet? Within that framework, its achievement in the transmogrification of educational into public radio was considerable. In the two decades following World War II, noncommercial radio on FM frequencies had remained largely isolated and marginal operations. After the Public Broadcasting Act of 1967, a coordinated CPB-NPR plan to provide stations with grants, interconnection, and programming succeeded in creating a national infrastructure for public radio. NPR, representing a federal form of public radio, had realized—albeit in an altered form—the aspirations of radio reformers reaching back to the 1920s to establish a national noncommercial radio system. Yet NPR was built and sustained largely from above and as such did not provide a significant new sphere for public participation and contestation. And NPR, in part by wooing Pacifica and other community radio stations and in part by overshadowing them in the public's consciousness, threatened to co-opt the community radio movement.

The Public Broadcasting Act of 1967 established a federal system of television as well as radio. The Act came relatively late in the development of the structure of American television. The television boom had followed World War II just as the radio boom had followed World War I. Proponents of noncommercial television were determined to avoid the fate of educational broadcasters who had failed to secure spectrum allocations on the AM dial during the interwar period. However, the climate after World War II resembled that after World War I: a period of political conservatism and rapid economic expansion inhospitable to government intervention in the marketplace to advance public policy. Also, educational broadcasters were not prepared to shift gears from radio to TV, and the general public, lacking exposure to a noncommercial radio system, had little sense of television's potential as a public resource.

As in the past, the institution of the private foundation, in this case the Ford Foundation, came forward to fill the breach. The Ford Foundation mounted a sophisticated, multifaceted campaign by channeling funds into studies, pilot projects, lobbying initiatives, and public information efforts that resulted in the reservation of channels for noncommercial use when the FCC lifted its four-year freeze on new licenses in 1952. The next phase of Ford's program, reaching into the 1960s, was to fund station construction, the National Educational Television network, and programming initiatives like the *Public Broadcasting Laboratory*. The Ford Foundation's indispensable support made possible, in the altered political climate of the 1960s, the transition from the foundation era to the federal era of noncommercial television.

The intervention of the Ford Foundation reflected the historic role of the private foundation in mediating between the private and public sectors of American society. Dating back to the ethos of Andrew Carnegie's "gospel of wealth," the major foundations were dedicated to providing guidance in public policy by an enlightened elite one step removed from day-to-day social and political conflict. Carnegie updated the Protestant ethic to address the social dislocations of the age of industrial capitalism. The great foundations like the Carnegie Corporation of New York and the Ford Foundation became linked to the centrist and reformist eastern establishment. During the interwar years, the Carnegie Corporation of New York had funded—and controlled—the movement to foster educational programming on commercial radio as an alternative to the reservation of noncommercial channels through the National Advisory Council on Radio in Education.

After World War II, the Ford Foundation, which had previously administered the philanthropies of the Ford family, received a vastly expanded endowment and mission. Robert M. Hutchins, president of the University of Chicago since 1929, resigned in 1951 to become associate director of the Ford Foundation. Hutchins, a long-standing critic of American educational and communication policy, had been a patron of the distinguished *University of Chicago Roundtable* radio series before the war. Disenchanted with the discredited doctrine of Cooperation for radio, Hutchins joined the Ford Foundation as its campaign to establish a noncommercial television system went into high gear. The reconstituted Ford Foundation enunciated broad objectives to promote peace, democracy, economic development, education, and knowledge of human behavior.

The prospect of social disorder in the transition from wartime to peacetime—of urban decay, racial conflict, and economic instability—was the context in which the Ford Foundation issued its important 1949 report upon which its postwar programs were based. According to Seybold (1978), the Foundation's "hidden political agenda" was to address a new legitimation crisis for the social system and its elite, as the United States increasingly became a mass society characterized by a lack of participation and growing alienation. Seybold argued that the Foundation's strategy for addressing postwar problems resided in "containing social problems and channeling discontent" (pp. 385-398). Mechanisms would be created through which grievances could be aired, brought into the mainstream, and eventually rectified—within the framework of the existing society.

The notion of a "third force" mediating between the state and society, the rationale for the private foundation itself and for institutions it nurtured like public broadcasting, is fundamentally at odds with extending the public sphere, despite appearances to the contrary. Two incompatible strategies are at play. One seeks to create a platform open to dissenting voices, a venue that affirms pluralism and serves as a social safety valve but precludes popular direction. The other attempts to establish a more independent sphere of communication over which counterpublics exercise greater control for the purpose of an untrammeled exchange of ideas and as a means of self-organization. For the former, public television is seen as supplementing the commercial television system, highlighting its inadequacies, to be sure, but at the same time rendering its reform less necessary, ultimately reinforcing the industry status quo. The latter, more democratic and participatory in nature, is inherently critical of the gatekeeping functions of mainstream television, both commercial and noncommercial.

The report of the Carnegie Commission on Educational Television, which provided the foundation for the Public Broadcasting Act of 1967, was predicated upon the same principles that animated the Ford Foundation. The 1967 report (Carnegie I) appealed for support of public television because of its great promise as an agent of public enlightenment and social progress. Emphasis was placed on its potential to reaffirm, at once, American pluralism and unity, to "help us know what it is to be many in one":

> It should show us our community as it really is. It should be a forum for debate and controversy. It should bring into the home . . . occasions where people of the community express their hopes, their protests, their enthusiasms, and their will. It should provide a voice for groups in the community that may otherwise be unheard. (p. 92)

Although sharing a common frame of reference with the Ford Foundation, the Carnegie Commission served as a bridge between the foundation world and the state. By the 1960s, the Kennedy and Johnson administrations provided the opportunity for a transition from a foundation-supported to a government-supported system. Ralph Lowell, a scion of the eastern establishment, had taken the first steps that led to the creation of a blue-ribbon panel on educational television. Officially independent, Carnegie I had close links to the Johnson administration and to the Cambridge, Massachusetts/Washington, D.C., nexus of advisors and policymakers.

One of the most prominent members of that nexus was MIT's James Killian, Jr., chairman of the original Carnegie Commission. A remarkable number of members of the Commission and later of top CPB officials were close associates of Killian, who had been appointed to sensitive advisory posts regarding technology and national security by Truman, Eisenhower, and Kennedy prior to his stewardship of Carnegie I. Mooney (1980) suggested a connection between Killian's past government service in the intelligence and communication field and his pivotal role in public broadcasting. According to Mooney, Killian's work for the Psychological Warfare Strategy Board in the early 1950s was instrumental in the establishment of the USIA and the Voice of America, propaganda instruments of the United States during the cold war.

Killian was an admirer of the BBC, especially how its World Service eschewed overt propaganda in favor of a prestigious news and cultural service that enhanced Britain's image and influence overseas. However, unlike the BBC, the USIA and Voice of America were forbidden from engaging in programming within the United States so as to avoid the threat of government-sponsored domestic propaganda. The Voice of America, established in imitation of the BBC World Service that rebroadcast BBC programs, lacked a comparable direct link to national cultural institutions and the ability to coordinate domestic and foreign broadcasts. Mooney argued that Killian helped create the CPB in part as a substitute for the lack of a domestic arm of the USIA, enabling programming produced domestically for NPR and PBS to be distributed abroad by the government.

A key behind-the-scenes organizer of the original Carnegie Commission and architect of the Public Broadcasting Act of 1967 with the Johnson administration was Leonard Marks, then director of the USIA. Former officials of the USIA assumed important positions at the CPB. Henry Loomis had worked with Killian on the Psychological Warfare Strategy Board and had served as director of the broadcasting service of the Voice of America (1958-1965) and as deputy director of the USIA (1969-1972) prior to his six-year tenure as president of the CPB. Richard Carlson had directed the Voice of America from 1986 to 1991 before becoming the CPB's president; he appointed as his second-in-command at the CPB Robert T. Coonrod, an employee since 1967 of the USIA, where his last post had been deputy associate director of the USIA's Bureau of Broadcasting.

In 1993, Carlson proposed to make the link between the CPB and the promotion of America's image abroad more overt. He circulated a memorandum recommending that in the post-cold-war environment the U.S. government's foreign broadcast services, including the Voice of America and Radio Free Europe/Radio Liberty, be reorganized into a unified international network administered by the CPB. Carlson, offering the BBC as a model, argued that public broadcasting programming would serve as a better cultural ambassador than the sitcoms and game shows distributed around the world by U.S. commercial broadcasters. He stressed that a unified international radio and television network operated by the CPB "could transform disparate foreign affairs tools into an 'electronic peace corps' " (cited in Wilner, 1993a, p. 1). Douglas Bennet, NPR's president and a former official of the U.S. Agency for International Development, indicated his support of the proposal.

Carlson's recommendation was not adopted by the Clinton administration, but distribution abroad of American public broadcasting continued to increase. In 1993, NPR began direct broadcast of *ATC* and other news and public affairs programs throughout Europe. Ken Sale of Worldnet indicated that at least 80% of the television programs acquired by the USIA for distribution worldwide via satellite originated as public television programs (personal communication, July 24, 1994). According to Sale, public television provided more programming relevant to the USIA's mission than any other source. To indicate the USIA connections and the desire to employ public broadcasting to enhance America's image abroad is not to assert the reductionist proposition that the CPB was created primarily as a tool of government foreign propaganda. The original Carnegie Commission made it clear that the fundamental focus of the new public broadcasting system would be domestic. Social and cultural traditions in the United States mitigated against a state-run broadcast entity like the BBC. Instead, the creation of the CPB can be viewed as a quasi-official "chosen instrument" of the government—like the establishment of RCA a half-century earlier—in addressing certain domestic and foreign communication needs in which the state had an interest.

The CPB, as recommended by Carnegie I, was designed as both a nongovernmental and a noncommercial institution charged with insulating public radio and television from political pressure. However, a key Carnegie recommendation—that funding be separated from the political process through a tax on broadcast licenses—was rejected by the Johnson administration. As Lashley (1992) emphasized, congressional appropriations as well as presidential appointments of CPB board members meant that organizational survival required compliance with the expectations of the legislative and executive branches of government. Financial insulation through a dedicated tax was rejected to avoid the opposition of commercial broadcasters to the 1967 Act, but Rowland (1976) speculated about a more broadly political motive: "If greater insulation were achieved, public broadcasting might emerge with sufficient strength to allow aspects of it to become a consistent source of controversy and challenge to various elements of the nation's dominant political, economic and cultural forces" (p. 129).

CHAPTER 14

The Attack of the Right and the Future of Public Radio and Television

Soon after passage of the Public Broadcasting Act of 1967, powerful conservative political forces placed public broadcasting under a more or less continuous siege that has lasted up until the present. In this undertaking, the new right had powerful allies in the White House and in Congress, from Richard Nixon in the late 1960s and early 1970s and Ronald Reagan in the 1980s to Senator Robert Dole and House Speaker Newt Gingrich in the 1990s. Hence, besides the system's funding and bureaucratic structure, pressure from the political right put political constraints on the development of public broadcasting's flagship news programs. *All Things Considered* began as an innovative news magazine both in form and in content but became more mainstream in its coverage as NPR evolved from a supplementary to a primary news source. Official Washington increasingly set the agenda in coverage of domestic and foreign affairs and provided a significant share of the program's news sources and commentators. The same could be said about PBS's *MacNeil/Lehrer NewsHour.* Robert MacNeil's and Jim Lehrer's roots in public broadcasting dated back to the National Public Affairs Center for Television in Washington, which had provoked the ire of the Nixon administration. And expanding *MacNeil/Lehrer* to make it the first hour-long national news broadcast on television was a bold step. Still, independent and especially oppositional voices from minority organizations, organized labor, environmental or consumer groups, and the peace movement were absent or received token representation on the *NewsHour. ATC* and *MacNeil/Lehrer* sought to avoid controversy by positioning themselves as meticulously centrist in orientation.

On both NPR and PBS news programs, public policy issues were ordinarily examined within the ideological confines of the two-party system, with discussion by representatives of the political elite supplemented by the purportedly dispassionate analysis of established experts. Indeed, the limitation of passion and controversy was seen as a virtue. Hence, as noted earlier, Linda Wertheimer hailed *ATC* for providing "an island of calm discourse," and Charles Kuralt heralded *ATC* for creating an "air of reason and good humor." Along the same lines, Robert MacNeil indicated his desire to bring "a quieter, more thoughtful, more civil atmosphere" to the *NewsHour.* Such journalistic values worked against the inclusion of discordant, oppositional voices. What Ryan (1993) wrote about *ATC* held also for the *NewsHour*: Both programs framed political debate largely in terms of intergovernmental or expert-driven rather than public discourse. Quantitatively, by virtue of the length and detail of their reports, *ATC* and *MacNeil/Lehrer* were superior to the news programs of the commercial networks. Despite some promising early initiatives, this was not the case qualitatively in terms of extending the scope of coverage topically and methodologically.

ATC and the *NewsHour,* like the CPB/NPR/PBS institutionally, yearned to be politically neutral and all-inclusive. Public broadcasting, as conceived by the Ford and Carnegie foundations, was predicated on the notion that nonprofit institutions could function as a third force, mediating between government and the private sector in such a way as to foster greater civic discourse and to reaffirm American democracy and pluralism. However, because the initiative came from above and government and other elite groups exercised ultimate control over the system established in 1967, public broadcasting has functioned largely as a pseudo- or hegemonic public sphere. McLaughlin (1994) noted how critics of Habermas have applied the Gramscian concept of hegemony to demystify the bourgeois public sphere as a neutral arena for rational political discourse based on a general common good. In the official public sphere, public life is organized to serve dominant groups under a mantle of universal inclusion while engaging in exclusionary practices vis-à-vis oppositional groups that question the legitimacy of the established order. When public broadcasting is conceived as part of a hegemonic public sphere, the character and limits of political discourse on NPR and PBS become more comprehensible.

Moreover, the aspiration that "third force" institutions like the CPB contain and transcend political conflict in the United States inevitably proved problematic. Williams (1975) noted that a historically more cohesive social elite in Britain than in the United States made the paternalistic form of public service broadcasting represented by the BBC feasible. The transition from the foundation years to the federal years of public television took place during the Kennedy and Johnson administrations, which marked the end of a period of liberal political ascendency in the United States. The centrist faith in peaceful progress within the existing social order would be challenged by both the right and the left. In 1968, Richard Nixon, a sworn enemy of the eastern establishment, was elected president. The lack of insulation from the state would enable Nixon to mount a political assault against public television.

The political and financial constraints imposed by the Nixon administration provided an opening for an increased role for corporate underwriters in public television, which compromised the noncommercial character of the system. Public television became a major public relations vehicle for enhancing the image of corporations through noncontroversial programming. Following the oil crisis, for example, public television became increasingly associated with Mobil Oil's support of *Masterpiece Theater.* Such underwriting was part of a broad tendency defined by Schiller (1989) as *Culture, Inc.: The Corporate Takeover of Public Expression.* Mobil Oil's involvement in public television was part of its strategy of countering what it considered antibusiness views in the mass media. In general, corporate underwriting of prominent programs like the *Nightly Business Report, Adam Smith's Money World,* and *Wall $treet Week* created a favorable business climate on public television. At the same time, labor and consumer perspectives were often absent or underrepresented on PBS.

The commercialization of public television took a quantum leap forward during the Reagan administration, which placed a premium on market solutions and deregulation. This inaugurated a period of experimentation with a host of ancillary commercial ventures and increased collaboration with private entities. Underwriting guidelines were relaxed in 1984, permitting corporate identification and display of products so that credits increasingly resembled advertising on commercial television. Jackson (1993) depicted typical post-1984 corporate "tags" by banking institutions on public television:

> A luxury car tools along a mountain road. A Citicorp bankcard gleams behind the slogan, "Anyhow. Anywhere. Anytime. Right Now." Chase Manhattan advises viewers: "We believe that helping our customers realize their dreams is the best investment we can make." . . .
>
> According to PBS, these are not commercials, but "enhanced underwriter acknowledgments." (p. 17)

The federal era of public television had yielded to the corporate era.

There were precedents in the history of American broadcasting for the turn taken by public television. The progressive expansion of allowable limits of advertising on public television replicated a process in the early years of commercial broadcasting. The double standard forbidding parties other than corporations from underwriting program topics in which they had a direct interest paralleled the distinction, made by Herbert Hoover and federal regulators during the interwar period, between "general interest" commercial radio stations and "special interest" nonprofit outlets. Leach (1983), who studied the movement in the 1930s to provide educational programming under the auspices of the commercial networks, observed that "the spirit of Cooperation lives on, though in guises very different from the original" (p. 2).

The doctrine of Cooperation, originally used to oppose the reservation of noncommercial channels, had been turned on its head: Programming on the public broadcasting network was now increasingly sponsored—and shaped—by private interests. Among those interests were some of the founding fathers of commercial broadcasting. AT&T, a partner in the creation of RCA, owner of WEAF, the first commercial radio station, could use the public television system as part of its public relations campaign for domestic and international expansion by underwriting PBS's premiere news program *MacNeil/Lehrer.* Another original RCA partner, General Electric, the scandal-ridden military contractor and owner of the commercial NBC network, could help shape the views of public television's influential audience by serving, for example, as the exclusive national underwriter of the conservatively oriented *McLaughlin Group*.

In 1994, independent producer Danny Schecter argued that the combination of political constraints and corporate underwriting contributed to a climate within public broadcasting comparable to that within the networks in the 1950s. Schechter noted that the smear campaigns against *South Africa Now* and *Rights & Wrongs* by David Horowitz's publication *COMINT* caught the ear of conservative board members of the CPB and Senator Robert Dole and how the attacks escalated to include Bill Moyers and the overall balance of programming aired by PBS. Such pressure made programs that "temper the tone, calm the waters" like *MacNeil/Lehrer* more palatable within the public TV bureaucracy but mitigated against controversial public affairs programming: "PBS will air endless programs on the civil rights movements of the past but not the human rights movement of the present. There was a history of the Civil War, but not the Gulf War" (p. 3). Schechter (1994) continued,

> The chilling effect *today* is more subtle but just as real. There are no loyalty oaths to swear to, or Congressional investigators to placate. Yet a fusion of conservative political ideology and conventional market-driven wisdom continues to guide media gatekeepers in decisions about what to buy, fund, commission and broadcast. Only no one talks about the political effects of the process. It is largely invisible . . . a Red Scare without the Reds. (p. 3)

Programs like *South Africa Now* and *Rights & Wrongs* produced by independent producers were too controversial and unpredictable to receive the corporate underwriting necessary for a secure niche in the PBS schedule.

The financial dependency of public television on corporate underwriting should be seen in perspective. According to CPB statistics, by 1990, corporations supplied about 16% of public television's total budget and 27% of PBS's national programming costs. About 40% of public television funds were provided by local, state, and federal government from tax revenues; viewer contributions amounted to about 25%. However, a considerable portion of taxpayer and viewer funds were used for fixed expenses and station operations, whereas corporate funds were earmarked to produce and promote specific programs. Hence, corporate funds had a disproportionate impact on creating and sustaining as well as publicizing programming: Some underwriters spend millions of dollars to promote public awareness of programming they have underwritten. Aufderheide (1991a) stressed that the significance of underwriting transcended corporate support for specific programs: "More important, corporate funding conditions what *doesn't* get made—or even imagined" (p. 62).

The exploitation of public television as a vehicle for corporate public relations and advertising also confused the mission of public television and had a chilling effect on broader public support and participation. Thus, public television came to reinforce rather than challenge the proposition stated by Barnouw (1978): "The sponsor, the merchant, has been living at the summit of our communication system" (p. 182). Illustrative is the example of *The Nightly Business Report,* the longest running and most watched financial news program on American television, distributed internationally by the USIA and underwritten by the nation's fifth largest brokerage firm and by a major financial services organization. As a result, the concept of a discrete public domain became obscured in relation to both public and commercial television. The periodization of public broadcasting history into the foundation, government, and corporate years is meant to accent the phases of public television history. Of course, these forces were always simultaneously at play and intertwined: Often, the broadcast of a given program was the result of financial support from all three sources together with viewer subscriptions. Thus, a public radio and television system chartered as nongovernmental and noncommercial nonetheless served important interests of the state and of business. What emerged was a quasi-public, quasi-governmental, quasi-commercial system.

The public's relationship to the public broadcasting system has been problematic from the outset. The reservation of channels for noncommercial television came about primarily as the result of the machinations of the Ford Foundation and its allies, not as a result of a more broadly based popular campaign like that in support of the Wagner-Hatfield Bill of 1934 to reserve noncommercial channels on AM radio. The 1967 report of the Carnegie Commission on Educational Television, in effect the CPB's mission statement, did not contain an expansive view of the public's role, stating simply that "we seek for the citizen freedom to view, to see programs that the present system, by its incompleteness, denies him" (p. 99). Blakely (1979) suggested that this narrow definition of the role of the citizen, virtually excluding the public from active participation, revealed a fatal flaw that haunted public television:

The report does not include the concept of television as the people's instrument to present grievances, to be heard and seen, to explain, to express, to use television as a means of communication in action to pursue the most serious personal and social goals. (p. 179)

Rowland (1976) made a searching critique of the failure to make "public" broadcasting a democratic institution. The absence of a principle of popular participation was compounded by the CPB's audience research methodology, which was rooted in the quantitative and qualitative criteria of commercial broadcasting. The CPB, PBS, or local station boards, made up largely of political and economic elites, were not broadly representative of American society:

A direct consequence is that battles like those over funding and the shape of the national institutions continue to be fought rather silently, albeit ferociously, well behind the scenes, without any substantial questioning of the assumptions underlying the terms of the dispute. Since they all speak essentially the same language, these power brokers on the different boards find it all too easy to reach decisions . . . that are worked out privately, not through any form of open, public debate. . . . Even national conventions and annual meetings, which ought to provide forums for developing a dialogue among differing professional and public interests, tend to serve as vehicles for rubber stamping compromises previously, and often secretly, arrived at. (p. 184)

Groups represented in the Advisory Council of National Organizations, established to lobby for the CPB, were denied meaningful participation in the public broadcasting system. In the mid-1970s, important constituencies represented within the ANCO—the women's movement, organized labor, and minorities—broke with the CPB over hiring and programming practices. By failing to mobilize their listeners, and instead alienating natural allies, public broadcasters made themselves more vulnerable to the political attacks mounted by the Nixon and Reagan administrations. As Rowland (1976) observed, the failure to create "any widespread collective self-awareness" (p. 111) of a noncommercial public community of viewers represented a fundamental flaw in the federal form of public television.

The CBP, attacked from the right by the Nixon administration, received increasing criticism from the left during the mid-1970s. Community groups across the nation—from New York to Texas to San Francisco—challenged the way public television stations were managed through confrontations with station officials and local boards and legal challenges. National organizations brought charges of fiscal irresponsibility, discrimination, and elitism to the attention of Congress and the public. Among those organizations were many of the same constituencies that had spearheaded the broadcast reform movement of the 1930s: educators, civil libertarians, church groups, and labor leaders. New elements, especially representatives of the women's movement, minority organizations, and independent producers, joined the revived coalition, whose efforts at legislative reform—unlike those a generation earlier—were seemingly crowned with success. The Public Broadcasting Financing Act of 1978 promised a new level of accountability and participation. However, the objectives of the legislation remained largely unrealized. During the 1980s, the members of the media reform coalition, which was no longer intact, experienced a growing sense of disappointment and betrayal.

In weathering the attacks from the right and the left, the public broadcasting system demonstrated a remarkable resiliency. It survived Nixon's political offensive, Reagan's attempt at defunding, and the broad-based public insurgency. If public broadcasting served the interests of the state and the corporation, it also created its own new class of bureaucrats. According to Lashley (1992), "As citizen participation waned, the power, influence, and role of the station professionals, particularly station managers, steadily increased" (p. 63). Applying organization theory to her examination of public broadcasting, Lashley posited that public broadcasting professionals defined their interests bureaucratically in terms of maintaining their positions and funding by adjusting to changing political circumstances. Rowland (1976) charged that public television executives invoked the "public" only as a rhetorical device to legitimate appropriations of taxpayers funds.

Disenchantment with the federal form of public broadcasting as a democratic communications system contributed to the movement for an alternative form of public access on cable television. As with radio, a fundamental divide separated community and federal forms of public television. "Access" became the rallying cry for a new, more participatory model of public television. Just as the advent of FM afforded Lewis Hill the opportunity to create a new form of public radio, cable television and portable video equipment permitted the emergence of a different, nonbroadcast form of public television. This departure had its antecedents during the latter half of the 1960s in the Challenge for Change program of the National Film Board of Canada.

Drawing on a unique theoretical and practical tradition in Canada of viewing mass media as public resources, Challenge for Change originally sought to use film as a tool for citizen mobilization and communication with government officials in Canada's war on poverty. The program expanded with the use of new communication technologies for social protest as well as for citizen-government collaboration. The introduction of portable video equipment and cable TV systems with channels reserved for the public permitted what was formerly considered impossible: television production by ordinary citizens and community groups.

The possibilities for public access demonstrated in Canada were brought to the United States by George Stoney, who together with Red Burns founded the Alternative Media Center in 1971. The Center led the movement for public access during the early 1970s, a period of crisis for the CPB and PBS when many of the original aspirations associated with the Public Broadcasting Act of 1967 were dashed. Community television on cable systems seemed to promise a purer, more independent form of public telecommunication. Nonetheless, many of the same forces that had shaped public broadcasting— for example, the private foundation—were again at play. The John and Mary R. Markle Foundation provided seed money and continuing support for the Alternative Media Center and Theadora Sklover's Open Channel. The 1971 report of the Sloan Commission on Cable Communications, a blue-ribbon body comparable to the Carnegie Commission on Educational Television, discussed cable television's potential social benefits and helped legitimate public access channels. The Ford and Rockefeller foundations also made strategic interventions in the development of public access.

The public access movement also had to contend with commercial and political forces. From 1968 to 1972, the FCC deliberated about standards for the development of cable television, as it had for broadcast television during the license freeze from 1948 to 1952. Early support for public access by cable operators came at a time when an emerging cable television industry, vulnerable financially and politically, needed to establish its legitimacy vis-à-vis "free" broadcast television. For a brief moment, the interests of the cable industry and the video freaks of the radical video collectives coincided. Red Burns was brought in as codirector of the Alternate Media Center because of her contacts in the cable industry, which provided early allies of the community television movement. Only a minority within the community television movement sounded a warning. Paskal (1971) argued in a sobering and prescient polemic in the summer 1971 issue of *Radical Software* that "whoever believes that gaining access to cable will enable him to control his destiny in any meaningful way is a fool" (p. 3). He accused public access advocates who dutifully testified before the Sloan Commission of ignoring the broader strategy behind the offer of access channels: to pave the way for a new frontier of consumer capitalism in which banking, shopping, information services, and entertainment would be supplied through the cable. "So," Paskal wrote, "community cable becomes the free gift and everyone packs in to the information supermarket" (p. 4). Public and corporate agendas intersected, albeit for a limited period of time. The cable industry championed public access, just as the commercial networks supported the Public Broadcasting Act of 1967, out of enlightened self-interest.

The corporate-community TV alliance broke down as the cable industry became more established. The cable industry's challenge to the right of the FCC to require public access was upheld by the U.S. Supreme Court in 1979. Further attempts were made to weaken public access through legislation and obstructionist practices at local cable franchises. Some cable companies reneged on commitments of resources to public access centers. Others replaced public access on a first-come, first-served basis with a system of "local origination," in which cable companies controlled public access. Once again, the old doctrine of Cooperation reared its head; once again, the distinction between public and private control of noncommercial television was obscured, a process parallel to that within PBS.

The Cable Communications Policy Act of 1984 weakened public access by sharply limiting the regulatory powers of state and local authorities. In a changed political and communications environment, Michael Shamberg, the ideologue of "guerrilla television," went to Hollywood to produce commercial films. Red Burns became sole director of the Alternate Media Center, which was rechristened the Interactive Telecommunications Program and reorganized to prepare students for careers in the high technology sector of the communications industry. The Alternate Media Center had relinquished its name, its leadership role in public telecommunications, and even its historical record. By the 1990s, public access channels persevered on fewer than one sixth of the nation's cable systems.

Besides opposition from without, the community television movement was constrained from within by the theory and practice of public access. An acceptance of the assumptions of American pluralism together with highly individualistic and fragmented programming undermined the capacity for collective and oppositional uses of public access. Sholle (1994) emphasized how a multiplicity of voices drowned one another out in an environment of disjointed discourse, resulting in "the fragmentation of the public sphere into multiple, isolated partial publics" (p. 28) which were unable to communicate with one another and forge coalitions. "As a result," Sholle wrote, "the collective basis of access is lost" (p. 25).

The *Paper Tiger Television* project provided an impetus for overcoming the theoretical and practical limitations that threatened to define public access by the 1980s. By building a bold and refreshing critique of mainstream media, the *Paper Tiger TV* series challenged the premises of American liberalism and pluralism. By virtue of its collective character and its organization of the *Deep Dish* network, *Paper Tiger TV* transcended the individualism and political fragmentation that plagued much of public access. The creation of the first national public access network in 1986 represented a milestone in the history of public radio and television. It occurred 20 years after the inception of Challenge for Change, transforming the Canadian model for employing video and cable technology for social change for the era of satellite communication. *Deep Dish TV* harked back even further to the aspirations of the first generation of amateur broadcasters, exactly a half century after Hiram Maxim's creation of an experimental national ham relay in 1916. As a result of *Deep Dish,* the New York-based *Paper Tiger* collective spawned an open-ended national collective of public access programmers able to share their work and collaborate on joint ventures.

The *Gulf Crisis TV Project* took the public access network to a new level, elevating it to an international plane. By using mass media as an instrument of peace and international understanding, the *Gulf Crisis TV Project* belonged to a strain of the media reform movement reaching back to Joy Elmer Morgan in the 1930s and Lewis Hill in the 1950s. The experience of *Deep Dish TV* and the *Gulf Crisis TV Project* affirmed the axiom stated by Nicholas Garnham: "It is cultural distribution, not cultural production, that is the key locus of power" (cited in Blau, 1992, p. 26). Wallner (1991) suggested that the *Paper Tiger/Deep Dish/Gulf Crisis TV Project* provided a model for reinvigorating public radio and television as a whole:

> *Deep Dish* has become a laboratory for new ways of making media and distributing it. We are constantly asking what are the most democratic, the most empowering models for media production and distribution? Under what circumstances will local activists start using their access stations more? How can we make the programs more interactive with viewers? How can *Deep*

> *Dish* collaborate with other media outlets, including PBS affiliates willing to take some risks, community TV and radio broadcasters, progressive print journalists, and the growing number of colleges and universities equipped with satellite dishes? (p. 34)

* * *

Deep Dish TV represented an important final step in the creation of public radio and television systems in the half century following World War II. The period was framed by the creation of a system of community radio by Pacifica at the outset and by the creation of a national and international community television network at the end. During the same era, a federal form of public radio and television was fostered by the foundation world and institutionalized by Congress. The sheer quantity and range of public radio and television activity in this period—despite all the constraints and compromises—represented a significant accomplishment within a social system in which commerce reigned supreme.

However, the apparent fulfillment of the movement to create noncommercial radio and television networks, defeated during the interwar years, was challenged in the 1990s. Shortly after the Republican Party gained control of both houses of Congress in 1994, House Speaker Newt Gingrich endorsed the crusade by the Christian Coalition and other organizations of the radical right to eliminate the CPB. In January 1995, a bill to repeal the statutory authority for the CPB was introduced in the House of Representatives. At the same time, Senator Larry Pressler, chairman of the Senate Commerce, Science, and Transportation Committee, sent a letter to CPB President Henry J. Cauthen insisting on the need to defund and privatize the CPB: "CPB officials must face this reality and reinvent their system" (Pressler, 1995).

Attached to the letter was a hostile 15-page, single-spaced questionnaire with leading questions based on the premises of the right-wing critique of public broadcasting. The inquiry was also submitted to all CPB board members, PBS, NPR, CTW, and the Pacifica Foundation. Pressler sought documentation for virtually every aspect of public broadcasting—from its contractual relationships and personnel practices to the use of funds and programming decisions. For example, information demanded about NPR included job descriptions and salary of all full-time employees, proof of balanced coverage of controversial issues, and explanation for allocations of

NPR's National Radio Production Fund. Similar questions were asked about every facet of public television, requiring exhaustive documentation of contracts, correspondence, and memoranda. Many queries zeroed in on public affairs programming: the mechanisms that ensure balance for PBS's National Program Service, the criteria used by the ITVS in evaluating proposals, and the reason for the CPB's selection of *P.O.V.* as the principal vehicle for documentaries with a point of view. The CPB was asked to provide its correspondence with *Frontline* and *The American Experience* in regard to issues of balance and objectivity and to respond to complaints by the National Rifle Association and other organizations about a variety of specific programs.

Although the questionnaire addressed to the CPB's president focused on NPR and PBS, Pacifica Radio was also singled out as a source of controversial programming and of personnel for mainstream public broadcasting. Had the CPB reviewed Pacifica programming for objectivity and balance, and if not, why not? Furthermore, in contrast to evangelical Christian stations, "How many NPR staff have previously worked for Pacifica stations? Please list them by name and job category" (p. 18). The query was a throwback to the Senate Internal Security Subcommittee hearings on Pacifica a quarter century earlier and evoked the language of the witch hunts of the 1950s, asking in effect, "Are you now, or have you ever been, associated with Pacifica?" People for the American Way characterized Pressler's inquiry as an effort to "chill political speech . . . not seen since the era of Sen. Joe McCarthy" (cited in "Pressler Stocking Up," 1995, p. 1). The climate of political restraint and self-censorship surrounding public broadcasting, what independent producer Danny Schechter called a "Red scare without Reds," became more overt.

How is one to interpret the new attack on public broadcasting and the lessons to be derived for media activists? The attack from the right is not new but part of a continuum from the earliest days of the CPB during the Nixon administration through the Reagan presidency of the 1980s to the present. This pattern underscores the defensive position of public broadcasting since 1967 and its institutional resiliency in weathering attacks through a pattern of strategic compromises. However, the assault of the mid-1990s represents a greater threat than those of the past when Nixon's political purge and Reagan's program of privatization were blunted. Now, a Congress controlled by the radical right, bearing the torch of cultural warfare and highly attuned to communication issues, is in a position to dismantle rather than protect public broadcasting. Moreover, by the 1990s not only were the foundation and government years long gone but the corporate years were winding down as public broadcasting became less important as an ideological and public relations vehicle for big business.

Indeed, there was a hint that interest in the corporate world might shift from underwriting to more direct forms of investment. At the end of 1993 it was announced that Liberty Media, a subsidiary of TCI, the largest cable system in the United States, was buying a two-thirds interest in the production company of the *MacNeil/Lehrer NewsHour.* The program, a past beneficiary of underwriting by corporate giants, is now owned by one. TCI is headed by archconservative John Malone, an admirer of Rush Limbaugh who has expanded carriage of the right-wing National Empowerment Television on TCI systems. Although TCI has been called the most discriminatory company in the telecommunication industry by the NAACP and is being investigated by the FCC for antitrust violations, the corporate takeover of public TV's flagship news program was welcomed by PBS (FAIR, 1995, p. 1).

Early in 1994, Senator Pressler disclosed that the Bell Atlantic Corporation, a regional Bell company in the eastern United States considering the distribution of television programming over its network, expressed interest in acquiring a stake in the CPB (Andrews, 1995). The disclosure in January 1995 by Pressler, chairman of the Senate Commerce Committee, was made within days of his jeremiad addressed to Henry Cauthen about the need to privatize the CPB. A new question was on the horizon for public broadcasting as it approached the 21st century: not whether public broadcasting would sell out but whether it would sell off (i.e., permit entities with commercial potential within its system to be acquired by the private sector). Wally Smith (1995), president of KUSC-FM/Los Angeles, suggested that defunding was part of a broader strategy to render public television ripe for takeover: "The debate about funding is a distraction from the real motive: to sell off the airwaves to private, for-profit commercial interests" (p. 12).

The public was largely a bystander in the most recent political conflict over the future of public broadcasting, which pitted the approach of the old eastern establishment against that of a new right with geographical roots in the South and the West. Indeed, the lack of genuine public involvement in the affairs of the CPB/PBS/NPR rendered these bureaucracies vulnerable to political attack. Now, belatedly and out of desperation, the call went out from the managers of the system seeking to rally public support for continued funding of the CPB. Cockburn (1995a) suggested in *The Nation* magazine that media activists abandon the ship of mainstream public broadcasting, which he deemed not worth defending, declaring "I'm with Gingrich on this one" (p. 299). In response, independent radio producer David Barsamian reminded Cockburn that CPB funds were also critical for the survival of small, independent community stations as well as for public broadcasting's major production centers, adding, "I share your disdain for PBS and NPR but there is a larger principle at stake, the notion of public airwaves" (cited in Cockburn, 1995b, p. 589).

Whether popular forces should be mobilized to defend the federal form of public broadcasting in its current crisis is related to a larger strategic dilemma facing media activists: infiltrating dominant media systems like PBS and NPR versus building independent distribution networks. Sholle (1994) suggested that such a dichotomy can be overdrawn and misleading, that no mass media in an advanced capitalist state can be wholly autonomous of dominant forces, so that the struggle for alternative practice should be waged on both fronts. If PBS and NPR represent a hegemonic public sphere with strong ties to the state and business, they cannot function in a monolithic fashion. A narrow yet significant margin of freedom exists due to structural contradictions, bureaucratic rivalries, and the democratic rhetoric intrinsic to public broadcasting—factors that can be capitalized on by independent forces within the system and public interest groups on the outside. A modest example: Criticism of the limited range of perspectives on *MacNeil/Lehrer* led to the inclusion of a regular commentator from the left, the late Erwin Knoll, editor of *Progressive* magazine. Hoynes (1994) insists that, as a unique system of national mass communication in the United States at least partially independent of the market and the state, public broadcasting represents "a key site in the struggle for a reinvigorated public sphere and a more healthy civil society" (p. 165).

Independent producers have demonstrated the possibilities of maximizing the openings within the highly restrictive confines of public television. Yet such successes occur rarely and against great odds and usually are of limited duration. They require extraordinary creativity and sacrifice, a willingness to struggle in a hostile environment, and a participatory vision of public telecommunication. At such moments, pseudopublic spheres become more open, even oppositional sites of communication and action. The mere possibility of an occasional breakthrough in programming such as Globalvision's *South Africa Now* is anathema to the new right, driving its attack on the very notion of a public sphere and on the rights of minorities and other counterpublics. So are those documentaries on *Frontline, P.O.V.,* or *The American Experience* and the reports on *MacNeil/Lehrer* or *ATC* that transcend the usual topical or ideological limits of commercial news and public affairs programming.

The attack on public broadcasting is part of a larger campaign against all institutions with some degree of autonomy from the market. PBS President Ervin S. Duggan (1995) noted that the congressional attack on public broadcasting's expenses was essentially symbolic, for the CPB's budget amounted to 1/50th of 1% of the federal budget, the equivalent of $1.09 per person. He added,

> That word "public" in public broadcasting refers to . . . a mission that cannot be replaced by commercial operators any more than your public library can be duplicated by Crown Books, a public school replaced by a New England prep school, or a national seashore duplicated by a commercial theme park. (p. 24)

The question is whether the last vestiges of independent mass communication systems will be destroyed along with a notion of citizenship distinct from the consumership. The struggle over public broadcasting, involving the public's right and ability to engage in informed political debate independent of private commercial forces, has crucial implications for the future of American democracy. "This," McChesney (1995) observes, "was precisely how the 1930s broadcaster reformers understood the long-term implications of the fight for the control of broadcasting; it remains the fundamental question before us" (p. 10).

This is an opportune moment for media reformers to revive the broad coalitions of the 1930s and the 1970s. "First, and perhaps most important," Hoynes (1994) writes, "is the need for a renewed grassroots movement as the carrier of a vision for change" (p. 178). Himmelstein (1984) suggests that the American people loom as a great potential base of support because "their pent-up frustration through years of enforced electronic silence craves an outlet" (p. 321). Halleck notes,

> There are thousands out there who did not come from NYU film school, but who come from the grassroots, who know what it means to produce community programming on public access, who can get involved in their local public television station. If they do so, the prospects for public TV will be much brighter. (personal communication, July 14, 1986)

The programming initiatives of Jack Willis at Twin Cities Public Television and of the Nitty Gritty City Group likewise suggest a potential convergence of community and public television. The attack on public broadcasting represents both an opportunity for and a threat to its future development. Recently, PBS has temporized, engaged in self-censorship, and made overtures to the right—in 1995, to give but one recent example, with *Peggy Noonan on Values,* hosted by the former Reagan and Bush speechwriter—to no avail. The failure to placate conservative adversaries could liberate public broadcasting to take greater risks and to engage the full spectrum of the American public as envisioned by the Carnegie Commission in 1967.

At this juncture, the federal system of public radio and television must choose whether to become more or less like commercial broadcasting. Public broadcasters are divided in their response to the threat of federal defunding. Some public television officials, including the station managers of WHYY/Philadelphia, WTTW/Chicago, and KCET/St. Louis, advocate dispensing with the remaining constraints on underwriting credits and accepting full-fledged commercials (Kolbert, 1995). Conversely, the opportunity is also at hand for public broadcasting to distance itself more from commercial broadcasting and to become a greater resource for diverse popular constituencies. To this end, other public broadcasting policymakers and activists have reintroduced funding strategies similar to that proposed by the original Carnegie Commission but rejected by Congress: a permanent source of income derived from transfer fees on the sale of radio and TV stations or from fees for commercial users of the broadcast spectrum.

On the programming front, there is talk of moving away from costly commercial production values and increasing coverage of community-based political and cultural events—for example, town hall meetings and political debates with feedback from viewers and broadcasts of plays, poetry readings, and concerts. If public broadcasting is to withstand the political and commercial challenges to its existence, it must pursue new avenues of funding and programming and involve the public more directly in its affairs. Public television can apply the participatory practices of public access and the interactive formats of programs like NPR's national call-in show, *Talk of the Nation.* Paradoxically, as Berger (1995) observed in regard to public TV, "Republican foes are forcing PBS to clarify its mission and perhaps save its life" (p. 1).

Radio Catskill WJFF-FM could serve as an example of a community radio station in a postfederal and postcorporate era. It began broadcasting in

1990 in Jeffersonville, New York, as the nation's first hydroelectrically powered station. Hydropower was initially harnessed from Callicoon Creek by two turbines in the home of Malcolm Brown and Anne Larsen, who subsequently built a nonprofit hydroelectric power station. They established the radio station, adjacent to the power plant, with volunteers originally mobilized through an advertisement in a local newspaper. The station received some federal, state, and local funding but owed its existence to an outpouring of local support. The community immediately realized that the station could serve as a vital resource in the Catskill area, which was suffering economically from its decline as a summer resort area. Larsen said that "it will be natural for us to talk about land trusts, eagle habitat, alternate sources of energy, land-use planning—the whole range of issues that we have in common" (cited in Gref, 1989, p, 7). The station raised over $20,000 in individual memberships prior to going on the air. Volunteers built the studio with materials discounted by local building supply companies. The satellite dish was received as a donation. By 1995, WJFF was receiving only about $11,000 in federal support annually. An affiliate of NPR and Public Radio International, 40% of its programming is produced locally, which includes reports on local events, a wide range of musical offerings, and a talk show called *The People Talk Back.* WJFF, in the tradition of popular technological experimentation of the first generation of radio and cable operators and the communitarian spirit of Lorenzo Milam, has created a new network and sense of community in a 60-square mile area of New York and Pennsylvania.

The frontal assault on public telecommunication has important ramifications for both the community and the federal form of public radio and television. Pacifica Radio has been singled out as a target not only by Senator Larry Pressler but by the new right in general. The congressional campaign to defund the CPB represents a vindication of sorts for the seemingly more marginal independent and alternative forces within public broadcasting. Community television and radio, despite a history of meager resources and instability, may be better positioned for long-term survival than mainstream public broadcasting, thanks to greater local participation and support and reliance on nonprofessional volunteers and low-cost production.

However, Pacifica must rise to the challenge posed by the conservative offensive and not temporize as it sometimes did in the past when under attack. Cockburn (1995b) complains that "the Pacifica HQ is waging war without pity on anything of radical or intellectually vivacious timbre" (p. 589). A study by Stavitsky and Gleason (1994) found a growing convergence in the journalistic practice of *All Things Considered* and Pacifica's expanded evening national newscast, which is competing with NPR for affiliates. Yet at the same time, local Pacifica stations have countered the cautiousness of the national office by taking significant initiatives in public affairs programming. For example, in April 1995, WBAI sponsored a public forum in New York on the continuing struggle for democracy in Haiti. The forum, taped for broadcast, was sponsored jointly by *The Nation* magazine and the Peasant Movement of Papay of Haiti and featured Noam Chomsky, a *Nation* reporter, a popular Haitian leader, and WBAI programmers along with a video presentation by Crowing Rooster Productions.

WBAI's Haiti forum was in keeping with Sholle's (1994) recommendation that "various counterpublics cohering around alternative media seek out potential connections with each other in order to establish a more comprehensive public sphere that can establish lines of communication blocked by dominant publicity" (p. 17). In terms of its sponsorship, participants and audience—which embraced dissident intellectuals, critics of U.S. foreign policy and racism, and representatives of the large Haitian community in New York—the Pacifica forum represented the kind of coalition building critical for the future of community radio and also community television. As Haight and Weinstein (1981) argued, media reformers "should spend less time negotiating the corridors of Washington and more time . . . involved in concrete struggles" of oppositional groups (p. 141).

The attack of the new right on public broadcasting will inevitably exacerbate tensions between the conservative and radical tendencies within the community television movement. The Alliance for Community Media, the national organization for public access programmers, needs to reevaluate its relationship to the cable industry. The use of public access channels to prepare for careers in the cable industry, and the acceptance of commercial production values, underscore the question posed by Aufderheide (1991b): Is the goal an improved version of commercial television or antitelevision? The proponents of the latter, like their counterparts in community radio, will need to take a leap forward: "Alternative media has challenged dominant conceptions of production and shown the potential of the democratization of the media, but this has certainly not lead to a sweeping revitalization of the public sphere in terms of its audience reach" (Sholle, 1994, p. 21).

Deep Dish TV, despite a small full-time staff in New York, aspires to start a national news bureau, include more public broadcasting stations in its network, and do more outreach and promotion to reach potential viewers.

Deep Dish TV's executive director, noting the precariousness of the funding it receives from foundation and government arts agencies, has appealed for new sources of funding and volunteer support: "Help us continue to build a television network that reflects the diverse realities and creative energies of our city, nation and world" (Barrow, 1993, p. 2). The future of the satellite network is far from assured. As one of its founders, Martha Wallner, emphasized, *Deep Dish TV* "has struggled to make the transition from a project to an institution" (personal communication, July 26, 1995). The success of ventures like *Deep Dish* that transcend a circumscribed conception of public access will have important implications for the fate of the community television movement.

Braderman (1991) has advocated that the community television movement "re-claim the utopian moment" (p. 20). Obviously, no useful purpose would be served by denying the seriousness of the crisis facing public broadcasting or by reviving technological romanticism. "What needs to be staked out and reclaimed is a different utopian moment," Braverman continues, "the larger one, the one we're not supposed to even dream about anymore" (p. 20). A utopian sensibility is necessary to see possibilities beyond the status quo and to shape the movement for change. As Hoynes (1994) suggests, "It is shortsighted . . . to allow short-term versions of 'realism' to inhibit the development of an alternative conception of public television" (p. 159).

The history of public radio and television has been one of struggle— from the earliest days of the ham operators to the congressional offensive of 1994-1995. On closer scrutiny, public radio and television have always been in crisis to one degree or another. Reinvigoration of the public sphere does not ultimately hinge on social engineering, on the correct legislative configuration or funding formula, or even on the outcome of specific initiatives of media reformers. Rather, the public sphere has been extended periodically over the past century through the process of struggle itself, at those moments when visionaries and constituencies act to defend and extend the use of radio and television as democratic instruments. As Aufderheide (1992) emphasizes,

> The public sphere in American society is nearly inchoate at a rhetorical level. But when members of the public have resources to raise issues of public concern, debate among themselves and develop ways to act upon them,

telecommunications becomes a tool in the public's organizing of itself. (pp. 53-54)

Media reformers, although under attack, have networks—producers, distributors, university programs, and advocacy groups—that provide a foundation for the struggle ahead. De Michiel (1991) states that the edifice of mainstream commercial media does not exist unchallenged: "Although minuscule by mass media standards, a tenacious alternative media culture thrives, mole-like, on the outskirts of this golden house" (p. 15).

Ironically, the new right in its rise to power co-opted many of the practices and insights of the alternative media movement of the 1960s. Indeed, DeeDee Halleck has chastised the left for its failure to get more engaged in alternative media. In 1986, when *Paper Tiger TV* organized the first national public access satellite network, she said in frustration,

> It has been very difficult to get a serious discussion about public communications on the left, which continues to focus on getting the attention of mainstream media. I couldn't believe the lack of understanding of the *Deep Dish* project. Despite being carried on perhaps a thousand stations across the country, neither *In These Times* nor the Socialist Scholars Conference took notice. Meanwhile, Pat Robertson's 700 Club and the other satellite networks of the religious and political right continue to grow. One of the historic problems in the media reform movement has been finding a constituency. We need to ask: how can we place media on the agenda of the left? (personal communication, July 14, 1986)

An important step for the media reform movement is the rediscovery of its history, which reaches back to the origins of broadcasting. That chronicle—including, for example, the true story of Joy Elmer Morgan's leadership of the NCER in the 1930s, or the documentation on community television discarded by the Alternate Media Center—needs to be retrieved from the dustbin of radio and television history. The media reform movement has deep roots in the American experience and in the Bill of Rights. Halleck has emphasized the importance of popular appropriation of the rhetoric of the First Amendment: "If you take the language seriously, it has radical implications" (personal communication, June 5, 1986). Contemporary political developments should foster a greater awareness of the importance of alternative media and the public sphere. The ascendency of the right and its attack on public broadcasting, as well as rapid consolidation within the communication industry, place media reform on the public agenda. McChesney (1994) argues that the factors that made it impossible to challenge the structure of American broadcasting since 1935 are changing. The possibility now exists, for the first time in over half a century, to renew the debate about ownership and control of the mass media and the desirability of fundamental structural change:

> Most important, the "American century" is literally and figuratively nearing an end and the halcyon days of a bustling capitalism may well be in America's past. This may eventually undermine the inability to criticize capitalism in U.S. political culture. This is clearly a decisive factor. If no other lesson emerges from the early 1930s, then let it be that any viable campaign to reconstruct the media system must be part of a broad-based mass movement that is attempting to reform the basic institutions of U.S. society. (p. 269)

Hoynes (1994) advances five broad principles for the reform of public broadcasting, and by extension, of American society. The goals embrace social ownership independent of both the market and the state, diversity as the hallmark of a true public sphere, direct participation of the public in the system's governance, interaction of the public in programming, and a critical or multiperspectival approach to major American institutions. Realization of these goals requires maximizing public control rather than public access to mass media, the twin poles in the history of the media reform movement. At the same time, reformers should not isolate themselves but forge and lead a broad coalition of constituencies with a stake in a public communications system. Kellner (1990) writes that the quest for a democratic communications system and a democratic society are one and the same: "The technologies are there, but imagination, will, and struggle will be needed to realize the democratic potential that still exists in a system organized for the hegemony of capital in an era of conservative political rule" (p. 222).

Braderman's (1991) call for the public access movement to reclaim the utopian moment—indeed, to see itself as part of a continuum of emancipatory moments in American communication history—can be applied to noncommercial radio and television in the United States as a whole. To heed this call will help demystify the hegemonic aspects of the public sphere advanced by the political center and help counter the campaign of the right to delegitimize *any* form of the public sphere. It will also assist the strengthening of a counter or oppositional public sphere that is open to a wide spectrum of citizens and to unfettered discourse, affirming the autonomy of civil society vis-à-vis the state. Devine (1992) links the destiny of community media to the very survival of the public as a category. We need to resist the privatization of the benefits of new communication technologies in the age of the information superhighway: "What we are currently experiencing is a re-feudalization of the public sphere" (p. 8). Conversely, Devine continues, public access involves private citizens in public life, builds coalitions, and promotes collective action:

> In the process, public access shields participants from economic or state intimidation, allowing all ideas to be discusssed and tested through rational public debate. . . . In short, public access is the last best hope for a public sphere and for an active and enlightened polity. (p. 9)

The utopian impulse is rooted in a notion of radical democracy in which a vital public sphere of communication can foster free and diverse speech, a sense of community, and purposeful action. A strain of utopianism persists throughout the history of telecommunication in the United States, ranging from Walt Whitman's hope that the telegraph would unite a young democratic republic to the spirit of universal brotherhood linking amateur ham radio operators. A dream to use radio as a progressive social instrument inspired the pioneering radio stations of the land-grant universities of the Midwest and the crusade for the reservation of educational channels on the AM spectrum during the Great Depression. After World War II, echoes of the utopian tradition were heard in the mission statements for Pacifica Radio and NPR written by Lewis Hill and William Siemering. Despite a tendency to equate technological and social progress, great aspirations were also articulated for public uses of television in key texts such as the original Carnegie Commission on Educational Television and Michael Shamberg's (1971) *Guerrilla Television.* The models of community television developed by George Stoney and DeeDee Halleck likewise reflected the connection between public access and the quest for social transformation. It is essential that the utopian tradition be reaffirmed to counter corporate and state control of mass media and to animate the renewal of public radio and television in the United States.

References

A station in search of a character [Editorial]. (1977, February 28). *New York Times,* p. 26.

AIVF [Association of Independent Video and Filmmakers]. (1977, November 18). *Independent film/video artists testify at Carnegie Commission hearings on PBS* [Press release].

AIVF [Association of Independent Video and Filmmakers]. (1978). *The outsiders get a bigger piece of the pie* [Flyer].

Allen, F. L. (1964). *Only yesterday: An informal history of the 1920's.* New York: Harper & Row.

Allison, J. (1992, May 25). Our words affirm that we are committed to what Montiegel and "Soundprint" stand for. Our actions do not. *Current,* p. 14.

Alverez. (1984). Atlanta union energized by access efforts. *Community Television Review, 6*(4), 12-13.

Andrews, E. L. (1995, January 24). Bell Atlantic's (mild) interest in public broadcasting deal. *New York Times,* pp. D1, D18.

Anshien, C., Cohen, J., Klein, A., Levine, C., Meyer, L., & Skidmore, R. (1971). *Public access celebration: Report on public access in New York.* New York: Glad Day Press.

Arlen, M. J. (1967a, January 7). The air. *The New Yorker,* pp. 80-83.

Arlen, M. J. (1967b, November 18). The air. *The New Yorker,* pp. 143-148.

Arlen, M. J. (1967c, December 30). The air. *The New Yorker,* pp. 54-61.

Armstrong, D. (1981). *A trumpet to arms: Alternative media in America.* Boston: South End Press.

Aufderheide, P. (1991a, November/December). A funny thing is happening to TV's public forum. *Columbia Journalism Review,* pp. 60-63.

Aufderheide, P. (1991b). Public television and the public sphere. *Critical Studies in Mass Communication, 8,* 168-183.

Aufderheide, P. (1992). Cable television and the public interest. *Journal of Communication, 42*(1), 52-65.

Avery, R. K., & Pepper, R. (1979a). Balancing the equation: Public radio comes of age. *Public Telecommunications Review, 7*(2), 19-30.

Avery, R. K., & Pepper, R. (1979b). *The politics of interconnection: A history of public television at the national level.* Washington, DC: National Association of Educational Broadcasters.

Avery, R. K., & Pepper, R. (1980). An institutional history of public broadcasting. *Journal of Communication, 30*(3), 126-138.

Barlow, W. (1988). Community radio in the US: The struggle for a democratic medium. *Media, Culture and Society, 10*(1), 81-105.

Barlow, W. (1992). *Pacifica Radio: A cultural history.* Unpublished manuscript.

Barnes, F. (1986, October 27). All things distorted: The trouble with NPR. *New Republic,* pp. 17-19.

Barnouw, E. (1966). *A tower in Babel: A history of broadcasting in the United States: Vol. 1—to 1933.* New York: Oxford University Press.

Barnouw, E. (1970). *The image empire: A history of broadcasting in the United States since 1953.* New York: Oxford University Press.

Barnouw, E. (1978). *The sponsor: Notes on a modern potentate.* New York: Oxford University Press.

Barron, J. A. (1972). Access to the press: A new concept of the First Amendment. In M. C. Emery & T. C. Symthe (Eds.), *Readings in mass communication* (pp. 16-22). Dubuque, IA: William C. Brown.

Barrow, K. L. (1993, May). Help keep Deep Dish TV on the air!! [Fund-raising letter].

Becton, H., Jr., (1971-1972, Winter). Broadcast TV as community television. *Challenge for Change/Société Nouvelle Newsletter,* No. 7.

Bedford, K. E. (1994, July 4). Seeking funds in Senate will be "trip to Hades." *Current,* pp. 1, 6, 11.

Bednarczyk, S. (1986). NFLCP: The way it was. *Community Television Review, 9*(2), 19-58.

Behrens, S. (1992, March 16). Now it's NPR's turn to face dues critics. *Current,* pp. 1, 10-11.

Behrens, S. (1994, July 4). How will PBS make underwriting "user-friendly"? *Current,* pp. 1, 8.

Behrens, S. (1995, January 16). The defense: It's all up to the listeners and viewers. *Current,* pp. 1, 12.

Berger, W. (1995, January 29). We interrupt this program . . . forever? *New York Times,* Sec. II, pp. 1, 27.

Berkman, D. (1980, July/August). Localism and freedom— Natural enemies? *Public Telecommunications Review,* pp. 24- 25.

Blakely, R. J. (1979). *To serve the public interest: Educational broadcasting in the United States.* Syracuse, NY: Syracuse University Press.

Blau, A. (1992). The promise of public access. *The Independent, 15*(3), 22-26.

Bogart, B. (1980, August 12-26). "Passive censorship" of international news. *In These Times,* p. 21.

Boyle, D. (in press). *Subject to change: Guerrilla television revisited.* New York: Oxford University Press.

Boyle, D. (1986). *Return of guerrilla television: A TVTV retrospective* (Video Feature Program Notes, November 14, 1986-February 22, 1987). New York: International Center for Photography.

Boyer, P. J. (1987, December 17). Once an embattled show, "Newshour" gains friends. *New York Times,* p. C26.

Braderman, J. (1991). TV/video: Reclaiming the utopian moment. In *Roar! The Paper Tiger Television guide to media activism* (pp. 19-21). New York: Paper Tiger Television Collective.

Brewin, B (1980, February 27-March 4). Channel 13's flimflam. *Soho Weekly News*, pp. 8-9.

Brewin, B. (1982, January 12). WNET's cable grab. *Soho Weekly News*, pp. 16, 18.

Brown, L. (1977, June 21). Public TV eagerly awaits Carnegie Commission study. *New York Times*, p. C67.

Burke, J. E. (1979). *An historical-analytical study of the legislative and political origins of the Public Broadcasting Act of 1967*. New York: Arno.

Burns, T. (1979). *The BBC: Public institution and private world*. London: Macmillan.

Buske, S. M. (1986). The development of community television. *Community Television Review*, *9*(2), 12-13.

Buzenberg, B. (1993, March 29). *NPR responds to FAIR report* [Memorandum to NPR station managers, program directors and news directors]. Washington, DC: National Public Radio.

Calhoun, C. (Ed.). (1992). *Habermas and the public sphere*. Cambridge: MIT Press.

Carey, J. (1968). Harold Adams Innis and Marshall McLuhan. In R. Rosenthal (Ed.), *McLuhan: Pro & con* (pp. 270-308). New York: Funk & Wagnalls.

Carnegie Commission on Educational Television. (1967). *Public television: A program for action*. New York: Bantam.

Carnegie Commission on the Future of Public Broadcasting. (1979). *A public trust*. New York: Bantam.

Caron, A. H., & Taylor, J. R. (1985). Cable at the crossroads: An analysis of the Canadian cable industry. In R. M. Negrine (Ed.), *Cable television and the future of broadcasting* (pp. 47-73). New York: St. Martin's.

Carter, B. (1994, October 11). MacNeil to retire from "Newshour" in '95 after 20 years. *The New York Times*, pp. C15, C18.

Cater, D. (1964). *Power in Washington*. New York: Random House.

Charlton, L. (1981). Upwardly Mobil. *Channels of Communication, 1*(3), 28-30.

Cockburn, A. (1995a, March 6). Beat the devil. *The Nation*, pp. 299-300.

Cockburn, A. (1995b, May 1). Beat the devil. *The Nation*, pp. 588-589.

Cockburn, A. (1995c, November 13). Beat the devil. *The Nation*, pp. 563-564.

Cohen, J. (1993, April 19). *FAIR's study of NPR news* [Memorandum to all public radio staff].

Cohn, R. (1990, November 18). "South Africa now" ponders its uncertain future. *New York Times*, Sec. II, pp. 33-34.

Committee to Make Public Broadcasting Public. (1980, March 26). *Issues of affirmative action compliance and federal funding as they concern the WGBH Educational Foundation, Boston* [Statement to the United States Commission on Civil Rights].

Corry, J. (1985, August 1). TV review: MacNeil/Lehr shift. *The New York Times*, Sec. III, p. 18.

Covert, C. L. (1992). "We may hear too much": American sensibility and the responses to radio. In J. Folkerts (Ed.), *Media voices: An historical perspective* (pp. 300-315). New York: Macmillan.

Czitrom, D. J. (1982). *Media and the American mind from Morse to McLuhan*. Chapel Hill: University of North Carolina Press.

Dates, J. L., & Barlow, W. (Eds.). (1990). *Split image: African Americans in the mass media*. Washington, DC: Howard University Press.

Daviss, D. (1986, March/April). The $3 million giveaway. *Emmy Magazine*, pp. 53-55.

De Michiel, H. (1991). Re-visioning the electronic democracy. In *Roar! The Paper Tiger Television guide to media activism* (pp. 14-15.). New York: Paper Tiger Television Collective.

De Sola Pool, I., & Alexander, H. E. (1973). Politics in a wired nation. In I. de Sola Pool (Ed.), *Talking back: Citizen feedback and cable technology* (pp. 64-102). Cambridge: MIT Press.

Dean, S. W. (1970, July 20). Television in New York: Hitches in the cable. *The Nation,* pp. 41-45.

Deep Dish TV (1986a, April). *Press release.* New York: Paper Tiger TV.

Deep Dish TV (1986b). *Deep Dish directory—A resource guide for grass roots television producers, programmers, activists and cultural workers* (First series, cablecast April-June 1986). New York: Paper Tiger TV.

Del Solar, D. (1976). Toward "unfringed" and open programming: Some workable solutions. *Public Telecommunications Review, 4*(4), 30-33.

DeLuc, D. R. (1973). *Cable television and the FCC: A crisis in media control.* Philadelphia: Temple University Press.

Devine, R. H. (1991). Consumer video, the First Amendment and the future of access. *Community Television Review, 14*(2), 6-11.

Devine, R. H. (1992). Access in the 21st century: The future of a public. *Community Television Review, 15*(6), 8-9.

DiGiacomo, R. (1995, June 16-23). Public television on the edge. *Philadelphia City Paper,* pp. 12-13.

Do it yourself TV. (1972, January 3). *Newsweek,* pp. 49-50.

Dodge, C. (1981). Masterpiece p.r. *Channels of Communication, 1*(3), 31.

Dougherty, P. H. (1982, December 10). Advertising: Chemical bank on public TV. *New York Times,* p. D15.

Douglas, S. J. (1987). *Inventing American broadcasting, 1899-1922.* Baltimore: Johns Hopkins University Press.

Downing, J. (1984). *Radical media: The political experience of alternative communication.* Boston: South End Press.

Doyle, P. K. (1990). *National Public Radio's* All Things Considered*: Origins and early history.* Unpublished doctoral dissertation, University of Tennessee, Knoxville.

Drummond, B. (1993, February 15). To rouse its news reporting from a midlife malaise. *Current,* p. 13.

Duggan, E. S. (1995, February 6). Spare that living tree. *Current,* pp. 24-26.

Elman, R. M. (1965, March 1). Educational TV: The timid crusaders. *The Nation,* pp. 217-221.

Endrst, J. (1991, October 7). In 10th season on PBS, "Frontline" still a beacon. *Hartford Courant,* pp. B1, B3.

Enzensberger, H. M. (1974). *The consciousness industry: On literature, politics and the media.* New York: Seabury.

Ewen, S. (1989). Advertising and the development of consumer society. In I. Angus & S. Jhally (Eds.), *Cultural politics in contemporary America* (pp. 82-95). New York: Routledge.

FAIR [Fairness and Accuracy in Reporting]. (1990). No place for labor on PBS? *Extra!, 3*(7), p. 13.

FAIR [Fairness and Accuracy in Reporting]. (1995, February). MacNeil/Lehrer sells out. *Extra! Update,* p. 1.

FCC v. Midwest Video Corporation, 440 US 689 L Ed 2d 692, 99 Sct 1435.

Ferretti, F. (1970, July 24). City delays its decision on CATV policy. *New York Times,* p. C63.

Fisher, M. (1989, May). Pacifica's next wave. *Mother Jones,* pp. 50-52.

312 PUBLIC RADIO AND TELEVISION IN AMERICA

Fox, M. (1994). *The history of the Independent Television Service (ITVS)*. 4th draft. Unpublished manuscript, pp. 1-18.

Fox, N. (1991). NPR grows up. *Washington Journalism Review, 13*(7), 30-36.

Fox, N. (1992, January/February). Public radio's air wars. *Columbia Journalism Review*, pp. 9-10.

Francis Spiller Associates. (1983). *Cable community programming in Canada*. Nepean, Ontario: Author.

Frederickson, S. G. (1972). *John F. White: One man's contribution to educational television in the United States*. Unpublished master's thesis, University of North Dakota, Grand Forks.

Frontline: A brief history. (n.d.). Boston: Frontline.

Fuller, L. K. (1994). *Community television in the United States*. Westport, CT: Greenwood.

Gever, M. (1983). Meet the press: On "Paper Tiger Television." *Afterimage, 11*, 7-11.

Gibson, G. H. (1977). *Public broadcasting: The role of the federal government, 1972-1976*. New York: Praeger.

Gillespie, G. (1975). *Public access cable television in the United States and Canada*. New York: Praeger.

Gitlin, T. (1980). *The whole world is watching: Mass media in the making and unmaking of the new left*. Berkeley: University of California Press.

Goldstein, R. (1980, February 25). The fight to open WNET. *Village Voice*, pp. 33, 49.

Good, L. (1989). Power, hegemony, and communication theory. In I. Angus & S. Jhally (Eds.), *Cultural politics in contemporary America* (pp. 51-64). New York: Routledge.

Gref, B. (1989). Catskill public radio on the air soon. *Catskill Center Newsletter, 18*(4), pp. 6-7.

Gwyn, S. (1975). Citizens communications in Canada. In B. D. Singer (Ed.), *Communications in Canadian society* (2nd ed., pp. 407-428). Montreal: Copp Clark.

Habermas, J. (1989). *The structural transformation of the public sphere: An inquiry into a category of bourgeois society*. Cambridge: MIT Press.

Haight, T. R., & Weinstein, L. R. (1981). Changing ideology on television by changing telecommunications policy: Notes on a contradictory situation. In E. G. McAnany, J. Schnitman, & N. Janus (Eds.), *Communication and social structure: Critical studies in mass media research* (pp. 110-144). New York: Praeger.

Halberstam, D. (1979). *The powers that be*. New York: Dell.

Hall, L. S. (n.d.). *A look inside the making of the 1978 Public Telecommunications Financing Act*. Unpublished manuscript.

Hall, L. S. (1979). Controlling public telecommunications: Theory and practice for human management of electric literature. In T. Haight (Ed.), *Telecommunications policy and the citizen* (pp. 169-199). New York: Praeger.

Halleck, D. (1979a). Mind power: Collective action for media reform. In Rockefeller Foundation (Ed.), *Working papers: Independent television-makers and public communications policy* (pp. 109-118). New York: Rockefeller Foundation.

Halleck, D. (1979b, April). Term paper from the president. *The Independent*, pp. 4-5.

Halleck, D. (1980, February). Catch 13. *The Independent, 3*(10), 3.

Halleck, D. (1981). Media makers in Bonzoland. *The Independent, 4*(1), 5-6.

Halleck, D. (1984). Paper Tiger Television: Smashing the myths of the information industry every week on public access cable. *Media, Culture and Society, 6*, 313-318.

Halleck, D. (1985, July). *Local origination does not mean public access*. Paper presented at the annual meeting of the National Federation of Local Cable Programmers, Boston.

Haney, J. M. (1981). *A history of the merger of National Public Radio and the Association of Public Radio Stations.* Unpublished doctoral dissertation, University of Iowa, Iowa City.

Hardt, H. (1994, September). *Access for whom? Contours of a cultural history of communication and participation in America.* Paper presented at the European Institute of Communication and Culture Colloquium, Piran, Slovenia.

Head, S. W. (1972). *Broadcasting in America.* New York: Houghton Mifflin.

Heitler, B., & Kalba, K. (Eds.). (1972). The cable fable. *Yale Review of Law and Social Action, 2*(3).

Hénaut, D. T. (1971-1972, Winter). Powerful catalyst. *Challenge for Change/Société Nouvelle Newsletter,* No. 7, 2-4.

Henwood, D. (1990). Public TV's elite market. *Extra!, 3*(7), 13.

Herman, E., & Chomsky, N. (1988). *Manufacturing consent.* New York: Pantheon.

Hertsgaard, M. (1988). *On bended knee: The press and the Reagan presidency.* New York: Farrar Straus & Giroux.

Hill, L. (1966). The theory of listener-sponsored radio. In E. McKinney (Ed.), *The exacting ear* (pp. 19-26). New York: Pantheon.

Himmelstein, H. (1984). *Television myth and the American mind.* New York: Praeger.

Hochheimer, J. L. (1993). Organizing democratic radio: Issues in praxis. *Media, Culture and Society, 15*(3), 473-486.

Hollins, T. (1984). *Beyond broadcasting: Into the cable age.* London: British Film Institute.

Hoynes, W. (1994). *Public television for sale: Media, the market, and the public sphere.* Boulder, CO: Westview.

Hoynes, W., & Croteau, D. (1990). All the usual suspects: MacNeil/Lehrer and Nightline. *Extra!, 3*(4), 2-15.

Hoyt, M. (1993, September/October). Danny Schechter's "Rights & Wrongs." *Columbia Journalism Review,* pp. 29-32.

Hulser, K. (1985, March). VideoFile: "Paper Tiger Television." *American Film,* pp. 61-63.

Hyder, J. (1971-1972, Winter). Some recommendations on community TV. *Challenge for Change/Société Nouvelle Newsletter,* No. 7, 13.

Ianacone, E. (1980). Public broadcasting: A citizen perspective. *Citizen Participation, 2*(2), 5, 10-11.

Innis, H. A. (1971). *The bias of communication* (2nd ed., introduction by M. McLuhan). Toronto: University of Toronto Press.

Isay, D. (1992, November 16). Invites a radio revolution [Letter to the editor]. *Current,* p. 20.

Jackson, J. (1993). When is a commercial not a commercial? *Extra!, 6*(6), 17-18.

Jensen, E. (1994, June 1). PBS may ease rules as way to increase corporate support. *Wall Street Journal,* pp. A3-A4.

Josephson, L. (1979, March/April). Why radio? *Public Telecommunications Review, 7*(2), 6-18.

Josephson, L. (1992, April 27). We're drunk on numbers, boring to our listeners. *Current,* pp. 31, 34.

Kellner, D. (1990). *Television and the crisis of democracy.* Boulder, CO: Westview.

Kinderman, G. (1992, February 17). Proposals disappointing: No aid for new rural stations. *Current,* p. 17.

King, J. C. (1992, April 27). Too many programmers are thralls of research gurus. *Current,* p. 30.

Kinsley, M. E. (1976). *Outer space and inner sanctums: Government, business and satellite communication.* New York: John Wiley.

Kirkish, J. B. (1980). *A descriptive history of America's first national public radio network: National Public Radio, 1970-1974.* Unpublished doctoral dissertation, University of Michigan, Ann Arbor.

Kirsh, D. (1993). The struggle for the soul of public radio. *Extra!, 6*(3), 27.

Kolbert, E. (1995, May 30). Public broadcasting is anguishing over commercials. *New York Times,* pp. C13, C16.

Kopkind, A. (1986, April 8). MacNeil/Lehrer: The news as snooze. *Village Voice,* pp. 51, 53.

Land, J. R. (1994). *Active radio: Pacifica's "brash experiment."* Unpublished doctoral dissertation, University of Oregon, Eugene.

Land Associates, H. W. (1967). *The hidden medium: A status report on educational radio in the United States.* New York: National Association of Educational Broadcasters.

Lashley, M. (1992). *Public television: Panacea, pork barrel, or public trust?* New York: Greenwood.

Larson, M. S. (1985). *A content analysis of National Public Radio's* All Things Considered. Unpublished doctoral dissertation, Northern Illinois University.

Lashley, M. (1992). *Public television: Panacea, pork barrel, or public trust?* Westport, CT: Greenwood.

Leach, E. E. (1983). *Tuning out education: The cooperation doctrine in radio, 1922-38.* Washington, DC: Current.

Lee, M. A., & Solomon, N. (1990). *Unreliable sources.* New York: Lyle Stuart.

Lewis, P. M., & Booth, J. (1990). *The invisible medium: Public, commercial and community radio.* Washington, DC: Howard University Press.

Linfield, S. (1983, January/February). A world of their own. *The Independent, 6*(1), 10-12.

Looker, T. (1995). *The sound and the fury: NPR and the art of radio.* Boston: Houghton-Mifflin.

Lumpp, J. A. (1979). *The Pacifica experience—1946-1975: Alternative radio in four United States metropolitan areas.* Unpublished doctoral dissertation, University of Missouri at Columbia. (University Microfilms No. 78-3738)

MacNeil, R. (1985). *The mass media and public trust* (Occasional Paper No. 1). New York: Gannett Center for Media Studies.

Mahler, R. (1993, March/April). Cheap air: Hard times for public radio producers. *Columbia Journalism Review,* pp. 17-18.

Mander, J. (1978). *Four arguments for the elimination of television.* New York: Quill.

Marcus, D. (1991). Tales from the tiger den: A history of our deconstruction. In *Roar! The Paper Tiger Television guide to media activism* (pp. 31-32.). New York: Paper Tiger Television Collective.

Margulies, L. (1980, April 25). KCET board is under fire. *Los Angeles Times,* Sec. VI, p. 14.

McChesney, R. W. (1987a). Crusade against Mammon: Father Harney, WLWL and the debate over radio in the 1930s. *Journalism History, 14*(4), 118-130.

McChesney, R. W. (1987b, August). *Free speech and democracy: The debate in the American legal community over the meaning of free expression on radio, 1926-1939.* Paper presented at the annual meeting of the Association for Education in Journalism and Mass Communication, San Antonio, TX.

McChesney, R. W. (1990). The battle for the U.S. airwaves, 1928-1935. *Journal of Communication, 40*(4), 29-57.

McChesney, R. W. (1992). Labor and the markeplace of ideas: WCFL and the battle for labor radio broadcasting, 1928-1934. *Journalism Monographs,* No. 134, 1-40.

McChesney, R. W. (1994). *Telecommunications, mass media, & democracy: The battle for the control of U.S. broadcasting, 1928-1935.* New York: Oxford University Press.

McChesney, R. W. (1995). Public broadcasting in the age of communication revolution. *Monthly Review, 47*(7), 1-19.

McGraw, W. (1977). *Toward the public dividend: A report on satellite telecommunications and the Public Interest Satellite Association.* New York: PISA.

McKinney, E. (Ed.). (1966). *The exacting ear: The story of listener-sponsored radio, and an anthology of programs from KPFA, KPFK, and WBAI.* (Preface by Erich Fromm.) New York: Pantheon.

McLaughlin, L. (1994, September). *The feminist counterpublic sphere and the media: From identity politics to access.* Paper presented at the European Institute of Communication and Culture Colloquium, Piran, Slovenia, and published in revised form in the winter 1995 issue of *Javnost—The Public, 2*(4), 51-61.

McLuhan, M. (1964). *Understanding media: The extensions of man* (2nd ed.). New York: Signet.

Minor, D. (1970). *The information war.* New York: Hawthorn.

Minow, N. (1962, September 16). ETV takes a giant step. *New York Times,* Sec. VI, pp. 32-33, 37, 39-40.

Mooney, M. M. (1980). *The ministry of culture: Connections among art, money and politics.* New York: Wyndham.

Morgan, T. (1986, April 7). Is public TV becoming overly commercial? *New York Times,* p. C26.

Moss, M. L. (1978). The development of two-way cable television: Applications for the community. In M. C. J. Elton, W. A. Lucas, & D. W. Conrath (Eds.), *Evaluating new telecommunications services* (pp. 199-214). New York: Plenum.

National Film Board of Canada. (n.d.). *All about us!* Montreal: Author.

Negt, O., & Kluge, A. (1993). *Public sphere and experience: Toward an analysis of the bourgeois and proletarian public sphere* (Foreword by M. Hansen). Minneapolis: University of Minnesota Press.

Network Project. (1971). *The fourth network.* New York: Author.

Nord, D. P. (1978). The FCC, educational broadcasting, and political interest group activity. *Journal of Broadcasting, 22*(3), 321-338.

Noton, P. (1994, March). Independent radio's problems and prospects: An interview with Peter Franck, former president of Pacifica Radio. *Z Magazine,* pp. 51-57.

NPR [National Public Radio]. (1993, May 3). Extend your tentpoles [Advertisement]. *Current,* p. 2.

NPR [National Public Radio]. (1995). *National Public Radio 1995 member station list.* Washington, DC: Author.

Pacifica Foundation. (1989). *Minutes. Meeting of the National Board of Directors of the Pacifica Foundation, January 27-29, Los Angeles.* Berkeley, CA: Author.

Paskal, T. (1971, Summer). Which side has power? *Radical Software,* No. 4, Canadian Section, pp. 3-4.

PBL on the brink. (1967, November 6). *Newsweek,* pp. 102, 104.

PBS [Public Broadcasting Service]. (1994). *Facts about PBS.* Washington, DC: Author.

Peck, A. (1985). *Uncovering the sixties: The life and times of the underground press.* New York: Pantheon.

Pember, D. R. (1987). *Mass media law* (4th ed.). Dubuque, IA: William C. Brown.

"People's satellite." (1967, August 15). *Newsweek,* pp. 76-77.

Phillips, A. (1993). *Pacifica radio's fading vision.* Unpublished manuscript carried on PeaceNet.

Pierce, R. (1979, February 26). Indies rap the new PBS. *Village Voice,* p. 39.

Porter, B. (1990, September/October). Has success spoiled NPR? *Columbia Journalism Review,* pp. 26-32.

Post, S. (1974). *Playing in the FM band: A personal account of free radio.* New York: Viking.

Potter, D. M. (1954). *People of plenty: Economic abundance and the American character.* Chicago: University of Chicago Press.

Pressler, L. (1995, January 27). [Letter and questionnaire addressed to Henry J. Cauthen, chairman, Corporation for Public Broadcasting], pp. 1-18.

Pressler stocking up on ammunition. (1995, February 6). *Current,* pp. 1, 10.

Prinn, E. (1971-1972, Winter). Video as an organizing tool for poor people. *Challenge for Change/Société Nouvelle Newsletter,* No. 7, 14-15.

Rauber, P. (1993, March 5). Off-mike: Mid-life crisis at KPFA. *East Bay Express,* pp. 1, 10-18.

Revolutionary engineering: Towards a counter-technology. *Radical Software, 4,* 12.

Robertson, J. (1979-1982). *TeleVisionaries: In their own words, public television's founders tell how it all began.* Charlotte Harbor, FL: Tabby House.

Rogoff, C. (1986). Deep Dish TV—More than pie in the sky. *Community Television Review, 9*(1), pp. 30, 38.

Rosenberg, H. (1982, February 5). "Let Poland be Poland": Has Reagan gone too far? *Los Angeles Times,* Sec VI, pp. 1, 14.

Rosenthal, R. (Ed.). (1968). *McLuhan: Pro & con.* New York: Funk & Wagnalls.

Rovere, R. (1962). *The American establishment and other reports, opinions, and speculations.* New York: Harcourt Brace.

Rowland, W. D., Jr. (1976). Public involvement: The anatomy of a myth. In D. Cater & M. J. Nyhan (Eds.), *The future of public broadcasting* (pp. 109-139). New York: Praeger.

Rowland, W. D., Jr. (1986). Continuing crisis in public broadcasting: A history of disenfranchisement. *Journal of Broadcasting and Electronic Media, 30*(3), 251-274.

Russell, T. (1992, April 27). We're not talking entitlement here. *Current,* p. 29.

Ryan, C. (1993). A study of National Public Radio. *Extra! 6*(3), 18-21, 26.

Ryan, P. (1988). A geneology of video. *Leonardo: Journal of the International Society for the Arts and Technology, 21*(1), 39-44.

Salniker, D. (1994, May). [Letter to the editor]. *Z Magazine,* p. 4.

Salyer, S. L. (1993). Monopoly to marketplace—Competition comes to public radio. *Media Studies Journal, 7*(3), 176-183.

Schechter, D. (1989, December 8). [Letter to the George Polk Awards Committee]. Unpublished data.

Schechter, D. (1994). *Anatomy of a smear: Political discrimination and ideological exclusion in public television.* (Unpublished manuscript.) New York: Globalvision.

Schiller, H. I. (1989). The privatization and transnationalization of culture. In I. Angus & S. Jhally (Eds.), *Cultural politics in contemporary America* (pp. 317-332). New York: Routledge.

Schmidt, B., Jr. (1976). *Freedom of the press vs. public access.* New York: Praeger.

Scott, P. (1994, May). [Letter to the editor]. *Z Magazine,* p. 4.

Severin, W. J. (1978). Commercial vs. non-nommercial radio during broadcasting's early years. *Journal of Broadcasting, 22*(4), 491-504.

Seybold, P. (1978). *The development of American political sociology—A case study of the Ford Foundation's role in the production of knowledge.* Unpublished doctoral dissertation, State University of New York at Stoney Brook.

Shamberg, M. (1971). *Guerrilla television.* New York: Holt, Rinehart & Winston.

Sholle, D. (1994, September). *Access through activism: Extending the ideas of Negt and Kluge to American alternative media practices.* Paper presented at the European Institute of Communication and Culture Colloquium, Piran, Slovenia, and published in revised form in the winter 1995 issue of *Javnost—The Public, 2*(4), 21-35.

Siemering, W. H. (1969). Public broadcasting—Some essential ingredients. *Educational/Instructional Broadcasting, 2*(9), 65-69.

Siemering, W. H. (1970). National public radio purposes. In J. M. Haney (1981), *A history of the merger of National Public Radio and the Association of Public Radio Stations* (Appendix D, pp. 247-263). Unpublished doctoral dissertation, University of Iowa.

Siemering, W. H. (1979, March/April). Public radio in the 1980s: Making connections. *Public Telecommunications Review, 7*(2), 35-7.

Siemering, W. H. (1991a, January/February). Still tuned to NPR [Letter to the editor]. *Columbia Journalism Review,* p. 60.

Siemering, W. H. (1991b). WBFO and the genesis of public radio. Unpublished paper, pp. 1-2.

Siemering, W. H. (1992a, May 25). There's more at stake than "Soundprint." *Current,* p. 14.

Siemering, W. H. (1992b, November). *The future of public radio programming.* Speech delivered at the annual meeting of the Association of Independents in Radio, Fort Worth, TX.

Silk, L., & Silk, M. (1980). *The American establishment.* New York: Basic Books.

Sklover, T. (1971, Summer). Cable: Letters and inquiry. *Radical Software,* No. 4, p. 23.

Sloan Commission on Cable Communications. (1971). *On the cable: The television of abundance.* New York: McGraw-Hill.

Smith, R. L. (1970, May 18). The wired nation. *The Nation,* pp. 577-606.

Smith, W. (1995, March 6). The real motive: Grab for spectrum. *Current,* p. 12.

Sobel, R. (1986). Television as invention and business. In R. Atwan, B. Orton, & W. Westerman (Eds.), *American mass media: Industries and issues* (3rd ed., pp. 334-341). New York: Random.

Spark, C. (1987). Pacifica radio and the politics of culture. In D. Lazere (Ed.), *American media and mass culture* (pp. 577-590). Berkeley: University of California Press.

Sparkes, V. (1985). Cable television in the United States: A story of continuing growth and change. In R. Negrine (Ed.), *Cable television and the future of broadcasting* (pp. 15-46). New York: St. Martin's.

Stamberg, S. (1982). *Every night at five: Susan Stamberg's* All Things Considered *book* (Foreword by Charles Kuralt). New York: Pantheon.

Stavitsky, A. G. (1990). *From pedagogic to public: The development of U.S. public radio's audience-centered strategies—WOSU, WHA, and WNYC, 1930-1987.* Unpublished doctoral dissertation, Ohio State University, Columbus.

Stavitsky, A. G. (1995). "Guys in suits and charts": Audience research in U.S. public radio. *Journal of Broadcasting and Electronic Media, 39*(2), 177-189.

Stavitsky, A. G., & Gleason, T. W. (1994). Alternative things considered: A comparison of National Public Radio and Pacifica Radio news coverage. *Journalism Quarterly, 71*(4), 775-786.

Stebbins, G. R. (1978). *Listener-sponsored radio: The Pacifica stations.* Unpublished doctoral dissertation, The Ohio State University. (University Microfilms No. 70-14, 102)

Stephens, M. (1988). *A history of news: From the drum to the satellite.* New York: Viking.

Sterling, C. H., & Kittross, J. (1978). *Stay tuned: A concise history of American broadcasting.* Belmont, CA: Wadsworth.

Stoney, G. (1971-1972). The mirror machine. *Sight and Sound, 41*(1), 9-11.

Storm, J. (1995, May 30). In "Through the Lens," sights of artistic vision from independents. *Philadelphia Inquirer,* pp. D1, D5.

Task Force on Minorities in Public Broadcasting. (1978, November). *A formula for change.* Washington, DC: Corporation for Public Broadcasting.

Tebbel, J. (1967, November 11). Latest hope for television. PBL: The great experiment. *Saturday Review,* pp. 85-87, 98.

The *NewsHour* format. (1993). [MacNeil/Lehrer *NewsHour* press information]. New York: MacNeil/Lehrer Productions.

Twentieth Century Fund Task Force on Public Television. (1993). *Quality time?* (with background paper by R. Somerset-Ward). New York: Twentieth Century Fund Press.

Unger, A. (1991). *Frontline*'s David Fanning: Upholding the documentary tradition. *Television Quarterly, 25*(3), 27-41.

Wallner, M. (1991). Deep Dish TV: Tigers sprout wings and fly! In *Roar! The Paper Tiger Television guide to media activism* (pp. 33-34.). New York: Paper Tiger Television Collective.

Watson, P. (1970). Challenge for change. *artscanada, 27*(142/143), 14-20.

Weeks, E. (1966). *The Lowells and their institute.* Boston: Little, Brown.

Werden, F. L. (1985, August 13-September 10). Watchdogs bay over bias of National Public Radio news. *Current,* pp. 1, 3.

Wicklein, J. (1986, January/February). The assault on public television. *Columbia Journalism Review,* pp. 27-34.

Williams, R. (1975). *Television: Technology and cultural form.* New York: Schocken.

Willis, J. (1979, October 16). *Discussion of draft proposal on the issue of independents and public television.* Unpublished transcript.

Willis, J. (1995a). *The role of Twin Cities Public Television in the mega-channel environment* [Press release, pp. 1-4]. St. Paul: Twin Cities Public Television.

Willis, J. (1995b). *Public TV needs public support* [Press release, pp. 1-2]. St. Paul: Twin Cities Public Television.

Wilner, J. (1992a, August 3). Hockenberry departure viewd as "sign of success" for NPR. *Current,* pp. 1, 23.

Wilner, J. (1992b, November 2). Siemering leaves "Soundprint" for international gig. *Current,* p. 8.

Wilner, J. (1993a, February 1). Carlson: CPB should lead "electronic peace corps" with VOA, other services. *Current,* pp. 1, 12.

Wilner, J. (1993b, March 15). Bennet leaves NPR in April for State Dept. position. *Current,* pp. 1, 16.

Wilner, J. (1993c, March 29). FAIR study sees NPR as voice of establishment. *Current,* pp. 1, 3.

Wilner, J. (1993d, May 17). APR, NPR tout separate overseas radio channels. *Current,* pp. 1, 16.

Wilner, J. (1993e, August 9). NPR shows debut in Europe through direct satellite. *Current,* pp. 1, 25.

Witherspoon, J., & Kovitz, R. (1987). *The history of public broadcasting* (J. J. Yore & R. Barcieri, Eds.). Washington, DC: Current.

Wolin, S., & Schaar, J. H. (1970). *The Berkeley rebellion and beyond: Essays on politics and education in the technological society.* New York: New York Review Books.

WPFW. (1977, February 13). *Statement of WPFW, Pacifica Washington, on WBAI takeover* [Press release].

WYBE-TV. (1995). *Mission statement* [Press packet].

Zimmerman, P. R. (1982). Public television, independent documentary producer and public policy. *Journal of the University Film and Video Association, 34*(3), 9-23.

Zuckerman, L. (1987). Has success spoiled NPR? *Mother Jones, 12*(5), 32-45.

Transcript Compilations and Archives

Pacifica

Documents

The following is contained in Pacifica Foundation (n.d.), *Documents and papers about Pacifica.* Berkeley, CA: Pacifica.

Johnson, N. (1969, March 26). Separate statement of FCC Commissioner Johnson: Letter to Mr. Dan Sanders, United Federation of Teachers.

Policymaking

The following are contained in Pacifica Foundation (1989), *Underwriting: An evaluation of Pacifica policy.* Berkeley, CA: Pacifica.

National Federation of Community Broadcasters [NFCB]. (n.d.). Underwriting on your community radio station is a way to reach your market (pp. 65-69).
Pacifica Radio News. (1983). Position statement (pp. 101-102).
Raimi, J. (1979). Lewis Hill and the first years of Pacifica (pp. 48-51).
Smith, C. (1988). Report to KPFA board on underwriting (pp. 21-38).
WORT. (1989). What is underwriting?

Interview Transcripts

The following are contained in J. Robertson (1979-1982), *Oral history of educational television, 1948-1967*. Madison: Mass Communications History Center, State Historical Society of Wisconsin.

Armsey, J. (1981, June 19). An interview with James Armsey (pp. 1-37).
DuBridge. L. A. (1981, April 14). An interview with Lee A. DuBridge (pp. 1-24).
Gunn, H. N. (1981, April 7). An interview with Hartford N. Gunn (pp. 1-59).
Hudson, R. (1982, January 26). An interview with Robert Hudson (pp. 1-42).
Killian, J. R., Jr. (1981, September 11). An interview with James R. Killian, Jr. (pp. 1-27).

Author Index

Subject Index

About the Author

Ralph Engelman is a professor of journalism and chair of the Journalism Department at the Brooklyn campus of Long Island University. He is a member of the selection committee of the George Polk Awards, which are conferred by LIU, and coordinator of the annual George Polk Awards Seminar. Prior to joining the LIU faculty in 1985, he taught at Hofstra University and at the District 65 Institute of Applied Social Sciences, a labor college in New York City. He has been a guest lecturer at the Multinational Institute of American Studies at New York University.

A specialist in communication history, he received his PhD from Washington University in St. Louis, where he was a Danforth History Teaching Fellow. He has published articles and reviews in *The Yale Review, Journalism Quarterly, Journalism Monographs, American Journalism, Dictionary of Literary Biography,* and the *Approaches to Learning* series of the Modern Language Association.

His affiliations embrace both scholarly and professional organizations in the communication field. He is a member of the Union for Democratic Communications and the European Institute for Communication and Culture. He has served on the editorial board of *American Journalism,* published by the American Journalism Historians Association. He is also a member of the Association of Independent Video and Filmmakers and the Alliance for Community Media. A former member of the board of directors of the Pacifica

Foundation, which operates a national network of five noncommercial radio stations, Engelman was part of a Pacifica delegation that testified before Congress against broadcast deregulation in 1979. He has presented papers based on his research on public radio and television at communication conferences hosted by the universities of Texas, Montreal, and Ljubljana and by Temple University.

Ralph Engelman lives with his wife and two children in the Park Slope section of Brooklyn, New York.